A Movement Without Marches

The John Hope Franklin Series in African American History and Culture

Waldo E. Martin Jr.
and Patricia Sullivan,
editors

THE UNIVERSITY OF
NORTH CAROLINA PRESS
Chapel Hill

LISA LEVENSTEIN

A Movement Without Marches

*African American Women
and the Politics of Poverty
in Postwar Philadelphia*

*This book was published with the assistance of
the Anniversary Endowment Fund of the University
of North Carolina Press.*

Designed by Jacquline Johnson
Set in Whitman
by Keystone Typesetting, Inc.

The paper in this book meets the guidelines for permanence
and durability of the Committee on Production Guidelines for
Book Longevity of the Council on Library Resources.

The University of North Carolina Press has been a member of
the Green Press Initiative since 2003.

Library of Congress Cataloging-in-Publication Data
Levenstein, Lisa.
A movement without marches : African American women and
the politics of poverty in postwar Philadelphia / Lisa
Levenstein.
p. cm. — (The John Hope Franklin series in African American
history and culture)
Includes bibliographical references and index.
ISBN 978-0-8078-3272-1 (cloth: alk. paper)
ISBN 978-0-8078-7164-5 (pbk.: alk. paper)
1. African American women—Pennsylvania—Philadelphia—
History—20th century. 2. Poor women—Pennsylvania—
Philadelphia—History—20th century. 3. African American
women—Pennsylvania—Philadelphia—Social conditions—
20th century. 4. African American women—Pennsylvania—
Philadelphia—Biography. 5. African Americans—
Pennsylvania—Philadelphia—Economic conditions—20th
century. 6. Poverty—Political aspects—Pennsylvania—
Philadelphia—History—20th century. 7. Urban policy—
Pennsylvania—Philadelphia—History—20th century.
8. Philadelphia (Pa.)—Race relations—History—20th
century. 9. Philadelphia (Pa.)—Politics and government—
20th century. 10. Philadelphia (Pa.)—Social conditions—
20th century. I. Title.
F158.9.N4L485 2009
305.48'89607307481109045—dc22   2008041130

For my parents,
Harvey and Mona

Contents

Illustrations, Tables, and Maps

Illustrations

Tables

Maps

Acknowledgments

In writing this book, I relied on many people who believed in this project and shared their time and energy to help bring it to fruition. Some of them were drawn into my life through their involvement with the book; others were drawn into the book through their involvement with the rest of my life. It is with great pleasure and gratitude that I acknowledge their contributions.

I began my research in archives and libraries where I met people who went out of their way to help me find the materials I needed. My greatest debt is to the staff at the Urban Archives at Temple University, who helped make Philadelphia feel like a home away from home. Thanks in particular to Brenda Galloway-Wright, whose friendship made my months at the archives productive and also a lot of fun. At the Philadelphia City Archives, Gail Farr facilitated my use of court records and Ward Childs provided important assistance. Thanks also to the archivists and staff at the African American Episcopal Church of St. Thomas, Bryn Mawr College Archives, Center for African American History and Culture at Temple University, Center for the Study of the History of Nursing, Free Library of Philadelphia, Library of Congress, Medical College of Pennsylvania Archives, Mother Bethel Church, National Archives and Records Administration, Pennsylvania State Archives, Philadelphia Board of Education Pedagogical Library, Philadelphia Family Services, Philadelphia Jewish Archives, University of North Carolina Interlibrary Loan Department, University of Pennsylvania Archives, University of Pennsylvania Library, University of Wisconsin Interlibrary Loan Department, and the Wisconsin Historical Society.

After spending several years alone in the archives, I turned to interviewing older women in Philadelphia, and our conversations played a pivotal role in my thinking. I am grateful to the staff at the Golden Slipper Senior Center, Pennsylvania Home, Philadelphia Senior Center, and St. Rita's Senior Center for facilitating the interviews. I promised the women I spoke with that their names would remain confidential, so I cannot mention them individually; but I am tremendously indebted to them for generously sharing their life stories. I have been profoundly affected by their words and experiences and hope that this book conveys the respect that I have for the stories of their lives.

I am grateful for the financial support that gave me time to devote to this book, especially postdoctoral fellowships from the Center for African American Urban Studies and the Economy and the American Association of University Women. Thanks also to the Jacob K. Javits Fellowship Program, the University of Wisconsin History Department, the University of Wisconsin Graduate School, the Feinstein Center for American Jewish History, and the University of North Carolina at Greensboro. Equally important are the remarkable group of young women who helped care for my children over the years: Emily Gresham, Emily Hatfield, Heather Hayes, Madeline Huey, Gini Potts, Meaghan Riordan, and Jennifer Scism.

I have been deeply touched by the generosity of the people who agreed to read and comment on my work. I am particularly grateful to Eileen Boris, Tera Hunter, Alice O'Connor, Annelise Orleck, Wendell Pritchett, Tom Sugrue, and Joe Trotter, all of whose comments on the manuscript improved it immensely. Jack Dougherty, D. Bradford Hunt, Kate Masur, Rhonda Y. Williams, and Michael Willrich provided thoughtful readings of portions of the manuscript and extremely helpful follow-up conversations. Other individuals generously commented on papers and early drafts of chapters: Jason Brent, Sarah Elvins, Arnold Hirsch, Judith Walzer Leavitt, Harvey Levenstein, Walter Licht, Joanne Meyerowitz, Tony Michels, Gwendolyn Mink, Premilla Nadasen, Margaret Nash, Dylan Penningroth, Brenda Gayle Plummer, Steve Schlossman, Karen Spierling, Marc Stein, Lisa Tetrault, and Heather Thompson.

When I began this project in Madison, Wisconsin, Linda Gordon challenged me to develop my own analytical voice even when it led to conclusions that differed from her own. I have benefited greatly from her model of politically engaged and intellectually rigorous scholarship and am extremely grateful for her steadfast support. Steve Kantrowitz's keen mind improved the project, and he has offered sage advice and support throughout my career. Jeanne Boydston provided a model of committed scholarship and teaching, and challenged me to think hard about the meaning of gender. Tim Tyson helped me appreciate the political implications of my work and provided good humor and encouragement. Nan Enstad offered insights on politics, incredible generosity of spirit, and a wonderful friendship. Other friends in Madison also provided crucial assistance. Mariamne Whatley, and especially Nancy Worcester, have been two of my greatest supporters, and it means a great deal to have them in my corner. Long conversations with anu jain inspire me and remind me of what is important. Lisa Tetrault has been a steadfast friend and colleague, and I treasure her honesty and sense of fun. My relationship with Svetlana Karpe began over a decade ago when I told her about my "Sunday night blues" and she began sending me an e-mail message every Sunday evening. Svetlana has become my rock and my lifeline—the friend who signs her messages "always on your side."

From my very first visit to Philadelphia, Tom Sugrue took a keen interest in my project and established himself as a crucial sounding board for my ideas. That Tom's reaction to my arrival in the city was not a polite chat over coffee, but an afternoon-long tour of Philadelphia's neighborhoods that left me with a deeper understanding of the city, as well as several great restaurant tips, speaks volumes about his generosity as a scholar and his spirit as a person. In subsequent years, I have shared many wonderful and stimulating meals with Tom and Dana Barron. Other people in, around, and connected to Philadelphia provided much appreciated support: V. P. Franklin, Gloria Gay, Verdie Givens, Caroline Golab, Janet Golden, Julie Goldsmith, Sarah Barringer Gordon, Walter Lear, Guain McKee, Stephanie Stachniewicz, and Norma Van Dyke. Jane C. Kronick generously spoke with me about her research and shared unpublished materials. For assistance with statistical data, I am grateful to Mark Stern, Benjamin Field, and Jeff Kojac.

I finished the first draft of this book in the fabulous cities of Toronto and Pittsburgh, where I rekindled old friendships and forged new ones. In Pittsburgh, I relied heavily on Tera Hunter's support as well as her great taste in restaurants and wonderful cooking. Tera has been an important friend and mentor, providing wise advice and wonderful all-encompassing conversations. Joe Trotter, Paul Eiss, and Michal Friedman made me feel welcome at Carnegie Mellon and offered great company. Rhonda Y. Williams visited from Baltimore, enabling us to forge a strong intellectual and personal connection. I encountered Marc Stein in an archive in Philadelphia and was fortunate to overlap with him in Toronto, where I benefited from his support and encouragement and spent many enjoyable evenings with him and Jorge Olivares. In Toronto, I also relied on Catherine Carstairs, Sarah Elvins, and Molly Ladd-Taylor. Rebecca Dent remains an anchor despite her multiple—and crucially important—commitments to cancer patients and research. Maia Aziz has been my friend since I was two years old and remains a vital and absolutely irreplaceable part of my daily life.

Fellow North Carolinians have made Greensboro a warm and engaging place to work. At the University of North Carolina at Greensboro, Laurie O'Neill, Doris Corbett, Dawn Sallie, and Kristina Wright provided crucial administrative assistance. Jennifer Scism and Lindsey Hinds-Brown were excellent research assistants and Anna Tapp meticulously prepared the maps. I have also relied on the friendship and support of Chuck Bolton, Ken Caneva, Mary Ellis Gibson, Phyllis Hunter, Jeff Jones, Tom Jackson, Felicia Kornbluh, Bill Link, Cheryl Logan, and Hepsie Roskelly. Benjamin Filene and Rachel Seidman have been wonderful new additions to my life. Pete Carmichael is a supportive and fun colleague and friend and I miss him and his family immensely. Watson

Jennison and Susanna Lee have made me laugh as hard as they have made me think, and I derive great pleasure from our lively discussions of scholarship, families, and politics. Time spent with Madeline Huey has taught me about struggle and resilience. My first meeting with Heather Thompson was an instantaneous personal and intellectual connection that has developed into a friendship that I treasure.

Elsewhere, Kate Masur is as brilliant in analyzing child rearing and family relationships as she is in discussing history. We have turned to each other during both personal and professional challenges, forging a unique and multi-faceted bond that I cherish. Eileen Boris has become a mentor and friend, whom I can call on for all sorts of advice. Grey Osterud helped me find the right words and made the final stage of writing and revising a challenging and collaborative experience that I will never forget. It has been a privilege to work with someone as smart and compassionate as Grey, who is guided by such a strong moral compass.

At the University of North Carolina Press, Chuck Grench expressed interest in the project from the beginning and consistently offered good humor, insight, and support. Katy O'Brien deftly helped me negotiate the final stages of manuscript preparation, Kenneth Graham copyedited the manuscript, and Paula Wald patiently answered numerous questions and provided wise advice.

It is impossible to imagine writing this book without my family. My grandparents, Marie Croatti and the late Aldo Croatti, have respected the choices that I made in my life and offered unwavering love and assistance. My children, Anna and Owen Brent-Levenstein, accepted that I sometimes needed to work instead of play and offered kisses, hugs, and stories when I returned. My sister, Monika, offered laughter when it was possible. The book is dedicated to my outstanding and devoted parents, Mona and Harvey Levenstein, whose sense of humor and unconditional love and support have made all the difference.

Jason Brent has made this a better book, and me a better person. Through snowstorms in Toronto and long hot summers in North Carolina, he has read and revised countless sentences and encouraged me to develop and articulate my vaguely formed ideas. He has kept our household running, helped me laugh at myself, and challenged me to think deeply about the implications of my work. Jason has been with me through it all, and I continue to be inspired by the breadth of his intellectual curiosity, deep compassion for others, and critical engagement with the world around him. As Jason's favorite artist writes, "I'm giving you a longing look. / Everyday I write the book."

A Movement Without Marches

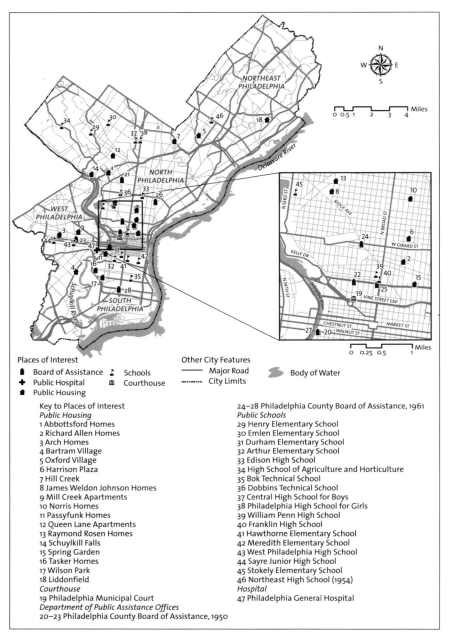

Places of Interest

- ⬛ Board of Assistance
- ✚ Public Hospital
- ⬛ Public Housing
- ♪ Schools
- 🏛 Courthouse

Other City Features

- ── Major Road
- ----- City Limits
- 〰 Body of Water

Key to Places of Interest

Public Housing
1 Abbottsford Homes
2 Richard Allen Homes
3 Arch Homes
4 Bartram Village
5 Oxford Village
6 Harrison Plaza
7 Hill Creek
8 James Weldon Johnson Homes
9 Mill Creek Apartments
10 Norris Homes
11 Passyunk Homes
12 Queen Lane Apartments
13 Raymond Rosen Homes
14 Schuylkill Falls
15 Spring Garden
16 Tasker Homes
17 Wilson Park
18 Liddonfield
Courthouse
19 Philadelphia Municipal Court
Department of Public Assistance Offices
20–23 Philadelphia County Board of Assistance, 1950

24–28 Philadelphia County Board of Assistance, 1961
Public Schools
29 Henry Elementary School
30 Emlen Elementary School
31 Durham Elementary School
32 Arthur Elementary School
33 Edison High School
34 High School of Agriculture and Horticulture
35 Bok Technical School
36 Dobbins Technical School
37 Central High School for Boys
38 Philadelphia High School for Girls
39 William Penn High School
40 Franklin High School
41 Hawthorne Elementary School
42 Meredith Elementary School
43 West Philadelphia High School
44 Sayre Junior High School
45 Stokely Elementary School
46 Northeast High School (1954)
Hospital
47 Philadelphia General Hospital

Map 1. Postwar Philadelphia

Source: Adapted from PASDA, http://www.pasda.psu.edu/.

Note: The institutions shown here are those discussed in this book rather than all the public facilities in the city.

The Multidimensionality of Poverty in a Postwar City

On a hot summer day in 1999, Catherine Sanderson* recalled the challenges she faced decades earlier, caring for her son while working full-time as a domestic for white families in Philadelphia. Wearing a patterned dress and a yellow hat with a narrow brim, she spoke slowly and deliberately with a strong southern accent. "I would go to work in the day, and I would put a key around his neck, and then he'd come home from school," she explained. Afraid her son would get into trouble, she "was always . . . saving up to give him some money and send him to the movies, and tell him to be home at six o'clock, because that's when I'd be home." Sitting erect, with her hands clasped on the table in front of her, Mrs. Sanderson spoke in a warm, measured voice as she recounted the sacrifices she made to ensure that her son graduated from high school and recalled the numerous problems she faced securing basic necessities when he was young. "Well, I had a miserable life," she observed matter-of-factly, "but thank God He brought me through it."

Catherine Sanderson was born in 1911 in Darlington, South Carolina. Her

*Like most of the names used to identify women in this book, Catherine Sanderson is a pseudonym.

mother, who had fifteen children, died in childbirth in 1914, when Catherine was three years old. Her father quickly remarried a woman whom Catherine considered her mother and who bore him an additional seven children. Like most African Americans in Darlington, Catherine's father was a sharecropper. His wife and children joined him in the fields to plow, plant, hoe, and pick the staple crops. On Sundays, they took their only break from field work. In the mornings, they dressed in their finest clothing and attended church. In the afternoons, the children played jump rope and hide-and-seek, while the adults mingled with friends and relaxed.

Catherine's father exerted considerable control over her life, enforcing strict rules in an authoritarian fashion. Although she appreciated his strong religious values and work ethic, she described him as a "mean" man who "hit me . . . when he was bringing me up." Aside from her weekly visits to church and her few years of elementary schooling, her father rarely allowed her to leave home until she turned eighteen and he let her "take company." She fell in love with a man from town, whom her father deemed unacceptable as a husband. Her father insisted that she date a "country boy" instead, and she married a man who fit this description when she was twenty-one. "I didn't love him," Mrs. Sanderson explained; "I married him to get out from under my father."

Mrs. Sanderson described a troubled relationship with her husband. "We said we'd stay together until death do us part," she recalled, "but we didn't because he was mean." Her husband "loved to hit" her and left her and their son for another woman after nine years of marriage. After the separation, Mrs. Sanderson took her son and moved with a female friend to New York City, where she held low-wage jobs in hotels, restaurants, and people's homes. She missed living near family, so when her brother encouraged her to join him in Philadelphia, she moved again. In 1945, at the age of thirty-four, Mrs. Sanderson and her twelve-year-old son arrived at her brother's apartment, ready to make a new life for themselves in Philadelphia.

Corrine Elkins, who also migrated to Philadelphia in 1945, came from different circumstances. A generation younger than Mrs. Sanderson, Mrs. Elkins was born in New York City in 1935. She came to our interview wearing casual clothing—solid-color pants and a plain top—and carried herself confidently. Mrs. Elkins spoke eloquently and animatedly with what she described as a "New England" accent. Her recollections were so intricate that we scheduled a second interview to provide her with ample time to tell the story of her life.

Corrine Elkins's family had lived in the North for decades, largely supported by women who performed domestic work for white families. She believed several children in her family, including her mother and her sister, had been fathered by their mothers' employers—a fact that her relatives did not speak about but that was widely known. "When you were in service and somebody wanted to take a little bit of nookie, you didn't say 'no,'" she explained; "not if you wanted to keep your job."[1]

Corrine spent her childhood in a working-class African American neighborhood in the Bronx. Her father died from a heart attack when she was three, leaving her mother to raise four small children alone. Corrine's mother applied for welfare to help compensate for the loss of her husband's income and worked "under the table" cleaning offices and private homes. Visits from welfare caseworkers became major sources of stress. "We had a dog," she remembered, "and you weren't allowed to have animals on welfare, so every time the welfare lady came by . . . we had to hide the dog." Corrine learned to act "cute and nice for the welfare lady," but she despised watching caseworkers scour her home for signs of rule-breaking. "It was very demeaning," she explained; "You had no privacy."

When Corrine's mother had a hysterectomy to remove a tumor, the family moved to Philadelphia to live with her maternal grandmother. "I took an instant dislike to my grandmother," she recalled, "because she was . . . a snob." Her grandmother had disapproved of her mother's marriage to her father because he was "too dark." "I never could understand that," Mrs. Elkins observed. "People who were prejudiced against, who turn around and be prejudiced. It just makes no sense." In Philadelphia, Corrine's grandmother supported the family by doing domestic work, while Corrine, the eldest daughter, took responsibility for her mother's care. Corrine struggled to stay in school, looking after her mother with little help from her sister and two brothers, who began to run "wild." "My brother was out on the street acting like a hooligan, [and] my sister was out on the street acting like a wannabe hooligan," she explained. "It was just one great big mess."

At seventeen, Corrine Elkins graduated from Philadelphia's William Penn High School and got a job at Bell Telephone, which had recently begun to hire African American workers. Working outside the home became very difficult when she began to suffer from heavy vaginal bleeding. A doctor diagnosed endometriosis and told her that to treat it she had to have an operation, take expensive drugs, or get pregnant. The last option sounded like the best one to Corrine, who began dating the brother of a friend of hers whom she found attractive. Six weeks later, she was pregnant with his child. Upon hearing of the pregnancy, her boyfriend said, "'Well, I guess we'll have to get married.' And so that's how I ended up getting married," she recalled. "This was not a mighty love story."[2]

Over the course of their lives in Philadelphia, both Catherine Sanderson and Corrine Elkins confronted severe poverty and turned to public institutions for assistance. Struggling with various combinations of low wages, poor health, joblessness, inadequate housing, and domestic violence, they joined a "movement without marches": the assertive pursuit of resources from public institutions initiated by low-income African American women in the 1950s and early 1960s. In Philadelphia and cities across the North, ever-increasing numbers of African American women claimed services from local welfare departments, municipal courts, public housing, public schools, and public hospitals. They traveled across the city to seek assistance from public institutions, filling out sheaves of papers in crowded state offices and entering into complicated negotiations with admissions personnel. For decades, black women and their children had used schools, public hospitals, and municipal courts, and they quickly made claims on New Deal programs such as welfare and public housing. However, it was in the 1950s that all of these institutions and programs in Philadelphia began to serve a predominantly black female clientele. By the early 1960s, when African Americans comprised 26 percent of the city's population, black women comprised over 85 percent of those served by the Aid to Dependent Children (ADC) program and at least half of the tenants in public housing, patients at Philadelphia General Hospital, plaintiffs in municipal court, and mothers of students in the public schools.[3] Seeking dignity and respect, and in face of numerous obstacles and personal hardships, these women struggled to use public institutions to improve their lives and secure better futures for their children.

The movement without marches was not a social movement in the ordinary sociological sense of the term. Its participants did not describe themselves as part of a movement, nor did they self-consciously seek to enact large-scale social or political change. Yet the term "movement" is apt because it captures what was literally a mass movement of African American women to claim the benefits and use the services of public institutions, and it underscores the struggles they engaged in to secure assistance. Movement participants did not develop formal political platforms or engage in militant collective protests, but through their interactions with public institutions, they asserted a deeply rooted set of ideas about the responsibility of the state to provide them with basic resources and protections. The cumulative effect of their interactions with these institutions transformed the culture and political economy of modern urban life, altering the landscape of cities and the configuration of state policies and modern racial politics.

African American women's interactions with public institutions played a major role in what historians have called the "origins of the urban crisis": the growing concentration of poverty among African Americans in postwar cities. Most urban historians view black men's joblessness, stemming from deindustrialization, racial inequalities in the labor market, and public policies that confined African Americans to deteriorating housing in segregated neighborhoods, as the driving force behind the economic decline of the "inner city."[4] Their approach emphasizes the significance of racial discrimination and provides a historical perspective on William Julius Wilson's pathbreaking 1987 book, *The Truly Disadvantaged*, which focused on the structural causes of chronic black male unemployment. Wilson's work suggested that providing African American men with jobs would encourage marriage among the poor, thereby improving the social standing of both black men and black women.[5]

Examining the situation of black city-dwellers from a gendered perspective that foregrounds women's positions, actions, and viewpoints changes our understanding of the urban crisis significantly. Although black women supported efforts to find jobs for men and suffered when black men were unemployed, men's unemployment was not the sole or even primary cause of their poverty. They expected to hold jobs themselves and sought to acquire the resources they needed to support themselves and their families. Poor black women faced distinct challenges in postwar cities. They suffered not only from racial discrimination in housing and employment but also from sex discrimination. They were susceptible to domestic violence, vulnerable to health problems at a young age, and usually the primary caregivers for children. Black women were treated differently from black men by the public institutions that maintained African Americans in impoverished circumstances and the public discourse that blamed them for their predicaments. These distinctive struggles that poor African American women confronted reveal a heretofore unexamined component of the urban crisis: the gendered construction of racialized urban poverty.

Understanding the impoverishment of black residents of postwar cities as a gendered process that women and men experienced in different ways impels us to move beyond the focus on race, housing, and employment that dominates the historical literature on the urban crisis. This narrow approach has distorted our understanding of the production of inequalities in U.S. cities because it ignores many crucial components of women's and men's struggles. Deindustrialization and racial discrimination in employment and housing played important roles in shaping people's lives, but so did sex discrimination, health problems, inadequate education, domestic violence, lack of child care, the public discourse on poverty, and the policies implemented by public institutions. These social forces and structures interacted in various ways: Lack of child care hindered the acquisition of jobs; unemployment restricted access to health care; welfare assistance enabled women to care for children; domestic violence inhibited women's abilities to pursue employment; dilapidated housing contributed to health problems; and public portrayals of African Americans as welfare "cheats" and criminals created a social environment that impeded their access to jobs and housing. Scholars who focus narrowly on the production of racial inequalities in employment and housing obscure these multidimensional roots of postwar urban poverty and underestimate the extent of poor people's efforts to improve their lives.[6]

Women's attempts to claim resources from public institutions left indelible marks on the postwar urban landscape, bringing a range of government benefits and services into poor black communities. Whether they held jobs or relied on other forms of income, the majority of the women and children in low-income African American neighborhoods used at least one public institution besides the schools; many women combined resources from several different government agencies. They secured an unprecedented range of resources from public institutions, supplementing or replacing some of the long-standing survival strategies that had helped sustain working-class communities for decades. These resources helped women care for themselves and their children and achieve more leverage in their relationships with employers and with men. Yet public institutions also introduced new problems into women's lives. State programs rarely helped them escape from poverty and frequently subjected them to intense surveillance and public humiliation. Looked at as a whole, then, women's use of public institutions both alleviated and intensified the inequalities in postwar cities.[7]

Women engaged in struggles with state authorities over their right to pursue adequate and respectful government assistance that produced several changes in public policies. Although a rich historical literature explores black women's collective activism in welfare rights and tenant rights organizations in the late 1960s and 1970s, as Robin D. G. Kelley has observed, "some of the most dynamic struggles take place outside—indeed sometimes in spite of— established organizations."[8] In the 1950s and early 1960s, when large numbers of poor African American women in Philadelphia turned to public institutions seeking upward mobility, dignity, and respect, the collective weight of their efforts put pressure on state authorities to respond to their demands. Women achieved the most success at Philadelphia General Hospital, which sought to accommodate their requests for neonatal and obstetrical care and treatment for complications from illegal abortions. Many other public institutions responded to women with hostility, dismissing their efforts or implementing restrictive policies that made it even more difficult for them to secure resources. In several instances, government officials refused to appropriate adequate funds for programs that served large numbers of African American women. The insufficient funding of programs such as welfare and public housing led to inadequate services that kept women and children in poverty instead of helping them escape it. As women struggled to obtain the resources and respect they believed they deserved from public institutions, their efforts sometimes prompted state authorities to implement policies that made it even more difficult for them to secure adequate assistance.

African American women's movement into the halls and offices of public institutions provoked fierce public opposition that exposed the fault lines and limitations of the postwar liberal and civil rights agendas. In Philadelphia, as elsewhere, although a contingent of liberal whites supported the civil rights movement, many other whites responded to African American in-migration and civil rights activism by opposing the integration of their neighborhoods, recreational facilities, and schools and by escaping to the suburbs where they hoped to avoid African Americans completely. In the 1950s and early 1960s, the media and the police in Philadelphia reinforced whites' fears by focusing public attention on black crime. In this highly charged political climate, African American women's use of state resources drew intense public criticism, particularly from prominent Democratic public figures.[9] Democratic municipal court judges berated African American women for neglecting their numerous "illegitimate" children and taking unfair advantage of the resources they could garner from the city's education, health, and welfare systems. Even those liberals most likely to sympathize with poor African American women's predicaments did not fundamentally challenge the terms of the debate. Civil rights activists tried to avoid the highly charged public discussions of black "illegitimacy" and concentrated on the problems confronted by middle-class African Americans and working-class African American men. Social welfare advocates sometimes defended single mothers but focused most of their attention on reducing the number of women who relied on government assistance. No one publicly questioned the widespread belief that public institutions "gave charity" to the "dependent" poor while government benefits such as old-age pensions and unemployment insurance were "earned" by hardworking "taxpayers."

Although Philadelphia Democrats took the lead in publicly decrying African American women's use of public institutions, Republicans consistently portrayed government efforts on behalf of African Americans as a threat to whites' social standing. In 1951, a landmark Democratic victory that ended thirty-five years of Republican rule in Philadelphia city government left Republicans without a strong platform in municipal politics. Nevertheless, prominent Republicans helped incite opposition to the construction of public housing, and the city's two major newspapers, both Republican, encouraged white resistance by publishing inflammatory editorials condemning black women's reliance on welfare and public health care.[10] In subsequent years, Republicans would use the sensationalist claims about African American women's "promiscuity" and "abuse" of state programs that emerged in the 1950s to help build a powerful social movement that relied on racialized antigovernment rhetoric and appeals to conservative ideals of gender, sexuality, and the family.[11]

Confronting Poverty in Postwar Philadelphia

The difficulties Catherine Sanderson and Corrine Elkins faced during their lives in postwar Philadelphia illuminate the multidimensionality of urban poverty and its gendered, as well as racialized, construction. Many African American men faced enormous difficulties providing for themselves and their families. Yet women's problems differed from men's because women usually held the primary responsibility for raising children, encountered both race and sex discrimination in housing and employment, were vulnerable to domestic violence, and were more likely than men to need medical attention before old age.[12] Informal community networks, churches, and private social service agencies lacked sufficient resources to address these problems, leading thousands of women like Mrs. Sanderson and Mrs. Elkins to turn to public institutions for assistance.

In 1945, Philadelphia was the nation's third largest city, with two million residents. Tens of thousands of working-class African Americans migrated to the city during and after World War II in search of new opportunities. In 1940, foreign-born immigrants (primarily from Russia, Ireland, Germany, Italy, Great Britain, and Poland) comprised 15 percent of the city's population, African Americans comprised 13 percent, and native-born whites comprised 72 percent. Over the next two decades, the proportion of foreign-born residents decreased to 9 percent, while the number of African Americans more than doubled, from a quarter million to more than half a million people; by 1960, African Americans comprised 26 percent of the city's population (see Table I.1).[13] Most African Americans who migrated to the city were low-income young adults in their prime wage-earning and child-rearing years, who came as part of a chain migration of family and friends.[14] Three-quarters came from the South Atlantic region: South Carolina, North Carolina, Georgia, Virginia, and Washington, D.C. The rest came from northern or border states: New York, New Jersey, Ohio, other parts of Pennsylvania, Maryland, Delaware, and West Virginia.[15]

Over the course of their lives, Mrs. Sanderson and Mrs. Elkins lived in many different apartments scattered throughout Philadelphia's working-class African American neighborhoods. At the turn of the century, Philadelphia had earned a reputation as a "city of homes" because of its high-caliber housing and high

Table 1.1. African American Population of Philadelphia, 1930–1960

Year	Total Population	African American Population	Percentage African American	Increase
1930	1,950,961	219,599	11.3	—
1940	1,931,334	250,880	13.0	14.2%
1950	2,071,605	376,041	18.2	49.9
1960	2,002,512	529,239	26.4	40.7

Source: *Population of Metropolitan Area Counties: 1790–1960; Population of Philadelphia Sections and Wards, 1860–1960* (Philadelphia: Philadelphia City Planning Commission, 1963), 2-1.

rates of home ownership. Even low-income residents frequently rented detached or semidetached houses instead of large tenements. Mrs. Sanderson's first apartment was in South Philadelphia, the city's oldest African American neighborhood and the site of W. E. B. Du Bois's famous 1896 study, *The Philadelphia Negro*. African Americans in South Philadelphia frequently lived in two-story brick-row houses south of Spruce Street, from the Schuylkill almost to the Delaware River. In the postwar period, although the neighborhood had a few vacant lots, it was generally lively and bustling. The streets were filled with people, children played on the sidewalks, and residents could purchase meats and produce from a large open-air market. The neighborhood had several small businesses including an ice manufacturer, a paper and publishing company, and men's and women's apparel factories. Of all the neighborhoods where African Americans lived, South Philadelphia was the most racially mixed. In some areas, African Americans lived on all-black blocks directly adjacent to all-white blocks inhabited mostly by Italians. A few blocks housed African Americans on one side of the street and Italians on the other.[16]

Mrs. Sanderson moved every few years, never finding a place she could afford where she felt safe and comfortable. Her second apartment was in North Philadelphia, the neighborhood with the largest and densest concentration of African Americans that extended from Poplar Street north to Lehigh Avenue, between the Delaware and the Schuylkill Rivers. Some North Philadelphia blocks were in good condition, with relatively high rates of African American home ownership and active community groups. Others were controlled by absentee landlords and extremely run-down. The neighborhood had crowded streets with large numbers of vacant lots and abandoned houses. Many families rented small two-room apartments in two- or three-story brick row houses. Some lacked running water and private bathrooms. Ridge Avenue, a central thoroughfare, housed a farmers' market, a butcher shop, and a supermarket

In the 1950s, North Philadelphia was the poorest neighborhood in the city, but it maintained a vibrant street life. Temple University Libraries, Urban Archives, Philadelphia, Pa.

known to local residents to stock poor-quality goods. As factories, warehouses, and breweries closed down, the parts of North Philadelphia close to Center City retained some small industries, while the sections further from the downtown core had more movie theaters and bars (locally called "taprooms") than places of employment.[17]

North Philadelphia had a reputation among whites as a dangerous area, a black "jungle" dominated by crime, immorality, and liquor; but residents of the neighborhood frequently emphasized the presence of block groups working to improve the community and the large number of stable, hardworking families.[18] Corrine Elkins, who lived in North Philadelphia during her teenage years, described the neighborhood in the 1950s as "nice," at least in comparison to subsequent years when it became even more run-down. Yet she also confronted sexual harassment and the threat of rape while living there. "Say you just gotta walk three blocks to a grocery store; somebody's going to say something to you," she recalled. The young black men who congregated on corners in her neighborhood frequently teased her when she passed, telling her she was "built like a brick shithouse." "If you couldn't handle the repartee, they're backing you up somewhere. . . . And everybody was not going to jump to your defense." Onlookers would "just sit back and grin at you," she explained, leaving her to fend off assaults alone.

As an adult, Mrs. Elkins moved to the African American neighborhood in West Philadelphia. Here, families lived in two-story brick-row houses, side-by-side duplexes known as "twin houses," and converted apartments in larger homes that had once been the most exclusive mansions in the city but had become extremely neglected. The African American neighborhood in West Philadelphia extended between Market Street, Mantua Avenue, Wyalusing Avenue, and Girard Avenue, and between Fairmount Park and 64th Street. Many small businesses were integrated into the residential area, and there was a great deal of life on the streets. Neighbors sat on their steps, and children were disciplined collectively by mothers who punished anyone they caught misbehaving on their blocks. Mrs. Elkins lived in a "wreck" of a building in the area of West Philadelphia that African Americans called "the bottom" because of its location below 52nd Street. "The bottom," Mrs. Elkins explained, accurately described the physical condition of the neighborhood. Compared to the more prosperous area above 52nd Street called "the top," it was "pretty degraded."[19]

Although African Americans had always occupied run-down housing in Philadelphia, prior to World War II their living conditions had not differed substantially from those of the immigrants and poor whites who lived near them.[20] However, in the postwar period, African Americans lived in increasingly racially segregated neighborhoods and began to predominate among those who lived in dilapidated and crowded conditions. Across the country, racist government initiatives, banking practices, and real estate policies facilitated white home ownership and suburbanization while confining African Americans to old housing in segregated or "transitional" neighborhoods, which whites were leaving as African Americans were moving in. Almost all mortgages for new housing underwritten by the Federal Housing Authority and the Veterans Administration went to whites, not African Americans, and private banks frequently discriminated against African Americans seeking mortgage assistance. Slum clearance and urban renewal projects were dubbed "Negro Removal" because they disproportionately uprooted working-class African Americans. The locations chosen for public housing further confined poor African American families to segregated neighborhoods. Women found it particularly difficult to find places to live because many landlords refused to rent to single mothers.[21]

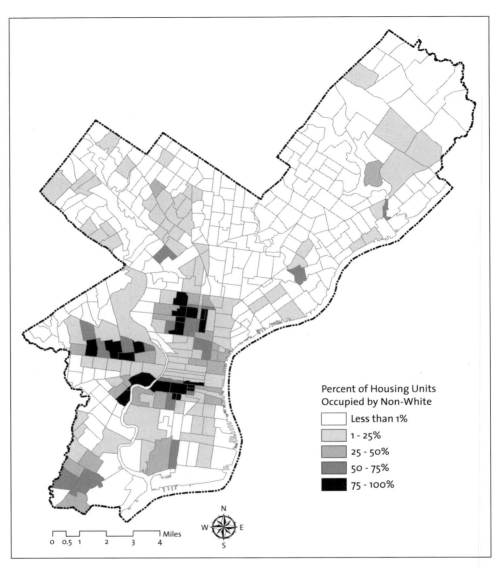

Map 2. Racial Composition of Philadelphia, 1950 Census Tracts
Sources: National Historic GIS, http://www.nhgis.org/; PASDA, http://
www.pasda.psu.edu/; U.S. Department of Commerce, *U.S. Census of Population: 1950,*
Census Tract Statistics, 154–204.

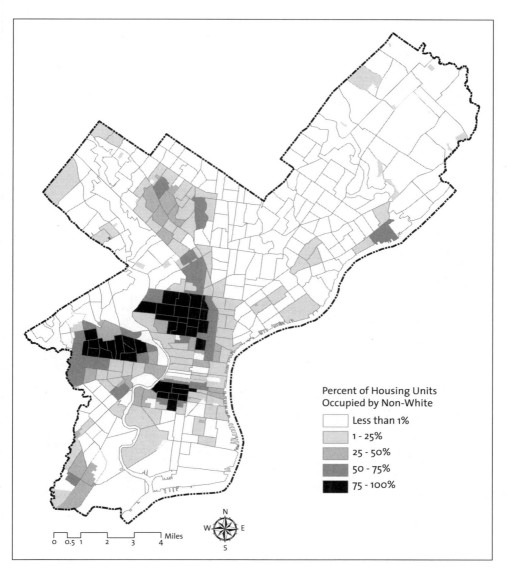

Map 3. Racial Composition of Philadelphia, 1960 Census Tracts
Sources: National Historic GIS, http://www.nhgis.org/; PASDA, http://
www.pasda.psu.edu/; U.S. Department of Commerce, *U.S. Census of Housing: 1960,*
City Blocks, 1–169.

Poplar Street in North Philadelphia had some shops and businesses in the 1950s.
Temple University Libraries, Urban Archives, Philadelphia, Pa.

By 1960, African Americans inhabited 75 percent of all dilapidated units in Philadelphia, mostly crowded together in census tracts that were more than 50 percent black.[22]

Mrs. Elkins and Mrs. Sanderson both combined marriage and motherhood with continued participation in the labor force. They held jobs after they married and returned to the labor force after the births of their children. Mrs.

Sanderson wanted a large family, but she was unable to conceive again after bearing her son. Mrs. Elkins, who had five pregnancies and three surviving children born eleven months apart, quickly became "sick of babies." In returning to the labor force when they had small children, Mrs. Sanderson and Mrs. Elkins joined thousands of other African American mothers who did not have the means to stay home with their children full-time and viewed employment as a way to fulfill their maternal responsibilities.[23]

The labor market that Mrs. Sanderson and Mrs. Elkins confronted in Philadelphia was undergoing major structural shifts. Throughout the nineteenth century, the city had been a thriving manufacturing metropolis, well-known for its diverse array of goods—textiles, clothing, paper, glass, furniture, shoes, and hardware—produced in comparatively small shops and factories. However, in the first decades of the twentieth century, the city lost thousands of manufacturing jobs as the national shift in the location and nature of work—from center cities to suburbs, from the Northeast to the South and West, and from manufacturing to service industries—began to take its toll.[24] The tide turned briefly during World War II when, thanks to federally funded plant expansion, factories hired over 27,000 new workers.[25] After the war, Bucks County, the city's northeast suburban area, experienced an "industrial boom," becoming the site of seven new industrial plants opened by large firms such as U.S. Steel and Philco.[26] Yet within Philadelphia proper, where most African Americans lived, the job losses continued. Between 1952 and 1962, a period of national prosperity, Philadelphia lost 90,000 jobs, as factories either went out of business or moved away. The city's unemployment rate fluctuated between 8 and 12 percent compared with a national average of 4 to 7 percent.[27]

The loss of manufacturing jobs hit working-class African Americans particularly hard because they were concentrated in the factory and service-work sectors within the city and nearly completely excluded from most professional jobs and skilled trades (see Table I.2). This skewed occupational distribution resulted in part from African Americans' relatively lower levels of formal education and lack of access to job training. Widespread discrimination in hiring and promotion and racist barriers around entire occupational categories also played a significant role in limiting their employment opportunities. By 1960, the black unemployment rate was 11 percent compared to only 5 percent for whites. A survey of some of the poorest African American neighborhoods in the city found 37 percent of the labor force jobless and 42 percent employed only irregularly as domestics, service workers, and common laborers.[28]

Women, like men, scrambled to find even low-paying, physically demanding jobs. Mrs. Sanderson's employment history was typical. With only a fourth-grade education, she went from employer to employer, performing "any type of

Table 1.2. African American Labor Force Participation in Philadelphia, 1960

Percentage of male labor force	22.4%
Professional and technical workers	8.7
Craftsmen and foremen	14.4
Clerical workers	19.3
Salesworkers	7.1
Operatives	26.5
Private household workers	78.0
Service workers	37.0
Percentage of female labor force	29.8
Professional and technical workers	18.3
Craftsmen and foremen	19.9
Clerical workers	11.3
Salesworkers	10.5
Operatives	34.5
Private household workers	86.5
Service workers	43.6

Source: U.S. Department of Commerce, *U.S. Censuses of Population and Housing: 1960*, 243, 317.

job I could get my hands on," sometimes in manufacturing but mostly cooking and other domestic work. She held several positions as a domestic for white families, which paid very little, isolated her, and required her to work under intense scrutiny. Mrs. Sanderson recalled lunches consisting of a boiled potato and a glass of milk, provided by women employers who set their clocks back an hour to keep her until six instead of five o'clock, without paying her for the extra hour.[29] She rarely made enough money to eat properly and became "so weak that I could hardly work." Losing weight at an alarming pace, Mrs. Sanderson began taking large quantities of Bufferin (a brand of aspirin) to help manage the chronic pain and exhaustion she experienced. A typical day involved her waking up early in the morning, taking a "bunch of Bufferins," drinking a Coke or a Pepsi, sometimes some coffee, and then going to her job. She took Bufferin throughout the day and came home in the evening to cook dinner for her son, clean her house, and wash and iron clothes. Since she rarely had enough money for her and her son to eat dinner each day, like many mothers, she went without.

Corrine Elkins fared better than most in the labor market, helped by the education she received at William Penn High School. While most Philadelphia public schools that served large numbers of African Americans were overcrowded, underfunded, and understaffed, William Penn was unique. Under Dr. Ruth Wright Hayre, the first black high school principal in the city, it offered a challenging curriculum and a serious and supportive environment that cultivated academic success. After Corrine graduated from William Penn, she learned that Bell Telephone was hiring African American women as operators and decided to apply. To get the job, she had to pass a series of tests and participate in a home interview. She had no problem with the tests, and she smiled when she described the home visit. Her mother had just died, so the interviewers from Bell had to deal with her grandmother. Their first question was a big mistake. They asked her grandmother, who had been born and raised in Philadelphia, when she had arrived in the city. Highly insulted, her grandmother disdainfully responded, "Do you assume all black people are from the South?" "I got the job," explained Mrs. Elkins, chuckling. Her grandmother's "snobbishness came in handy that time."

Corrine Elkins worked at Bell Telephone for five years and described it as "a very prejudiced place." She did not recount a specific incident of racism, but explained that "they let you know that you were not quite up to par." Despite the hostile environment, Mrs. Elkins loved her job because it was "complex" and you "had to be good at what you did." She found holidays like Christmas especially rewarding because she fielded calls from people living far away, wanting to speak with their loved ones. "I traveled all around the world by telephone," she recalled.

Bell Telephone opened jobs to African American women in the postwar period because of the pressure exerted by local civil rights organizations. Philadelphia's civil rights movement was spearheaded by the city's branch of the National Association for the Advancement of Colored People (NAACP) and received assistance from the Armstrong Association, renamed the Urban League in 1957. Both organizations were "liberal" insofar as they sought to equalize opportunities for black and white Philadelphians while working within the existing political and economic system.[30] The NAACP focused primarily on eliminating barriers in employment, housing, and education, while the Armstrong Association paid particular attention to the struggles of working-class Philadelphians, especially newcomers to the city. Interracial organizations such as the Philadelphia Fellowship Commission, a liberal group that sought to promote "intergroup understanding," and the Commission on Human Relations (CHR), the city government agency responsible for the enforcement of antidiscrimination laws, frequently supported African Americans' organizing efforts.[31]

Most of the activism orchestrated by Philadelphia's postwar civil rights movement focused on opening the city's labor force to African Americans.[32] In the immediate postwar period, the NAACP broke many important employment barriers, securing positions for African Americans as operators at Bell Telephone, "salesgirls" in department stores, meter readers at gas companies, and interns at Philadelphia General Hospital.[33] In the 1950s, the CHR successfully pressured employers such as the Pennsylvania Railroad and two national loan companies to hire African Americans.[34] Philadelphia's labor force was desegregated even further in the early 1960s, thanks to a "selective patronage" campaign launched by the 400 Ministers, an organization of black clergy led by Reverend Leon Sullivan, a civil rights leader who was the pastor of the Zion Baptist Church. Drawing on a long history of African American consumer activism and "don't buy where you can't work" campaigns, the ministers presented Philadelphia firms that had discriminatory practices with specific demands regarding the hiring of African Americans. If the firms refused to comply, the local women who shopped for their families refused to buy the companies' products. The selective patronage campaign opened up over two thousand jobs to African Americans, and Reverend Sullivan estimated that an additional three hundred companies changed their hiring practices after the ministers threatened boycotts.[35]

The most significant employment gains that African Americans achieved in the postwar period came in the municipal sector. In 1948, Philadelphia became one of the first cities in the nation to establish a fair employment practices law, and in 1951, a coalition of civil rights activists and liberal reformers succeeded in incorporating into the new city charter clauses explicitly banning racial discrimination in municipal employment, services, and contracts.[36] After the black vote provided the margin of victory for the Democratic coalition that came to power in city hall, the new administration headed by Mayor Joseph S. Clark rewarded African Americans by enforcing these equal rights provisions in the civil service.[37] Rather than awarding municipal jobs on a patronage basis, the prevailing practice before the 1950s, Democrats began to award them on the basis of standardized exams and application processes that did not discriminate by race.[38] Many African Americans gained access to municipal jobs, coveted positions that provided workers with good salaries, standardized sick leaves, vacations, health insurance, and job security. By the early 1960s, when African Americans constituted 26 percent of the city's population, they comprised 39 percent of its municipal labor force.[39] Although they did not gain access to the upper echelon of municipal jobs (almost all city employees who earned more than $7,000 were white), those who secured city jobs frequently achieved upward mobility and job security, helping propel the growth of the African American middle class. The increase in rates of home ownership illustrates black families' growing attainment of middle-class status: Between 1940 and 1960, the proportion of African Americans owning a home rose from 10 to 43 percent.[40]

Mrs. Elkins was one of the many African Americans who benefited from the opening up of municipal employment. After the births of her sons, she taught herself to type and applied to work for the city. Describing why she was attracted to municipal employment, she explained: "I wanted security. And in those days, city jobs were security. Once you got the job, you had it for life." After she obtained her first municipal job, classified as a Clerk-Typist I, Mrs. Elkins took advantage of the opportunities the city provided for its employees to achieve upward mobility. She moved up to a Clerk-Typist II, and, building on her previous job experience, she eventually obtained coveted positions as a telephone operator and municipal radio operator.

In the early 1960s, Mrs. Elkins's life changed dramatically when she left her philandering and abusive husband, who had started whipping her with belts soon after they married. After "one too many beatings," she recalled, "I got to the point I wanted to kill him. And I said no, because I remember during some women talk . . . the way they put it, if you want to hear in the vernacular: don't let no nigger get you mad enough where you want to kill him—then it's time to leave." So Mrs. Elkins finally decided, "I am out of here—I am not going to jail for this man." She packed some clothing in a suitcase and took her three young boys to her sister's house. She had hoped to live with her sister until she could afford a place of her own. Her sister, however, was raising six children on welfare in a very small apartment with two German shepherds and a "crazy" husband who drank too much, resented Mrs. Elkins's presence, and threatened her with guns. Recognizing that their living situation was untenable, Mrs. Elkins and her sister decided to pool resources and move to West Philadelphia, where they found a vacant dilapidated house in "the bottom" large enough to accommodate all nine children. It had no running water or electricity and was overrun with "water bugs." "God, that place . . . was terrible," Mrs. Elkins recalled; "I hated it."

After several months, Mrs. Elkins finally saved enough money to leave her sister and move her children to another West Philadelphia apartment. Although the new apartment had water and electricity, it still lacked basic necessities because when Mrs. Elkins had escaped from her husband, she had to leave behind all the appliances, towels, sheets, blankets, dishware, and furniture that she had accumulated over the years. "I was . . . going from place to place, and all I had was clothes and kids," she recalled. Her paycheck from her clerical job with the Water Department barely covered food, clothing, and rent, leaving her unable to replace essential household items. Lacking money to ride the bus, she would have lost her job if her coworkers had not agreed to drive her back and forth to the Water Department each day. Purchasing big-ticket items like beds or tables was out of the question. "I did a lot of floor sleeping," Mrs. Elkins explained. "I became real familiar with floors."

Employment did not solve the multidimensional problems that Mrs. Elkins and Mrs. Sanderson confronted. Both women had steady jobs—Mrs. Elkins even had a good one—yet they still faced severe poverty. For Mrs. Elkins, a marital separation sparked by domestic violence led her to forfeit almost all of her material possessions. Once she became poor, the expenses that accompanied her responsibility for her children made it extremely difficult to save the money she needed to improve her circumstances. Mrs. Sanderson spent her entire life in poverty, the result of her lack of education, limited employment prospects, health problems, and the burdens she faced raising a child by herself. Neither she nor Mrs. Elkins could pinpoint a single cause of their poverty because of its multiple and interlocking roots.

The survival strategies that working-class African Americans had long employed to help make ends meet were inadequate for women such as Mrs. Elkins and Mrs. Sanderson, who were struggling to overcome many problems simultaneously. Although scholars have illuminated the importance of community and family support networks to working-class families, many low-income women described their limitations.[41] Mrs. Elkins tapped into support networks, living temporarily with her sister after she left her husband and relying on her friends at the Water Department to chauffeur her to her job each day. But most of her friends and relatives were also struggling to get by, so the assistance they could offer—and that she could reciprocate—was short-term or small-scale. Mrs. Sanderson relied even less on social networks to resolve her problems. "I wasn't much of a talker," she explained. Although she had a small circle of friends at church, her shyness prevented her from engaging in the casual socializing that took place on the streets and inhibited her from joining other local women in exchanging food and clothing and sharing child care responsibilities. Mrs. Sanderson did not regard depending on men as an option either. Although she had a "couple" of boyfriends over the years, she did not trust them to treat her well and did not want to rely on them for her survival. "I don't depend on no man," she boasted, "and he can't tell me what to do." Some working-class Philadelphians participated in the informal economy—taking in boarders, engaging in prostitution and the numbers racket, making repairs on automobiles, sewing, baking, and running speakeasies—but these pursuits rarely enabled them to achieve significant upward mobility.

Meanwhile, private social service agencies did not provide much help. Although some white social service agencies served African Americans, many others either closed down when whites left their surrounding neighborhoods or discriminated against the black Philadelphians who sought assistance. On shoe-string budgets, agencies that catered to African Americans such as the Wharton Centre (a settlement house) and the black Young Men's Christian Association

(YMCA) and Young Women's Christian Association (YWCA) pieced together an impressive array of community programs and services. Yet on the whole, institutions that served African Americans were poorer than those that served whites and could not afford to provide much direct financial support to those in need. As Mrs. Elkins put it, "Social services . . . were just not equipped" to deal with the extent of poverty in her neighborhood.

African American churches traditionally served as a support system for struggling congregants. In 1950, Philadelphia had hundreds of black churches: 275 were storefront churches (small, independent congregations gathered around a charismatic preacher); 247 had 200 or more members; and 28 had at least 1,000 members. Men served as the leaders of most of these churches, although women comprised the bulk of the members.[42] Many churches had distinctive membership bases, with most of their congregants belonging to a similar social class or sharing similar southern origins. Although the African Methodist Episcopal (AME) Church, founded in Philadelphia, had long been the most influential denomination in the city, southern migration bolstered the ranks of Baptists. By 1955, Philadelphia had 225,000 African American Baptists in 362 churches, and several Baptist churches grew to over 3,000 members.[43] The proliferation of storefront churches was another way that new arrivals made their mark on the urban social landscape.[44]

For many African American women, the church was at the center of their lives. They attended services every Sunday, sent their children to Sunday school, and returned during the week to attend meetings, participate in recreational events, practice singing, and engage in community service. Churches provided women with a social outlet and sense of community as well as the ability to fulfill the responsibilities they felt to God and to their communities. "I was raised up in church," Mrs. Sanderson explained, "and I . . . couldn't stay out of church." Churches offered recreational opportunities and sometimes provided congregants with services such as home loans, scholarships, and libraries.[45] Mrs. Sanderson credited her religious involvement for increasing her self-esteem, providing her with a sense of community, and bolstering her faith and morale. Yet when she needed substantial material aid, she recognized that her church could not provide the kind of sustained assistance she required. Other women, like Mrs. Elkins, rarely attended church at all because they lacked interest, had no spare time, or did not own appropriate clothing.

Employment often did not lift mothers out of poverty, and informal mutual aid networks, churches, and private social service agencies had insufficient resources to solve the major problems they confronted. So when Mrs. Sanderson and Mrs. Elkins faced severe difficulties in their lives, they turned to Philadelphia's network of public institutions for assistance. From their claims on the Freedmen's Bureau during Reconstruction to twentieth-century civil rights activists' pursuit of social welfare services, African Americans have historically taken a strong stand in favor of public institutions.[46] In this tradition, many poor black women used postwar public institutions to secure resources that they were otherwise denied, including health care, financial support for child rearing, protection from domestic violence, housing, and education.

When women contemplated approaching public institutions for assistance, a host of factors came into play: their experiences as children and young adults, their family's and community's understandings of the nature of the services provided by various government programs, and the specific problems they faced. Both Mrs. Sanderson and Mrs. Elkins first came into contact with Philadelphia's public institutions when they enrolled their children in the public school system. Mrs. Sanderson deeply regretted her lack of education. Her father had forced her to leave school at a young age because her stepmother became sick and the family needed her to care for the younger children. "I wanted to finish [school] but I couldn't," she explained, recalling the disappointment she felt when she learned that she would have to forgo her education. Believing that she had missed out on a crucial opportunity to obtain knowledge and credentials, Mrs. Sanderson resolved that her son would receive an education at all costs. For Mrs. Elkins, her own employment history testified to the power of education. Her high school diploma enabled her to obtain a municipal job, and she wanted her sons to have access to similar opportunities.

Mrs. Elkins and Mrs. Sanderson engaged in a great deal of deliberation before approaching other public institutions. After Mrs. Elkins left her husband, she considered applying for welfare, which would have enabled her to focus her attention on finding a new apartment and spend time helping her children adjust to their new living arrangement. However, after recalling her sister's and her mother's humiliating experiences with public assistance, she decided to continue with her job, which provided more money than welfare and did not involve demeaning invasions of privacy. When Mrs. Elkins's friends learned about the financial difficulties she faced trying to support her family on her paycheck alone, several of them suggested that she seek child support from her husband through the municipal court, assuring her that judges in such cases almost always ruled in women's favor. Mrs. Elkins had hoped to limit her contact with her husband after she moved out, but her need for money outweighed her reluctance to see him in court. She took her friends' advice, and, after a series of interviews with the court's staff and a great deal of paperwork, she successfully pressed charges against her husband and received a court order for child support.

Mrs. Sanderson made a different set of decisions about seeking welfare and child support. After her arrival in Philadelphia, her husband migrated to the city. "A lot of people [told] me I should go into the courts and have him support [my son]," she recalled, but "I was too stiff and stubborn." Mrs. Sanderson feared her husband would view her taking legal action as a sign of weakness, an indication that she could not support herself on her own. Instead, when Mrs. Sanderson faced a health crisis she could not cope with alone, she approached the welfare department for assistance. A few years after her move to Philadelphia, her years of overwork and poor nutrition caused her to collapse. She consulted a doctor who told her that she needed to stop working completely and encouraged her to apply for welfare. Mrs. Sanderson took his advice, and, after convincing caseworkers of the severity of her illness, she qualified for Aid to Dependent Children (ADC). Welfare enabled her to quit her job and regain her health while supporting her son. It prevented her from losing her home and her family and possibly saved her life.

The predicaments in which working-class African American women like Mrs. Sanderson and Mrs. Elkins found themselves led them to seek assistance from public institutions. Denied access to adequate education in the South and to decent employment in Philadelphia, Mrs. Sanderson toiled to support herself and her son beyond the limits of her physical endurance. Mrs. Elkins's reliable job did not keep her out of poverty when she left her husband and tried to raise her children alone. Domestic violence, marital separations, inadequate wages, and responsibility for children plunged both women into precarious living situations, forcing them to teeter on the brink of financial and familial disaster.

Reconceptualizing Poverty and Working-Class Life in Postwar Cities

This book explores the gendered construction of racialized poverty in postwar Philadelphia by examining the experiences, perspectives, and actions of African American women who sought assistance from the city's public institutions. The women in this book were in their childbearing years, mostly mothers, and either married, separated, divorced, or never married. Many had been born in the South and moved to Philadelphia as children or young adults. While some women attained a modicum of financial stability, most were very poor, often chronically and occasionally acutely so. Many scholars and political commentators would later describe them as part of an emerging urban "underclass," a term used from the early 1960s to the present to refer to severely impoverished people who have no connection to the labor force, often use drugs and alcohol, and hold values that differ starkly from the majority of U.S.

residents. The term is usually assumed or asserted to apply primarily to African Americans and is highly differentiated by gender: The men designated as members of this "underclass" are often described as violent criminals or drug dealers who have chosen not to hold jobs, while the women are depicted as single mothers who have no aspirations beyond dependence on welfare.[47]

This book rejects the term "underclass" and redefines the working class to include women who pursued various forms of government assistance in combination with, or instead of, employment. Many of the women in this book did exhibit some of the characteristics commonly associated with the "underclass": They received public assistance, became pregnant unintentionally, suffered from depression, or used drugs and alcohol. Yet rather than holding a unique set of immoral values, most women who sought assistance from public institutions did so to fulfill goals shared by people of all classes: to mother their children, live in decent housing, receive effective and respectful health care, ensure their children acquired an adequate education, and secure protection from violence. Many placed a high value on social respectability and sought upward mobility for their children. The term "underclass" not only paints a false portrait of poor women's goals and values, but it also severely misconstrues their work habits. Regardless of their employment status, women who sought and retained assistance from public institutions were workers, first and foremost, because they labored to care for their households and their families with few financial resources. Their involvement with public institutions constituted another important form of unpaid labor that they performed to help sustain their families in postwar cities.[48]

The "state" that women confronted was not monolithic. An expansive set of institutions came together to help create the fabric of women's lives, not only the public housing programs examined by urban historians and the public assistance benefits explored by historians of the welfare state, but also the municipal court, public schools, and the public hospital.[49] Each institution had a unique understanding of the causes of poverty and the needs of the poor. The lack of a comprehensive federal social welfare system, or even much coordination among institutions, meant that when women sought assistance from government programs, they encountered many different kinds of eligibility requirements, regulations, and resources. Women frequently described Philadelphia General Hospital as the most generous and respectful institution in the city. The public schools were the most inflexible and unresponsive, and the welfare department and municipal court were the stingiest and most demeaning. Women sought to master the requirements and institutional cultures of each branch of the state in order to capitalize on the resources public programs offered.

A mother irons with one baby balanced on her hip and another child on the floor in her apartment in North Philadelphia in 1954. Temple University Libraries, Urban Archives, Philadelphia, Pa.

Women who experienced troubled relationships with men appear frequently in this book because of their strong presence in the archival records and oral histories. Since several public institutions offered services particularly valuable to single mothers and victims of domestic violence, they attracted women who experienced difficulties with relationships. Many working-class African Americans had loving, stable partnerships, and those who had conflicts were no different from many other Philadelphia couples. What set the women in this book apart was that the conflicts in their relationships often became public when they tried to secure assistance from the state. The decades of racist scholarship and public discourse on the alleged "dysfunctions" of the African American family, blaming "deadbeat dads" and "promiscuous" single mothers for black poverty, have produced a political environment in which any analysis of African American gender conflict or single motherhood runs the risk of being misinterpreted or taken out of context by those who wish to blame poor black people for their predicaments. I take this risk because we cannot understand the struggles African Americans faced in postwar cities or the profound ramifications of women's use of public institutions without exploring elements of their personal lives. Women's experiences with domestic violence and single motherhood helped shape their approach to public institutions, and their interactions with the state in turn altered their relationships with men. At times, the policies enacted by public institutions provided women with more leverage in marital conflicts. Such policies also sometimes led men to become less involved in child rearing, exacerbated tensions in relationships, and forced marital separations. Ignoring these issues would provide an incomplete portrait of African Americans' struggles with poverty and would not help extinguish racist assumptions about working-class black culture and African American family life.[50]

I focus on African American women rather than men because their demands on public institutions increased significantly during the postwar years. The unique struggles that led many women to turn to public institutions and the problems they faced while receiving government assistance provide an important window into the way that their experiences often differed from those of men. Although I do not provide a comprehensive study of the black community, I do attempt, wherever possible, to take men's actions and viewpoints into account and to explore how women's perspectives sometimes derided or slighted men's predicaments. Ultimately, though, this is primarily a story about African American women. A multidimensional and gendered history of working-class African American men's struggles in postwar U.S. cities remains to be written.[51]

It is not my intention to suggest that only black citizens used public institutions or that many whites did not experience severe economic and social problems. Throughout the twentieth century, many working-class whites struggled with various combinations of unemployment, dilapidated housing, domestic abuse, poor health, and inadequate education. By the early 1960s, whites retained a strong but diminishing foothold in several of Philadelphia's public institutions, and they remained the majority of recipients of welfare benefits on the national level. Although I explore how working-class whites frequently constructed their racial and class identities by defining themselves in opposition to African Americans who depended on public institutions, ordinary white people do not play a central role in my study. In the postwar period, working-class whites increasingly withdrew from and criticized public institutions. They did not launch a movement without marches that transformed the postwar urban landscape through their ever-increasing use of the state.[52]

Although this study focuses on Philadelphia, its findings demonstrate the value of incorporating gender analysis, working-class women's activism, and public institutions into our understanding of postwar U.S. history writ large. No city can be presumed to be "typical" of urban areas across the nation. Philadelphia's economy was relatively diverse, unlike cities such as Detroit that relied primarily on a single industry. In the 1950s, New York City, only ninety miles away, experienced a large Puerto Rican in-migration, but the primary racial divide in Philadelphia remained between whites and African Americans. Although Puerto Rican migration to Philadelphia increased significantly in subsequent years, in 1960, Puerto Ricans still comprised less than 1 percent of the city's population.[53] Still, many of the characteristics of racialized urban poverty that took shape in Philadelphia—growing residential segregation and social isolation, high rates of unemployment, and the increased importance of public institutions—were similar to those in other northern cities with large numbers of impoverished African Americans. Poverty certainly looked different in regions where it was concentrated among whites or new immigrants and where local government officials were more restrictive in their distribution of resources. Nonetheless, throughout the nation, when growing numbers of women sought and received assistance from public institutions, their efforts substantially shaped the landscape of postwar cities.

Over the course of the 1950s and early 1960s, all of the institutions examined in this book became deeply enmeshed in the construction of racialized poverty, all of them began to serve a majority of African American women and children, and all of them became sites of public controversy. Yet each institution underwent a unique trajectory. African American women penetrated some institutions more deeply than others, and their actions elicited a range of reactions from state authorities, political commentators, and civil rights activists. Each chapter of the book explores women's pursuit of resources from a specific institution in the 1950s and early 1960s, revealing how they developed strategies tailored to each institution's policies and procedures and encountered different types of responses.

The first chapter investigates women's life circumstances by examining those who turned to welfare to help support their families. It illuminates how the gendered construction of racialized urban poverty shaped women's need for welfare and explores recipients' evaluations of the benefits and burdens that ADC entailed. Women expended considerable labor to secure welfare, as well as to raise their children on its inadequate benefits. They developed strategies to use what the system offered while avoiding its restrictions. Placing women's experiences with ADC in the context of postwar urban racial politics, the chapter demonstrates how public condemnations of welfare policies became integral to the public opposition to black migration and African Americans' agitation for civil rights.

The second chapter examines how women sought child support and protection from domestic violence in the municipal court. Since women pressed charges against their husbands or boyfriends, their involvement with the court significantly shaped the lives of working-class men. Women employed complex reasoning when deciding whether and how to use the court to pursue goals they determined for themselves. Many needed both economic support and physical protection, but legal authorities often forced them to choose between seeking financial assistance and defending their bodily integrity. Over the course of the 1950s, judges and welfare authorities increasingly restricted women's abilities to maneuver within the court, providing a vivid example of how women's activism could inadvertently inspire repressive changes in public policies.

Housing is taken up in the third chapter, which shows how working-class African American women were deeply enmeshed in the postwar transformation of public housing. Women initially approached public housing in Philadelphia with great enthusiasm because it offered a pleasant and affordable place to live in a city with few decent options for working-class African Americans. However, during the 1950s, the quality of life in public housing rapidly deteriorated, and tenants began to face major difficulties when they tried to cultivate safe and supportive communities. Civil rights activists and working-class African American women focused their attention on different problems in public housing. Civil rights organizations sought to eliminate discrimination against two-parent African American families, while women tenants frequently complained about the restrictions on the admission of single mothers, the policies that limited their autonomy, and the location of public housing in poverty-stricken and dangerous neighborhoods.

The fourth chapter explores how working-class African American women retained their deep faith in education as a tool of upward mobility in the face of the racist policies adopted by the Philadelphia public school system. Of all the institutions that women approached, the public education system was the most discriminatory and unresponsive, and it played a powerful role in shaping African Americans' future prospects. While civil rights activists sought to eliminate the racial segregation within the school system, most working-class mothers focused their attention on performing the daily labor required to facilitate their children's education. Mothers tried to maintain some limited contact with the schools, even after encountering teachers and principals who viewed them with contempt and blamed them for their children's problems. Some women looked outside of the school system to secure resources that they needed to educate their children. They tried to convince the municipal government to help them address problems in their neighborhoods that impeded their children's successful pursuit of education.

The last chapter turns to publicly provided health care at Philadelphia General Hospital (PGH), which was of critical importance to poor African American women who needed a safe and respectful place to care for their own and their children's medical needs. This hospital was the most successful institution in the city in terms of the quality of the services it provided and the loyalty it commanded from a wide range of citizens. Its effectiveness stemmed from its high standards of care, its policies mandating respectful and equitable treatment of all patients regardless of their financial circumstances or marital status, and its responsiveness to patients' needs. As increasing numbers of African American women sought and received subsidized treatment at PGH, critics charged that its policies encouraged "illegitimacy" and irresponsible state expenditures. Yet these same policies played a vital role in encouraging and enabling working-class African American women to choose PGH over all of the other hospitals in the city and turn it into a place they called their own.

The book ends in the early 1960s, before women started formal organizations demanding welfare rights, tenants' rights, legal protections, and more responsive public education. Through grassroots mobilization, political lobbying, pickets, and demonstrations, the members of these activist groups pressed for additional resources from the state, more respect from government authorities, access to good jobs, greater authority within public institutions, and support for the labor they expended mothering their children. The women in this book desired and fought for many of the same resources that women demanded in the late 1960s and 1970s, but they did not engage in militant collective activism. Theirs was a movement without marches that took shape in the thousands of daily efforts they engaged in to improve their lives through their interactions with public institutions.[54]

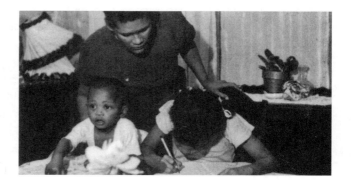

CHAPTER ONE

"Tired of Being Seconds" on ADC

In 1962, Ada Morris walked out of her run-down apartment in search of an unoccupied pay phone where she could place a call to her welfare caseworker. She did not own a phone because the welfare department considered it a "luxury," and she could not afford to buy one anyway. When Mrs. Morris got through to her caseworker, she informed him of the urgency of her situation: "I don't call up very often and complain about my finances to you people, but I would like some sort of assistance." Mrs. Morris explained that her husband had defaulted on several child support payments and she was sinking into debt. Her most recent welfare check was "only $47.80, which I entirely owed the whole check to the rent man." She had defaulted on her $65.00 rent to "pay the food bill, which was $42.00 for two weeks for six people, which I think is very good, don't you?" Mrs. Morris's caseworker agreed that her $42.00 food bill demonstrated remarkable thrift. However, he told her that he could not provide her with supplementary income until the "halfway mark" of the month. With not a penny to her name and her debts piling up, Mrs. Morris had exhausted all options and had nowhere else to turn for assistance. "When people say 'Oh, you're on relief' [welfare], they think the average person that's on relief is sitting down with nothing to do," she told researchers in the early

1960s. "Being on relief is a . . . strain, whether anybody knows it or not. Physically, mentally—a strain."[1]

Women like Mrs. Morris endured the "strain" of welfare because it was an improvement over their previous living arrangements. Most of them had at one time supported themselves and their children through employment, but health problems, lack of child care, or layoffs had prevented them from keeping their jobs. Since their relatives, friends, and neighbors were also poor, mutual support networks could not solve their problems. Most women viewed depending on men for survival as an impossible or unattractive solution, given their past experiences with nonsupport, infidelity, and abuse. Raising children in poverty was laborious and stressful, and the Aid to Dependent Children (ADC) program provided only minimal financial support for women's efforts. Yet by the early 1960s, testament to the extent of poverty among African Americans in Philadelphia, over one-tenth of the city's African American population and one-quarter of its African American children were receiving ADC. Since each year 40 percent of recipients left the program and were replaced by others, the number of people who received assistance from the ADC program at some point in their lives was even higher than these percentages would indicate.[2]

Working-class African American women and welfare authorities held fundamentally incompatible understandings of the ADC program. Women focused on expanding and capitalizing on the opportunities the program provided. They believed ADC should help them live autonomously, pay their bills on time, rent clean and safe apartments, obtain health care when needed, and purchase adequate food and clothing for their families. State and local welfare authorities focused their efforts on containing the program's expenditures by preventing fraud and keeping costs low. They enforced policies that made life on ADC as unattractive as possible in order to ensure that only the neediest women would seek assistance. Women had to deplete all their savings and assets to qualify for ADC, and the program's restrictions on securing additional resources prevented them from rising above a subsistence level of living. Prohibitions against living with men placed roadblocks in women's efforts to cultivate intimate relationships.

Women sought dignity and autonomy by challenging the constraints the welfare department placed on their lives. Most believed any job was preferable to welfare, but some refused to give up ADC for low-wage employment they deemed exploitative. Some viewed domestic work as particularly demeaning and saw little benefit in leaving ADC for jobs that yielded comparable or even lower income. Others insisted on obtaining more money than either welfare or low-wage jobs provided and earned income secretly, "under the table," while receiving ADC. Relationships with men also became points of contention. Welfare policies prohibited women from living with men because state authorities assumed the men would, or should, provide women with financial support. They believed women who lived with men should give up welfare and get married. Many women refused to sacrifice the steady income they received from ADC to marry men whom they considered unreliable. They had steady boyfriends while receiving welfare, relying on ADC to provide them with more leverage in their relationships.[3]

In the years after World War II, in Philadelphia and cities across the nation, African American women's pursuit of ADC inspired fierce public opposition. In a climate of white resistance to civil rights, several outspoken Democratic legal authorities in Philadelphia began to advocate restricting women's access to ADC, charging that welfare programs took money from upstanding "taxpayers" to support mothers who had "illegitimate" children and depended on public assistance as a "way of life." Over the course of the 1950s, their harsh criticism was echoed by many ordinary whites and African Americans who exhibited both disdain for ADC recipients and resentment of their allegedly "easy lives." Even prominent civil rights activists tempered their support of ADC, expressing in their reservations the gender- and class-based limitations of their visions of social justice. When liberal advocacy groups and state and local welfare authorities tried to defend the program, they failed to challenge many of the assumptions that lay at the core of the antiwelfare discourse. By the late 1950s and early 1960s, although women managed to retain and even expand their foothold in the ADC program, they faced increasingly strident public resistance.

The burgeoning opposition to African American women's use of welfare inspired a significant body of academic scholarship documenting the lives of Philadelphia's ADC recipients. The most extensive work was compiled and directed by Jane C. Kronick, a professor of social work at Bryn Mawr College who received her Ph.D. from Yale University. Between 1959 and 1962, Kronick conducted a study of a random sample of 239 Philadelphia ADC recipients. She analyzed their casework files and hired two African American women to conduct interviews with 119 of the women. Kronick wrote several reports exploring her findings, and many social work graduate students at Bryn Mawr based their Masters' theses on the information she compiled. In their work, Kronick and these students critically interrogated the negative images of African American "illegitimacy" and the "culture of poverty" found in white newspapers and academic discourse by exploring ADC recipients' employment histories, personal relationships, material circumstances, and survival strategies. The mothers who participated in the study were also well aware of the demeaning images of welfare recipients that were circulating in the press. Many of them tried to show the interviewers that their lives did not conform to popular stereotypes by emphasizing their commitment to their children. Yet they also described how the stigma of ADC and the severe poverty they confronted prevented them from properly fulfilling their familial obligations. Several of the studies include excerpts from the interview transcripts that allow us to hear and interpret these women's own words. Read critically, and in conjunction with other primary sources, the studies provide us with rare insight into ADC recipients' past struggles and daily lives. (For more information on the Bryn Mawr studies and other first-person accounts in this book, see the Appendix.)

The Racialization of Welfare

In 1935, when the federal government created the ADC program as part of the Social Security Act, no one predicted that it would become the largest welfare program in the nation or that African American women would become major beneficiaries of the grants. The women social reformers who drew up the blueprint for ADC modeled the program on state Mothers' Assistance grants, which were instituted in the early twentieth century primarily to serve small numbers of white and immigrant widows.[4] Gendered and racialized ideas about poverty undergirded the sharp stratifications in the welfare programs created by the Social Security Act. Old-age pensions and unemployment insurance disproportionately benefited whites and men with stable employment histories. State authorities portrayed these benefits as based directly on recipients' past earnings or "right" to assistance, even though the proportion of workers' wages they provided was calculated according to a sliding scale that benefited those who earned lower incomes. The ADC program, by contrast, served single mothers who, instead of receiving benefits as a "right," had to pass strict means and morals tests to receive meager grants accompanied by state supervision.[5]

In 1937, Pennsylvania changed the name of Mothers' Assistance to Aid to Dependent Children, and African American women quickly became the primary clients of Philadelphia's program. The Pennsylvania legislature provided two-thirds of the funding for ADC, and the rest came from the federal government, which imposed very few requirements on state authorities. The Philadelphia Department of Public Assistance (DPA) administered ADC, but state-level authorities made all of the important policy decisions.[6] In Philadelphia, many of the first African American women who received ADC entered the welfare system in the 1930s through the state's General Assistance (GA) program, which provided grants to needy persons regardless of their marital status. Since Pennsylvania welfare authorities conserved funds by moving women off GA and onto the new federal program, they increasingly opened ADC to unmarried, separated, and deserted women, many of whom were African American.[7]

As early as 1940, African Americans comprised 13 percent of Philadelphia's population, but 62 percent of its ADC recipients. Throughout the postwar period, whites comprised the majority of ADC recipients on the national level, but in northern cities such as Philadelphia, black women maintained a strong presence in the program.[8] By the early 1960s, when Philadelphia administered ADC grants to more than 65,000 single mothers and children, African Americans comprised at least 85 percent of the recipients.[9]

Many public officials linked the large numbers of African Americans who relied on welfare with black migration, suggesting either that welfare benefits attracted new migrants or, slightly more sympathetically, that migration caused black poverty. Neither position accounted for African Americans' strong presence in welfare programs. African Americans migrated to Philadelphia in search of employment, not welfare benefits.[10] They frequently faced difficulties finding jobs not because they were born in the South but because of their relatively low educational levels, racial discrimination, and the diminishing numbers of entry-level jobs in the city. Many longtime black residents faced similar problems.[11] In 1960, 65 percent of ADC recipients were born outside Philadelphia, a figure to be expected in a city that was a frequent destination for southern migrants. However, most of them had lived in the city for more than five years. The one-year residency requirement meant that those who had recently moved to Philadelphia could not receive ADC benefits even if they tried to apply.[12] In the early 1960s, when Rhode Island and New York State eliminated residency requirements, newcomers did not suddenly flock to welfare offices in search of assistance, despite public anxiety that the policy shift might attract large numbers of new applicants.[13]

Southern origins did give many African Americans a unique perspective on welfare policies. From its inception, racial discrimination has permeated the U.S. welfare state. Working-class African Americans were largely shut out of the most generous and publicly respected programs such as old-age pensions, and in the South, many African American women with children could not even gain access to ADC, especially during seasonal labor shortages when white landlords needed cotton pickers. In the postwar period, several states enacted strict restrictions on ADC ranging from "suitable home" laws to employment requirements that especially targeted blacks.[14] As a result, many African Americans in Philadelphia did not take the availability of ADC for granted. They appreciated the availability of welfare and viewed it as an essential safety net for struggling families.

Black women received ADC benefits far more frequently than white women because of their disproportionate poverty and the DPA's insistence that only the poorest of the poor should receive assistance. In 1960, 46 percent of Philadelphia's African American households lived in poverty, with annual incomes under $4,000, compared to 20 percent of white households. Since the poor white households frequently consisted of older persons living either alone or in couples, while the poor black households often consisted of younger and larger families with children, poverty was even more widespread among African Americans than household-based statistics suggest.[15] The DPA took out liens on welfare recipients' homes and placed strict limits on the value of their savings, life insurance, and cars. These policies discouraged and disqualified more whites than African Americans from receiving public assistance because whites were more likely to have such assets.[16] Similarly, because more whites than African Americans had relatives who could support them, whites were disproportionately disqualified by policies forcing applicants to obtain financial assistance from relatives deemed capable of contributing to their households. The structure of unemployment insurance also contributed to African Americans' significant presence in welfare programs because it did not cover most unskilled, part-time, or seasonal forms of employment in which they were concentrated, forcing them to turn to welfare when they were laid off. The exclusion of domestic workers from unemployment insurance penalized black women in particular.[17]

A relatively high proportion of African American women in Philadelphia were single mothers with young children, another factor that contributed to their overrepresentation in the ADC program.[18] In 1960, nearly one-quarter of all black women headed households compared to just under one-tenth of white women. Some of these women had children out of wedlock: 22 percent of black children but only 2 percent of white children were born to unmarried parents.[19] While white unmarried women were often stigmatized and pressured to marry or give up their children, the same social pressures were not brought to bear on black women. Most African Americans did not welcome unwed motherhood; they valued stable partnerships and family ties. Out-of-wedlock pregnancies were often stressful, particularly for young unmarried women whose parents were concerned and sometimes deeply disappointed.[20] However, few African American women who had children out of wedlock faced pressure to marry or confronted stigma for an extended period of time. Their children were rarely stigmatized, and unmarried women could earn respect by being good mothers.[21]

Women's Need for Welfare

Working-class African American women who decided to apply for welfare faced multidimensional problems. Most had once been married and had once held jobs. They turned to welfare reluctantly. "Not because I want[ed] to," explained Ada Morris, "but because conditions and situations forced me on."[22] Women sought ADC when they could no longer support themselves through employment and had primary responsibility for their children. Most lacked child care that would enable them to combine wage-earning with single motherhood. Some had been victimized by domestic violence, and many looked after sick family members or suffered from debilitating health problems themselves. With little access to affordable housing, the apartments they could rent were often dilapidated. Few could obtain enough material assistance from social service agencies, churches, friends, neighbors, and kin. They understood how hard it was to care for children in poverty, but felt morally obligated to keep and raise their children themselves.

Like most working-class African American women, ADC recipients had expected and wanted to support their families through wage-earning. Almost all had held jobs in the past, and they considered employment the best way to provide for their children.[23] Their jobs, however, had generally not been good ones. Most, like Catherine Sanderson, had not finished high school and had toiled as low-wage workers. In 1960, 74 percent of employed black women but only 32 percent of employed white women held jobs as factory workers, service workers, laborers, and domestics. Some did not qualify for unemployment insurance and turned to ADC when they lost their jobs. In 1960, 10 percent of African American women in Philadelphia were unemployed, and 11 percent of ADC recipients stated that layoffs precipitated their turn to welfare.[24] Acute and chronic health problems prevented even more women from holding jobs. Two-thirds of ADC recipients told interviewers that they were injured or ill, and nearly one-third stated that poor health had made them unable to seek or retain jobs.[25] Bell Jackson had to leave a position as a sewing machine operator because an "ailment in my back" prevented her from operating "the heavy power machines." In a few cases, alcoholism, drug addiction, depression, and mental illness may have hindered women's abilities to successfully pursue employment. Mrs. Jackson stated that she had lost several jobs because "before I got a good check on my emotions, they was popping forth on me."[26]

For healthy women who could have found jobs, the impossibility of finding child care frequently impeded their participation in the labor force.[27] By the early 1960s, almost half of ADC recipients had large families of four or more children, with two or more below school age.[28] Half had at least one child with chronic health problems.[29] Affordable and reliable day care was very difficult to find. Although the Philadelphia Board of Education ran thirteen day care centers (which had been started by the federal government during World War II) and private agencies operated an additional fifty centers, these facilities served only a tiny fraction of the families in need throughout the city. The situation was particularly dire in working-class African American neighborhoods in which rates of female employment were high and the number of day care centers particularly low. Informal centers in basements and backyards were hard to find, and some had inadequate numbers of staff, poor equipment, and unsanitary conditions.[30] "It's hard out here scuffling with these children," explained Irene Barry; but she refused to give up welfare to "stick [her children] in strange people's houses, and get a job and hope and pray" they would be taken care of properly.[31]

Although most ADC recipients participated in mutual support networks, their relationships with other people often could not provide them with reliable or long-term child care. Some of the other women who lived in their neighborhoods had family members or friends who could take care of their children during the day, but ADC recipients usually did not have access to such assistance. Anna Baylor explained that she had people she could call on to care for her children for an afternoon or an evening, but "you can't ask a person every day to watch your child."[32] Mrs. Jackson had family members who lived nearby, but they did not provide her with much help caring for her four small children. Her grandmother wished she could help but was too old. Her sister, who suffered from tuberculosis and "partied" a lot, would "take care of my children for, say, maybe a week or two. . . . Then she gets tired." Mrs. Jackson received even less assistance from her mother, who "doesn't have very much interest in me" and "isn't particularly fond of children."[33] A few women stated that when they were pregnant and went into labor they had to call the police to take their children because they did not have anyone to provide child care while they were giving birth.[34]

Although ADC recipients could have given their children up for adoption or placed them in foster care, many sought welfare because they felt obligated to raise their children themselves. Patricia Bell described her commitment: "If you have a child, bring it up. Take the responsibility. Hard or easy, it's yours."[35] Helen Lawson explained, "It never crossed my mind to give [my children] away, no matter how tough a struggle I had. I seen some pretty bad times even with ADC, but I would never give them up."[36] Joelle Wright declared, "I sure don't think much of giving babies up for adoption. God wouldn't put it into the world without making a way to care for it. The mother might not be able to give it the finest and best in the world, but she could find a way."[37] Many mothers spoke of the struggles they faced but still refused to give their children away. Mrs. Jackson explained that she had gone through periods in her life when she "didn't care how I kept [my children] or my house" and believed that she still had "a long way to go" in her efforts "to do right" for her family. Nevertheless, Mrs. Jackson chose to raise her children herself instead of sending them to live with strangers.[38] Even when ADC recipients could not live up to their own expectations for motherhood, they felt compelled to care for their children themselves.

Women's resistance to giving their children away partly reflected the unattractive options available to them. While a wide range of family and child welfare organizations, government agencies, and maternity homes encouraged and facilitated the adoption of white women's children, black women did not have access to such services or did not trust them.[39] Even if reliable institutions had existed, many women would have refused to use them. "You put your child away, you might as well kill him; he'll think no one wants him," explained Emma Spells.[40] Some of the other mothers in their neighborhoods relied on "informal adoptions," which they considered preferable to giving their children to the state. "If you had a child and you couldn't take care of it, you gave it to your sister, aunt, or lady down the street who you considered to be 'cousin so and so,'" recalled Gloria Gay.[41] Most ADC recipients did not have anyone who could informally adopt their children and chose ADC because they felt personally compelled or morally obligated to keep and raise their children themselves.

To qualify for ADC, women had to be the primary providers for their children, which meant that they were usually single mothers. Three-quarters of ADC recipients had once been married, and they had hoped to have lasting relationships with men. However, by the time they turned to welfare, most were in their late twenties, thirties, and forties and had experienced several relationships that had ended in painful desertions or separations. Their experiences in relationships had often been so unpleasant that they found it difficult to trust men. Viola Stanley explained, "I'm afraid another man will do to me the same thing that my husband [did]."[42] Many ADC recipients had boyfriends, but even those who got pregnant rarely married. In the early 1960s, two-thirds of Philadelphia ADC recipients had had at least one child born out of wedlock.[43]

The most common problem women reported confronting in their relationships was men's inability or refusal to provide financial support.[44] Many scholarly analyses of marriage and nonsupport rely on an employment-centered model that describes poor couples splitting up because unemployed men cannot support their wives and children.[45] ADC recipients recounted more complex experiences of nonsupport that did not stem solely from men's unemployment. In their neighborhoods, families survived through various combinations of temporary and informal jobs, pawning and bartering, theft, gambling, selling drugs or liquor, and assistance obtained from friends, relatives, social service agencies, and churches. Men who did not have formal jobs could still contribute to women's households through these informal economic pursuits or by assisting with child care or household labor. Marcelle Blackwell recalled that even when men only managed to obtain a "piece of a job," many women considered them "good men" worth sticking with if they were committed to helping out and collaborated with their wives in the task of obtaining adequate resources.[46]

Most women defined nonsupport as men purposely not sharing their resources or not putting forth enough effort to help out. They complained most vehemently about employed men who withheld their earnings. Joyce Winters grew enraged when her husband spent his earnings on "flashy cars," while she and their five children struggled to find enough food. Others charged that their husbands spent their money in bars, on clothes for themselves, or on other women, instead of helping support their families.[47] Women with unemployed husbands who complained of nonsupport usually stated that it was not simply men's lack of jobs that was the problem, but that they believed the men had not tried hard enough to obtain resources. Some of these women underestimated men's efforts to find jobs. Others complained when men grew demoralized after numerous failed attempts and stopped looking for employment. Lucille Williams blamed her husband for not trying harder to find a job or to make money in the informal economy. She recalled that when he started drinking and "wouldn't work," she finally decided, "I ain't taking care of no man." Mrs. Williams told her husband, "You ain't gonna run on top of me and eat my food and drink my coffee. . . . You either work or go from me." Not all women responded to men in this way. Mrs. Williams knew women who stayed with men who did not contribute to their households because they loved them. She herself never "love[d] a man that much."[48] When women did not receive what they personally believed to be adequate assistance and cooperation from men, they often complained of nonsupport.

Women described many breakups with men that could not be explained solely on the basis of nonsupport. Domestic abuse had loomed large in many relationships. One in four ADC recipients told interviewers that she had been physically assaulted by the father of her children. Given the extent of domestic violence in their communities, many others worried that their boyfriends would become violent at some point in the future.[49] Women's experiences with domestic violence cannot be understood apart from men's experiences with racism, poverty, and unemployment, which caused depression, anger, and shame. However, domestic violence cannot be explained solely as a result of the economic and social problems that affected men because many poor men did not beat their wives and middle-class men sometimes did.[50]

Many ADC recipients had also felt the effects of the high incarceration rates of African American men. In 1950, when African Americans comprised 18 percent of Philadelphia's population, they comprised 40 percent of its prison inmates. Sociologist Leonard D. Savitz's study of crime in postwar Philadelphia found that racial discrimination permeated the entire judicial system: "At every stage of the criminal procedure . . . differential administration of justice . . . operates continually and prejudicially against Negroes."[51] With a disproportionate number of working-class African American men becoming ensnared in the criminal justice system, nearly one-quarter of ADC recipients had been in relationships with men who were put in prison.[52]

Other issues that women identified as contributing to their breakups included jealousy, alcoholism, drug addiction, and infidelity. Fourteen percent of ADC recipients described the fathers of their children as addicted to drugs or alcohol.[53] Men's infidelities and their suspicions of women's infidelities caused great distress. Catherine Sanderson, recalling her husband's jealousy, explained, "Oh boy, every time you'd talk with a person, he'd say you were making plans to go out with him." Her husband refused to go to church himself but would "accuse me of going to church to see a friend, see a man." Mrs. Sanderson contended with her husband's suspicions by avoiding other men when they socialized. However, she refused to let his jealousy interfere with her attendance at church.[54]

Women were not just victims in their conflicts with men. They also got jealous, cheated, and provoked violent disagreements. Some women sympathized with men's predicaments in a city with few decent employment opportunities. Others blamed men for having problems and exhibited little sympathy for their struggles. For men who themselves felt angry, frustrated, and even ashamed about their inability to provide for their families, women's criticisms only exacerbated their difficulties.[55]

The availability of ADC sometimes facilitated or forced the dissolution of marriages. By providing women with the resources to run independent households, it enabled some poor mothers to escape relationships in which they were being beaten or otherwise mistreated. In other instances, perhaps 10 to 15 percent of the caseload, women wanted to stay with men but separated in order to qualify for ADC.[56] Although welfare policy officially stipulated that women who lived with "able-bodied" unemployed men could obtain ADC as long as the men were looking for jobs, few women in these situations were actually granted public assistance for a sustained period of time. The rules changed briefly in the early 1960s when Philadelphia adopted the ADC-UP program that made women with unemployed husbands officially eligible for ADC. However, the DPA quickly reverted to the old system of excluding most women who lived with unemployed men. Many couples who separated so the women could receive ADC insisted on secretly staying together. Still, by requiring couples to live apart, the ADC program hindered their abilities to cultivate their relationships and made it more difficult for men to participate in child rearing.[57]

Women's status as single mothers enabled them to qualify for ADC, but it did not single-handedly push them onto welfare. In the 1980s, social scientists discovered the "feminization of poverty"—the disproportionate and increasing concentration of poverty among women. Although many scholars assumed that single motherhood itself was a powerful predictor of poverty, comparisons of single mothers across racial lines have complicated this view. While many white women fell into poverty when they became single mothers, most black single mothers did not experience the same radical drop in their standard of living.[58] In Philadelphia in 1950, white women who separated from their husbands were two-and-a-half times as likely as married white women to live in poverty, while for black women, marital separations increased their rate of poverty only by slightly over one-half.[59] Many black women had also been poor when they were married: Their husbands rarely earned much money, and they themselves were confined to low-wage jobs, in need of child care, struggling with health problems, and hindered by discrimination and lack of education. Single motherhood created additional struggles because it was expensive, laborious, and stressful, particularly when children misbehaved or became sick. However, it was not the sole or even primary cause of women's poverty. The struggles women faced raising children as single mothers combined with their difficulties finding jobs and housing, poor health, lack of child care, and limited education to force them to resort to welfare.[60]

The Application Process

Most women avoided applying for welfare for as long as they could because of its stigma, meager assistance, and invasions of privacy. When they incurred a crisis such as the loss of a job or health problems, they first relied on the survival strategies that had helped sustain their communities for decades. Many sought assistance from private social service agencies, tried to borrow from family, friends, and neighbors, pawned furniture and other household goods, and spent whatever savings they had. Emma Counts "waited until the last minute" before applying for ADC, trying to find another way to support her children.[61] Only after exhausting all of their resources and calling in every last favor did most women embark on the application process.[62]

When women finally decided to apply for welfare, they faced the daunting task of getting an appointment with the DPA. Many spent hours standing at pay phones because they could not afford their own phones and the phone lines at the DPA were notoriously busy. Once they managed to make an appointment at one of the welfare offices located throughout the city, they often had to walk long distances with young children in tow since they rarely owned cars or had money for bus fare. Welfare offices were crowded, the waits long, and the chairs uncomfortable. When women met with caseworkers, they learned that to qualify for ADC, they had to collect a seemingly impossible number of official documents: rent books and leases, birth certificates, Social Security cards, separation agreements, life insurance policies, bank statements, hospitalization records, and old pay stubs. The welfare rights groups of the late 1960s and 1970s provided applicants with a detailed list of requirements that enabled women to plan ahead, bring the correct papers the first time, and avoid having to make several visits to the office. Before that movement, women rarely brought all the necessary documents to their initial appointments.[63] Mrs. Jackson described her frustration with the system: "I had a hard time getting on [welfare]. . . . I had to get papers from this place and that place. . . . I went down there about six or seven times before I was put on."[64] By constructing intricate and laborious application requirements that usually necessitated repeat visits, the welfare department sought to limit the number of women receiving assistance.

The longer women tried to avoid applying for welfare, the more difficult it became to qualify for grants. When some time had elapsed between women's applications and their loss of wages or male support, caseworkers forced them to disclose how they had made ends meet in the interim and to prove why those strategies were no longer effective. Many women had to sign affidavits swearing that their relatives could no longer support them. If caseworkers decided that the fathers of their children or any of their family members might be able to contribute to their support, women had to press charges in the municipal court to try to get support payments, which were then subtracted from their welfare grants.[65]

In the face of these challenges, neighborhood women shared information to help one another negotiate the system. At kitchen tables and on doorsteps, those familiar with the ADC program provided others with the welfare department's phone number, explained which documents were required, and told them what to expect from the initial interviews. Newcomers were often informed of the one-year residency requirement for welfare, which prevented recent arrivals to the city from receiving assistance. In their conversations, women frequently used the term "DPA" to refer to both welfare grants and the welfare department itself. Describing themselves as "DPA people" or women who were "on DPA," they informed potential applicants of the types of questions they would face when they visited welfare offices and warned them that they would have to hold their ground when intake workers discouraged them from applying for assistance.[66] In the mid-to-late 1950s, with large numbers of women sharing information about welfare, enrollment in Philadelphia's ADC program grew by 40 percent. Although an increase in federal monies available to states facilitated the rising caseload, women's assertive requests for services created the demand for public assistance that federal authorities sought to help states meet.[67]

Sustaining Women in Poverty

In the 1950s, the Pennsylvania legislature appropriated such minimal funds for the ADC program that the stipends mothers received barely allowed them to achieve a subsistence level of living. Each year, state welfare authorities submitted a budget request that the legislature almost always refused to fully grant, appropriating less money than was required to fund the program adequately. Welfare authorities tried to make do with insufficient resources by restricting benefits. In 1960, they estimated that ADC provided women with just two-thirds of the estimated cost of living at a minimum standard of health and decency.[68] With such limited financial assistance, women faced major difficulties finding decent apartments to rent. The fact that many landlords refused to rent to welfare recipients hardly helped. In 1956, over half of the city's public assistance recipients lived in substandard housing, and one-fourth lived in conditions that the Philadelphia Housing Association deemed hazardous to their health and safety.[69] Their buildings had inadequate heat and plumbing, leaky roofs, missing plaster, and rooms infested with rats, rodents, and bed bugs.[70]

Mere survival required tremendous labor and expense. Many mothers constantly worried about how to feed their children adequately, especially when they had teenage sons with big appetites. Without cars they could drive to affordable grocery stores, most women had to shop at the stores in their neighborhoods, which frequently charged higher prices than the stores in middle-class neighborhoods for inferior goods.[71] Beginning in 1955, the federal government provided surplus food, but women often had to travel to and from the distribution centers by taxi (sometimes splitting the cost with friends) so they could transport the large packages of food back home.[72] Finding shoes and clothing for children was a difficult and time-consuming chore that required women to visit secondhand stores and social service agencies on a regular basis. Maude Seibert explained, "The Outgrown Shop, the Goodwill, Salvation Army—all these places have been a blessing because otherwise I wouldn't have been able to keep [food in] the refrigerator and keep the house halfway decent and keep something on the children."[73] Prioritizing food and clothing, many women stated that decent furniture was out of the question. It was not unusual in ADC recipients' families to find three to five people sharing one bed. Meals usually had to be eaten in shifts because few families had enough chairs, cutlery, or dishes for everyone to eat at the same time.[74] The lack of adequate kitchen facilities, baths, and toilets turned small tasks such as showering, brushing teeth, and washing dishes into arduous chores. Most mothers purchased a television, considering it a necessity because of their restricted social lives, the lack of safe recreational opportunities in their neighborhoods, and their crowded quarters. However, since the only way they could afford a TV was through installments, they usually had to pay three times the normal cost of the set.[75]

Welfare policies designed to ensure that only mothers "truly in need" received ADC kept women in poverty. To weed out applicants who could survive without welfare, authorities restricted the savings, life insurance, and property that recipients could own. Such policies forced women to liquidate their assets before receiving ADC, making it even more difficult for them to survive when they tried to leave welfare.[76] To prevent women from becoming too comfortable on ADC, a significant proportion of any additional income and of the value of any gifts that they reported receiving were subtracted from their grants.[77] Such policies served as a disincentive for women to take jobs or engage in the informal economic pursuits that had sustained working-class families for decades, such as taking in boarders, baby-sitting, styling hair, and selling liquor.

Caseworkers frequently encouraged ADC recipients to find jobs even though they knew women would receive few financial benefits from employment. In the immediate postwar period, welfare policy stipulated that recipients could choose whether or not to hold jobs while receiving ADC. By 1953, employment was a condition of eligibility for healthy women whose children were away at school all day.[78] This employment requirement was not strictly enforced. While other states restricted women's access to ADC when low-wage jobs (particularly in agriculture) became available, mothers in Philadelphia who refused to seek jobs rarely lost their grants.[79]

Women frequently discussed the perversity of the DPA's insistence on keeping them poor while encouraging them to secure gainful employment. Many stated that their poverty prevented them from finding a job. Cassandra Wilson believed that "with a little help," she could be "very successful." However, she blamed welfare's small stipends for preventing her from improving her situation. "Look, let's face it," she explained; "I haven't got the proper clothes, I don't get the proper food—nothing right, you know, that would help me. I can't go out and try to better my position without the proper clothes, shoes, food."[80] Other women resented ADC for hindering their attempts to get job training. Welfare "holds a lot of people back," complained Lenora Hill after her caseworker prevented her from pursuing further education. Mrs. Hill's mother had offered to pay for her to take a "course in IBM," but her caseworker would not allow it, stating that if her mother could afford to pay for a course, she should contribute to Mrs. Hill's support checks instead.[81] Women who found a way to pursue an education ran into many of the same problems they faced when they tried to hold jobs. Many could not find people to care for their children because their family and friends were often overwhelmed by their own responsibilities.[82]

Since 89 percent of ADC recipients reported having at least one family member with health problems, the health care that was an integral part of public assistance programs was essential to their well-being.[83] Some women were reluctant to give up ADC precisely because they valued their ability to get medical care when they needed it and the jobs they could get rarely provided health insurance. Beginning in 1938, welfare policy stipulated that ADC recipients could go to a doctor or hospital when they became ill and receive treatment and medicines free of charge. Doctors and pharmacists sent the bills to the DPA, which then submitted them to a local committee composed of medical professionals who made certain that doctors had not provided clients with more than the "minimum consistent with good professional practice."[84]

In practice, the ADC program's health care provisions did not completely meet either doctors' demands or patients' needs. The Pennsylvania Department of Public Assistance had a fixed monthly budget for medical care, and if the bills submitted by doctors and pharmacists exceeded the department's available funds, the department only partially compensated medical professionals for their services.[85] Over the course of the 1950s, state authorities tried to improve medical professionals' compensation, and in 1956, the federal government began to contribute funds for welfare recipients' health care.[86] Still, some doctors refused to treat public assistance recipients, and others placed restrictions on the services they offered. After viewing signs in a doctor's office stating "No DPA Patients in the Evening" and "No DPA Patients on Saturday," Ella Maxwell observed, "What are we supposed to do . . . plan our sickness?"[87] Other women complained that because of their welfare status, doctors examined them hastily and did not prescribe adequate drugs.[88] Although the health care women received with ADC surpassed what they could have obtained without it, they did not acquire the respectful medical attention from private doctors that they believed they deserved.

Pushing the Boundaries of the System

Women applied for welfare because they had exhausted all of their resources and ADC provided them with a more stable source of income than they were otherwise able to obtain. Yet once they gained access to the program, they rarely dwelled on the conditions that had led them to seek ADC, such as the constraints of the labor market, day care shortages, and chronic illnesses. Instead, they blamed ADC for not helping them solve their problems. Women did not expect private employers or landlords to respond to their needs, but they saw great potential in ADC, a program that specifically addressed their concerns, and they believed it should enable them to care for their children properly.

Many women tried to turn ADC into a program that better met their needs by using their grants in ways that authorities did not condone. The strategies they developed became integral features of daily life in working-class African American neighborhoods and ranged from earning money "under the table" to engaging in clandestine relationships with men. These expedients entailed breaking the program's rules and living with the fear of losing their grants. Women took their chances because they were firmly committed to determining for themselves whether and how to participate in the labor force and become involved in intimate relationships with men.

One of the most highly charged decisions concerned employment. For many women, employment was not an option: Their health problems were too severe, or they were never able to find reliable child care. Other women who recovered from their illnesses or found people to look after their children left ADC as soon as jobs became available. In 1960, nearly half the women who left ADC entered the labor force.[89] Like Catherine Sanderson, many took positions as domestics, waitresses, and hospital aides that paid less or only slightly more than welfare, but allowed them to escape the rules and surveillance of ADC. "I love working," explained Sandra Ross. She preferred even low-wage employment to ADC because she could "do just what I wanted to do" with her salary and did not have to answer to welfare authorities.[90]

Other women found that ADC provided them with some bargaining power that enabled them to avoid taking the worst jobs available. This newfound leverage became particularly evident when some began to refuse work as domestics. African American women had for decades resisted the exploitative nature of domestic work through acts of resistance ranging from quitting, going on strike, and working slowly, to warning friends about abusive employers and refusing to take live-in positions.[91] ADC provided them with a new avenue of resistance: the ability to leave the occupation altogether. Women like Lenora Hill categorically refused to take low-paid positions in "domestic work, hospital aide, or something like that. . . . I don't want *those* types of jobs."[92] Similarly, when a caseworker encouraged Alice Jones to leave welfare for a job cleaning houses, Mrs. Jones jokingly replied, "My goodness, I need somebody to come and help *me* clean!" In cities like Philadelphia that did not enforce strict employment regulations for ADC, welfare grants gave women like Mrs. Hill and

Mrs. Jones a degree of bargaining power with employers, enabling them to resist taking absolutely any job available regardless of pay or working conditions. Employers who relied on large numbers of working-class African American women recognized the increased power that women enjoyed as a result of the availability of ADC and advocated policies that limited access to welfare and forced women to take jobs. Their success in convincing welfare authorities to implement new restrictions in many southern and some northern states prevented many African American women in rural areas from using ADC to avoid low-paid, backbreaking agricultural labor.[93]

In Philadelphia, African American women did not leave domestic work entirely. In 1960, 23 percent of employed African American women in the city still held positions as domestics, which was a significant decrease from the 60 percent in 1940 but not a complete retreat from the occupation.[94] Other women staked out a middle ground. Given the insufficiency of their welfare stipends and the meager wages they could earn through employment, they believed that both were absolutely necessary for their families' survival. These women performed a variety of low-wage jobs in both the formal and the informal economy, ranging from baby-sitting and domestic work to selling liquor and styling hair. Viewing the outside income they obtained as a necessary supplement to ADC, not a replacement for it, they rarely reported their earnings to the DPA as regulations required.[95]

The welfare department tried to prevent women from earning unreported income by assigning caseworkers to monitor their households. The casework component of ADC had long-standing roots. The Mothers' Assistance program had relied on caseworkers who were committed to a holistic approach to poor families' problems and made frequent home visits to assess recipients' living conditions and provide extensive "advice" on employment, child rearing, homemaking, and finances. When ADC replaced Mothers' Assistance in 1935, casework remained part of the program, even though none of the other welfare programs created by the Social Security Act maintained such strict surveillance over their clients. Because of the large numbers of ADC recipients and the inadequate funding of the program, Philadelphia's caseworkers had extremely high caseloads of 120 to 200 clients each. Most did not have the time to attempt to understand women's problems or help them improve their lives.[96] They acted mainly as fraud checkers who focused on monitoring eligibility and making sure through interviews and annual or semiannual home visits that ADC recipients were adhering to the program's rules. The overwhelming workload and low wages frustrated caseworkers, many of whom were college-educated. In the early 1960s, 50 to 60 percent of them resigned each year. Since it usually took at least six months for caseworkers to learn the ropes, the staff was both overburdened and inexperienced.[97]

The casework relationship varied widely depending on the individuals involved, but most ADC recipients found it demeaning and invasive.[98] Although state-level authorities made almost all of the policy and budgetary decisions, local staffers had "great flexibility in terms of what we can do in helping a family." Caseworkers could not sanction huge expenditures of money or enact significant policy changes, but they had the power to determine who qualified for assistance and how much aid they received.[99] Recognizing that welfare grants were utterly insufficient in meeting women's needs, some caseworkers tried to help women secure the most assistance possible and turned a blind eye to signs of rule breaking. Others were committed to keeping caseloads and costs low by ferreting out fraud and wrongdoing. One ADC recipient, Charlotte Palmer, explained that some caseworkers "will help you, will talk to you, will try to comfort you," while others were "moody, hateful, haven't got enough time for you, think anything they tell you, anything they do for you, should be accepted."[100] Given the high turnover rates, even the most committed workers rarely formed deep or trusting relationships with their clients. Louise Smith explained, "They're strangers to you and they change them so fast. You might have one visitor this six months, and the next six months, here come another face."[101] Each caseworker met with women in their homes, inspected their rent books, and had the authority to rifle through their possessions for signs of rule breaking. Jacqueline Richards observed, "[We] have *no* privacy. Period."[102]

Women who had boyfriends found the lack of privacy particularly difficult to negotiate, but they refused to leave ADC to get married or officially move in with men. No matter how much women liked their current boyfriends, they considered it highly unlikely that their relationships would last or that their boyfriends would consistently be able to earn enough money to support them, be good to their children, and abstain from violence.[103] Mrs. Williams explained her reluctance to remarry: "I ain't taking no chances. . . . I went through hell with the first one [husband] and I won't go through hell with the second one."[104] Women appreciated ADC for giving them a certain degree of power in their relationships with men that they had not had when they had been more dependent on men for their livelihood. With ADC, they maintained control over their households, they did not need to worry quite as much about men's contributions, and they could more easily leave men who became abusive, unfaithful, or otherwise unreliable.[105]

Women formed interdependent relationships with their boyfriends that did not conform to welfare authorities' expectations about men's roles as breadwinners. At the beginning of each month, when ADC checks first arrived, instead of men supporting women, women usually purchased and prepared food for men and sometimes even bought them small gifts. Then, over the course of the month, as funds dwindled, women began to look to men to buy groceries. Men also sometimes helped women purchase more expensive items such as clothes, furniture, and toys for their children.[106] Mrs. Jackson discussed the reciprocal ties of dependency between ADC recipients and their boyfriends. "You get to wanting a skirt," she explained, "and some man or another you'll meet, he'll promise to give you those things, and maybe for a little while he'll give them to you." However, men's support frequently came with strings attached. Mrs. Jackson described most men as "like leeches, they only want to hang on to you for that check."[107]

Some women valued ADC for helping them avoid depending on men altogether. After weighing their options, they believed that the benefits of being in a relationship with a man were not worth the costs. "I'm very independent," explained Barbara Cook, who did not have a boyfriend. Although Mrs. Cook regretted her inability to receive financial support from a man, she chose to stay single because "I have a mind of my own . . . [and] I have my own ambitions." She appreciated welfare because it enabled her to be the "boss" in her house and not have to answer to anyone else.[108]

Recognizing that many women broke the rules and had boyfriends while receiving ADC, caseworkers sometimes arrived unexpectedly at their homes and looked through their laundry hampers and closets for articles of men's clothing. Women responded by keeping their boyfriends' clothes out of their closets and encouraging men to stay out of sight during the day. Louise Smith explained, "Dear God, if you have a boyfriend, and he come and go, you better scurry him out in the daytime—you better not let him in—because you never know when they're coming through after you meet them. They just pop up sometime and you can't have [a] man's clothes around."[109] Women's success in hiding men's presence in their homes led caseworkers to start making surprise visits in the middle of the night. Although these "midnight raids" were humiliating and invasive, many women insisted on their right to make their own decisions about their personal lives by continuing to form intimate relationships with men.[110]

Neighbors tried to collectively outsmart the welfare department by warning one another of impending casework visits. Especially in the summer, when people sat out on their stoops to escape the stifling heat in their apartments, word spread fast whenever a newcomer appeared on the street. One welfare department employee, Frances Hopkins, noted that her "coming was heralded two squares away." She added, "As soon as we got off a trolley car some kind neighbor would carry the word," giving recipients just enough time to hide signs of illicit activities.[111] By joining together to inform one another of caseworkers' arrivals, friends and neighbors tried to resist the DPA's attempts to monitor and control their personal lives.

Welfare authorities tried to break neighbors' solidarity by encouraging them to inform on one another. By exploiting and exacerbating the interpersonal tensions and resentments in local communities, they convinced some residents to turn their neighbors in. One study described "frequent reports of neighbors' spying on each other and reporting untoward behavior to DPA."[112] Mrs. Smith observed, "A next-door neighbor can see your boyfriend coming and going and drop a line: 'Louise is living with a man.' And they [caseworkers] believe all this."[113] Neighbors with low-wage jobs that paid less or only slightly more than ADC often resented welfare recipients. ADC recipients may have also sometimes snitched on each other, feeling envious of women whom they believed were flagrantly breaking the rules of the program, particularly if they themselves were following the regulations more closely.

Many ADC recipients responded to the DPA's rewarding of informants by devising strategies to keep their neighbors at bay. They participated in casual banter and exchanged resources with their neighbors, but avoided discussing much personal information. "I don't like to be too friendly with my neighbors," explained Mrs. Jackson. "I don't want them to know my business, and if they know I'm on DPA—even if they see my uncle come in and visit me once a week, he'll become a 'boyfriend,' and I'll have a lot of explaining to do." Although not everyone on her block was an informer, Mrs. Jackson observed, "You find a few busybodies. They're always watching you to see who you have coming in and coming out, and they're the first to report to the DPA."[114] With many women making a conscious effort not to get too close to people on their blocks, three-fifths of ADC recipients reported having no neighbors whom they would call close friends.[115] By placing firm limits on social interactions with their neighbors, women sought to protect their ability to make autonomous decisions about their income-earning activities and their relationships with men.

The degree to which women managed to capitalize on the resources provided by ADC varied. Younger recipients who had small families and were educated and in good health could sometimes successfully use ADC in conjunction with other resources to help them through a rough time. Those who found it extremely hard just to survive on ADC often lacked education, had large families, and faced problems such as ill health, alcoholism, drug addictions, and mental illness.[116] Some lived in extremely dilapidated apartments and found the grants so meager that they could barely manage to feed and clothe their kids. "I've tried all the tricks of environment [sic] to keep the children nice," explained Ethel Wright. "And somewhere along the line, you gradually feel that you're batting your head against a brick wall."[117] Some mothers grew depressed and lacked hope for the future. "It's no use making plans," observed Delores Graham; "they get all fouled up."[118] No one found life on welfare pleasant or easy. Women like Mrs. Wright and Mrs. Graham found ADC's small stipends wholly inadequate to meet their multifarious needs.

Welfare and Postwar Racial Politics

During the 1950s, women's struggles to achieve a measure of dignity while receiving ADC benefits intensified as the city became embroiled in heated public debates about African American women's use of welfare. The conversations began in earnest in 1952, the year after the political landscape of Philadelphia was transformed by the Democratic victories in the municipal election. In 1951, the electorate approved the new city charter designed to reduce political patronage and graft, creating a strong-mayor form of government and a relatively weak city council. The Republicans, who had become identified with corruption, were voted out of office, a result spurred by a strong turnout of black voters. Joseph S. Clark, an elite Philadelphian with a racially egalitarian ethic who had received his law degree from the University of Pennsylvania, was elected mayor, and Democrats took over the city council. For the first time, North Philadelphia was represented by an African American—Raymond Pace Alexander, a Harvard-trained lawyer who was a staunch advocate of civil rights and whose wife, Sadie Tanner Mossell Alexander, had served on President Truman's Committee on Civil Rights. Mayor Clark sought to put an end to the machine politics that had run the city for decades. He enforced the new charter and replaced many political appointees in City Hall with qualified young professionals. In 1955, when Clark stepped down as mayor to run for the U.S. Senate, his district attorney, Yale-educated lawyer Richardson Dilworth, replaced him. A supporter of African American rights, Dilworth sought to continue the progressive reform agenda.[119]

The growth of postwar racial liberalism was accompanied by growing white resistance to African American advancement. In the first six months of 1955 alone, there were 213 racial conflicts over housing in Philadelphia, which frequently involved whites opposing African Americans moving into their neighborhoods. In some cases, crowds of whites greeted African Americans with heckling, pickets, and vandalism.[120] Similar resistance developed when African Americans tried to integrate parks, swimming pools, and other municipal recreation facilities.[121] The police arrested large numbers of African Americans, and the media fueled whites' fears by printing numerous articles about black men's criminality and black children's juvenile delinquency.[122]

Beginning in 1952, African American women came under fire for their receipt of ADC, which critics portrayed as a prime example of the threat that African Americans posed to the white city.[123] The public assistance caseload was at an all-time low, but after an inquiry into welfare corruption conducted by Robert Lowe Kunzig, the Republican deputy attorney general of Pennsylvania, the Philadelphia DPA joined welfare authorities in cities throughout the North and West in launching a drive to crack down on relief "chiseling." Philadelphia authorities concentrated on prosecuting cases of welfare fraud; other cities stepped up their surveillance of women suspected of living with men, introduced stricter rules denying welfare to nonresidents, and sought to expel mothers deemed "employable" from their caseloads.[124] The Philadelphia welfare department's own studies ultimately concluded that cases of welfare fraud were extremely rare. Still, as in cities throughout the nation, white newspapers created the perception that thousands of welfare recipients were purposely cheating the government.[125] Municipal court judge Adrian Bonnelly was one of the first to publicly discuss the issue in explicitly racial terms. Bonnelly was a Democrat, born and raised in a working-class Italian American family on New York City's Lower East Side, who was well-known in Philadelphia as a supporter of the downtrodden. However, in 1952, he made it clear that his sympathies did not extend to African American welfare recipients. Bonnelly linked welfare fraud to black migration, criticizing the DPA for "throwing money away" on those "who have been brought here from the South to take advantage of the munificent bounty of Pennsylvania."[126]

Over the course of the 1950s, welfare became increasingly racialized in the public mind, and women became the main targets of public criticism. The initial press coverage of fraud had focused on recipients of all types of public assistance, but by the late 1950s, it focused almost exclusively on the ADC program. "Of all the categories, the aid to dependent children is the one that beats the devil out of us," observed Ralph Havens, supervisor of restitutions collections for the DPA. "The blind and the aged don't cheat—there the need is obvious. On general assistance, most people are honest . . . but the dependent children category is a headache."[127]

Echoing many of the themes in postwar social scientific scholarship, considerable public attention focused on ADC recipients' "illegitimate" children.[128] Several local magistrates and municipal court judges, mostly whites from European immigrant backgrounds, joined Bonnelly and became deeply involved in the controversy, issuing numerous inflammatory statements based on their frequent contact with African American single mothers in court. In 1959, one of the most outspoken municipal court judges, Edward A. Kallick, a Jewish Democrat, claimed that ADC recipients had "ten or 11 illegitimate children by ten or 11 different fathers." Articulating an image that featured centrally in the notion of a "culture of welfare dependency" that emerged in subsequent years, Kallick described black women's lives as part of "a circle; just illegitimacy handed down generation after generation, fostered and sponsored by the state."[129]

Philadelphia's two major newspapers, the *Evening Bulletin* and the *Inquirer*, picked up where Kallick left off. Although the papers were Republican, they were not extremely conservative; both supported Democratic candidates in the 1951 and 1955 municipal elections.[130] Their inflammatory rhetoric about ADC recipients cemented the place of the antiwelfare discourse in the political mainstream. Headlines on the front page of the *Inquirer* decried the "Wanton Illegitimacy" that characterized the ADC program, while the editors of the *Bulletin* disparaged the "hundreds of second generation reliefers in Philadelphia" for whom "living on relief comes naturally." "It's been called 'chain reaction relief,'" they observed; "illegitimacy . . . relief . . . more illegitimacy . . . more relief."[131] By the late 1950s, the idea that ADC promoted African American "illegitimacy" had become so firmly established in the public mind that some judges in Philadelphia began to advocate the adoption of suitable home laws to deny welfare to women who had more than two children out of wedlock. One former judge even advocated forced sterilization.[132]

Legal authorities did not publicly advocate employment for ADC recipients, but instead criticized women for not properly fulfilling their maternal roles. In 1958, Democratic magistrate Elias Myers told reporters that ADC recipients "simply don't care a rap about [their] kids except as an excuse to claim bigger relief payments."[133] District Attorney Victor Blanc also seized on the issue. A Jewish lawyer who was active in Democratic Party politics and had worked with the American Civil Liberties Union, Blanc complained about ADC families with "children . . . left alone in their houses while their mothers were in neighborhood taprooms drinking liquor, smoking marijuana cigarettes and playing the numbers."[134] By 1961, the editorial page of the *Bulletin* described the typical ADC recipient who abused the system as a "drunken wench . . . paid more for each hapless offspring." In such ADC recipients' families: "The mother may be a mother only biologically. The fathers of her assorted children may be missing primarily because she never is sure who they are. Her pathetic children may stay with her only because she needs them to keep the ADC relief checks coming in. They may even die of neglect or malnutrition because the money intended for their care is entrusted to the trollop who happened to beget them."[135]

Portraits of African American women as promiscuous, unfit mothers who cheated the government suggested that white taxpayers were being exploited by immoral black city-dwellers. Newspapers described the relationship between

ADC recipients and Philadelphia's taxpayers as one of dependency, in which African American women drained resources directly from the pockets of hard-working and law-abiding whites.[136] A 1958 *Bulletin* editorial warned that "taxpayers do not want to support mothers living in repeated degradation." "No one local sore point seems to be more irritating to the ordinary citizen," reported the *Bulletin*, "than the use of tax money to support low-living slatterns on relief."[137] By portraying honest taxpayers as subsidizers of immoral welfare recipients, the discourse masked the labor it took for women to raise children in poverty and the massive amounts of assistance "taxpayers" received through federal home-ownership programs, highway construction, and old-age insurance. It suggested that hardworking men were being taken advantage of by wasteful government authorities and irresponsible African American women.[138]

The discursive juxtaposition of upstanding white taxpayers and immoral black ADC recipients helped foster the overrepresentation of African Americans on welfare by encouraging working-class whites to avoid ADC at all costs in order to claim the social privileges of whiteness. Many working-class whites had already been deterred from welfare because they had access to alternative resources and wanted to avoid the program's restrictions on savings, home ownership, and life insurance. As the ability to identify as a "taxpayer" became an important marker of Philadelphians' race and class identities, struggling whites became even more motivated to avoid ADC so that they could define themselves as superior to the growing numbers of poor African Americans who relied on welfare.[139] In the 1960s, community workers noted that white residents of the working-class Kensington neighborhood were averse to applying for benefits from government programs because to accept social services "might be to admit that they're not all they claim to be." They championed their own thrift and industriousness by describing African Americans as "too lazy to work and earn a living." An element of resentment, and even envy, entered into some whites' perceptions of ADC recipients because they believed that women who received welfare led lives of leisure that they themselves could not attain. One older man remarked, "We had to do without, why can't they?"[140] In comparing themselves to ADC recipients, white Kensingtonians expressed both a sense of superiority and deep resentment toward the growing numbers of African Americans in the city.

Many African Americans joined whites in distancing themselves from welfare recipients by claiming identities as taxpayers. Summing up this sentiment, the headline of a 1959 article in the African American *Philadelphia Tribune* declared: "58 Million Taxes Paid by Negro." The article responded to the widespread belief "that Negroes accept assistance from the government but play no part in sharing the expense of maintaining the agencies of Philadelphia, Pennsylvania and the United States" by calculating the local, state, and federal taxes paid by African Americans.[141] In a similar vein, the *Philadelphia Afro-American* noted significant antiwelfare sentiments among its audience. "I think all public assistance to unwed mothers should be eliminated . . . if the same mistake is made repeatedly," Molly Blackwell told reporters. "After all, those of us who are working have to pay the bill."[142] Others expressed resentment about the perks allegedly received by women who relied on welfare. ADC recipient Lulu Bridges observed, "My family has said to me many a times, 'I wish I was in your shoes. . . . Do y'all realize that y'all don't have to do nothing?' " Mrs. Bridges's relatives frequently told her, "You don't have to work, you can sit right here and the mail man will bring y'all money, and you don't have nothing to do, and I wish I could do it."[143] By implicitly or explicitly juxtaposing their hard work with the laziness and immorality of welfare recipients, some African Americans joined whites in defining themselves in opposition to black women who received ADC.

African Americans who did not receive welfare were sometimes particularly critical of ADC recipients because they suffered from the racist images that surrounded the program. Many confronted disdain from whites who assumed that they received welfare just because they were black and looked like they did not have much money. Angry at their own vulnerability to racist treatment, some of them criticized ADC recipients for engaging in behaviors that conformed to public stereotypes. One letter published in the African American *Philadelphia Independent* lamented the "women and young girls on Public Assistance for two or three generations, some with four or five children with different fathers," and added, "We find these mothers sitting in taprooms drinking, and their little children are being neglected."[144] Juanita Kidd Stout, a Philadelphia municipal court judge who was the first African American women appointed to a court of record in the nation, was outspoken about her support of suitable home laws, and other African Americans agreed with her. "I believe that welfare support of these mothers should be cut out, and that's that," argued Mamie Ashton.[145] When African Americans who did not rely on public assistance sought to differentiate themselves from ADC recipients, they often reinforced the demeaning images of black women that permeated public discourse.

Civil rights activists found it particularly difficult to negotiate the new racial politics of welfare. In 1960, when 29,000 women and children in Louisiana were suddenly cut from the ADC program, the Urban League and many local African American community groups fought for their reinstatement. Viewing welfare politics as integrally linked to racial politics, many activists condemned white politicians for using ADC cutbacks as retribution for civil rights organizing.[146] Yet in face of the growing public uproar over welfare, civil rights activists often felt compelled to temper their support for ADC.[147] Many viewed single motherhood and women's reliance on welfare benefits as unfortunate symptoms of what they considered a much more important problem: chronic male unemployment, which prevented black men from fulfilling the dominant masculine ideal.[148] Family and sexual politics were an important component of the Black Freedom Struggle, and civil rights leaders feared that whites would equate any defense of African American women's receipt of welfare with support for "promiscuity" and single motherhood. In 1961, the executive director of the National Association for the Advancement of Colored People, Roy Wilkins, noted that although he supported ADC, to advocate for single mothers publicly would mean political death for civil rights organizations. Given the widespread public disapproval of "illegitimacy," Wilkins explained, to defend women with children born out of wedlock "would be regarded by the Negro's opponents as an admission on our part that our people are not yet worthy of the status we demand for them."[149]

The Urban League stood out among civil rights organizations for the sympathetic attention it paid to ADC recipients. Led on the national level by social workers Lester Granger and Whitney M. Young Jr., the league devoted a great deal of attention to welfare policy. In 1962, Young expressed his outrage at the "erroneous" images of welfare circulating in the press that misrepresented ADC recipients' efforts to provide for their children.[150] Insisting that African Americans received welfare in high numbers because they suffered from racial discrimination, the Philadelphia Urban League (PUL) consistently attempted to increase ADC grants and engaged in community networking and lobbying on behalf of welfare recipients.[151] Yet while campaigning for increased welfare allowances, the PUL emphasized that more generous grants would help women "get the most out of marriage" and achieve "marital stability." (How that would occur was never made clear.)[152] This advocacy of marriage placed the PUL and ADC recipients at odds. While the PUL viewed women's status as single mothers as a moral problem that needed to be solved, working-class African American women appreciated welfare precisely because it enabled them to mother their children while heading their own households.

Local and state welfare authorities and some liberal civic groups joined in defending ADC recipients, and labor unions and caseworkers sometimes offered their support as well. High-ranking welfare officials issued numerous statements that emphasized not only the falsity of the derogatory images of ADC recipients, but also the need for higher grants. William P. Sailer, executive director of the Philadelphia DPA, told the press that the extent of public misunderstanding about the ADC program was "enormous." Norman V. Lourie, deputy secretary of welfare in Pennsylvania, defended women even more explicitly. "To assume that a mother has a financial inducement to have more dependent children is a myth," charged Lourie. "The more children she has, the deeper she goes in debt."[153] Liberal organizations such as the Philadelphia Health and Welfare Council conducted research to back up welfare authorities' statements. Their studies investigated whether recipients migrated to receive welfare, had high numbers of children out of wedlock, or engaged in fraud. In all three arenas, the studies concluded, popular stereotypes were categorically wrong.[154]

Welfare advocates' attempts to dispel the growing myths about welfare received some coverage and support from the mainstream press. Prior to World War II, white social reformers had cultivated support for welfare for single mothers by portraying recipients as impoverished, "deserving" white widows and "innocent" children, and these ideas did not disappear from the public consciousness overnight.[155] Even the *Bulletin* could be swayed by sympathetic tales of women in need. In 1959, in response to the calls for higher welfare grants, it ran an article headlined "It's Possible to Live on Relief, but High Rents Make It Tough," which described ADC recipients living in deplorable conditions and expending an extraordinary amount of time and energy just to feed, clothe, and house their families.[156] Illustrating that older, more positive conceptions of public assistance for single mothers had not completely vanished, the same *Bulletin* editorial page that described ADC recipients as "subsidized slatterns" and "drunken wenches" argued that if taxpayers were shown "how niggardly the payments made to those in need are in relation to today's inflated costs," Pennsylvania Welfare Secretary Harry Shapiro's requests for increases in the payments to welfare recipients would command extensive public support. Contrasting a more favorable understanding of ADC with the newer racialized images, the *Bulletin* stated that "Pennsylvanians approve of aid to dependent children. . . . [They are just] incensed at cases in which wanton living appeared to be tax-subsidized."[157]

Even the most ardent defenders of ADC did not challenge the assumptions at the heart of the antiwelfare discourse. No one called into question the dichotomies drawn between the rights of "taxpayers" and those of welfare recipients, nor did anyone explicitly oppose the public condemnations of "illegitimacy." Many welfare advocates argued that the main problem with ADC stemmed from its inadequate funding, which prevented local authorities from hiring more caseworkers and assigning them smaller caseloads. Workers who had more manageable caseloads would be able to provide women with the individualized attention and access to community resources that they needed to leave the program.[158] In the late 1950s, the Philadelphia DPA tested this theory by constructing a pilot project in which caseworkers supervised thirty-five cases each and collaborated with physicians and other social service agencies. After two years of the program, local authorities championed their new approach not by discussing ADC recipients' improved health and housing conditions, but by emphasizing that 98 of the 349 women left welfare completely, resulting in a considerable savings to taxpayers.[159] Welfare advocates sometimes conceptualized their calls for higher stipends in the same way—not as a moral or civil rights issue, but as evidence of their commitment to fiscal restraint, since higher grants would enable more families to acquire the resources they needed to get jobs and leave public assistance.[160] The push to diminish caseloads and cut costs stigmatized and marginalized mothers whose health problems, inadequate education, or need to care for young children prevented them from securing gainful employment.

The emphasis on helping women get jobs and leave ADC was shared by welfare advocates working to shape policy on the national level. In the 1950s, with the growing acceptance of employment as a viable and necessary option for middle-class white mothers, many professionals became reluctant to support poor African American women engaging in full-time mothering work. Prominent reformers such as Wilbur Cohen and Elizabeth Wickenden increasingly advocated "rehabilitation" programs to provide women with the tools to leave welfare and achieve "self-sufficiency." In the 1960s, the federal government answered the call for rehabilitation by introducing employment incentives and job-preparation programs for ADC recipients.[161]

Ultimately, then, although critics and defenders of welfare held radically different views of the mechanisms needed to help women leave ADC, with critics advocating suitable home laws and defenders championing the need for increased resources, by the late 1950s, both sides agreed that welfare policies should aim to reduce caseloads. In the postwar period, neither group succeeded in significantly reshaping Pennsylvania welfare policy. Funding levels remained low, caseworkers remained overworked, and the number of women who received ADC in Philadelphia increased sharply. Public condemnations of ADC recipients intensified, making it increasingly difficult for working-class African American women to negotiate the postwar city.

"Hungry for Things"

ADC recipients experienced the rhetorical attacks on welfare viscerally and felt deeply humiliated by the stereotypes that circulated in the mainstream press. "The peoples who are on DPA—have no one to stand up for them," observed Jacqueline Richards. "We're actually looked down upon."[162] Several women complained that when they and their children took city buses, the drivers would make loud comments about their promiscuity and lack of initiative and chastise them for undeservedly living off "taxpayers'" money.[163] Clerks, secretaries, and health care professionals were notoriously disrespectful to ADC recipients, and women dreaded public interactions with them.[164] Mrs. Ross described her experiences by noting, "People that have a little something and can, are lucky enough to have jobs and stuff, are downing us like mad—so you're just afraid to say anything."[165]

In face of the barrage of criticism, women tried desperately to preserve their dignity and privacy by hiding their receipt of welfare from public view. They placed a high priority on obtaining clothing for themselves and their families in the hope that it would camouflage their poverty and receipt of welfare. Mrs. Ross explained, "Just because you are on DPA, you don't want to go around advertising it all over the streets."[166] Women frequently sacrificed money for food and rent to obtain decent clothing so they could join churches and participate in community organizations such as block groups without feeling ashamed. Yet no matter how hard they tried to save money and shop efficiently, they could rarely afford to purchase a fraction of the new clothing and consumer goods that they desired. Many mothers became particularly distressed when their children complained about having to wear used clothing. Jocelyn Carter's children were "tired of being seconds," and it pained her to disappoint them: "When you go out and calls yourself shopping, and come back with some second hand clothes every time, it makes them feel pretty bad."[167] Elsa Bell described her children as "hungry for *things*—not food, not a home to live in. . . . They're hungry for the trimmings."[168]

Many mothers asserted their right to more than basic subsistence by refusing to purchase the cheapest items available. This happened most frequently when they bought and prepared food for their families. Unable to afford steaks or fresh vegetables, their diets consisted mostly of starchy foods and inexpensive meats such as pigs' feet and chicken wings. Still, they made a great effort to serve what Rossalyn Dickenson described as "good, nourishing meals" for their children.[169] Some mothers described the surplus food program as particularly inadequate and demeaning. The staff at several of the distribution centers would not let them pick the foodstuffs that they wanted, forcing them to take large quantities of all the available goods. Thousands of pounds of flour, beans, and powdered eggs went to waste because women could not—or would not—use the ingredients in their cooking. After receiving surplus food for several months, Theresa Trader complained about the cans of powdered eggs, which sat accumulating dust on her porch. "You couldn't use them in baking, you couldn't use them in cooking. Well, in fact, you couldn't scramble them." Lois Brooks found the rice particularly unappetizing. "It's like tapioca. . . . They used to give you long-grain rice, which was alright, but now it's like gum. . . . I give it to the neighbors or somebody that can use it, because I don't like it."[170] In their refusal to make do with whatever food they were given, no matter how unappealing, women insisted that their families deserved to eat decently, like everybody else.

In the rapidly growing consumer culture in which citizens' identities were inextricably linked to their ability to consume, mothers regretted and resented that their inability to participate in mainstream consumer culture publicly marked and stigmatized their families. Many sought to gain a small measure of respectability and status by purchasing new consumer goods. They could not afford sparkling new kitchen appliances or automobiles, but they could sometimes purchase smaller items that helped lift their spirits and build their self-esteem. Mrs. Dickenson did most of her shopping at secondhand stores, but insisted on purchasing brand-new winter coats at specialty shops for her unusually tall daughter. "I have to pay a little extra or I don't get the fit in the waistline where it should be," she explained. "I have to get proportioned things or she looks slightly funny."[171] In the late 1960s, welfare rights groups sought to secure access to consumer goods for women by making credit at department stores (which was denied to welfare recipients) one of their central demands. Before the welfare rights movement, many women insisted on their right to experience the pleasures and social benefits of mass consumption through small purchases of clothing, jewelry, and other consumer goods.[172]

Tens of thousands of working-class African American women in Philadelphia viewed ADC as an essential resource in their struggle against poverty. They understood that welfare was not a panacea: ADC sustained them in poverty instead of helping them escape it, and small stipends did not solve their problems with illness, dilapidated housing, lack of child care, and restricted employment prospects. Yet many women appreciated ADC for enabling them to keep and raise their children themselves. Some women found that the program helped them care for their health and avoid taking exploitative, poorly paid jobs. Others insisted that they deserved more money than welfare provided and pursued jobs illegally to increase their standard of living. Refusing to cede control over their households by moving in with men, many women achieved more leverage in their intimate relationships.

During the 1950s, public attacks on ADC threatened to derail women's efforts to use welfare to meet their needs. In a climate of resistance to African Americans' growing presence and influence in northern cities, critics charged that ADC promoted immorality and fiscal irresponsibility. Contempt for welfare and those who depended on its benefits became a crucial source of identity and pride for many whites. Some African Americans, sensitive to a dynamic that was equating the entire race with dependence on public assistance and damaging their own tenuous hold on social respectability and political citizenship, repeated the antiwelfare discourse. With ADC recipients constituting the "other" against which Philadelphians from a range of backgrounds sought to define their own position, supporters of welfare rarely mounted an effective defense of the program.

Yet even as state and local authorities faced tremendous pressure to restrict access to welfare, women continued to seek and receive ADC in ever-increasing numbers. As public opinion of ADC recipients sank, the number of women benefiting from the program rose. No one had anticipated African American women's rapid movement into the city's welfare offices, and authorities were not willing or able to ban qualified applicants from receiving assistance. Yet over time, the welfare department slowly began to chip away at the ADC program. The move to limit women's access and sense of entitlement to ADC became most evident through a burgeoning alliance between the welfare department and the municipal court.

CHAPTER TWO

Hard Choices at 1801 Vine

In a Philadelphia criminal courtroom on November 18, 1947, Judge Gay Gordon called Janice Carson, an African American woman in her early twenties, to take the stand. Mrs. Carson walked to the podium to testify in an assault and battery case that she had brought against her husband. When questioned, Mrs. Carson told the court that she and Vince Carson had had a rocky marriage with constant domestic violence both before and after he served in the army during World War II. The most recent incident had occurred after she told Vince that she was pregnant with their second child: He "beat me and he struck me. . . . He was choking me and he knocked me against a radiator, and the night after that I had a miscarriage."

When Vince Carson took the stand, he admitted that he had beaten Janice. However, he stated that the incident had occurred during an argument "about her allowance" and that he had hit her in self-defense. "She slapped me first," he testified, "and I just lost my head and slapped her—" "Your Honor, I never struck him first," interrupted Mrs. Carson. "Everyone knows he fights me." At this point, Judge Gordon intervened in the dispute. "You talk too much," he told Mr. Carson. The judge proceeded to call Mr. Carson a "brute," told him that the "seeds of murder" were planted in his home, and warned him that he would end up in the electric chair one day.

After a few more questions, Judge Gordon turned to Mrs. Carson and asked, "Madam, what do you want me to do with him?" Mrs. Carson explained that although she had separated from Mr. Carson, she still needed his financial support because she had been in poor health since the miscarriage and could not seek employment to support herself and her son. She asked for a "peace bond," a type of bail that would give Mr. Carson freedom and allow him to look for a job as long as he did not beat her. The judge told Mrs. Carson that Mr. Carson belonged in jail, but that he would grant the peace bond. The day after his release, Vince Carson attacked his wife, tore her clothing, and beat her up.[1]

Working-class African American women like Janice Carson turned to the Philadelphia Municipal Court for economic support and protection from domestic violence. They pressed charges of nonsupport to obtain financial assistance from the fathers of their children or charges of assault and battery to obtain physical protection from abusive men. The legal system was geared toward preserving two-parent families and limiting Aid to Dependent Children (ADC) payments, but since judges strongly believed that men needed to fulfill their roles as breadwinners and owed women physical protection and financial support, women could harness the court's biases to work in their favor.[2] Most women won their cases, often obtaining either a small amount of money or limited protection from domestic violence.

Of all the public institutions in the city, it was in the municipal court that the intimate connections between poverty and domestic abuse became most clearly visible. During years when civil rights activists focused on violence outside the home, and well before middle-class feminists would interpret spousal abuse as a political issue, working-class African American women placed the issue of domestic violence squarely on the public stage.[3] Like Mrs. Carson, many viewed their need for protection from violence as integrally linked to their need for financial assistance and struggled because the municipal court separated charges of assault from charges for support. They had to choose between freedom from violence and freedom from hunger, even though gaining one often meant sacrificing the other.

Women's use of the municipal court profoundly shaped men's lives and reconfigured gender relationships within working-class communities.[4] When women sought redress through the legal system, men had to meet with probation officers and interviewers and appear in court, where they usually faced monetary demands, strong rebukes, or jail sentences. In many cases, men temporarily limited the abuse or began to pay child support after women pressed charges. In other cases, just by threatening to take legal action, women managed either to diminish men's violence or to elicit voluntary financial contributions from the fathers of their children. Although most men ultimately defaulted on their payments or resumed the abuse, women's involvement with the legal system usually, at least briefly, gave them more leverage in their relationships with men.

In the early 1950s, the large and growing numbers of women receiving assistance from the municipal court and the welfare department inspired legal and welfare authorities to implement restrictive new policies governing women's use of the legal system. Pennsylvania welfare authorities grew concerned about the large numbers of ADC recipients refusing to seek support orders that could be deducted from their welfare grants and mandated stricter enforcement of policies requiring women to press charges against the fathers of their children. Such policies made it more difficult for ADC recipients to provide for their families since men rarely regularly paid their support orders and the state did not compensate women for the missed payments. A similarly constraining new policy originated within the municipal court in response to the unexpectedly large number of domestic violence cases brought by women. Judges instituted policies that discouraged women from pressing assault charges and encouraged them to reconcile with violent men after receiving counseling in the domestic relations court.

The new policies attempted to enforce the male breadwinner/dependent housewife model on African Americans in the face of concrete evidence that it was economically unattainable and in cases in which the domestic partnership had irretrievably broken down. Welfare authorities jeopardized ADC recipients' financial well-being, and judges ignored women's constitutional right to protection from violence, making it clear that they believed that assault was not a serious problem if it took place within the home. While many women continued to insist upon their right to make their own decisions about whether and how they used the court, the new policies made it more difficult for them to secure adequate resources.

Judges' and Working-Class Women's Differing Perspectives on Court Policies

Impoverished African American women had long viewed the legal system as a crucial tool in their efforts to gain control over their lives. In the first half of the nineteenth century, courtrooms were an integral part of urban culture, and working-class whites and African Americans used them to settle community problems. Over the course of the century, the legal system expanded and became more bureaucratic, more professional, and more focused on monitoring and controlling low-income citizens.[5] By the early twentieth century, Philadelphia had twenty-eight magistrates' courts, five courts of common pleas (civil courts), a quarter sessions court and oyer and terminer court (criminal courts), a municipal court, and an orphans' court. Working-class whites and African Americans continued to use the courts to solve problems that they faced in their daily lives. Women regularly appeared in court, defending their interests when accused of crimes such as prostitution and illegal liquor-selling and pressing charges to settle disputes over property, seek redress for violence, and resolve conflicts in personal relationships.

In the years after World War II, most working-class African American women who initiated legal action sought assistance from the Philadelphia Municipal Court, which was created by the state legislature in 1913 in response to agitation by white middle-class social reformers. Instituted in early twentieth-century cities throughout the country, municipal courts worked under the assumption that common crimes should be addressed in a comprehensive manner that promoted individual and social rehabilitation. Reformers rejected long-standing conceptions of crime as a product of free will, flawed character, or sinfulness, and embraced the radical notion that it was a *social* phenomenon; in their way of thinking, crime arose from the interaction between individuals' biological makeup and their socioeconomic circumstances. Although the Philadelphia Municipal Court was a court of record and had the power to imprison offenders, like most twentieth-century municipal courts, it sought not only to punish, but also to assist, educate, and discipline its clients. Legal authorities conducted thorough investigations of their clients' life circumstances and provided medical testing, counseling, and other social services.[6] To provide specialized attention to different types of cases, the court was divided into five divisions: civil, criminal, domestic relations, juvenile, and misdemeanant. The civil division had concurrent jurisdiction with other courts in the city over civil actions and equity claims up to $5,000. The criminal division saw, and had concurrent jurisdiction over, all but the most serious crimes in the city. The misdemeanant division, known as the "morals court," had exclusive jurisdiction over cases involving "disorderly street walkers" as well as "disobedient, idle, and disorderly" minors between sixteen and twenty-one years old. The juvenile division had exclusive jurisdiction over all cases involving children, and the domestic relations division had exclusive jurisdiction over most cases of desertion and nonsupport.[7]

African American women's legal dealings usually took place in the courthouse that handled domestic and juvenile cases, which they referred to by its address as "1801 Vine." Marcelle Blackwell, who grew up in postwar Philadelphia, described 1801 Vine as the "most famous address in the city of Philadelphia" because of the frequency of women's visits.[8] Opened in 1940, on the eighteenth block of Vine Street, a wide, central thoroughfare for municipal

The Philadelphia Municipal Court at 18th and Vine Streets was modeled after government buildings in Paris. Temple University Libraries, Urban Archives, Philadelphia, Pa.

buildings in Philadelphia, its architecture exuded a formality that distinguished it from most other public institutions in the city. The imposing limestone structure had a colonnaded front. Grand front doors opened onto an expansive main hallway with high ceilings, chandeliers, murals, and terrazzo floors. Trials took place in the courtrooms on the first floor, which had painted ceilings, cork floors, several rows of wooden chairs, and windows framed with curtains and venetian blinds. The waiting rooms had stone walls, stenciled beams, and patterned rubber tile on the floors. A series of murals throughout the building symbolized the "uplifting" work that the court envisioned itself performing— reuniting families and rehabilitating juvenile delinquents.[9]

Since pursuing legal action was less stigmatized than receiving welfare and court policies did not require women to deplete their assets before receiving assistance, the municipal court attracted a broader spectrum of the working class than the welfare department did, including some women who had income from family members or their own jobs. While welfare provided demeaning "handouts," the legal system was open to everyone and offered women "justice." The formal architecture and elaborate decoration of 1801 Vine conveyed a sense of dignity that the city's welfare offices lacked. Legal rituals underscored the court's function as an institution that enforced the rule of law. Although most trials were conducted without juries, women had to swear before signing petitions or testifying in front of judges, and their statements were carefully recorded by court employees. They interacted mainly with middle-class, often college-educated, interviewers and probation officers who were the foot soldiers of the court's efforts to collect and organize personal and demographic information about clients. African American women did not have as strong a presence in the municipal court as they did in the welfare system, but they were still disproportionately represented: In the mid-1950s, African Americans comprised less than one-quarter of the city's population, but black women were half of the plaintiffs in nonsupport cases and two-thirds of the plaintiffs in assault and battery cases. Although African American and white women both experienced domestic violence and nonsupport, black women had less access to alternative resources than did white women and were more likely to take legal action against men.[10]

Women who pressed charges in the municipal court confronted judges whose outlooks exemplified some of the limitations of postwar liberalism in meeting their needs. In the 1950s, the court had fourteen judges, elected by city voters to ten-year terms. All of the judges who worked in the domestic relations court were white men, usually Democrats from Italian American, Polish American, or Jewish backgrounds.[11] Although many of them were active in a range of civic organizations and known for their humanitarianism, they felt little sympathy for the plight of struggling African Americans. Most believed that two-parent families with male breadwinners were superior to other family forms. They looked down on unmarried mothers and expressed contempt for fathers who could not adequately support their wives and children.

Most women who approached the municipal court sought child support or protection from domestic violence.[12] Their suits took three main forms. Unmarried women's suits against the fathers of their children for financial support, called fornication and bastardy, were handled in the women's criminal division, making it ambiguous exactly who legal officials believed should be on trial.[13] In the 1950s, on average, nearly two thousand women pressed these charges each year.[14] The domestic relations court handled married women's financial support cases, usually in the form of nonsupport charges against their husbands. These cases numbered over four thousand each year (for statistics on all child support cases, see Table 2.1).[15] Finally, assault and battery charges brought by women against violent men were handled in the criminal division until 1952, when the domestic relations division took control of their adjudication. The court usually handled over six hundred of these cases each year.[16] Although women did not press charges of assault as often as they pressed charges of nonsupport, the large number of assault cases challenges feminist scholarship

Table 2.1. Cases of Fornication and Bastardy and Nonsupport, Philadelphia Municipal Court, 1940–1960

Year	Fornication and Bastardy	Nonsupport
1940	698	2,474
1941	721	2,589
1942	611	2,247
1943	550	2,118
1944	504	2,020
1945	560	1,896
1946	742	2,686
1947	787	2,967
1948	1,297	2,992
1949	1,660	2,871
1950	1,643	4,076
1951	1,839	3,571
1952	1,466	3,889
1953	1,516	4,163
1954	1,835	3,927
1955	2,203	4,159
1956	2,133	4,728
1957	2,220	4,079
1958	2,406	3,705
1959	2,427	4,331
1960	2,338	3,548

Source: Philadelphia Municipal Court Annual Report, 1960, 306; Philadelphia Municipal Court Annual Report, 1964, 221.

that has portrayed this period as a time when women rarely used the legal system to prosecute domestic violence.[17]

The rulings in women's assault and battery cases varied widely because judges did not have formal procedures in place for dealing with them. Prior to 1952, the municipal court sent abused women to the magistrates' courts for an initial hearing. Some women settled their cases with the magistrates, securing warnings, peace bonds, and occasionally jail sentences for their husbands. Those not satisfied with the magistrates' hearings could pay a $10 fee to obtain a warrant for their husbands' arrest and press assault and battery charges in the criminal division of the municipal court. During the criminal trials, municipal court judges almost always tried to reconcile couples. However, when reconciliation proved impossible, judges used their own discretion to settle the disputes, finding some men not guilty and requiring others to post peace bonds or go to jail.

Many women found fault with the court's handling of domestic assault cases because judges separated cases of abuse from cases of financial support, forcing them to choose between physical protection and monetary assistance even though these two aspects of their lives were integrally linked. The legal system did not address or help remedy the connections between poverty and domestic abuse: women who were financially dependent on their husbands were more vulnerable to abuse, and abuse could reinforce women's poverty by injuring and isolating them. If women with abusive husbands chose to seek support orders, they were left without protection from violence. If they pressed criminal charges and their husbands ended up in jail, they were left without financial support.[18] Faced with this impossible choice, some abused women who relied on men's financial support sought a compromise: They pressed assault charges and then asked judges to give their husbands a warning or put them on probation, hoping that this would allow men to continue earning money while helping curb subsequent episodes of violence.[19] As Mrs. Carson's case illustrates, this strategy could backfire by making men so furious that they continued the abuse.

Nonsupport and fornication and bastardy cases had far more predictable outcomes. Married women seeking to press nonsupport charges met with an interviewer, usually a woman, who recorded detailed information about their cases and their backgrounds. The interviewer then contacted women's husbands and requested their presence in court. Probation officers investigated men's places of employment to verify their wages and sometimes conducted home visits to inspect couples' living arrangements. Seven to ten days after the women's initial contact with the court, most men came in for their meetings with interviewers. Interviewers spoke individually with the men and then met with the couples together in one or more joint conferences. No matter what interviewers learned about the men's and women's relationships, they tried to convince couples to reconcile. Most women refused and insisted on filing a formal petition for a trial. The cases then joined a line of hundreds of other similar cases waiting for a trial, a backlog caused by the large numbers of women pressing nonsupport charges and the limited number of judges assigned to the cases. On average, it took ten to fourteen weeks before women received hearings. The trials themselves usually lasted less than five minutes because judges were under tremendous pressure to move quickly. Even when men painted unflattering portraits of women's behavior by complaining about their promiscuity, failure to perform domestic chores, or excessive nagging, court policy was formulated so that judges almost always ruled in women's favor and awarded them financial support.[20]

Fornication and bastardy cases, which concerned unmarried couples, involved similar procedures, but were usually settled more quickly. To secure benefits, women had to press charges within two years of the conception of a child. Because the couples were not married, interviewers did not try to persuade them to reconcile. Instead, during the initial meetings and fieldwork inquiries, court workers pressured men to admit paternity and agree to pay child support. Most men recognized that they had a slim chance of winning their cases, acknowledged that they had fathered the child, and agreed to comply with a support order. Fewer than one in ten cases went to trial, and the mothers who testified were usually awarded financial support.[21]

The legal priorities that undergirded the policies favoring reconciliation and men's support of women and children reflected judges' commitment to the family-wage system and to preventing women's dependence on the state. Family-wage ideology envisioned men earning a wage that was sufficient to support a wife and children at home. This ideal was unattainable for most working-class African Americans; men could rarely obtain stable, well-paying jobs, and many women with young children were gainfully employed.[22] State authorities recognized that African American women held jobs because African American men's wages were insufficient, but they did not believe that women should be the primary breadwinners for their families or head their own households. Judges claimed that households with married couples and male breadwinners were morally superior to those headed by single mothers. They also preferred two-parent households for fiscal reasons because most married women did not qualify for welfare. The court's *Annual Reports* noted that interviewers tried to "effect a reconciliation . . . and a reestablishment of wholesome family relationships" to save "the community many millions of dollars" in welfare payments.[23] In cases in which reconciliations proved impossible, judges promoted support orders in order to diminish women's welfare checks. "Someone must support each family," the 1957 *Annual Report* stated, adding, "This obligation is the father's, however, and not the community's."[24]

Women often faulted the court for failing to ensure that they received adequate financial assistance. Many criticized the judges' practice of calculating support orders according to men's wages, which typically awarded them one-third of men's pay. Since most men who came before the court held low-wage jobs, most women received very small stipends. Jessie Redd observed, "When you take a man into court you hardly get enough to pay a baby-sitter."[25] The fact that the court was notoriously slow and inefficient in delivering support checks on time exacerbated the problem.[26] Men could either send checks through the mail or pay cash in person at the Department of Accounts at 1801 Vine. Neither route resulted in women receiving their checks promptly. Clerks had to verify that men's checks had cleared before they sent stipends to women, and the cash payments were usually "shunted about the office" and not immediately processed.[27] Even more troubling for many women was the court's failure to compensate them for the high rates of male noncompliance. In 1960, 70 percent of the support orders in effect were not being paid.[28]

To address the problem of noncompliance, judges advocated changing men's behavior, a solution that did not take into account many working-class men's precarious economic circumstances. *Annual Reports* attributed men's default to willful neglect, charging that men found "devious and sundry" ways to "escape their family obligations."[29] Claiming that the "withholding of support, personal extravagance and profligacy, rather than the inability to acquire economic substance are usually the basis of the nonsupport problem," the court's 1957 *Annual Report* implied that the problem would be solved if men faced up to their responsibilities and fulfilled their breadwinner-provider roles.[30] This approach did not take into account how unemployment and low-wage jobs made it difficult for many men—especially African American men—to support families. The unusually high rates of men's defaults during the Depression suggest that unemployment and underemployment played a significant role in men's noncompliance. Similarly, when there was a sharp increase in the cost of living just after World War II, many men returned to court to get their support orders decreased. That many women returned to have their orders increased for the very same reason illustrates a fundamental problem with court policies that made poor women and children directly dependent on poor men for their livelihood.[31]

Many men charged that they suffered from the court's financial support policies.[32] Those who had remarried, lost their jobs, or had to care for parents or other family members usually found support orders financially burdensome. Particularly in cases involving unmarried mothers, the court's policy of ruling in favor of women was so entrenched that men had little chance of being found innocent even if they did not believe that they had fathered the child.[33] Throughout the postwar period, legal officials engaged in periodic crackdowns on delinquent accounts in which field-workers tracked down men and sometimes even arrested them at their places of employment. Authorities experimented with jail terms and garnished wages; in 1959, 463 men were jailed for nonpayment of support orders.[34] Judges justified the crackdowns by emphasizing that men's avoidance of child support resulted in increased welfare payments to women, claiming that it was "the state—and not the wife—who suffers when the husband fails to meet the court order."[35] By laying part of the blame for welfare expenditures on unpaid support orders, judges suggested that African American men contributed to the immorality and fiscal irresponsibility that they associated with ADC.

Working-class African American women insisted that they, not the state, were the victims of men's noncompliance. Thousands of women lived in precarious situations, never assured of receiving financial support because the legal and welfare system forced them to depend on men's irregular contributions. Arlene Starks remarked: "Maybe the next week I'll get a check. Maybe the following week I'll get a check. Now the next two weeks I don't get no check. See, that keeps me off base all the time."[36] Court policies stipulated that men had to default on four consecutive payments before women could issue a complaint at the Department of Accounts. After women reported the nonpayment, probation officers often instructed them to track down men themselves to find the reason for the defaults.[37] Mrs. Starks explained: "I'll go down to the court, and I'll tell them 'Mr. S. has missed out for four checks this month. I haven't received any money from him.' And they'll say, 'Now . . . have you been to his job to find out if he's working or not, have you been to his home to find out if he's sick or anything?' "[38] Throughout the 1950s, nearly seven thousand women returned to court each year to complain of men's noncompliance (see Table 2.2).[39] Many women needed their small support checks so desperately that they returned five to fifteen times over the course of several years when men refused or were unable to pay.[40]

Even when women managed to get their husbands back into court, they did not always receive compensation for missed payments. Several years after Corrine Elkins pressed charges, her husband stopped paying his support order. When she took him back to court, "he was $4,800 in arrears." To Mrs. Elkins's dismay, "The judge dismissed $2,000 of it. He said, 'Well, just get rid of $2,000 of it, and you owe $2,800, and you can pay $5.00 extra each week.' " Knowing that this ruling would have little effect on her husband's behavior, Mrs. Elkins said that she "came to the conclusion, you've got to do things yourself, girl" and started putting in more overtime, working twelve to sixteen hours a day, six or seven days each week. With her arduous schedule and decent city job, Mrs. Elkins could get by without her missed support payments.[41] Most poor mothers could not.

When the court advocated policies that ensured women's financial dependence on men, why did it fail so consistently in enforcing them? First, enforcement procedures were expensive since, as women knew from experience, it could take weeks to track down men and verify their wages. By forcing women

Table 2.2. Cases in Which Plaintiffs Returned to Court to Report Nonpayment of Support Orders, Philadelphia Municipal Court, 1940–1960

Year	Nonpayment Cases
1940	2,383
1941	3,027
1942	2,288
1943	2,088
1944	1,758
1945	2,249
1946	2,276
1947	3,289
1948	3,659
1949	4,694
1950	4,409
1951	3,837
1952	4,326
1953	4,108
1954	4,364
1955	5,054
1956	4,992
1957	4,546
1958	5,197
1959	5,337
1960	5,211

Source: Philadelphia Municipal Court Annual Report, 1964, 221.

to find and discipline men themselves, the court saved money and still collected support payments: by the 1950s, the sum amounted to over $9 million each year.[42] Second, because welfare administrators decreased women's ADC checks after they pressed nonsupport charges, the state conserved money simply by issuing a support order, regardless of whether or not judges enforced it.[43] Third, as historian Anna R. Igra has argued, in an era in which the "taint of corruption . . . adhered to state spending," the court's financial support policies performed an important symbolic function. By strongly advocating support orders, public authorities who were often criticized for encouraging the breakup of families and wasting funds could demonstrate both their desire to conserve state monies and their adherence to social norms concerning men's responsibilities to their wives and children.[44]

Deciding Whether to Pursue or to Avoid Legal Action

In most cases women made carefully calculated decisions about their use of the court. Taking legal action was an ordeal, requiring regular visits to court, several interviews, and a great deal of paperwork. Those with small children found the process particularly difficult. Bell Jackson described a typical visit: "My children and I spent almost six hours in court. I took them at 9:30 that morning and we didn't get out until 3:00 that afternoon. . . . I spent my last money getting there, and all that time. And what happened? Nothing, except we discussed why he wasn't staying with us and how come we broke up, which I've been over a lot of times."[45] Prior to initiating such frustrating procedures, women took stock of their circumstances and tried to decide whether the assistance they could receive from the court was worth the costs.

Before women took legal action, they usually spoke with other women in their communities who shared similar struggles. The welfare department, social service agencies, and hospitals sometimes encouraged them to press nonsupport charges, and the police occasionally referred victims of domestic violence to the court; but most women turned to their peers before making decisions about their use of the legal system. Friends, neighbors, and family members told them about the court's long waits, in-depth interviews, and frequently unenforced support orders. Women also learned that they had a good chance of winning their cases—that the court, as Mrs. Elkins put it, generally ruled "for the woman."[46]

When contemplating pressing nonsupport charges, healthy employed women who earned decent wages usually decided not to bother because the money they could obtain from a support order paled in comparison to their incomes.[47] Edwina Jordan, who raised her son with help from her mother, described her first and only visit to court: "The lady explained, 'well, we only give you ten dollars.' . . . And I said, 'I'm not going to come to court . . . for ten lousy dollars— that don't make no sense.' . . . If I've got my health and strength, and I can take care of my child, hey, I don't need it. The minute I get sick, I'll be back." Miss Jordan could avoid taking legal action because she had a well-paid city job and child care for her son. Yet she anticipated that if sickness struck her family, she would have to return to court.[48]

Most ADC recipients tried to avoid going to court because they risked losing money by pressing charges. The fathers of their children usually could not keep up with support orders, and since welfare caseworkers subtracted the dollar amount of support orders from their ADC checks and rarely provided compensation when men defaulted, taking legal action was a potential financial burden, not a help. Mrs. Jackson said she decided not to press support charges against the father of her children because she imagined that if she did, "maybe he'll send money for a little while, my [welfare] check will get cut, [then he'll stop contributing], then it's a long time getting the money back."[49] Women on decent terms with the fathers of their children generally preferred to receive full welfare grants with no court order, supplemented "under the table" with informal gifts from men.

Some women tried to avoid getting involved with the court because of the humiliation that frequently accompanied the process of taking legal action. Pursuing assistance from the court was never publicly maligned in the way that seeking welfare was, but it was still tarnished by its association with low-income Philadelphians. When Hazel Weinberg, a Jewish woman, went to court to press nonsupport charges, she did not return after her first visit because the interviewers were rude and condescending and she found the process "degrading."[50] Many African American women dreaded testifying before the same judges who condemned their receipt of welfare in the mainstream press. Although those who had not married the fathers of their children and relied on ADC received the most criticism, all black women felt vulnerable to judges' wrath. Joan Park, a financially secure working-class African American woman, explained that she "wouldn't be caught dead in court" because she considered herself an upstanding member of her community and did not want to subject herself to the indignities involved in pursuing legal action.[51]

The women who decided to press nonsupport charges frequently had financial troubles that led them to believe that even a meager court order would make a positive difference in their lives. African American women's poverty explains why, in the mid-1950s, they comprised 50 percent of all nonsupport and fornication and bastardy cases when they made up just over 21 percent of the city's population.[52] Ada Morris, a welfare recipient, explained the importance of her small support check to her livelihood: "I sit down on the first of the month . . . and I count my money up—to who I owe. . . . My rent comes first. My gas comes next. My food bill . . . comes next. . . . If I don't get nothing from him—well, I can't pay." For women like Mrs. Morris, who struggled each month to make ends meet, even a small stipend made a difference.[53]

Women who pressed domestic abuse charges tended to come from slightly more financially stable homes than those who pursued nonsupport charges and considered their need for physical protection to be their most pressing concern. They were rarely middle-class, but they were often not completely impoverished either.[54] Although some very poor abused women like Mrs. Carson pressed assault charges, others were either deterred by the $10 fee (until 1952, when the fee was waived) or prioritized financial support over protection from violence. Some women who pursued physical protection had experienced such severe abuse that they feared for their lives. Pauline Barnett took her boyfriend to court after getting six stitches on the back of her head and eight on her arm because he had cut her with a broken beer bottle in a drunken, jealous rage.[55] Even if men did not receive jail sentences, women hoped that the experience of court proceedings would intimidate them and help prevent subsequent episodes of abuse.

Most abused women decided to avoid legal action completely. Some lived in an acute state of terror with extremely violent and volatile husbands. They were unable or unwilling to leave their marriages and feared that pressing charges would only make the abuse worse. Charlotte Elkins decided to "hang in there" with her husband while "getting my butt beat" for thirteen years because of the "mental abuse" that accompanied his physical violence. She stated that her husband's verbal and physical assaults made her feel worthless and convinced her that she would be unable to survive on her own. Many women who did not go to court resisted the abuse in other ways, escaping to friends' and relatives' houses, attempting to protect their children, and fighting back. Catherine Sanderson recalled standing up to her husband when he beat her. "I sure would . . . hit him back," she explained. "He wasn't my father." Corrine Elkins never fought back until the night that she decided to leave: "He came home . . . and got crazy, and I went for the kitchen knife . . . and . . . really tried" to kill him.[56]

When women made decisions about their pursuit of legal action, they considered their responsibility for children, access to alternative resources, employment opportunities, and experiences of domestic violence. They also took into account a wide range of facts about their husbands and boyfriends: how much money men made, whether they were abusive or unfaithful, and how involved they were with their children. Most women only pressed financial support charges against men who had jobs because they knew that unemployed men did not have any money to give them. While legal authorities assumed that all African American men who did not provide for their families were irresponsible, African American women had a different and more nuanced definition of nonsupport. Recognizing that racial discrimination made it difficult for the most dedicated husband and father to earn enough to support his wife and children, they did not condemn all men who failed to provide them with financial resources. Instead, most African American women reserved charges of nonsupport for cases in which men deliberately withheld funds from their families, complaining about men squandering their wages on alcohol, other women, or luxury items, instead of rent, food, and clothing for their families.[57] For some married women, the discovery that their husbands had been cheating on them further galvanized them to press nonsupport charges.[58] Unmarried women sometimes responded similarly when they learned that their boyfriends had wives. In other cases, unmarried women may have only had casual contact with the father of their children and pressed charges in court because they had nothing to lose.[59]

Some married women sought support orders to help them cope with domestic violence. Unable to pursue both physical protection and monetary assistance simultaneously from the court, they made financial support their first priority. *Annual Reports* acknowledged that the "husband's brutality against his wife [stood] out" in a significant number of nonsupport cases and that these cases revealed that "spousal assault and battery [was] a major family problem."[60] Twenty-four percent of all women involved in nonsupport cases reported physical violence, which they often linked with men's excessive drinking.[61] Some of the others had experienced abuse but chose not to report it to interviewers.[62]

Many women who maintained cordial relationships with the fathers of their children found that even the threat of legal action provided them with considerable leverage when negotiating financial support. Because of the strength of their community information networks, women and men who had never set foot in court knew from other people's experiences that women would almost always win financial support cases. Men understood that they would be saddled with a court order and subjected to humiliating treatment from legal authorities, and women knew that men would be angry and would rarely pay regularly. Many women decided that, rather than alienate men by pressing charges, they were better off having men feel indebted to them for not pursuing legal action.[63] The undesirability of legal action gave some leverage to women like Beverly Jordan, who was separated with one child and worked in a coat factory in postwar Philadelphia. Every year, Mrs. Jordan was laid off for two to three months during slow seasons around Christmas and Easter. When this occurred, she would phone her ex-husband and ask for money for food and for her daughter's Christmas present, threatening to take him to court if he did not comply. Like Mrs. Jordan, many women found that by threatening to take legal action, they obtained specific contributions from men that surpassed what poorly enforced court orders could have provided.[64]

Women who struggled with domestic violence sometimes employed a similar strategy: They pressed assault charges to intimidate men but then withdrew the charges at the last minute. In 1953, in approximately one-third of all domestic abuse cases, women told judges that they no longer wanted to prosecute.[65] When these couples came before the court, the women usually said that they had changed their minds because their husbands had stopped the abuse. In some cases, women may have withdrawn the charges because men intimidated them. It is also likely that some men at least temporarily stopped beating their wives after women pressed charges in court.

"White Man's Law"

Most African Americans viewed the entire legal system as racist. It began with the police, with whom they interacted more frequently than the court. In the postwar years, the *Philadelphia Tribune* published a steady stream of articles criticizing racial discrimination in police hiring, promotions, and job assignments, and many African Americans charged that they were unfairly targeted by unexpected arrests and raids on their homes, bars, and restaurants.[66] Black middle-class community leaders fought for racially sensitive police training, fair tribunals for African Americans bringing complaints against law enforcement officials, and the elimination of the racial identification of criminals in newspapers.[67] Many working-class African Americans participated in acts of grassroots community resistance targeted at the police. In 1951, the *Bulletin* described a typical incident that began when police arrested a man in a North Philadelphia taproom for a robbery that many believed he did not commit. A large group gathered and tried to prevent the arrest by throwing the police officers to the ground. The police responded with clubs, blackjacks, and their fists, while onlookers expressed their support for the resistance by throwing "bottles and other missiles," which "rained down from windows" surrounding the scene. Two hundred spectators attended the hearings for the men and women arrested during the confrontation, becoming so disruptive that the magistrate ordered them to leave the police station. The onlookers then stood outside and "alternatively cheered and jeered" and "let loose a mock cheer when the prisoners . . . were taken to prison vans." Many similar occurrences took place in the postwar period, revealing a deep current of African American mistrust of the police.[68]

Some of the conflicts between African American women and the police were gender-specific, involving officers who raped women or refused to protect them from domestic violence. Over the course of the 1950s, several African American women who were sexually assaulted by policemen brought their cases to public attention, including Lenora Kidd, a twenty-three-year-old mother of three whose husband was in Eastern State Penitentiary. In 1959, Mrs. Kidd charged that two policemen came to her apartment to investigate a fight she was having with her upstairs neighbor. Learning that her husband was away, they asked her if she ever "got lonesome" and then forced her to perform sodomy, threatening to cut off her ADC checks and make it hard for her husband in prison if she did

White police officers frisking young black men suspected of belonging to a gang. In the 1950s, African Americans frequently complained that they were unfairly targeted by the police. Temple University Libraries, Urban Archives, Philadelphia, Pa.

not comply.[69] Other women faulted the police for failing to take domestic and sexual assault cases seriously. It was widely known that the police typically responded to reports of domestic violence in women's homes by either blaming the women involved or walking the men around the block and threatening to beat them up. Even the court's *Annual Reports* acknowledged that the police often refused to make arrests in domestic violence cases.[70]

Within the courts themselves, many African Americans believed that judges favored whites. G. Gordon Brown's 1947 study of Philadelphia African Americans' relationship to the legal system concluded that in the face of an epidemic of adverse jury verdicts, many African Americans believed that courts practiced "white man's law." This bias was especially evident in magistrates' courts, where the preliminary hearings were held. Many African Americans complained about white magistrates using explicitly racist language in court. In the municipal court, white judges such as Gay Gordon humiliated African Americans on the stand and used the courtroom to promote their prejudices regarding African Americans' innate criminality.[71]

Judges, magistrates, and lawyers directed some of their most vehement attacks at African American women whose children engaged in wrongdoing. In the postwar years, juvenile delinquency became a major concern in cities throughout the nation, and in Philadelphia's racially charged environment, the panic became intimately tied to the antiwelfare discourse. Before World War II, middle-class professionals often blamed mothers' employment for juvenile delinquency, but in the postwar years, Philadelphia judges blamed southern migration and women's use of ADC for their children's misbehavior.[72] "Most of the juvenile delinquency in Philadelphia is committed by illegitimates," charged Victor Blanc, the Jewish district attorney who helped lead the campaign against welfare.[73] During children's trials for curfew violations and juvenile delinquency, magistrates called on mothers to testify, fined them, scolded them for their children's behavior, and sometimes even put them in jail. Magistrate Elias Myers, another antiwelfare Democrat, who became well-known for advocating the Mummers' right to wear blackface in their annual parade, complained vociferously about the fact that the mothers he chastised for their children's curfew violations received "between $160 to $200 a month off the welfare." "Instead of using the money in some bar, as many of them do," Myers charged, "they should help the kids."[74] When one mother told Myers that her son was in South Carolina visiting relatives, Myers replied: "Good. . . . If you guarantee to keep him there, I'll only charge you $5. . . . Only make sure you keep him there. We don't want him here."[75]

Despite the problems working-class African American women faced at every level of the criminal justice system, they refused to give up on the courts. Building on decades of African American legal assertiveness, they sought to harness a system that they viewed as racist to work on their behalf. Had black women testified against white men, judges' racial prejudices might have served as more of a deterrent to their use of the court. However, since most African American women pressed charges against African American men, they knew that the verdicts would usually be in their favor. Although women did not receive very much money or physical protection from their legal victories, most of them faced such severe problems and had so few alternative sources of support that even the small amount of assistance they secured from the court made a difference. Mrs. Elkins recalled, "In those days, the women didn't really have too much going for them. Except 1801 Vine."[76]

Seeking Autonomy and Privacy

Working-class African American women who approached the municipal court insisted that their difficulties with men who abused or refused to support them constituted legitimate concerns of the state. Yet, as with seeking welfare benefits, demanding assistance from the legal system left them vulnerable to unwarranted intrusions into their private lives. Court interviewers and judges often tried to dictate the decisions women made about their intimate relationships and asked them probing and humiliating questions. In the face of these intrusions, women fought to protect their privacy and make their own decisions about their personal relationships by interacting with legal authorities in carefully calculated ways.

One of the most basic rights of privacy that women pursued was the ability to make autonomous decisions about their relationships with men. Many women chafed when interviewers pressured them to reconcile because they had come to court after deciding that they wanted to leave their relationships. Believing that they knew best whether or not their marriages were worth preserving, most women insisted on pursuing legal action instead of reconciliation. In 1950, three-fourths of the women who approached the court to press charges of nonsupport refused to reconcile, attesting to interviewers' flexibility in interpreting the guidelines and women's persistence in resisting the legal system's attempts to shape their private lives.[77]

In women's dealings with the court, they frequently challenged legal authorities' attempts to collect detailed personal information. Interviewers sought to compile extensive files documenting women's backgrounds and grievances, while field-workers investigated men's earnings and employment records and made home visits to ask about children's school attendance and inspect women's living conditions.[78] Unmarried mothers had to provide detailed descriptions of their relationships with the fathers of their children, the date of the sexual intercourse that produced the child, and accounts of their previous sexual experiences.[79] Many women refused to give court interviewers full access to their private lives, falsifying information or refusing outright to answer questions that they deemed too personal. One of the most common falsifications came from abused women pressing nonsupport charges who refused to disclose their experiences with domestic violence. Some of them likely felt embarrassed or ashamed about the abuse; others considered it none of the interviewers' business or feared that if their husbands found out that they had told legal authorities, it would make their beatings worse.[80] A few women directly challenged legal authorities who interrogated and demeaned them. In 1958, Judge Sydney Hoffman criticized Mary Sapp for "spawning juvenile delinquents" and challenged her to defend her decision not to marry. Miss Sapp retorted, "The business of my getting married is a private affair . . . and is no business of the court."[81]

One of the only times that interviewers and judges did not attempt to challenge or pry into women's decisions about their private lives was when women withdrew their assault and battery charges against their husbands, which occurred in approximately one-third of all abuse cases.[82] On the witness stand, these women usually minimized the abuse and told judges that they had changed their minds and did not want to press charges. Even when women testified that their husbands had "busted my head open" or stabbed them with knives, if they stated that they wanted to return home with their husbands, judges made no attempt to dissuade them.[83] Most judges feared that if couples separated or the men received jail sentences, the wives would seek public assistance.

When women testified in court, they sometimes shared aspects of their private lives selectively to try to elicit sympathy. Some tried to win favorable settlements by capitalizing on judges' and interviewers' interest in their marital problems. They steered their testimony to subjects they felt comfortable discussing, complaining about men's mismanagement of money or decrying men's abuse and philandering. A few women lied outright on the stand. Recognizing the prejudices many judges harbored against them, particularly if they received welfare, they feared that if judges suspected them of "promiscuity," they would not receive favorable settlements. When testifying in her daughter's fornication and bastardy case, ADC recipient Barbara Cole did not want the judge to think that her daughter had been brought up in a morally deficient home or to blame her for her daughter's pregnancy. Consequently, Mrs. Cole, a mother of five, told the court that her deceased husband had fathered all five of her children, when in fact, her children had multiple fathers.[84] Women themselves did not see a contradiction between being good mothers and having children by several fathers, but they recognized that public officials often did. To win favorable settlements they tried to paint simple and superficially consistent portraits of their identities in court.

Policies Change, Options Narrow

During the 1950s, judges and welfare authorities responded to women's deliberate and assertive use of ADC and the courts by implementing two policy changes that restricted women's abilities to selectively pursue legal action. One of the policies involved state and local welfare authorities forcing ADC recipients to obtain support orders. The other involved judges implementing policies that made it more difficult for women to press criminal assault charges against men. Neither policy signaled an abrupt change in institutional philosophy; rather, each was an attempt to bolster the original missions of the court and welfare systems. Both policies made women's lives more difficult by intensifying their economic struggles, introducing new tensions into their relationships with men, and leaving them vulnerable to domestic violence.

The first policy change originated in the welfare department and provided an opportunity for legal and welfare authorities to work together. In the early twentieth century, municipal court judges and Mothers' Assistance administrators had both expressed concern about poor women draining state coffers but had proposed different solutions to the problem. Judges regarded the Mothers' Assistance program as stingy and inefficient because women who did not qualify for grants or were placed on the program's waiting list often turned to the court for help placing their children. Because caring for women's children in publicly funded boarding homes and institutions was much more expensive than paying for Mothers' Assistance, judges sometimes granted their own support orders to women, eliciting strong criticism from welfare officials who viewed these actions as an infringement on their turf.[85] In 1937, legal and welfare authorities began to work together when the Pennsylvania Public Assistance Law made it mandatory for men and women seeking public assistance to press charges for support against legally responsible relatives.[86] The welfare department encouraged women who sought ADC to press charges against the fathers of their children and enlisted indigent parents who sought Old Age Assistance to press charges against their children.[87] The court strongly supported these policies by making sure that the vast majority of plaintiffs won their cases.

When authorities first implemented the Pennsylvania Public Assistance Law, they only loosely enforced it, enabling ADC recipients to avoid pressing nonsupport charges without putting their welfare grants in jeopardy. If women told welfare caseworkers that the father of their children had died or that they did not know where he was or even if they could identify him, they were usually not forced to pursue legal action.[88] However, in the late 1940s and early 1950s, in response to the mounting public criticism of ADC and policy changes at the federal level, state welfare authorities began to require local authorities to enforce support policies more strictly. Pennsylvania joined most other states in complying with the 1950 Notification of Law Enforcement Officials Amendment (NOLEO) to the Social Security Act, which encouraged local welfare authorities to notify law enforcement authorities in cases of desertion so that men could be called into court and forced to pay child support. While fourteen states applied NOLEO to women already receiving ADC, Pennsylvania and eighteen other states took a middle of the road approach, applying the policy only to new applicants. From 1953 on, women in Pennsylvania who were already receiving ADC and had avoided legal action were not forced to go to court, but all new applicants had to comply with NOLEO regulations.[89] Throughout the 1950s, welfare recipients who were forced to go to court constituted a minority of all of the women in the city who pressed nonsupport and fornication and bastardy charges. Still, the results of the new policy were impressive. In 1953, approximately two-thirds of ADC recipients in Philadelphia did not have a court order directed to the fathers of their children; by 1955, two-thirds did.[90]

The DPA's more vigorous enforcement of the court requirement diminished women's ability to survive on meager welfare grants and introduced new tensions into their relationships with men. Compulsory legal proceedings almost always reduced ADC recipients' monthly income because men's payments were rarely as reliable as the welfare department's stipends. Before pressing charges, some women had been able to pressure the fathers of their children to bring them food, toys, or school supplies. Once women took legal action, fathers usually stopped contributing such items and frequently defaulted on their support payments. Since many men then avoided visiting their children to spare themselves from women's anger, the new policy diminished fathers' involvement with childrearing.

The second restrictive policy change occurred in response to women's forceful pursuit of legal action in cases of domestic abuse. In the early 1950s, municipal court judges expressed concern that the state would limit their jurisdiction by creating a family court that focused exclusively on marital and juvenile cases.[91] To prove that Philadelphia had no need for a family court, they claimed that the municipal court already handled all of the city's family problems and offered the same kind of social work and psychological services provided by family courts in other cities. Suddenly, the large numbers of domestic violence cases handled in the magistrates' courts became a source of great concern for municipal court judges, who now felt more obligated to respond to abused women's assertive pursuit of legal protection. In 1952, judges introduced a new policy in which women who approached the municipal court complaining of domestic violence were no longer referred to the magistrates' or the criminal courts, but instead received attention from the domestic relations division.[92]

Judges heralded the new policy for handling domestic violence cases by claiming that it would help more women reconcile with their husbands. Insisting that magistrates' hearings created tensions and resentments among married couples that tended to "sunder the family forever, or create long lasting resentment over the wife's action," judges established uniform procedures for domestic abuse cases that emphasized reconciliation. Attempting to bypass the criminal division, which did not offer counseling, they sent abuse cases to the domestic relations division, where, as the 1953 *Annual Report* noted, "reconciliation of the spouses is attempted in a joint conference with husband and wife . . . then, follow-up services are supplied through home visits by the field staff." When couples refused to reconcile, interviewers pressured women to seek support orders instead of pressing assault and battery charges. If women still insisted on pressing assault charges, the court waived the $10 fee.[93]

Although judges claimed that the elimination of the fee made legal action more accessible for poor women, it did not address the fundamental problem that they faced in court: their inability to secure support orders and physical protection simultaneously. Most very poor abused women did not attempt to press assault charges in the first place, deterred not by the fee but because they felt compelled to prioritize the obtainment of support orders over protection from violence. The waiving of the fee did not address their need for consistent financial support. Those who did press assault charges appreciated being able to prosecute their cases without the fee, but found that the financial benefits were accompanied by new drawbacks: added layers of bureaucracy and counseling designed to dissuade them from securing physical protection. By separating cases involving domestic violence from other criminal assaults and trying to dissuade women from pressing charges, judges made it clear that they did not consider domestic violence a serious offense worthy of criminal adjudication.

Many abused women refused to let judges and interviewers dictate the outcome of their cases, expressing especially strong opposition to reconciliation. Judges admitted that most couples had such severe marital difficulties that they "cannot be treated successfully" through counseling.[94] When unable to foster reconciliations, interviewers managed to convince many women to seek support orders instead of pressing charges of assault and battery. Still, a significant number of women refused to be dissuaded from having their husbands arrested on criminal charges. During 1958, the court acknowledged that in over one-third of the 521 spousal assault cases adjudicated, legal authorities had been forced "at the request of wives" to issue arrest warrants instead of petitions for support orders.[95] Even in face of tremendous pressure to avoid pressing charges, many women continued to insist on their right to protection from domestic violence.

Working-class African American women understood that the Philadelphia Municipal Court considered it more important to restrict state expenditures on welfare than to ensure that women received financial support and protection from violence. They sought to use the court selectively, pressing charges only when they believed that legal authorities' strong support for male breadwinning would work in their favor. Those who sought protection from domestic violence often succeeded in convincing their husbands to refrain from beating them for a limited period of time. Yet some violent husbands became so angry when women pressed charges that they responded by escalating the abuse. In financial support cases, women sometimes forced men who otherwise would not have contributed to their families to provide them with a small amount of money. However, many other women alienated the fathers of their children, received only a few payments from men, and then spent years trying to get the court to force men to comply with judges' rulings. Although most women received some limited assistance from the court, their involvement with the legal system introduced new forms of labor into their lives and did not help them achieve upward mobility.

Over the course of the 1950s, women grew increasingly frustrated with the outcomes of their dealings in court. Legal and welfare authorities contributed to the mounting white resistance to African Americans' use of Philadelphia's public institutions by enacting policies that hindered women's efforts to secure physical protection and financial support. Judges enacted procedures for domestic violence cases that made it more difficult for abused women to press charges against violent husbands. Welfare authorities began to compel ADC recipients to sacrifice part of their secure welfare grants in exchange for support payments that they usually received only briefly or intermittently.

Still, tens of thousands of working-class African American women continued to seek assistance from the municipal court. Although it was not the authorities' intention, they had provided women with rare glimpses of routes through which they could claim some limited authority over their lives. Women suffering from domestic violence and struggling to make ends meet valued even the meager assistance they could receive from the court and insisted on pressing assault and nonsupport charges, even when interviewers and judges tried to encourage them to reconcile with their husbands. Those who received welfare often attempted to avoid pressing charges altogether in an effort to retain their full ADC grants. In all their dealings with the court, women sought to acquire physical protection and financial resources while refusing to grant authorities full access to their private lives. They struggled to secure assistance from the state on their own terms while asserting their right to keep aspects of their lives shielded from public view.

CHAPTER THREE

Housing, Not a Home

In 1954, Mildred and Joseph Spencer moved with their four children into sparkling new public housing at Raymond Rosen Homes in North Philadelphia. Mrs. Spencer had stood in line for hours to submit an application to the Philadelphia Housing Authority (PHA) and had managed to obtain one of the coveted apartments for six-person families. Like almost all of the public housing constructed in postwar Philadelphia, Raymond Rosen was racially segregated. Serving African American tenants in a predominantly black neighborhood, it combined high-rise towers with row homes, and the Spencers considered themselves fortunate to receive one of the low-rise dwellings. The Spencers and their neighbors appreciated the dramatic improvement in their standard of living and tried to put their mark on Raymond Rosen by decorating their homes and caring for its public spaces. Many of the women who lived in the low rises took particular pride in their yards and competed with one another over who had the "prettiest" garden.[1]

Of all the public institutions in the city, working-class African American women had the highest hopes for public housing. They envisioned the program providing not only the shelter that they desperately needed, but also a measure of the financial security and bodily integrity that they secured from the welfare department and the municipal court. The clean new apartments with modern conveniences provided trappings of respectability that women had long desired. Public housing offered them a chance to create real homes for their families, where they could live affordably and autonomously, surrounded by supportive networks of friends.

Federal and local housing authorities and liberal housing reformers had slightly different, but equally high, hopes for public housing, envisioning it serving as a temporary "way station" that would enable working-class families to achieve upward mobility.[2] They hoped that public housing would provide shelter for families displaced by slum clearance projects while improving the living conditions in run-down neighborhoods. Many also believed that public housing would serve a social function, fostering tenants' physical and mental well-being and eradicating crime and juvenile delinquency.[3] The media echoed these optimistic predictions in stories that featured enthusiastic tenants moving into attractive new homes in previously blighted neighborhoods.

Although the Philadelphia branch of the National Association for the Advancement of Colored People (NAACP) paid far more attention to public housing than it did to welfare or the municipal court, it did not address the unique struggles that African American women faced when they tried to gain admission. Women's attempts to secure welfare assistance and protection from domestic violence fell outside the purview of most male civil rights activists, but they saw programs used by men such as public housing, along with education and employment, as crucial components of equal citizenship. Along with other liberal advocacy groups, the NAACP lobbied for the construction of public housing for black families in stable neighborhoods and campaigned to convince the PHA to stop discriminating against African American applicants. Yet the NAACP's vision of the black applicants who deserved admittance to public housing was limited to two-parent families and excluded unmarried mothers. The organization never challenged the PHA's efforts to restrict unwed mothers from public housing, which prevented many of the neediest black families from securing decent homes. Only working-class women saw public housing as essential for everyone, regardless of their race or marital status. Single mothers fought their own battles to gain access to public housing by applying in large numbers and pressuring the PHA to let them in.

More than most other public institutions in the city, public housing's success depended on women's support. Welfare authorities purposely confined women to miserable poverty because they feared that if women became too comfortable receiving Aid to Dependent Children (ADC), they would never leave the program. Judges paid no penalty if the court's policies prevented women from making ends meet or trapped them in abusive relationships. Yet the success of public housing depended on tenants committing themselves to their homes and communities. Public housing could not flourish without residents who would respect and care for their apartments, keep public spaces in good condition, and cultivate respectful relationships with neighbors. Since women in working-class neighborhoods usually took the lead in performing these tasks, their investment in public housing mattered immensely.

Upon moving into public housing, women sought to claim ownership of their surroundings by decorating their apartments, maintaining public spaces, and forging relationships with neighbors. The management staff often undermined women's efforts, fearing that tenants would ruin public housing if they were not tightly controlled. Staff members discouraged and punished women for investing themselves in public housing and supervised their financial expenditures, personal relationships, and domestic labor. Relationships between tenants frequently grew tense in public housing's close quarters, particularly when managers encouraged neighbors to inform on one another. Many women quickly grew frustrated with their lack of ownership and control of their surroundings.

While women clashed with their neighbors and the management staff, policy makers on both the federal and local levels made decisions that further eroded tenants' commitment to their new homes. Federal authorities demanded low-cost construction, resulting in bare-bones apartments, increasing numbers of high-rises, and a dearth of facilities for children's recreation. As the tenant population became poorer, local authorities did not invest in the maintenance work and upgrades needed to keep public housing clean and efficient. Women found it difficult to take pride in outmoded appliances, unkempt public spaces, and walls with peeling paint. To accommodate working-class whites' demands to keep public housing out of their communities, the PHA located most public housing for African American families in or near black neighborhoods that were deteriorating and dangerous, undermining women's efforts to maintain clean and safe surroundings. As drugs and crime infiltrated public housing, many tenants began to fear for their safety.[4] Women who had once envisioned public housing serving as a linchpin in their struggles against poverty began to view it as a place of last resort.

"Undreamed of Luxury"

Public housing in the United States was first built by the New Deal's Public Works Administration to serve both working-class and middle-class families. In 1937, the Wagner-Steagall Act created a two-tiered system of housing subsidies that substantially shaped the production of inequalities in postwar cities. Like the distinctions made between welfare benefits and old-age insurance, public

Table 3.1. Philadelphia Public Housing, 1938–1956

Public Housing	Units	Year of Occupancy	Percentage Black 1956	Percentage Black 1964	Predominant Race in Neighborhood
Hill Creek	258[a]	1938	0.7	0	
James Weldon Johnson	589	1940	99.0	100.0	Nonwhite
Richard Allen	1,324	1942	100.0	99.3	Nonwhite
Tasker	1,007	1941	23.0	38.0	White
Abbottsford	700	1942	9.4	19.3	White
Bartram Village	500	1942	9.9	23.0	White
Oxford Village	200	1942	0.7	NA	White
Passyunk	994	1942	4.6	18.0	White
Arch	77	1952	74.0	98.0	Nonwhite
Wilson Park	746	1954	9.6	21.0	White
Norris	326	1954	100.0	97.0	Nonwhite
Raymond Rosen	1,122	1954	99.9	100.0	Nonwhite
Schuylkill Falls	714	1955	11.5	28.0	White
Liddonfield	412	1955	1.9	1.0	White
Mill Creek	444	1955	100.0	100.0	Nonwhite
Queen Lane	139	1955	92.5	98.3	Nonwhite
Spring Garden	203	1955	83.8	97.0	Nonwhite
Harrison Plaza	300	1956	98.6	97.0	Nonwhite

Sources: Committee on Public Housing Policy, "Basic Policies for Public Housing in Philadelphia" (1956), 34; "Developments of the Philadelphia Housing Authority: March 1964," Box 283, Folder 4953, HADVR1, UATU; John Bauman, *Public Housing*, 172–73.
[a]Later enlarged to 340 units.

housing was viewed as a form of charity, while more substantially funded mortgage-guarantee and tax-subsidy programs that encouraged middle-class home ownership were understood to be entitlements.[5] The United States Housing Authority (USHA) loaned money to local authorities to construct public housing and provided guidelines for site selection, building materials, tenant selection, and safety standards.[6] The Philadelphia Housing Authority, established in 1937, constructed Tasker, Richard Allen, and James Weldon Johnson between 1940 and 1942. After World War II, the PHA took over the federal government's emergency wartime housing: Abbotsford, Passyunk, Bartram Village, and Oxford Village. More public housing in Philadelphia followed the 1949 Housing Act, which called for the construction of 135,000 new units annually across the country for six years. Between 1952 and 1956, the PHA

A courtyard at James Weldon Johnson Homes in 1949. Women and girls usually took charge of the small garden plots assigned to tenants. Temple University Libraries, Urban Archives, Philadelphia, Pa.

opened Arch, Wilson Park, Norris, Raymond Rosen, Schuylkill Falls, Liddonfield, Mill Creek, Queen Lane, Spring Garden, and Harrison Plaza (see Table 3.1).[7]

When first constructed, public housing in Philadelphia looked extremely promising. The PHA employed innovative architects and encouraged them to improve the standards of urban design. In the 1940s, the city's public housing consisted mainly of low-rise buildings arranged in a "communitarian" fashion, facing a grassy court or common area where residents could gather. African Americans took particular pride in their 589-unit James Weldon Johnson Homes. Its 58 two- and three-story red brick buildings were located around pleasant courts and walkways. "Luxuries" such as gabled roofs, landscaped walkways, and white canopies over doorways made Johnson Homes uniquely warm and attractive.[8] Although the 1,324-unit Richard Allen Homes for African Americans was larger and had a less original layout, its 53 three- and four-story red and yellow brick buildings formed pleasant quadrangles with small courtyards, and it had a conveniently located community center and library.[9]

Inside new public housing, tenants found quarters more spacious and modern than their previous living situations. One of the first tenants at Richard Allen, Agnes Hawryluk, had lived with her two children in a one-room apartment with no sanitary facilities or running water. Her apartment at Richard Allen felt luxurious in comparison. Downstairs it had a living room and a kitchen with a gas stove, electric refrigerator, and built-in cabinets. The upstairs had two bedrooms, a bathroom with a sink, bathtub, and toilet, and a laundry tub for washing clothes.[10] Mrs. Hawryluk had paid $14 each month for rent and utilities for her one-room apartment. At Richard Allen, she paid $14.50 for her much nicer accommodations.[11] Because of strict federal budgets, public housing had no "frills." Apartments lacked dining rooms, closet doors, baseboards, and splashboards for the sinks. Floors were made of concrete, closets had steel shelves, and banisters were made of iron pipe. Still, because so many tenants who moved into new public housing had previously lived in the slums, they experienced a significant increase in their standard of living. Many considered new public housing an "undreamed of luxury."[12]

The media joined tenants in heralding the opening of new public housing. Even in the early 1940s, when Republican mayor Robert Lamberton tried to derail the construction of public housing, headlines in the *Bulletin* read, "New Homes, New Health, New Fun, New Happiness," and newspapers described tenants thriving in their new communities.[13] The real estate industry tried to link public housing with communism, but it still became more popular than welfare because it served both whites and African Americans and catered to two-parent families. Most tenants had jobs, and the public found the subsidized rents more tolerable than welfare's outright "handouts." Newspapers portrayed public housing as an essential component of urban redevelopment, describing how it improved the conditions in blighted neighborhoods. Throughout the 1940s, the *Bulletin* published glowing accounts of public housing, reporting in a typical article that the "First Housing Projects Pay Dividends in Happiness," providing well-maintained apartments to upwardly mobile white and black two-parent families.[14]

In the 1950s, high land costs, federal cost restrictions on construction, and a deluge of applicants led the PHA to build high-rises. However, the PHA continued to employ prominent architects and sought to create inviting neighborhoods that combined low-rise apartments with the taller buildings.[15] One of the most successful endeavors was Wilson Park, which served whites in the Point Breeze section of South Philadelphia. Wilson Park had four eight-story buildings surrounded by two- and three-story units. Its community building provided a child care center, well-baby clinic, and space for recreation. Raymond Rosen, where the Spencers lived, was higher and more sterile and imposing.

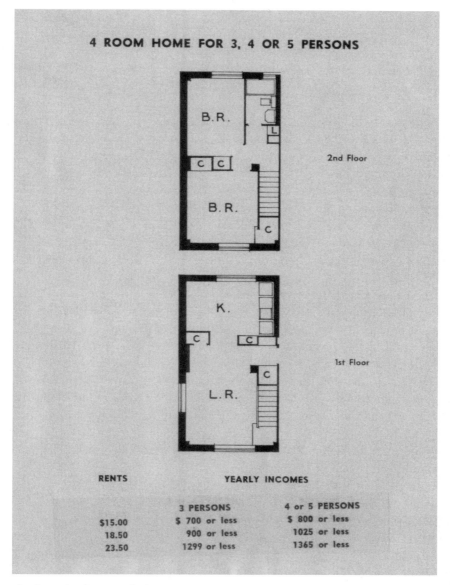

4 ROOM HOME FOR 3, 4 OR 5 PERSONS

B.R.

2nd Floor

B.R.

K.

1st Floor

L.R.

RENTS	YEARLY INCOMES	
	3 PERSONS	**4 or 5 PERSONS**
$15.00	$ 700 or less	$ 800 or less
18.50	900 or less	1025 or less
23.50	1299 or less	1365 or less

The floor plan for a two-bedroom apartment in Richard Allen Homes. Each of Richard Allen's 1,324 apartments included a living room, kitchen, bathroom, and bedrooms and came equipped with hot and cold water, central heating, electric lights, gas range, refrigerator, sink, toilet, laundry tub, bathtub, and closets. Temple University Libraries, Urban Archives, Philadelphia, Pa.

On twenty-seven acres of land stood 8 thirteen-story elevator buildings, 308 gable-roofed row houses, a community building with an auditorium, a day care center, and large open play areas for children.[16]

Public housing was federally funded, but it relied on cities to facilitate its construction and operation. The federal government raised the capital needed to construct public housing by selling U.S. Treasury Bonds and loaning the money to local authorities at relatively low rates. Federal authorities then provided local authorities with an additional subsidy each year to make payments on the loans. Rental income was expected to cover routine operations and improvements.[17] In Philadelphia, the Housing Authority was run by a citizen board of directors appointed by the mayor and city controller, who served voluntarily and helped set policy.[18] Between 1947 and 1959, the executive director was Walter E. Alessandroni, a prominent Republican lawyer who served as chancellor of the Philadelphia Bar Association and state commander of the American Legion. In the central office, the staff oversaw public housing's finances, admissions, construction, maintenance, and community relations.[19] The PHA administrators were in frequent contact with the numerous liberal organizations in Philadelphia that took a keen interest in public housing. The most influential was the Philadelphia Housing Association, an independent, nonprofit citizens' organization staffed by professionals who worked to improve housing conditions in the city through public education, research, and lobbying. In 1951, the Housing Association joined the Health and Welfare Council, Fellowship Commission, Council of Churches, and Citizens Council on City Planning to form a citizen advisory committee to monitor and evaluate PHA policy.[20]

Since emancipation, African Americans had viewed decent housing as a central component of citizenship, and civil rights activists joined liberal reformers' attempts to shape the policies adopted by the PHA.[21] In the early 1940s, leaders of the Philadelphia NAACP and Armstrong Association vigorously encouraged the city's plans to build public housing for African Americans. After World War II, the NAACP expanded its campaign from inclusion to integration by protesting racial segregation and attempting to influence the location of new public housing. African American block groups established committees to assess proposed sites and sent petitions to Washington to urge senators to vote to secure appropriations for new construction. In the mid-1950s, when the PHA announced that it had decided to locate Raymond Rosen Homes in North Philadelphia, its manager, Charles H. Kircher, noted that it was "regarded as a neighborhood triumph that the site was selected."[22]

Public housing comprised only one plank of African Americans' broad civil

Raymond Rosen Homes housed 1,122 families in stark high-rise buildings surrounded by row homes. Temple University Libraries, Urban Archives, Philadelphia, Pa.

rights agenda, but federal and local housing authorities and white liberal re-formers frequently envisioned that it would single-handedly ameliorate a wide range of urban ills. Employing an environmental and behavioral analysis of the causes of poverty, they claimed that the improved physical environment and wholesome atmosphere of public housing would lift tenants out of pov-erty by transforming their psyches and behaviors.[23] One 1952 PHA publica-tion explained: "The dwellings built by the Housing Authority . . . offer the chance for improved self-respect, health, and family life." Families who lived in public housing demonstrated increased "initiative . . . more responsibility for . . . property, better civic participation, and a stronger sense of citizen-ship."[24] Mayor Clark articulated even more unrealistic aspirations; he claimed that living in public housing would raise tenants' intelligence and educational levels while helping curb juvenile crime.[25] This array of promises made by white liberals played upon stereotypes of working-class Philadelphians as negli-gent and unintelligent, while creating expectations that public housing could never fulfill.

The Battle to Live in Public Housing

Public housing's affordable rents and modern conveniences inspired thousands upon thousands of working-class Philadelphians to seek apartments. By 1949, the PHA had a waiting list of over 10,000 families, and the list would have been even longer if more people thought they had a chance of getting in.[26] African Americans were overrepresented among the applicants because they were largely confined to the worst housing in the city. Many were single mothers, who faced particularly severe problems finding decent homes because private landlords often refused to rent to them.[27] Yet, as in other cities, African Americans did not gain access to public housing in proportion to the number of their applications. In 1956, they constituted nearly 90 percent of the applicants for public housing, but only 51 percent of its tenants.[28]

The PHA devised an intricate scoring system to rate public housing applicants in order to determine their eligibility for admission. Federal guidelines restricted public housing to families who had lived in Philadelphia for at least one year and whose incomes did not exceed specific maximums. Veterans received preferential treatment. So did families who had lost their homes because of slum clearance projects or who had lived in substandard housing for more than one year. The PHA also awarded high marks to steadily employed families who would help maximize rental income and create an upstanding clientele.[29] While the scoring system applied equally to both white and black applicants, it was coupled with a segregation policy implemented by President Roosevelt's secretary of the interior, Harold Ickes, mandating that the racial composition of public housing reflect the "prevailing racial composition of the surrounding neighborhood."[30] While Chicago authorities tried to integrate some early public housing by choosing racially mixed neighborhoods, the PHA designated its sites as either primarily white or African American.[31] By locating only half of Philadelphia's public housing in black neighborhoods, the PHA ensured that African Americans would have access to only a limited number of apartments, despite their enormous demand for affordable housing.

When it came to single mothers, the issue was not just the dearth of spaces allocated, but the sex discrimination that made many ineligible for admission. Authorities gave preference to two-parent families, accepted a limited number of separated women with small families, and sought to exclude unmarried mothers from public housing altogether.[32] In 1957, George J. Dunn, the director of Housing Management, described his resistance to accepting unwed mothers in a memo to his staff detailing the characteristics of "problem families" whom admissions officers were instructed to exclude. The list included any "unmarried mother of two or more children evidencing irresponsibility and

Two-parent families like this one at James Weldon Johnson Homes in 1951 were given preference in admissions to public housing. Temple University Libraries, Urban Archives, Philadelphia, Pa.

a continued illegitimacy pattern," along with applicants who had health or psychological problems; police records involving drugs, prostitution, rape, robbery, and assault; alcohol addictions; poor housekeeping skills; and delinquent children.[33] Dunn's description of "problem families" equated male criminality and female promiscuity and untidiness, viewing them as comparable justifications for denying admission to public housing.

Over the course of the 1950s, while the restrictions on unmarried mothers remained intact, the combined force of black political activism, local Democrats' civil rights agenda, and whites' increased avoidance of public housing forced the PHA to change its segregation policies. After World War II, an NAACP delegation pressured the PHA to abandon the neighborhood-composition formula.[34] Momentum built in 1952 with the election of Joseph Clark, who made civil rights liberalism—a commitment to equal opportunity and "color-blind" policies—the official creed of city government.[35] With the PHA's racially discriminatory admissions policy directly contradicting the new direction of the city government, municipal officials successfully pressured the Housing Authority to sign an agreement in which it promised not to discriminate by "race, color, creed, religion, or national origin" in its selection of tenants. Between 1952 and 1956, housing officials spent a great deal of time choosing and assisting 3,000 black families who moved into previously all-white public housing.[36] The PHA also made an effort to integrate its workforce. By the mid-1950s, the staff at the central office remained predominantly white, but two of the five board members and one-third of the housing managers were black.[37] Yet despite these efforts at integration, the PHA continued to designate most newly built public housing as either predominantly white or black and consistently refused to allow African Americans to gain admittance in proportion to their applications. Believing that public housing needed a strong white presence in order to preserve the reputation of the program, the PHA kept many apartments intended for whites empty, while thousands of African American applicants remained on the waiting list, eager to move in.[38]

The PHA's faith in its ability to preserve white public housing was shaken after its 1956 plan for constructing new public housing on twenty-one sites scattered across the city incited tremendous white resistance. Richardson Dilworth, who was elected mayor in 1955, joined the NAACP, the Housing Association, and the Health and Welfare Council in expressing strong support for the scattered-site plan.[39] Building on grievances that had been aired by Republican legislators in the early 1950s, white Philadelphians launched protests against the construction of public housing in their neighborhoods and employed racial code words such as "undesirables," the "less ambitious," and "people [not] like us" to describe public housing residents. At one particularly rambunctious 1956 community meeting, the attendees yelled, "Send them back to Georgia."[40]

The resolution of the site-selection controversy illuminates the incompatible agendas of Philadelphia's Democratic leaders and the city's working-class African American residents.[41] While several liberal organizations urged the PHA to stay the course, many Democratic city council members and ward leaders joined Republicans in backing the protesters.[42] The NAACP expressed support for the scattered-site plan only in private communications with Alessandroni, stating that it was remaining "silent" in public so as not to "bring [more] out in the open the race issue" that was fueling the protests.[43] Without forceful public opposition to the racist depictions of black public housing, resistance gained currency in many white neighborhoods. Under enormous pressure, the PHA shifted the sites to areas of the city that were less white. Between 1956 and

White women often took the lead in protesting proposed public housing in their neighborhoods. This protest occurred at a meeting about the Philadelphia Housing Authority's 1956 proposal to build public housing on twenty-one new sites scattered throughout the city. Temple University Libraries, Urban Archives, Philadelphia, Pa.

1967, it located all new public housing in working-class African American neighborhoods or neighborhoods in transition from white to black.[44]

The 1956 controversy gave public housing such a strong racial stigma that it became difficult for authorities to imagine many working-class whites ever considering public housing an attractive option.[45] White tenants had initially exhibited a strong commitment to public housing. After the war, they were among the first to protest when the government began to enforce policies evicting those whose incomes exceeded the prescribed maximum.[46] Yet the government's insistence on carrying out evictions and the increased stigmatization of public housing resulted in the waning of many whites' commitment. Henrietta Applegate, a white woman who lived at Hill Creek, explained that she had "always been proud of our Hill Creek community. . . . But since this controversy grew so heated and such dreadful things have been said about public housing residents, all of us can feel an icy chill in the air when we tell anyone where we live."[47] One of her neighbors, Jim Park, did not "like to be regarded as a lower-class citizen" just because he lived in public housing.[48] Demand for public housing plummeted among whites, while African Americans, for whom need trumped stigma, still consistently applied for admission. At the same time, liberal organizations such as the Housing Association and the Commission on Human Relations stepped up their pressure on the PHA, demanding that it accept more African American applicants. Over time, the PHA allowed increasing numbers of African Americans to move into formerly all-white public housing, much of which was now located in neighborhoods changing from white to black. By 1968, in most of the public housing that had once served whites, African Americans comprised half of the tenants.[49]

For many African American women, the decline in overt racial discrimination in public housing's admissions policies addressed only one dimension of their problem because the restrictions on unmarried mothers remained in place. Civil rights activists moved on to other issues after the 1956 debacle and never seriously considered advocating on women's behalf. Unmarried mothers did not gain the right to live in public housing until 1968, when Community Legal Services, a legal-aid agency for low-income Philadelphians, helped a group of thirteen unwed mothers win a suit against the PHA challenging the ban on their admission.[50]

During the 1950s and early 1960s, even with the restrictions on unmarried mothers, women became the majority of tenants in public housing. In some cases, separated or divorced women's persistence in applying to public housing resulted in their eventually gaining admission.[51] In other instances, women entered public housing with their husbands but broke up with them at some point after moving in. When marriages ended, the women and children usually remained in public housing, while men found new places to live. By the early 1960s, because of the frequency of marital breakups and the women without husbands who gained admittance, single mothers occupied almost half of all the units in public housing.[52]

The rising numbers of African Americans and women in public housing went hand in hand with an increase in the proportion of poor tenants. Public housing was particularly valuable to the poor because it substantially reduced the proportion of their income spent on rent. In 1960, on average, the poorest households in Philadelphia paid over 35 percent of their incomes in rent, while better-off households paid less than 20 percent.[53] Public housing's income-based rental policies helped correct this disparity by setting most rents at 20 and 25 percent of tenants' incomes. Those with the lowest incomes benefited the most from prorated rents. Upwardly mobile tenants claimed that they suffered because managers raised rents when they acquired additional income and evicted them when their reported earnings rose to more than 25 percent above the allowable maximum.[54] Elsa Price observed: "You can't get ahead in public housing. You get a little more money and they up your rent."[55] In the 1950s, the number of poor families in public housing grew because upwardly mobile tenants left, either by choice or because of rising incomes, while accelerating slum clearance projects displaced more of the poor whom authorities had an obligation to serve.

As more poor families lived in public housing, welfare recipients became a prominent and valued clientele.[56] The PHA had originally tried to avoid renting to welfare recipients, considering families who relied on wages from employment more respectable and lucrative tenants. Yet the Authority soon recognized that welfare offered a more reliable source of income than many of the unstable jobs to which working-class African Americans were confined. The PHA negotiated fixed rental rates for welfare recipients with the Department of Public Assistance that nearly equaled, and sometimes exceeded, the rents paid by employed tenants. As the tenant population became poorer and less able to hold steady jobs, welfare recipients became one of the PHA's more reliable sources of income. By 1960, welfare recipients occupied nearly one-quarter of all public housing units in the city.[57]

Poor tenants were unfairly scapegoated for the problems that developed in public housing. As early as 1953, when public housing still served many upwardly mobile families, PHA public relations director Drayton Bryant blamed deteriorating conditions on a "changed type" of tenant, one who lacked opportunity and subscribed to an "enforced pattern of [deviant] behavior over many generations."[58] Certainly, poor families frequently lacked education and faced health problems. And because local authorities often crowded them together, they had difficulty finding neighbors whom they could turn to for assistance.[59] Still, most of the problems that developed in public housing had little to do with tenants' personal struggles or behaviors. While some tenants did not supervise their children or maintain public spaces adequately, many of the most serious problems in public housing stemmed from the management's top-down approach, the inadequate budgets for construction and maintenance, and the poorly chosen locations. Problems began to develop in the early 1950s when many upwardly mobile tenants still lived in public housing, and they developed similarly among African Americans and whites in high-rises and in low-rises. In some sites, problems began to appear after only a few years of operation.[60] It was much cheaper and more politically expedient to place the blame for public housing's problems on its tenants than it was for authorities to acknowledge and remedy the flaws in their policies.

"If You Don't Like It, Get Out"

In the late 1940s and 1950s, most women who gained access to public housing invested themselves in their new homes. They sought to create safe havens for themselves and their families where they could feel comfortable and take pride in their surroundings. As in working-class communities throughout the city, although men frequently performed chores such as taking out the trash and washing walls and windows, women usually tackled most of the daily household labor. Similarly, although fathers baby-sat and talked with neighbors, mothers usually held primary responsibility for child care and social networking.[61]

When families first moved into public housing, women sought to personalize their sterile apartments to make them feel comfortable and inviting. On shoe-string budgets, they tried to obtain a few pieces of decent furniture and added homey touches such as knickknacks and pictures.[62] Those who had the means engaged in ambitious decorating projects—putting up curtains, buying rugs, and covering shelves with decorative paper. Edna Cooper explained, "All my life, I've been dreaming of a pretty little kitchen in red and white. I used to look at magazine pictures that showed the kitchen all white and shiny and plan how I'd make mine—someday." Mrs. Cooper had not been able to realize her dream "in the place we used to live." There, she said, "the kitchen was dark and musty, with nothing but an old gas range and a dilapidated wooden icebox that wouldn't keep anything cold." Mrs. Cooper claimed ownership of her new apartment in public housing by decorating the kitchen entirely in red and white. She put up homemade curtains, covered her shelves with paper, and carpeted her floor.[63]

Women with more limited means still sought to create respectable and comfortable homes for their families. Mrs. Felton Reddy took great pride in the working bathtub in her new apartment. "We had our own bath in the old place," she explained, "but no hot water. . . . Since we had to heat all our bath water on the gas range we couldn't take many baths; it cost too much." Mrs. Reddy told a *Bulletin* reporter that she bathed her five children daily in her new apartment at Richard Allen and sometimes gave them baths twice a day in warm weather.[64] Her bathing routine served as a key marker of respectability that signaled her commitment to raising her children properly.

Many women viewed the cultivation of community relationships as an essential part of their efforts to turn public housing into a real "home." As in other neighborhoods, they took the lead in establishing support networks and getting their families involved in organized activities. Many women formed close relationships with other mothers who lived nearby, shopping together and exchanging food, clothing, and child care. In 1955, shortly after moving into

This apartment at James Weldon Johnson Homes was carefully decorated, showing a personal touch. Temple University Libraries, Urban Archives, Philadelphia, Pa.

Raymond Rosen, Dorothy Medley described the bonds she had formed in her new community: "The neighbors here are all wonderful, after you have been here for a couple of months you feel as if you have known them all of your life."[65] Although the management staff usually did not get involved in planning recreational activities, tenants and community agencies stepped in to organize clubs and special events. They formed Mother's Clubs, Boys and Girls Clubs, and Scout troops, and organized sports and other recreational activities. The Department of Recreation ran playground activities; the Free Library of Philadelphia operated two branch libraries, three extension libraries, and one bookmobile in public housing. In 1955 alone, tenants made 10,097 visits to the library at Richard Allen and 15,756 to the one at James Weldon Johnson.[66] Historian Rhonda Y. Williams has argued that African Americans' participation in the civic groups within public housing served a political purpose, enabling tenants to counter negative public perceptions about their behaviors and values and demonstrate their respectability and suitability for first-class citizenship.[67] That was certainly the case at Richard Allen when, in 1958, after two months of fried-chicken dinners and other benefits, the community council raised

When first constructed, public housing offered clean and modern apartments like this one at Norris Homes in North Philadelphia in the mid-1950s. Temple University Libraries, Urban Archives, Philadelphia, Pa.

enough money to put on an afternoon concert by the Philadelphia Symphony Orchestra.[68]

In their attempts to make homes for themselves in public housing, women frequently encountered the PHA's on-site staff of managers, assistant managers, management aides, and maintenance workers, who sometimes sought to help tenants but frequently restricted their autonomy. Some PHA employees were unionized, and all of them received decent salaries and benefits almost comparable to the perks provided to municipal employees.[69] The on-site staff's main responsibility was to collect rent from tenants and maintain properties in good condition. A few African American men became managers, and many of the women staff members had clerical jobs or front-line positions that required them to frequently interact with tenants. As in other public institutions, staff members differed significantly in their approaches to their jobs, with some exhibiting more respect for low-income women than others. Black staff members were not necessarily more sympathetic than white staff members, nor were women always more understanding than men. All managers, African American and white, had to follow policy directives from the central office, and they could also create rules to meet specific needs. From the tenants' perspective, what stood out was the sheer number of rules, which frequently interfered with their abilities to make their own decisions about their households and personal relationships. Staff members could help them when they got sick or defaulted on rent, but tenants had virtually no voice in public housing's operations; managers neither consulted them before implementing new policies nor solicited their suggestions.[70] Theresa Davenport, a tenant at Richard Allen, described clashing with her manager whose "theme song" was "If you don't like it, get out."[71]

The PHA enforced strict housekeeping policies that many women resented. Even the most sympathetic staff members had to conduct surprise biannual household inspections. If tenants were not home when the staff arrived, they let themselves in with pass keys. Myrna Coulter protested that "they come in any time they want."[72] Women who were home when the staff members arrived described a wide range of experiences. Marcelle Blackwell recalled female staff members coming into her apartment, having a "cup of tea," and talking amicably about coming events at Raymond Rosen.[73] Other women complained about staff who inspected households much more thoroughly, turning down bedspreads to make sure beds had clean sheets, checking under cupboards for vermin, and judging the cleanliness of toilets and walls. Many women particularly resented the staff evaluating the neatness of their apartments. If they failed to wash their breakfast dishes, pick up toys, or make the beds, they could receive poor grades. Emma Taylor's apartment at Richard Allen received a rating of "fair" when it was inspected because she had certain household chores that she required her children to perform each day, and if they did not complete the chores before going to school in the morning, she purposely left the tasks unfinished. The staff member, Alice Moore, refused to take Mrs. Taylor's explanation into account and lowered her score because of her children's mess. Several of Mrs. Taylor's neighbors shared deep misgivings about Mrs. Moore. Barbara Watson observed that if Mrs. Moore could not "find anything wrong with your place, she starts pulling the beds apart and poking around until she finds something." Mrs. Taylor agreed that Mrs. Moore never "builds you up— always tears you down."[74]

Fearing that dirty and disorderly households would introduce vermin into public housing and set a bad example for other tenants, managers gave families judged to have poor housekeeping standards ninety days to improve. If their apartments were not then found to be neater and cleaner, they faced eviction. The women deemed "poor housekeepers" did not tend to be younger, poorer, less literate, or more likely to be on welfare than the average family in public housing. Most had large families with several preschool children who were constantly underfoot. Some suffered from health problems such as high blood pressure and obesity and had children who got sick frequently, requiring extra care. Several "poor housekeepers" did not agree with the PHA's definition of a well-maintained apartment. When they learned that they had failed their household inspections, they felt unfairly singled out and "picked on" by authorities.[75] In 1960, the Health and Welfare Council studied the situation and issued a report that legitimated women's complaints. It stated that the staff applied the poor-housekeeping label too freely, making judgments "on very shaky ground."[76]

Women frequently accused managers of sabotaging their attempts to create orderly and aesthetically pleasing apartments. Laundry became one of the biggest sources of contention. Many women avoided drying their laundry on the racks in the courtyards, which were often falling apart or located in heavily trafficked areas where clothes got dirtied by children playing. Managers infuriated women by prohibiting them from hanging their laundry out of their windows to dry, a sight that could tarnish public housing's "respectable" image. Unable to hang wet clothes outside, women had to drape them on the furniture in their apartments or on the stair rails in the hallways. Women wanted their homes to feel inviting, and the wet clothes hanging in and around their apartments were an eyesore. Mothers of asthmatic children, who needed to avoid damp conditions, complained that their inability to hang their clothes out of the windows threatened their families' health.[77]

Managers' focus on enforcing discipline discouraged tenants from trusting one another. Over time, as with any community of people, tenants formed friendships, gossiped, and fought with their neighbors. Managers undermined the bonds and exacerbated the hostilities between tenants by encouraging neighbors to spy and report on each other so they could take action against suspected cheaters. Managers encouraged tenants to report even small transgressions, forcing them to hide from their neighbors not only their acquisitions of pets (strictly forbidden in public housing) but also their failure to wash their supper dishes promptly.[78] More than simple jealousy inspired the spying and informing. By reporting wrongdoings to staff members, tenants made themselves appear law-abiding and trustworthy, which gave them more leverage and credibility when they asked managers for larger apartments, extensions on their rents, or household repairs. Getting on the good side of management could also help tenants when they themselves needed a second chance because their apartments were messy or they were caught breaking the rules.[79]

As with welfare, public housing's management staff exercised surveillance and control over the decisions women made about their intimate relationships. Many single mothers hoped that living in public housing would allow them to achieve more autonomy in their relationships with men. Having a decent place to live, with a lease in their own names, made them less dependent on men for their livelihood and enabled some women to break up with men who became abusive. However, single mothers faced new problems when they tried to sustain relationships with men while living in public housing. Housing Authority rules prohibited them from living with men who authorities suspected would contribute resources to their households. Sleeping over was strictly prohibited and frequently monitored. Although leases stipulated that managers could only enter women's apartments "at a reasonable hour" of the day, single mothers reported numerous middle-of-the-night visits from managers trying to catch them with men.[80] Even visits from male relatives aroused suspicion. Joan Richards received many warnings from the assistant manager at Richard Allen because her brother lived nearby and frequently dropped in to visit with his friends.[81] Many women defied the rules by allowing their boyfriends to stay overnight, but resented having to hide their relationships. Mrs. Jackson described living with her boyfriend in public housing as an exercise in constant "dodging." It was a "disgraceful way to live," she explained; "I just didn't want to live that way."[82]

Recognizing that most single mothers desperately needed public housing, staff members who caught them breaking the rules could try to take advantage of them. When Mrs. Jackson was in her early twenties, the white assistant manager of Richard Allen Homes caught her "entertaining" a man and used it as leverage to try to get her to have sex with him. "That man expected liberties that I knew I wasn't supposed to give him," she recalled. "One day he came in, and I had on some shorts and a tee shirt, and he wanted to take me to bed." After Mrs. Jackson repeatedly refused the manager's advances, he became "nasty," sending her extra electric bills and threatening her with eviction. Feeling unsafe, Mrs. Jackson moved out as soon as she could.[83]

Restrictions on overnight guests interfered with women's abilities to cultivate mutually supportive personal relationships. The PHA prohibited all guests, not just men, from sleeping over, preventing women from providing family members and friends with a place to stay when they were homeless, ill, or trying to escape from abusive relationships. Single mothers found the restrictions on overnight guests particularly difficult to accept because they so frequently needed other people's assistance. They were not allowed to ask their mothers, aunts, or friends to stay overnight to help them with their children, even when they got sick or had to work late at night. When housing authorities enforced the overnight-guest policy, they impeded women's ability to benefit from, and contribute to, support networks.[84]

Sharing the welfare department's fear that clients would earn unreported income, the PHA carefully monitored tenants' economic circumstances. Those who acquired big-ticket items such as new TV sets or telephones came under great suspicion from their neighbors and staff members. The PHA also prohibited tenants from using their apartments for informal economic pursuits such as styling hair, taking in boarders, and repairing furniture as well as illegal activities such as the numbers racket and bootlegging. Tenants believed that public housing, like welfare, limited their autonomy and restricted their ability to acquire the resources they needed to improve their lives.[85]

Managers frequently felt threatened by tenants' attempts to personalize and claim ownership of public housing. Perhaps nowhere was this more clearly evident than at Raymond Rosen in the late 1950s when a nearby factory burned down and tenants in the low-rises reused its bricks to edge their lawns. Members of each family made several trips to the factory, carrying armfuls of heavy bricks home. They believed that the aesthetic payoffs made their labor worthwhile, reporting that their gardens edged with bricks looked "beautiful," especially when viewed in a row. Raymond Rosen's manager did not agree. Without consulting the tenants, he sent trucks to take the bricks away. Tenants stood powerlessly while maintenance workers dug up their gardens before their eyes.[86] The conflict shattered the tenants' sense of ownership of their surroundings. It was as if the management staff said, "We're letting you live here out of charity," explained Mrs. Blackwell. "We no longer felt that the apartments were really ours."[87]

Alessandroni and the staff at the PHA Central Office knew that tenants became disgruntled when managers exerted invasive and seemingly arbitrary control over their lives.[88] The on-site staff witnessed the results firsthand as the tenants they managed showed resentment toward their rules and restrictions. Yet no one tried to change course. Authorities feared that if they loosened their grip, tenants would destroy their apartments and introduce immoral activities into public housing.[89]

The Inadequate Funding of Public Housing

The lack of adequate funding for public housing further diminished tenants' commitment to their homes. Federal legislation paired the construction of public housing with slum clearance, envisioning the two programs working together to house displaced families and improve the physical, social, and economic landscape of urban America.[90] However, the public housing agenda was constantly limited by Congress; less than one-fifth of the housing authorized in the 1949 Housing Act was ever built. In 1957, city authorities estimated that they could provide only one-fifth of the public housing needed in Philadelphia.[91] The problem was not just the inadequate number of units of public housing, but also the cost limitations imposed on new construction. An amendment to the 1937 Wagner-Steagall Act, written by Harry Byrd, the Democratic senator from Virginia, implemented strict spending restrictions on all new construction.[92] The USHA pushed cities to reduce costs even further by requiring local authorities to remove all "frills" and design innovations from their plans for new public housing.[93]

The federal restrictions on construction expenditures weighed heavily on tenants. Over time, many of them ceased remarking on the luxuries in public housing and began to complain about its inadequacies. Concrete floors were extremely cold, and closets without doors had to be in perfect order or else their contents spilled out onto the floors. Without dining rooms, families had to eat in their living rooms. The inadequate cupboard space forced many women to store canned food, dishes, and utensils in their bedrooms. Buildings lacked finished basements for storage, so tricycles, bicycles, and baby carriages usually ended up in the hallways or lodged in the tiny living rooms.[94] Tenants in older buildings resented not having on-site laundry facilities, and those who had them found them expensive and insufficient because members of the surrounding community frequently used them.[95]

The dwindling resources available for the upkeep of public housing had similarly deleterious effects on tenants' morale. Local authorities used the income they collected in rents to pay for salaries, utility bills, maintenance work, and modernization. When tenants' incomes were high, as they were during World War II, securing funding to keep public housing running smoothly was not difficult. However, as the number of two-parent, steadily employed families in public housing declined and the number of poor families increased, the income that the PHA collected from rents dwindled. At the same time, public housing became more expensive to maintain. Buildings and appliances aged, requiring costly repairs and upgrades.[96] As the booming postwar consumer economy made ranges and refrigerators considered luxurious in the early 1940s antiquated by the 1950s, tenants wished for newer items.[97] With little money to spend on upkeep, the PHA restricted the painting of the interior walls in public housing to every four years, even when apartments changed hands. Some tenants had to do the painting themselves. Families moving into apartments with marked-up walls and outmoded appliances did not view public housing as an inviting place to live.[98]

Fueling tenants' disgruntlement, managers conserved funds by forcing them to bear some of the costs of public housing's operations. Rents included utilities, but when a manager suspected that a family was using too much electricity, he installed a meter in their apartment and charged them for any use he deemed "excessive." To avoid getting stuck with extra electricity bills, many tenants felt compelled to turn off their lights and go to bed early in the evenings.[99] When apartments needed repairs, the PHA paid only for relatively inexpensive problems, typically busted locks and broken electric switches. Tenants usually had to pay for more expensive repairs and damage deemed to have been caused by their "heedlessness," such as smashed windows, out-of-order toilets, and broken doors. They also had to pay for damage caused by bad weather or other people. Tenants were angry about the expense of repairs, especially since the management prevented them from fixing problems themselves or shopping around for the cheapest handymen.[100]

The PHA's meager expenditures on public spaces inspired similar resentment. When public housing first opened, tenants kept its exteriors extremely clean. "One of the most spick-and-span spots in Philadelphia these days is the Richard Allen Homes," reported the *Bulletin*, five years after the site opened. "What little trash blows around there blows in from the outside and the residents are justifiably proud of the appearance of the area."[101] In an area of only eight city blocks, Richard Allen housed 6,100 people, over 3,000 of them children. Yet tenants took such good care of their surroundings that Richard Allen won an award from Philadelphia's Chamber of Commerce and Sanitation Squad for being one of the cleanest spots in the city. Women carefully swept the hallways outside their apartments; reporters noted that in "not a single hallway entered was there any accumulation of trash or even dust."[102] Although not every tenant maintained these high standards, the community ethos in support of cleanliness created neat and pleasant public spaces. Tenants in the new public housing that opened in Philadelphia in the 1950s similarly prided themselves on their clean and well-maintained surroundings.[103]

Over time, many tenants began to feel that the PHA did not support their efforts to keep up public spaces. When nonresidents and other tenants put graffiti on the walls, littered, and engaged in acts of vandalism, managers rarely provided assistance. One 1957 inspection found the landscape around Richard Allen Homes plagued by "erosion, water pockets, inadequate drainage, irregular surfacing, spindly plantings, makeshift fencing, [and] bare muddy spots." At Norris, water and urine had accumulated in the stairwells, creating a terrible stench. Even Raymond Rosen had begun to show signs of disrepair after only two years of operation.[104] Alessandroni acknowledged that the PHA did not spend nearly enough money on maintenance, but he blamed the federal government's refusal to provide adequate funds. When pressed by the Housing Association, Alessandroni admitted that with all of the problems the PHA faced, he did not consider maintenance funding a priority.[105]

The need to house as many people as possible for the lowest possible cost resulted in crowded and flimsy quarters where tenants felt as if they lived virtually on top of one another. "You're too congested in the projects," explained Mrs. Coulter; "it's just like one family—just like the whole people, everybody's living in one house."[106] The thin walls between apartments did not dampen sound. Tenants smelled their neighbors' food, heard neighbors' conversations, knew which TV programs they watched, and listened to their crying babies, fights, parties, and sexual relations. Gossip spread quickly and tempers wore thin. One of Mrs. Davenport's neighbors held a religious revival in her apartment, which lasted for several days until all hours of the night. When Mrs. Davenport complained, the neighbor left her speechless by retorting, "Why after all we are praying to God, you should too."[107] When managers intervened to quiet tenants, they made the noisemakers unhappy. Mrs. Coulter explained that "if you want to have a birthday party and you make a little bit too much noise, then they're ready to tell you everybody have to go."[108] Relationships among tenants, difficult in the best of circumstances, became even harder to negotiate inside the crowded quarters of cheaply constructed public housing.[109]

After living in public housing for several years, a core group of tenants usually remained engaged in organized social functions, sending their children to recreational activities, joining Mother's Clubs, and participating in community events. In 1961, more than one hundred children competed in Richard Allen's baby contest and four hundred onlookers attended the popular annual event. Yet thousands did not join any community activities whatsoever.[110] In 1955, the year after Raymond Rosen opened, its Boy Scouts and girls' "Golden Rings" clubs had about thirty members attending weekly meetings. Most other groups had far fewer members, and even the well-attended Scouts and Rings clubs drew only a tiny fraction of the thousands of children who lived in Raymond Rosen.[111]

The dearth of facilities for children weighed heavily on mothers who had to supervise and amuse them. Play areas rarely had enough equipment or space. Richard Allen had only two sets of swings and two jungle gyms for its 3,000 children. With the nearest public recreation center one mile away and no public parks nearby, children from the surrounding neighborhood also relied on Richard Allen's facilities.[112] At Raymond Rosen, the 200-seat auditorium provided the only indoor recreation space for 5,000 tenants. The PHA did not construct a gymnasium at Raymond Rosen because authorities assumed that tenants would be able to use the recreation facilities at the school across the street and at a nearby public recreation center. However, the school did not organize community programs in the afternoons or evenings, and the recreation center was already overcrowded and could not accommodate the thousands of new children from Raymond Rosen.[113] The few playgrounds and recreational activities that did exist in public housing usually did not attract teenagers, who began to hang out in the hallways because they had nowhere else to go. Even when women convinced managers to turn off the heat in the hallways to discourage young people from congregating, the loud and boisterous socializing often continued.[114] When Ruth Murphy sent her husband on one occasion to chase the youths away, "they retaliated by throwing stones."[115]

Mothers at home during the day frequently exacerbated problems. Some took turns watching children, but many developed the habit of sending young children out to play in the courtyards unsupervised while they performed their household chores. Chaos frequently ensued on the crowded playgrounds. On rainy days, mothers let children play in the hallways, where they used peashooters and created huge rackets, especially when they put on their roller skates. Children risked injuring themselves when they swung, as they often did, from the railings beside the stairs in the hallways over high drops to the cement floors below. Many mothers lamented that their children had gotten out of control in public housing. Refusing to acknowledge their own complicity in the process, they often blamed the "bad influence" of neighbors' children for their youngsters' misbehavior.[116]

The PHA's attempts to save money by switching its focus to high-rise living made the situation worse. High-rises did not in and of themselves cause public housing's difficulties. Many middle-class Philadelphians paid considerable sums to rent apartments in high-rise buildings, and Tasker and Richard Allen, which were low-rises, both became extremely run-down.[117] Still, high-rises did create new challenges for women. The buildings were large and impersonal, precluding many of the social interactions that took place between women in low-rises as they hung their laundry to dry, swept their stairs, and called their children in for dinner. Fearing that children would fall out of the windows of high-rises because of the inadequate window guards, many mothers sent them outside to play as much as possible.[118] The elevators added to the chaos because the children used them as toys, going up and down while hiding and chasing one another. Mrs. Coulter complained, "They're holding you up, they're running out the doors. . . . I just can't stand it."[119] These pranks often ended with broken elevators.[120] Many women dreaded using both the stairs and the elevators because they became prime locations for robberies and sexual assaults.

Boys play on a slide at Richard Allen Homes in the mid-1950s. The playground was usually overcrowded. Temple University Libraries, Urban Archives, Philadelphia, Pa.

When elevators broke, forcing women to lug toddlers, laundry, and groceries up numerous flights of stairs, they felt tired and vulnerable, making it impossible for them to take much comfort or pride in their surroundings.

Safety in Public Housing

Over the course of the 1950s, the working-class African American neighborhoods that hosted public housing confronted major challenges. While civil rights activists focused on securing greater access to housing for African Americans, neighborhood groups tried to enlist city authorities to help them eliminate the drug trade, crime, and bars in their communities. In the 1950s, with encouragement from the municipal government, the number of block groups in the city skyrocketed; by 1961, there were 1,500 groups in the city, many staffed primarily by working-class African American women.[121] Groups petitioned city officials to remove abandoned cars from their streets, inspect vacant houses, and provide their blocks with street repairs, fire hydrants, and police protection. Many groups organized neighborhood clean-up days and planted flower boxes outside their homes. Some converted vacant overgrown lots into "tot lots" where children could play.[122] When new bars opened in their communities, they launched protests, sometimes charging that white bar owners targeted African American neighborhoods, turning a profit at their expense. In one 1959 anti-taproom demonstration, 129 men, women, and children from the Strawberry Mansion neighborhood traveled to a State Liquor Control Board hearing in a bus, carrying placards demanding "Classrooms Not Taprooms." They testified for four-and-one-half hours against the granting of a liquor license to a nearby restaurant.[123]

With many neighborhood residents either experiencing or feeling vulnerable to robbery and rape, block groups sought to diminish the crime, gangs, and drug selling in their communities. In 1953, one North Philadelphia block group observed that "people don't feel safe from attack, purse-snatching, molesting or worse." The group sent petitions to the mayor and the city council asking for an increase in the police force assigned to their neighborhood and the restoration of foot patrolmen to their streets.[124] In South Philadelphia, a different group complained that drug "peddlers and pushers [were] very active" in their neighborhood and faulted the police for failing to enforce drug laws.[125] Although the extent of crime and the drug trade in working-class African American neighborhoods in postwar Philadelphia paled in comparison to later years, in 1960 there was a foreshadowing of what was to come: For the first time in the city's history, homicide was the leading cause of death among young African American men.[126]

Block groups frequently organized "clean-up, fix-up" days when neighborhood residents cleaned their windows and streets and attempted to clear vacant lots. Temple University Libraries, Urban Archives, Philadelphia, Pa.

Because of its location in segregated or transitional low-income neighborhoods, the fate of African American public housing was integrally linked to the fate of Philadelphia's working-class black communities. Although authorities had hoped that public housing would improve the standard of living in blighted neighborhoods, the boundaries between public housing and the neighborhoods surrounding it were permeable. Crime and the drug trade became an integral part of life in public housing, and the PHA became particularly concerned about the city's high-rises. "Problems in high-rise structures are mounting," observed Allesandroni in 1958. "There is vandalism from outsiders who get into the projects, which have no proper supervision, and nobody is willing to give [the] authority money to do the policing job. Women are raped." Many women began to avoid going out at night, and some even stopped sending their children outside to play during the day because they feared for their safety. Random acts of violence became increasingly common. In 1958, at Norris, when a group of people waiting for an elevator got frustrated because it was slow to arrive, they yanked the door loose and dropped it down the shaft. Nobody called the police for fear of violent retaliation.[127]

Over the course of the 1950s and 1960s, while the quality of life in nearly all public housing in Philadelphia declined significantly, James Weldon Johnson, which housed African Americans in North Philadelphia, and Hill Creek, which housed whites in the northeast, both remained clean, safe, and pleasant places to live. James Weldon Johnson was located on the edge of North Philadelphia, the most run-down African American neighborhood in the city. Yet families who lived in the surrounding blocks used its streets to park their cars, considering the streets much safer than those in their own neighborhoods. The success of James Weldon Johnson and Hill Creek stemmed partly from their architecturally distinctive and unusually attractive low-rise buildings, which were a source of great pride for tenants and managers. Their relatively small sizes and low turnover rates enabled tenants to develop close ties with one another as well as with members of their surrounding communities. James Weldon Johnson remained successful into the 1970s, when 90 percent of its tenants received public assistance. To accommodate the large teenage population, the staff acquired the funds to organize youth sports teams, which kept boys out of gangs and cultivated community spirit among the residents who cheered them on. Relationships between tenants and the management staff at James Weldon Johnson involved less friction than those elsewhere. The black manager orchestrated repairs and maintenance work promptly and assisted tenants in their efforts to keep the public spaces free from litter and graffiti. Rather than placing himself on a pedestal, he encouraged tenants to view him as "one of them."[128]

Situations like the ones at James Weldon Johnson and Hill Creek, however, were exceptional. Most tenants in Philadelphia's public housing became disillusioned as their relationships with staff members turned hostile and suspicious and their living conditions became run-down and dangerous. Although African Americans, and especially single mothers, continued to apply for public housing in large numbers because their options in the private market remained extremely limited, many doubted that it would improve their lives demonstrably. Once a source of tremendous hope, public housing became a reflection of their degradation.

Working-class African American women initially saw in public housing a rare opportunity to achieve a measure of upward mobility, bodily integrity, and personal autonomy. They hoped that public housing would provide a respectable and safe place to raise their children, surrounded by a community of like-minded friends. Many imagined that public housing would serve as the refuge that they had long desired, a place where they could close their doors and enjoy the security and comfort of a real home. They believed that well-maintained, affordable apartments would better equip them to deal with the multifaceted problems they faced in their lives.

By the early 1960s, women no longer enthusiastically embraced public housing. They continued to seek admission because it provided them with better and more affordable housing than they could obtain anywhere else in the city, but they no longer believed that it would provide them with real homes. When the PHA chose locations for public housing that placated working-class whites, it confined black tenants to segregated, low-income neighborhoods that threatened their safety. Federal funding policies mandated cheap construction and local authorities did not prioritize upgrades or maintenance. The on-site staff frequently undermined women's attempts to invest themselves in public housing by implementing rigid rules that limited their autonomy and allowed no room for their participation in the management's decision making. Tenants who had once sought to make public housing their own became disillusioned with their inability to take pride in and claim ownership of their surroundings. Therein lies the tragic missed opportunity of postwar public housing. Rather than nurturing working-class African American women's aspirations, it became yet another public institution that maintained them in poverty, sought to regulate their behaviors, and restricted their abilities to substantially improve their lives.

CHAPTER FOUR

"Massive Resistance" in the
Public Schools

In 1953, Hattie Parker, a forty-year-old mother, helped organize a Home and School Association in her South Philadelphia neighborhood. She and her husband had six children, aged five to eleven, and had fallen on hard times. Her husband had lost his job, and although he had recently found a full-time position as a garage attendant, the $36.00 he earned each week did not cover the family's food, clothing, utilities, and rent. Money had gotten so tight that Mrs. Parker had swallowed her pride and applied for welfare—only to have her application rejected. While dealing with these problems, Mrs. Parker agreed to serve as vice president of her local Home and School Association. She linked her strong commitment to her children's education to the difficulties that she had faced growing up in a poor neighborhood without a mother. Mrs. Parker explained to a social worker that her desire to provide a better life for her children "impels her to work in community organizations" that would help them pursue an education.[1]

The public school system that women like Mrs. Parker relied on to educate their children was the most damaging public institution in the city, plagued by a pernicious combination of mismanagement and deliberate racial segregation and academic tracking. By the early 1960s, the massive system, which served nearly one-quarter of a million students in 280 different schools, had the largest average class size and lowest proportion of permanently certified teachers of the nation's ten largest cities.[2] While racial discrimination in southern schools came under intense public scrutiny with the Supreme Court's 1954 decision in *Brown v. Board of Education*, the public schools in northern cities like Philadelphia had deeply ingrained inequalities that proved equally resistant to change. A few Philadelphia schools provided African Americans with a first-rate education, and many teachers strove to deliver excellent instruction. However, by confining African American students to segregated, underfunded, overcrowded, and understaffed schools, the system as a whole impeded teachers' efforts and made it difficult for most black students to succeed. A tracking system steered African American students toward vocational degrees, making it difficult for them to pursue academic courses successfully. School authorities refused to take responsibility for black students' struggles, describing them as "slow learners" whose academic problems stemmed from their poverty and their mothers' lack of interest in their education. Enormous numbers of African American students dropped out of school before high school graduation because they lacked institutional support. The deeply entrenched discrimination in the schools and the labor force meant that even high school graduates rarely achieved significant upward mobility.

Working-class African American women refused to abandon their deep and abiding faith in education. Recognizing that the schools were not uniformly deleterious or resistant to change, they tried to find openings in the system that they could use to improve the quality of the education that their children received.[3] Although many teachers and principals viewed low-income black mothers with disdain and mistrust, most women tried to maintain contact with their children's schools. They met with teachers and principals to discuss their children's progress and try to resolve classroom difficulties. Some attempted to transfer their children to better schools in the public or Catholic school system.

Mothers viewed the work they performed in their homes and neighborhoods as integrally linked to their children's success in school. They labored to secure financial resources, clothing, and after-school care for their children, believing that the provision of basic necessities would help their children's educational pursuits. At home and in their neighborhoods, they tried to prevent problems that impeded their children's schooling, seeking to stop their daughters from getting pregnant and to help their sons avoid becoming involved in gangs. Some women joined Home and School Associations in which they lobbied city authorities to make their neighborhoods safer for their children. In targeting unsafe streets as well as the classroom, women's efforts differed significantly from the educational activism engaged in by civil rights leaders and liberal reformers who focused on the school system's racial segregation. Working-class African American women connected the challenges their children faced within the schools with the struggles their families faced in their homes and neighborhoods.

Ultimately, neither mothers nor middle-class advocacy groups achieved much success in their efforts to improve black children's education. Democratic leaders largely ignored them, and education authorities actively resisted calls for change, isolating themselves from the community, stubbornly refusing to lobby the state for sufficient funds, and deliberately adhering to policies favoring middle-class whites. Still, most mothers remained firmly committed to education. Convinced by their circumstances that they would be unable to achieve significant upward mobility themselves, they refused to extinguish their long-standing hope that education would make a positive difference for their children.

Northern-Style "Massive Resistance"

Working-class African American women hoped that schooling would provide their children with opportunities that they had lacked. Many had not graduated from high school and believed that their limited education had impeded their ability to earn an adequate living. Anna Grier, a single mother on welfare, encouraged her children "every day to get an education so they don't have to bring up their children the way I do."[4] Emily Aford, another welfare recipient, believed that if she helped her children "go to school and learn like they should . . . they won't need public assistance."[5] Most mothers set their sights on high school graduation, believing that a diploma would open doors to decent jobs for their children. Others wanted their children to attend college. Juanita Hester, a welfare recipient, took great pride in her three children and supported their aspirations: "My oldest wants to enter the Army, learn a trade there and then go to college. The girl wants to be a nurse and the other boy a doctor."[6]

Although black people did not benefit from education to the same degree as white people did, securing a high school diploma did improve their standing in the labor force. The contribution of formal schooling to economic achievement has been debated by historians and policy makers, whose work directly addresses the hopes articulated by African American parents. Some scholars and political commentators have emphasized the democratic functions of the U.S. public education system, viewing it as enabling poor people to improve their circumstances and serving as a key tool in the creation of a meritocratic society. Others have argued that the school system has perpetuated inequalities by preparing nonwhite and low-income students primarily for low-status positions. Many studies of the construction of racialized poverty in postwar cities offer a completely different perspective, ignoring the schools and suggesting that deindustrialization and racism in the labor and housing markets had far more important effects on African Americans' job prospects than did the education they received. The historians who take this position envision the inferior schooling provided to African Americans as stemming from the impoverishment and racial segregation of the inner city and not as a primary or independent cause of poverty. The education and employment histories of African Americans in postwar Philadelphia illuminate the importance and limitations of all three perspectives, confirming black mothers' conviction that formal schooling was essential, while underscoring its insufficiencies in fostering significant upward mobility.[7]

Graduating from high school did improve African Americans' future prospects, but it rarely lifted them into the middle class. Black students were confined to schools with inadequate resources that steered them away from programs that prepared them for skilled jobs. When they left school, they confronted a discriminatory labor market that often excluded them from positions available to similarly educated whites. In postwar Philadelphia, black high school graduates were eight times as likely to be unemployed as white graduates, and their jobs tended to pay lower salaries and be less secure.[8] Still, their future prospects were much better than those of black high-school dropouts. In 1960, with low-wage jobs increasingly requiring a high school diploma, only one-quarter of the African American boys aged fourteen to seventeen in the labor force had full-time jobs, another quarter were unemployed, and half had part-time jobs. Black girls in the same age group had an even higher unemployment rate; one-third were jobless.[9] African Americans who graduated from high school fared much better, particularly if they were among the 24 percent who secured a college preparatory diploma. One survey of black high school graduates who obtained college preparatory diplomas in 1961 found that the year after they graduated, more than half had gone on to further education and nearly a third held jobs; very few were unemployed. Of those who earned vocational diplomas, almost two-thirds had jobs and 12 percent were unemployed (see Tables 4.1 and 4.2).[10] While a high school diploma did not guarantee that African American students would become gainfully employed, those with a diploma were in a much better position to get jobs than those without one, particularly if they had earned a college preparatory degree.[11]

The public school system impeded African American students' attempts to graduate from high school and earn the diplomas they needed to secure jobs. In the postwar period, as educators throughout the nation struggled to keep up with the rising demand for schooling, the situation in Philadelphia became

Table 4.1. 1961 Philadelphia High School Graduates' Future Prospects, Excluding "Other" and "Unknown"

	College Curriculum		Vocational Curriculum	
	Black	White	Black	White
Went to college	54%	60%	3%	2%
Entered another type of educational institution	8	11	7	5
Had gainful employment	29	23	60	85
Entered armed forces	5	4	5	8
Became a "housewife"	1	1	11	2
Unemployed	2	1	12	1
Died or became incapacitated	0	1	0	<1

Source: Odell, *Educational Survey Report*, 171.

Note: This table is based on a sample of high school students surveyed in the year after their graduation. Those graduates classified as "other" and "unknown," which include those who moved away or could not be located for other reasons, have been excluded. Black graduates, especially with vocational diplomas, were significantly overrepresented in this category. Accordingly, I calculated the percentages of the total number of graduates, shown in Table 4.2.

particularly dire. The city's entrenched educational bureaucracy resisted even the minimal expenditures required by increased enrollment. The problems began with the public school system's secretary business-manager, Add Anderson. With only a tenth-grade education, Anderson ran the school system from 1934 until his death in 1962.[12] Philadelphia journalist Peter Binzen described Anderson as "a legendary figure, a Scrooge with rolltop desk who blocked all efforts at liberalization and made the school system dance to his tunes."[13] The main funding for the public schools came from the city's real-estate taxes and a block grant from the state, both of which were set annually by the Pennsylvania legislature.[14] The schools remained chronically poor because Anderson, a Republican strongly committed to low taxes and limited state expenditures, refused to lobby for substantial increases in funding, and no one forcefully opposed him.[15] Throughout the 1950s, fiscal conservatism had enough appeal to white voters to ensure that significant pressure for school reform was not brought to bear on the system.

The city government allowed Anderson to maintain virtually free rein over the schools. Anderson handpicked the fifteen elite members of the Board of Education, all but one of whom were white. The board rubber-stamped his

Table 4.2. 1961 Philadelphia High School Graduates' Future Prospects, Including "Other" and "Unknown"

	College Curriculum		Vocational Curriculum	
	Black	White	Black	White
Went to college	47%	57%	2%	2%
Entered another type of educational institution	7	10	5	5
Had gainful employment	25	22	44	79
Entered armed forces	4	4	4	7
Became a "housewife"	1	1	8	2
Unemployed	2	1	9	1
Died or became incapacitated	0	1	0	<1
Other or unknown	13	5	26	7

Source: Odell, *Educational Survey Report*, 171.

Note: This table is based on a sample of high school students surveyed in the year after their graduation. Those graduates classified as "other" and "unknown," which include those who moved away or could not be located for other reasons, have been included. It is not safe to assume that the outcomes for students who fell into the "other" or "unknown" category resembled those for students who could be located. When this table is compared to Table 4.1, the racial disparities in this group of graduates' prospects are somewhat larger, especially in the proportions of vocational graduates who were gainfully employed and unemployed and in the proportions of college preparatory graduates who went on to college.

policies and rarely interacted with the community. Between 1955 and 1961, when local lawyer Leon Obermayer chaired the board, he was the only member whose children had even attended the public schools.[16] Democratic leaders' failure to intervene reflected the virtual absence of public education from their reform agenda, an omission central to their failure to grapple with the city's class and racial inequalities in a substantive, rather than merely rhetorical, way. Richardson Dilworth recalled his approach to the public education system during his tenure as mayor. "Nobody worried much about the schools," he explained in a 1967 interview. "We just didn't realize how neglected they were becoming."[17]

Although large numbers of white students suffered from the education system's mismanagement and lack of adequate funding, black students suffered at a higher rate because they were disproportionately represented in the public schools and concentrated in the poorest districts. Philadelphia's public schools were legally segregated until 1881. They became more integrated during the

Table 4.3. Percentage of African American Students in the Philadelphia Public Schools, 1944–1964

	1944	1957	1964
Elementary	NA	45	57
Junior high	NA	39	56
Senior high	NA	30	38
Technical high	NA	34	49
Total	24	41	53

Source: Committee on Nondiscrimination, *Report of the Special Committee on Nondiscrimination*, 2.

late-nineteenth and early-twentieth centuries, but as the city's black population grew over the course of the twentieth century, they became highly segregated again.[18] Between 1945 and 1962, as large numbers of white parents sent their children to parochial and private schools, the proportion of African American students in the public system rose from 26 to 51 percent, almost double their proportion in the population at large (see Table 4.3).[19] School board policies exacerbated the racial and economic disparities that arose from the segregation of Philadelphia's neighborhoods by consigning most black students and teachers to inferior, predominantly black schools. By the early 1960s, only 16 percent of the city's public schools were integrated (see Table 4.4). Eighty-five percent of African American students and 93 percent of African American teachers were in schools that were at least 80 percent black.[20]

Deliberate decisions made by the school board fostered the racial segregation of Philadelphia's public education system. Education authorities claimed that they assigned pupils and chose locations for schools on a "color-blind" basis, an assertion frequently echoed by those who have assumed that the racial segregation in northern schools stemmed from the segregation of neighborhoods. These assertions belie the numerous ways that the boards of education in Philadelphia and other northern cities played an active role in segregating their school systems.[21] One of the many instances in which Philadelphia authorities' commitment to segregation became clear occurred when they responded to the population changes in northwest Philadelphia. In the late 1950s and early 1960s, although both white and black schools in the northwest became filled beyond capacity, the board dealt with their situations in very different ways. When the white C. W. Henry school became overcrowded, education officials succumbed to pressure from parents, who asked them not to transfer students to a nearby black school that had openings, but to send them to a white school

Table 4.4. Racial Composition of Philadelphia Schools, 1963

Racial Composition	Percentage of Schools (N=263)
Under 30% African American enrollment	45
70% or more African American enrollment	39
30% to 70% African American enrollment	16

Source: Committee on Nondiscrimination, *Report of the Special Committee on Nondiscrimination*, 11.

further away instead. Several years later, when the black Emlen school in the same neighborhood confronted similar problems, authorities refused to let students transfer to the underutilized white Day school nearby and chose to relieve the overcrowding by adding six portable classrooms.[22]

The decision to enlarge the capacity of Emlen rather than allow black students to attend the white school galvanized the Philadelphia NAACP to launch a racial discrimination suit against the school board. Inspired by the 1961 federal district court case *Taylor v. Board of Education of New Rochelle*, which found New Rochelle's school board guilty of maintaining racially segregated schools, Philadelphia's NAACP joined civil rights organizations in forty-three cities in fourteen northern and western states in initiating suits challenging segregation and discrimination in their school systems. Civil rights activists' complaints included the racial gerrymandering of school zone lines; discriminatory transfer policies, feeder patterns, and teacher placement; the overcrowding of predominantly black schools and underutilization of predominantly white schools; and school-site selection that created or perpetuated segregation.[23] In 1963, the Philadelphia NAACP dropped its suit when the board of education (no longer run by Add Anderson) adopted a plan to foster increased integration.[24]

Philadelphia education authorities created stark disparities between white and black schools through the policies they enacted to regulate teacher and student transfers and determine the amount of per-pupil spending. Since the school board granted teacher transfers based on seniority, most of the experienced teachers transferred to white middle-class schools, leaving inexperienced teachers and vacancies concentrated in poor black districts.[25] In 1963, Philadelphia's African American schools had an average teacher-vacancy rate of 13 percent compared with a 5-percent rate in white schools. Almost one in three African American schools was overcrowded (operating at least 10 percent above capacity), compared to only one in twenty white schools.[26] School funding varied considerably throughout the city, and the board never publicly accounted for its spending policies. At the high school level, the average per-pupil

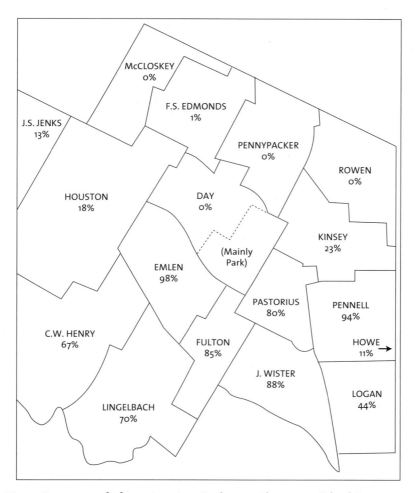

Map 4. Percentage of African American Students in Elementary School Zones in Northwest Philadelphia, 1961

In the early 1950s, when the pupil-transfer controversies began, C. W. Henry was a predominantly white school. The Emlen and Day school zones were separated by a railroad track. The board of education claimed that the boundary was not discriminatory because it had been instituted when the area mainly housed whites. Critics charged that when the boundary was drawn, the board could have anticipated the racial changes that would occur in the area and that an underpass constructed underneath the railroad allowed students from surrounding neighborhoods to easily travel to Day. In the 1950s, Day's boundaries were moved to include white students from other schools, but it did not accept students from Emlen.

Sources: U.S. Commission on Civil Rights, *Civil Rights U.S.A.*, 132–35; Clapper, "School Design," 249.

spending for African American schools was higher than was the spending for white schools. However, at the elementary school level, in which African American students were overrepresented, the school board exhibited a clear pattern of underfunding African American schools in several established and expanding working-class African American neighborhoods. In 1959, in District 4, which included the northern portion of West Philadelphia, seven of the nine schools with per-pupil budgets more than $250 served white students. All fifteen schools with per-pupil budgets less than $250 served African American students.[27]

Although the board spent more than $80 million on school construction and renovation during the postwar period, the new funding did not substantially improve the conditions for most low-income students.[28] Schools throughout the city were old and in very poor condition; more than one in five had been built prior to 1907. Peeling paint and crumbling plaster marred the walls, water seeped in through the windows and rotted the floors, and dingy basements housed rusty, clogged toilets. Parents worried because the buildings were firetraps. Heating and cooling systems were antiquated, and in several senior high schools, the laboratory equipment was more than fifty years old. Cafeterias were overcrowded; some neighborhood elementary schools had no lunchrooms. Libraries were either absent or inadequate. Many schools lacked auditoriums, playground equipment, and gymnasiums.[29] When addressing these problems, the board prioritized the needs of middle-class whites, particularly those who could afford to move to the rapidly growing all-white neighborhoods in the far northeast of the city. In one of the most blatant displays of favoritism, when African Americans began to move into the neighborhood surrounding Northeast High School in the early 1950s, the school's influential alumni persuaded the board to build a new Northeast school in an all-white, middle-class, mostly Jewish section of the city further north, six miles away from the old school. The board spent $7 million on the new Northeast facility, which was built in 1954. It renamed the old school Thomas Edison High (the remaining students staged a strike over the name change) and transferred the school's songs, color, athletic trophies, and alumni fund to the new school along with two-thirds of its teachers.[30]

When the school board provided new schools for African Americans, it usually located them in the middle of segregated neighborhoods, ensuring that they would only serve black students. The new African American schools were architecturally distinctive from the new white schools, with fewer and smaller windows and much smaller and less attractive grounds. In many cases, the board chose to fix old buildings or to add portable classrooms in African American districts rather than transfer African American students to white schools or

In 1958, the Philadelphia Board of Education demolished Benjamin Franklin High School (left) and replaced it with a modern structure (center). One of the few new schools constructed to serve African American students, the building was sterile and unwelcoming. Temple University Libraries, Urban Archives, Philadelphia, Pa.

construct new facilities. In one African American neighborhood, an entire new school consisted of twelve portable classrooms. The racially distinctive locations and architecture of the new schools ensured that any plans to desegregate Philadelphia's schools in the future would be extremely expensive and politically unpalatable for the majority of whites in the city.[31]

A noxious tracking system created further obstacles to African American students' academic success. In the early twentieth century, when the population of U.S. high schools expanded to include significant numbers of low-income and nonwhite students, educators began offering separate courses of study for students who were not from middle-class backgrounds and whom they did not expect to enter white-collar occupations or go on to higher education.[32] The tracking system was based on the premise that the majority of these nontraditional students were not suited for academic courses, and it reinforced the presumption by directing them away from intellectually demanding classes.[33] In the postwar period, tracking began as early as the first grade.[34] After failing to provide most African Americans with kindergarten, school authorities gave students intelligence tests and then used the results to determine whether or not they could handle first-grade work. Educators placed students who scored between 50 and 75 in state-subsidized "retarded educable" (RE) classes and saved money by adding to these classes students who scored higher than 75 but who exhibited behavioral problems or simply had difficulty keeping up with their peers.[35] Durham Elementary, an African American school in South Philadelphia, had four RE classes, serving one-quarter of its students.[36] With so many RE students, teachers found it difficult to give individualized attention to those who had genuine learning problems and nearly impossible to address the issues faced by students whose problems were behavioral rather than academic. Many students placed in RE classes in the early grades never escaped because they learned so little that it was impossible for them to reenter classes with their peers. Lucille Draper was one of those students. She quit school at seventeen when she was still in the seventh grade. After leaving school, she sought assistance at a job-training center where the staff described her as a capable worker of average or above average intelligence. Racial prejudice combined with tracking to create a vicious cycle that many black students found extremely difficult to surmount.[37]

Students placed in regular elementary school classes suffered from the system's low academic standards and lack of individualized attention. Teachers faced immense pressures in dealing with their schools' inadequate funding and overcrowded classes. Students who lagged behind their peers were promoted whenever possible; many students with academic problems never received the individual assistance that they needed. To help the unprepared students, educators simplified the curriculum, leaving the capable students bored and discouraged from achieving. In 1964, the Board of Education's Committee on Nondiscrimination found "a general sense of low expectancy in pupil performance . . . on the part of the staff," which led students to lose "any interest they might have developed in . . . learning."[38] The sobering result was that many Philadelphia elementary school students scored *lower* on IQ tests after four years of schooling than they had as preschoolers.[39]

In secondary school, the tracking system became more elaborate. Philadelphia had five specialized secondary schools. Students who wanted to focus on vocational training could attend the High School of Agriculture and Horticulture, Bok Technical School, or Dobbins Technical School, where the school board allowed construction trade unions to exclude African American students from their federally financed apprenticeship programs.[40] Students who wanted to take challenging college preparatory courses could compete to enter the Central High School for Boys or the Philadelphia High School for Girls, selec-

A chemistry class at the selective Philadelphia High School for Girls reflected the makeup of the student body, with a majority of whites and a small contingent of African Americans. Temple University Libraries, Urban Archives, Philadelphia, Pa.

tive schools that required good grades and high scores on achievement tests for admittance.[41] At the Philadelphia High School for Girls, African Americans comprised 20 percent of the student body, but at the Central High School for Boys, they comprised only 7 percent. Boys' relative underrepresentation at the selective high school partly reflected their greater likelihood of getting jobs before they finished high school. It also reflected the intense social pressure they faced in and outside of the classroom to assert themselves through violence and other forms of misbehavior.[42]

The majority of African American and white students bypassed the academic schools completely and attended one of the city's sixteen regular high schools, all of which offered both vocational and academic curricula. Entering students chose one of thirteen different curricula leading to seven different types of diplomas: college preparatory, commercial, clerical, homemaking, trade preparatory, vocational agriculture, and general.[43] Most African American students had been prepared in junior high to enter the vocational tracks, which were

Table 4.5. Black and White Student Enrollment in Philadelphia Senior High School Curricula, May 1963

Curriculum	Black Students	White Students
Academic	23.6%	45.6%
General	18.1	24.8
Commercial	29.3	20.1
Modified[a]	12.1	2.3
Trade preparatory/occupational shop	15.2	5.9

Source: Odell, *Educational Survey Report*, 140.
[a]The modified curriculum was only offered at select senior high schools. The school system defined it as a "special program for pupils whose abilities are in areas other than the subject matter of the regular classes in the high school."

largely segregated by sex, with boys preparing for the trades and girls directed toward secretarial work.[44] In 1963, 76 percent of African Americans pursued the nonacademic curricula, mainly the trade and commercial tracks, compared to 54 percent of whites (see Table 4.5).[45] The Armstrong Association had long championed vocational education as one of the best ways to improve African Americans' employment prospects, and many students and parents sought out and appreciated the vocational curriculum because it enabled children who did not thrive in academic courses to remain in school and receive a diploma. However, black students interested in the academic track were also steered toward vocational courses. Although some white educators encouraged African American students to pursue academic learning, many school officials openly acknowledged that they actively discouraged it. One counselor explained her position by asking, "What good is an academic course to them?" Because African American students were "too poor to go to college," she steered them toward "typewriting and bookkeeping so that they can get jobs when they get out."[46] While African American teachers and counselors were less likely than whites to discourage African American students' aspirations, they were under-represented at the high school level. In 1962, only 10 percent of high school personnel were black.[47]

The tracking system had a degree of flexibility, enabling some African American students to pursue academic learning. In 1963, nearly one-quarter of Philadelphia's black high school students followed the college preparatory curriculum. Many secured academic instruction through sheer determination, convincing high school counselors that they could handle difficult courses and working hard to succeed. A handful of public schools, staffed by groups of dedicated teachers and often overseen by African American principals, explicitly challenged the tracking system. At the Chester A. Arthur Elementary School, in South Philadelphia, despite meager financial resources and class sizes averaging thirty-seven pupils per teacher, the African American principal mandated high academic standards and helped the teachers—all but one of whom were black—implement them. By the fifth grade, students recited quotations from William Shakespeare's *Macbeth* and poems by William Butler Yeats and wrote stories and plays of their own. For the students who could not keep up with their peers, the school instituted special reading-adjustment classes in the fourth and fifth grades to give them extra help. Individualized attention helped many students improve their skills markedly; in a matter of months, several jumped from second- to sixth-grade reading levels.[48] Beginning in the mid-1950s, at William Penn High School, from which Corrine Elkins graduated despite her family's difficult circumstances, the black principal, Dr. Ruth Wright Hayre, strengthened the school's academic, vocational, and extra-curricular programs. With Dr. Hayre at the helm, teacher and student motivation improved significantly, students' attendance rates increased, and dropout rates declined.[49] Marcus Foster, another talented African American educator in postwar Philadelphia, worked as a teacher and became a highly esteemed principal and superintendent. One of his students, Edwina Jordan, described her experiences in his class as "fascinating." "I was privileged—and believe me, it was a privilege—to have him as my sixth grade teacher." After Mr. Foster gained a national reputation for his work in Philadelphia, the Oakland public school system recruited him to serve as its first black superintendent.[50]

In some schools, an infusion of outside funds improved the quality of the education African American children received. In the late 1950s and early 1960s, eight impoverished black schools became part of the Great Cities School Improvement Program and received extra funding from the Ford Foundation that was matched by the Philadelphia school district. Educators and white parents in the working-class Kensington neighborhood felt cheated because their schools had equally dismal conditions but did not get funding because Ford awarded grants to the neighborhoods with the lowest income as judged by the number of welfare recipients. The Ford Foundation encouraged teachers to experiment with the teaching of reading and writing, granted funds for school trips and extracurricular activities, and provided equipment and supplies such as filmstrips and projectors, records and record players, tape recorders, textbooks, and library books.[51]

Most schools that served working-class African Americans could not overcome the problems that they faced. Many teachers used their own money to buy supplies, mimeographed assignments to make up for the lack of books, and spent hours outside of the classroom organizing extracurricular activities, supervising students on playgrounds, and giving them individual help with their schoolwork.[52] Yet they could not compensate for their schools' outdated and run-down buildings, huge classes, and lack of academic materials. Students' frequent moves, precipitated by their families' poverty or their mothers' experiences with domestic violence, created extremely high turnover rates that made it very difficult for teachers to teach and for students to learn.[53] Textbooks and readers largely ignored or misrepresented African Americans' experiences. In one history textbook, the section on emancipation depicted newly freed slaves wanting to remain with their masters.[54] Large classes with inexperienced teachers sometimes became rowdy. In 1956, Alice K. Liveright, chair of the Philadelphia Federation of Teachers' professional committee, complained about "classes beyond the teacher's control in which audible comments, continuous extraneous conversation, ridiculing and mimicing [sic] are every day patterns."[55] Many of these classes were taught by the new teachers and substitutes concentrated in poor black districts. In 1956, Benjamin Franklin High School had thirty-seven substitutes on its staff of seventy-five teachers.[56]

Since schools, like public housing, were integral parts of urban neighborhoods, the problems in the communities around them became part of daily life within them. As in many other major cities, youth gangs became a major presence in postwar Philadelphia, and gangs with names such as the Villagers, Top Hats, Exiles, Wards, Black and Tans, and Pandoras roamed the streets in white and black neighborhoods, carrying razors, slingshots, knives, and guns.[57] Vandals damaged school property, students brought knives to school, gangs waited for children after school, and youngsters occasionally beat up teachers.[58] By 1958, ten Philadelphia public schools, white as well as black, had police stationed inside and outside to try to quell the gang violence and vandalism.[59]

A huge number of students responded to the poor quality of their educational experiences by leaving school altogether. Of all the African American students who began school in 1949 and did not transfer, move away, or die, over half of the boys and over one-third of the girls dropped out before high school graduation, more than double the proportions of white students (see Table 4.6). Fully 97 percent of the African American boys and 87 percent of the African American girls who dropped out had failed at least one grade.[60] While the gap between the dropout rates of African American boys and girls was never as high as the gap between African Americans and whites, African American boys' extremely high dropout rates illuminate the unique constraints they faced within and outside of the school system. Eric Schneider's study of low-income

Table 4.6. Dropout Rates for Students Who Enrolled in Philadelphia Public Schools in 1949

Students	Percentage Who Dropped Out
White boys	25
White girls	17
Black boys	52
Black girls	35[a]

Source: Odell, *Educational Survey Report*, 41, 45.

Note: Figures were calculated by excluding those who transferred to private school, moved away, or became incapacitated or died.

[a]The figure for African American girls was calculated by including most of the girls classified as "incapacitated or dead" as dropouts because most of the girls were classified as "incapacitated" because of pregnancy. See Odell, *Educational Survey Report*, 41.

teenage boys in postwar New York City explores how African American boys frequently chafed against the submission required in the public schools, viewing it as one of the many impediments that they faced in their efforts to become men in a racist society. Many young black men found school humiliating and did not believe that education would help them get good jobs in a labor market rife with discrimination.[61]

When Philadelphia educators publicly grappled with the problems African American students faced, they rarely discussed inadequate school funding, overcrowding, or the concentration of inexperienced teachers in poor black districts. Instead, they blamed African American students and their families for the problems in the schools. This viewpoint was encapsulated in a powerful series of front-page articles published in the *Bulletin* in April 1960, which all bore the headline "The Slow Learners." The first installment in the series featured the superintendent of schools, Allen H. Wetter, warning the public of a troubling new situation in the education system. According to a recent study, Wetter explained, one-third of the city's public school students were "culturally handicapped slow learners" who faced great difficulties mastering even the most basic skills necessary for academic learning.[62] The *Bulletin* made it absolutely clear that African Americans made up the majority of this group. Headlines announced "Migration from South Is a Cause of School Problem," and both school authorities and newspaper editors explicitly identified "slow learners" as African American children whose families were newcomers to the city.[63] These "unlovable characters," education officials claimed, had caused a "tragic deterioration of our schools."[64]

In the weeks following Wetter's announcement, educators and journalists engaged in extensive discussions about "culturally deprived slow learners" that absolved the schools of responsibility for educating low-income African American children. In Philadelphia, as elsewhere, they drew on the findings of a large body of liberal social-scientific studies that contradicted prevailing assumptions about the biological inferiority of nonwhite "races" and emphasized that it was the inadequacies of African Americans' families and neighborhoods, not their racial stock or genetic inheritance, that caused them to perform poorly in school.[65] The *Bulletin* observed that education professionals agreed that "pigmentation does not make a slow learner. . . . Slums breed slow learners."[66] While mentally retarded children were born that way, "true slow learners . . . though not mentally defective are, for a variety of reasons, subpar pupils. . . . These children . . . live in Negro ghettos . . . [and] lack a normal family life and a healthy environment in which to grow."[67] Even as educators sought to dissever the assumed ties between innate intelligence and race, their repeated emphasis on African Americans' poor performance in school reinforced long-standing ideas about black students' intellectual inferiority.

Popular depictions of the home as the root of African Americans' educational difficulties echoed and reinforced the growing public outcry about the deficiencies of black single mothers. School authorities conducted a widely publicized study of students' backgrounds that portrayed African American single mothers as incapable of properly raising their children. The study concluded that single-parent family structures impeded children's ability to learn and described many black parents as "indifferent to education."[68] One 1963 *Bulletin* article, titled "Schools Fight Parents Who Retard Pupils," reported that African American mothers even interfered with the progress of the few gifted black students. It featured a seventeen-year-old boy from a "broken home" in North Philadelphia whose mother would not allow him to accept a college scholarship because it would have resulted in a "cut in her relief check, which she could not afford."[69] In subsequent years, the notion that parents were the cause of students' problems would become even more widespread, reinforced by the publicity afforded to two influential national educational studies in the 1960s, one by James B. Conant and the other by James Coleman. While both studies explored a variety of factors that shaped students' achievements, the media coverage emphasized that students' backgrounds were the primary determinant of their educational prospects.[70] Damaging assumptions about African Americans' intellectual inferiority and inadequate family life became so deeply ingrained in both popular culture and educational institutions that many African American women who approached the schools in postwar Philadelphia did not know whom, if anyone, they could trust.[71]

Mothers' Interactions with Educators

When working-class African American women became involved with their local schools, they joined a wide range of liberal and civil rights organizations seeking to improve black children's educational prospects. Although low-income mothers participated in some organized campaigns against racial inequalities in the schools, middle-class African Americans and whites waged most of the formal battles. The oldest black educational advocacy group, Floyd L. Logan's Educational Equality League (EEL), formed in 1932, focused on eliminating racial discrimination in the hiring and placement of faculty, administrators, and board members.[72] In the early 1960s, the EEL expanded its purview, demanding that the schools adopt social studies textbooks that discussed African Americans' struggles and accomplishments and joining the 400 Ministers in challenging the tracking of children in elementary schools.[73] The interracial West Philadelphia Schools Committee, an umbrella organization of religious and civic groups, organized campaigns for school integration and lobbied the board for increased education funding.[74] Grassroots organizations in African American neighborhoods sought new schools, while liberal groups in white neighborhoods campaigned for racial integration.[75] The Teachers Union, which had a strong contingent of African American teachers, lobbied to decrease racial segregation in the schools and to improve the quality of education that African American students received.[76] The Urban League focused on vocational education, ran career conferences, sought rezoning to facilitate school integration, and lobbied for preschool programs and lunchrooms in schools that served large numbers of African American students.[77]

During the 1950s, although the EEL achieved a few significant victories in its attempts to integrate African American teachers and administrators into the public education system, most efforts to enact fundamental changes in the school system failed completely.[78] In 1960, the board published a response to criticism of its integration, tracking, and funding policies that claimed that the "progress of the Philadelphia Public Schools in the integration movement is among the best, if not the best, of those of the great cities of the Nation." Placing the blame for African Americans' low achievement in school on their homes and communities, the board stated that it had found "no evidence to indicate that any groups have been discriminated against or been given inadequate attention in connection with the instructional program."[79] The institutional racism embedded in the public school system and the rhetoric denying responsibility was a northern form of "massive resistance."[80]

Instead of fighting to change school board policies, many working-class African American mothers tried to serve as advocates for their children within the schools themselves. Many women met with teachers and principals to discuss their children's performance, and some attempted to transfer their children to different schools.[81] Fathers usually did not become as deeply involved as mothers in the day-to-day efforts required to facilitate and improve their children's education, but they also placed high value on the pursuit of formal schooling. Men sometimes joined women in their meetings with educators, and they contributed money and encouragement that helped their children succeed at school.

Parents hoping to improve the quality of their children's education found an important crack in the public school system's rigid organization that they could exploit: the school transfer system. Many parents were aware of the substantial disparities between white and black schools as well as the variations among the schools available to African Americans. Those who had children attending good schools tried not to move away, while those unhappy with their local schools sometimes tried to transfer their children to better ones. The Philadelphia system's "open schools" policy allowed students to cross boundary lines and attend any public school in the city that had openings. The board established this policy during the 1930s, before African Americans constituted a substantial proportion of the city's population. Board members never imagined that black parents would try to use the policy to improve their children's educational prospects or that whites would use it to avoid schools with growing numbers of black students.[82]

Although it was difficult for African Americans to secure school transfers, some parents were so dismayed by the quality of the education in their local schools that they made great efforts to get their children into better schools outside of their neighborhoods. The board did not advertise the open schools policy, but information spread through women's community networks. Parents requesting transfers had to apply on designated days each year; late applications were given lower priority.[83] If principals questioned the wisdom of the transfer, they scheduled interviews in which they informed parents of the potential problems they would encounter if their children changed schools, such as the cost of bus fare and the need for supervision at lunch. Parents had to convince principals that they could afford to pay the 15 cents for their children to take the bus and that they could arrange proper care for elementary school children at midday. After principals forwarded transfer applications to a central office, authorities granted transfers to a select group. The open schools policy guaranteed transfers to any student who applied to a high school from which their parents or grandparents had graduated, a rule that favored children from established white families. The other students competed in a mysterious way against all of the other applicants in the city for the available spaces. Education authorities never explained the criteria they used in deciding when to grant transfers to students not related to alumni, and they did not publish any statistics about the number of applicants they rejected. Published material stated only that transfers were granted according to the date of application, providing no description of how authorities chose among all of the requests submitted by the deadline. Those not granted transfers were placed on a waiting list that expired at the end of each term, forcing parents to reapply continually if they wished their children to be reconsidered.[84] In the early 1960s, the executive director of the Commission on Human Relations stated tactfully that "although it is very difficult to prove that principals actually discriminate . . . there is certainly not enough being done to dispel the feeling on the part of the Negro community that it is difficult to transfer."[85] Faced with such an opaque and frustrating process, a few parents tried to bypass the system completely by adopting false addresses near the schools that they wished their children to attend.[86]

A surprising number of black parents persisted in using the official channels to secure transfers for their children. Their success reconfigured the racial balance at several Philadelphia schools, although often not in the ways that they had intended. Racial integration in education had long been a contentious issue among African Americans. Some strongly advocated keeping children in schools staffed and attended primarily by other African Americans, believing that only all-black environments were free of racism. Segregated schools provided black teachers with jobs at a time when most white or racially mixed schools would not hire them in large numbers, and some African American parents wanted their children to learn from high-achieving members of their own group. Opponents of segregation, including most civil rights organizations, argued that it reinforced notions of inferiority, particularly since the schools that exclusively served African Americans were almost always underfunded and understaffed.[87]

In postwar Philadelphia, many African American parents who pursued transfers sought to build strong minorities of African American students at schools that had traditionally served whites.[88] School authorities and white parents frequently resisted their attempts, using transfers to create and maintain all-white environments. In 1958, *U.S. News and World Report* described school transfers in Philadelphia as a game of "musical chairs" in which African Americans enrolled their children in white schools with vacancies and whites responded by sending their children to schools that had fewer African Americans or moved to the suburbs to escape racial mixing completely.[89] Still, African American parents continued to pursue school transfers because even the resegregated schools were often an improvement over their previous situations.

By 1962, 6 percent of the public school population—15,309 pupils—had transferred to schools outside of their neighborhoods, and African Americans comprised just over two-thirds (10,633) of these students.[90]

Some parents opted out of the system completely by enrolling their children in one of the city's Catholic schools. In 1961, when 33 percent of Philadelphia's population was Catholic, 36 percent of the city's school children attended Catholic schools.[91] Because Catholic schools did not charge tuition, many were just as overcrowded and underfunded as the public schools in low-income neighborhoods. However, they prided themselves on the discipline and manners that they cultivated in their students.[92] While public schools had to accept all students who lived within their geographic boundaries, Catholic schools could dismiss students who exhibited behavioral or academic problems, allowing them to retain the more compliant students who did not need individual attention to keep up with their peers. Students in Catholic schools wore uniforms, stood up when teachers entered the room, and rarely talked back.[93] Many white parents chose the Catholic system because they valued its discipline. Some also wanted to escape the growing numbers of African Americans in the public schools. Yet African American parents did not allow whites to completely resegregate themselves in the Catholic system. Between 1953 and 1962, the proportion of African American students in parochial schools increased from 4 to 10 percent.[94] By 1969, the student bodies of nineteen Catholic schools in the city were at least 60 percent black.[95]

Like whites, the black parents who transferred their children valued the discipline of Catholic school classrooms and believed that parochial schools offered children a better education. Corrine Elkins came to that conclusion after learning that her local public school was switching to double shifts, a last resort to cope with the overcrowding of elementary schools in poor African American neighborhoods.[96] "That's ridiculous, half a day. . . . They could stay home," she recalled. "They didn't learn anything, so I decided to put them in Catholic school." Mrs. Elkins's sister shared her frustration, so they went together to discuss the situation with their local Catholic priest. Before the priest would agree to the transfer, he required the sisters, who were not Catholic or churchgoers of any kind, to attend religion classes. "So we went," recalled Mrs. Elkins. "We had a good time, arguing with the Catholic brothers. He said, 'You are my two worst students' [laughter]."[97]

Women who pursued school transfers for their children had the self-confidence and resources required to engage in byzantine application processes and to argue their cases in front of principals and priests. Many working-class African American mothers did not feel as comfortable or entitled in educational settings. Most had little formal education themselves. In 1951, at the predominantly black Benjamin Franklin High School in North Philadelphia, 80 percent of the parents had not graduated from high school, and one-third had not completed elementary school.[98] Some mothers did not know that they could try to transfer their children or felt too ashamed to negotiate with educators because of their shabby clothes or lack of literacy. Many women also knew that the system was designed to inhibit rather than encourage their success.

A more common way that black mothers interacted with educators was by meeting with teachers and principals to discuss their children's progress, solve problems, and facilitate student achievement. Despite obstacles, many women felt committed and compelled to engage in such interactions, hoping that their efforts would help their children succeed in school. A 1962 study of Philadelphia Aid to Dependent Children (ADC) recipients—all of whom had two or more children and had received welfare for more than two years—found that 90 percent had had contact with their children's schools on one or more occasions. Two-thirds had either attended at least one parents' meeting or open house or had taken the initiative to schedule a private appointment with teachers.[99] Some mothers looked forward to meeting with teachers. Bell Jackson claimed that she tried to give teachers "as much help as possible, because I know that they're helping my children."[100] Yet many other mothers viewed such interactions as uncomfortable obligations that they endured only for the sake of their children. They found their meetings discouraging, especially when they believed that teachers were blaming them for their children's struggles. Even teachers who sympathized with mothers' predicaments did not bear pleasant news when they discussed children's academic or behavioral problems. Unsympathetic teachers usually communicated with mothers only when their children were failing or misbehaved and then held them accountable for their children's difficulties.[101]

Many mothers found it logistically difficult to meet with teachers. Some never learned about opportunities for meetings because schools used notes as their primary form of communication with parents, and children often tore up the notes because they feared that the meetings would focus on their failures and wrongdoings. Many notices advertising open houses and interview nights never made it home.[102] For mothers who learned of opportunities to get involved, their jobs, their need to care for small children, or their lack of new clothing often impeded their participation.

Mothers who found it difficult or unpleasant to attend teacher conferences or other school functions often adopted a similar approach to their interactions with educators: They went into the schools when teachers called them in for special meetings or when they felt that teachers had done something to harm their children. One-third of the ADC recipients who had contact with schools did so only in response to teachers' requests that they come in to discuss their children's problems.[103] Other mothers confronted teachers and principals after finding out that teachers had made racist remarks to their children, treated them unfairly, or hit them. While mothers generally supported disciplining their own children with spankings, many disapproved of corporal punishment meted out by teachers.[104]

Sometimes mothers' anger at school officials boiled over. In 1963, at Sayre Junior High School, Dolores Watson, a mother of five, met with the vice principal to discuss her twelve-year-old daughter, Bernadette. The vice principal had slapped Bernadette and suspended her from school after she beat up another student and bit the student on the cheek. During the meeting, when the vice principal scolded Mrs. Watson for not disciplining Bernadette, Mrs. Watson became so enraged that she struck the vice principal in the face. One week later, a teacher at Stokely Elementary School complained that when she tried to break up a student fight, a mother of a fourth-grade girl punched her in the neck.[105] The violent confrontations between African American mothers and educators vividly illustrated the deep mistrust and frustration that many African American women felt in their dealings with the schools.

The Educational Dimension of Child Rearing

Mothers' involvement with the schools comprised just one piece of their educational activism. Many viewed their provision of shelter, food, and clothing for their families as a crucial component of their children's abilities to succeed in school. Some mothers lamented their inability to afford the desks, lamps, books, and enrichment activities that they knew would help their children. Mrs. Jackson wished that she could take her son who was "slow with reading . . . more often to places like the museum, and oh, say to the library, [that] would help him a great deal." Unable to afford the transportation costs and admissions fees, Mrs. Jackson strove to serve her children hearty and nutritious meals. "I try to feed them well, anyway," she explained. She took pride in her savvy shopping, which enabled her to serve dinners of "baked meats and vegetables" with jello for dessert.[106]

Mothers often emphasized the moral guidance they provided to their children. They taught their children about the importance of education and encouraged them to pay attention in their classes and to obey their teachers. Many sent their children to Sunday school, modeled good manners and sound values, and taught children to conduct themselves with dignity. Catherine Sanderson tried to attend movies with her son whenever possible, viewing it as an ideal educational opportunity. "I wanted to show him right from wrong," she

A mother helps one of her ten children with homework while her toddler amuses herself at the table in their North Philadelphia home in the 1950s. Temple University Libraries, Urban Archives, Philadelphia, Pa.

said, "so I'd sit in the movies with him, and when I'd come home, I'd teach him and show him what happened to the people that wasn't good, and what happened to the good people." Mrs. Sanderson also believed that physical punishment was a necessary component of good child rearing: "Sometimes you have to spank him, to let him know you love him and don't want him in trouble. You didn't hit him because you was mean to him; you hit him because you wanted him to be good."[107]

One of the most publicly invisible, yet crucially important, contributions that working-class mothers made to their children's education was their provision of shoes and clothing. Many women spent hours perusing church rummage sales and "second hand stores . . . [to] try to get something . . . good and repairable."[108] Maude Seibert described her search for decent secondhand school clothing as a year-round project: "In summertime I'm preparing for the winter—you know, piling up coats and skirts."[109] Marcella Clark, who only had one outfit for each of her children, stayed up late every night doing the laundry so that they could at least wear clean clothes to school each day.[110]

Women made clothing a priority because they viewed it as a public marker of respectability that would improve their families' social standing and help their children remain in school. Women who dressed their children in clean clothes that fit properly and did not have holes or stains countered the growing condemnations of their mothering by showing that they cared properly for their families.[111] They also believed that nice clothing would prevent their children from experiencing social humiliation. Joe Bonds, a thirteen-year-old, explained, "If you don't go dressed right to school . . . the whole class laughs at you—like they was better than you is." Another student, Richard Harris, observed that many students chose not to attend class at all "because they're ashamed of how they're dressed."[112] Recognizing the connection between clothing and social respectability, ADC recipient Harriet Moore searched "to find some little thing bright and new so that kids won't be ashamed to go to . . . school."[113] Another mother, Rossalyn Dickenson, hoped that fashionable clothes would enable her daughters to join the popular "clique."[114]

The run-down and dangerous neighborhoods in which many working-class families lived made women's efforts to get their young children to school safely a major challenge. Elementary school children usually walked to and from school twice each day because their schools did not have lunchrooms.[115] With the city not providing adequate streetlights, crossing guards, stop signs, or recreation areas, many women feared that their children would get hit by cars on busy streets or get injured in the abandoned cars and dilapidated buildings that became their playgrounds.[116] Gang members hanging out on street corners sometimes targeted children on their way to and from school, demanding money and threatening to beat them up if they did not bring cash the next day.[117] Some mothers tried to accompany young children to school, but those who had jobs or other responsibilities had to devise alternative strategies. Some let their children walk to school alone, teaching them the route and instructing them not to talk to strangers on the way. Others arranged for older siblings, neighbors, friends, husbands, or boyfriends to accompany them. At lunchtime and after school, they enlisted various combinations of friends and family members to supervise their children. Janet Beauford, a seamstress, sent her children to her sister's house for lunch every day. Beverly Jordan, who worked at a coat factory, sent her daughter to stay with the woman who lived in the next-door apartment. Grandmothers looked after several children at once, and un-employed husbands sometimes came home to stay with their kids.[118] Mothers who could not rely on friends or relatives for help had to leave their children unattended. Corrine Elkins experienced tremendous stress because "I didn't have baby-sitters or anything, so they had to get left in the house by them-selves." "I did a lot of praying," she recalled. "I really did."[119]

Mothers of teenagers developed gender-specific strategies to protect their children. Boys, who were most at risk of dropping out of school, were often tempted and threatened by the youth gangs in their neighborhoods. Many mothers tried to secure help from their children's fathers, hoping that male guidance and discipline would convince their sons to stay in school. Loretta Larson attributed her sons' successful pursuit of their education to her husband, who kept a firm watch over the boys and threatened to physically punish them if they joined gangs.[120] Catherine Sanderson, who shouldered the responsibility alone, forced herself to stay up late with her son, despite being exhausted from her full day of work at home and at her job. She played cards with her son at night, believing that keeping him occupied would help him stay away from gangs and enable him to remain in school until he graduated.[121]

Although the large numbers of boys who dropped out of school received the most public attention, girls' high dropout rates also worried their moth-ers. Philadelphia had several girl gangs; however, mothers' concerns for their daughters centered mostly on pregnancy and sexual violence. Many girls felt threatened by the street and bar culture in their neighborhoods. In 1961, a group of girls who attended West Philadelphia High stated that they feared walking home from school because "men and corner loungers molest us as we pass."[122] Mothers worried about assaults from strangers as well as consensual relationships with men that would result in their daughters getting pregnant. The Board of Education required pregnant students to leave school when they were starting to "show" at four months. They could return to school three months after they gave birth if they could prove that they had found someone to care for their infants. The schools did not have programs to assist mothers who wished to resume their education, and so, overwhelmed by the challenges of early parenthood, which were exacerbated by the stress of poverty, many young women never returned to school.[123] In the late 1950s and early 1960s, nearly half of all the girls who dropped out left school because they got pregnant, and more than 10 percent of the African American girls who started high school did not graduate because of pregnancy.[124]

The truncation of pregnant daughters' schooling disappointed mothers who believed that African American men's limited employment prospects made it

West Philadelphia High School at 48th and Walnut Streets. Young women feared for their safety walking to and from school. Temple University Libraries, Urban Archives, Philadelphia, Pa.

essential for African American women to acquire the tools to become financially self-sufficient. Yet the inferior conditions and invidious tracking system that young African American women encountered in the schools and the racial and sex discrimination they faced in the labor market prevented many of them from developing meaningful and attainable future goals that provided them with a strong motivation to avoid getting pregnant.[125] Most lacked access to contraception, which the government did not distribute to poor single African American women until the 1960s, when some federal and state policy makers began to enact policies aimed at halting their "excess reproduction."[126] In the 1950s, Edwina Jordan recalled, "Most black women did not know where to go and get" contraception; "I . . . think the white women did, but we didn't."[127] Some mothers taught their daughters to exercise great caution around men in the hopes of ensuring they would not become pregnant before they were grown. Joan Park recalled her mother warning her to stay away from boys because she would get pregnant if a boy so much as looked up her skirt. Her mother did not allow her to date and strongly discouraged even casual socializing with men, except at church.[128]

Mothers viewed summer vacation as a particularly vulnerable time for all of their children. Although many teenagers wanted summer jobs, the city's tight labor market for youth made employment extremely difficult to find, even for whites. In 1959, only one in every twenty-five students in Philadelphia between the ages of fourteen and eighteen successfully secured a summer job.[129] The city provided a few programs for children in local public parks and playgrounds, but it remained difficult for many mothers to find regular supervision. Unable to afford child care, some women sent their children to stay with southern kin.[130] Mrs. Jordan recalled, "In the summer, I was sent back down to my grandmother's, which is typically what was done by most people who had family in the South." Mothers relied on a southern "grandmother or an aunt or a cousin who was older . . . who ended up watching the kids."[131] Those who could not call on southern kin often tried to cobble together assistance from friends and relatives who lived nearby.[132]

Not all mothers managed to ensure that their children received adequate supervision. Some women could barely care for themselves because they suffered from severe health problems, drug addictions, alcoholism, domestic abuse, or mental illness. Others held one or more low-wage, physically demanding jobs that absorbed their time and energy. Working long shifts or double shifts impeded women's efforts to get their children to school, provide after-school care, prepare nourishing meals, and keep their households running efficiently. Single mothers found it particularly difficult. "The job I had was fascinating," Mrs. Elkins recalled; "you could work a lot of overtime there, so it was great." Yet the years of working long hours took its toll on Mrs. Elkins's family life. "There was nobody around" to look after the children, she explained. "That left those kids to raise themselves."[133]

Some women chose to receive welfare instead of taking jobs that would interfere with their parental responsibilities. Believing that they would not be able to perform all the labor required to properly raise and educate their children while holding the demanding, low-paid jobs to which they were confined, they used welfare to enable them to focus their energies on their children. Althea Combs, who received ADC benefits, described welfare as "a lesser evil than working and not giving proper care to the children."[134] Eleanor Allen agreed. In 1952, she faced a wrenching situation when her husband died suddenly. Like many other low-wage workers, Mr. Allen's job as a garbage collector did not provide Mrs. Allen with a pension, leaving her with no source of financial support after his death. Mrs. Allen, who prided herself on her work ethic, described her reluctant decision to seek welfare as one integrally connected to her strong desire to see every single one of her twelve children graduate from high school. She believed that they would not succeed at school without having her at home to wash clothes, cook meals, and supervise them at lunch and after school. Mrs. Allen received ADC until her youngest child reached the seventh grade, when she started working as a janitor at a nearby school. She chose the job because it enabled her to work in the early mornings and afternoons and still come home for her children's lunch and dinner.[135]

Like Mrs. Allen, many ADC recipients described their reliance on welfare as a sacrifice they made for the good of their children. While they did not believe that they would achieve upward mobility themselves, they hoped that welfare would enable them to provide their children with opportunities to achieve the educational credentials that they lacked. Many spoke disparagingly of welfare as a future choice for their children, insisting that they received ADC precisely to ensure that their children would avoid a similar fate. Josie Donnor explained that she certainly "wouldn't want" her children to rely on welfare, noting that "public assistance is a help but no pleasure."[136] When asked if she thought her children would turn to welfare, Annie Hite responded, "Unless there are no jobs in the world, they won't. . . . They don't want it and I don't want it."[137] Through their reliance on welfare, mothers sought to ensure that their children would avoid the humiliation and deprivation that life on public assistance entailed.

Neighborhood Activism as Educational Activism

Working-class African American mothers identified intimate connections between housing, health, and education that they sought to address by improving the communities in which they lived. They conducted some of this work in local block groups and churches, both of which offered a range of community services. Block group members believed that their "tot lots" and other neighborhood improvement projects would protect children from injuries and gang violence. Many large African American churches had community centers or gymnasiums that offered recreational activities for youth on weekends and after school. Some large churches provided scholarships for high-achieving youth, summer church schools, and day care centers to ensure that young children received proper care. Through block groups and churches, women worked to create social conditions conducive to African American children's pursuit of education.[138]

Some working-class African American women joined Home and School Associations to improve the conditions in their local schools and to address the problems that they encountered in their neighborhoods. In 1956, the directory of the Wharton Centre, a social settlement that served African Americans, listed eighteen Home and School Associations in the four North Philadelphia wards it served.[139] Records have survived from two associations whose membership included a critical mass of low-income African American mothers. They functioned in the mid-1950s at the Nathaniel Hawthorne and William M.

Meredith elementary schools in South Philadelphia and were initiated by field-workers on the staff of the United Neighborhood Association (UNA), a settlement house and community service organization.[140]

African American women's Home and School Associations were part of the citywide Home and School Council, an umbrella organization run by white middle-class mothers who had school-age children. The council coordinated projects and held an annual banquet, which was segregated until 1953. African American mothers sent delegates from their groups to attend the banquet and participated in workshops, gestures that demonstrated their commitment to their children's education to their white peers. White middle-class mothers organized donations of clothing, shoes, and canned goods for schools in low-income neighborhoods, but rarely worked together with African American women as coequals to address the specific problems black children faced in the schools.[141] In Philadelphia, as in other cities, the Home and School Council insisted that parents work with the schools as "partners" rather than "adversaries." The council tacitly supported Add Anderson's policies limiting expenditures on the schools and segregating black children in inferior ones; its bylaws prohibited members from opposing the board on any matter.[142] With such a conservative orientation, African American women recognized that the citywide council would rarely address their concerns.

Women forged more productive relationships with the field-workers from the UNA. In 1951, the UNA had three full-time field-workers on staff, two men and one woman, two of whom were white and one of whom was black. The field-workers held bachelor's degrees and sometimes worked in conjunction with college students pursuing internships. Although field-workers recruited members for Home and School Associations and helped coordinate meetings, they tried to encourage group members to develop their leadership capabilities and determine their own agendas. The UNA summed up its approach by explaining that field-workers were not supposed to provide "social aid" to low-income neighborhoods; "but rather the neighborhood, with guidance, becomes its own social aid."[143] A few women recognized that field-workers could serve as effective advocates outside the school system. After recounting their personal and financial problems to field-workers, they convinced the workers to put in a good word for them at the welfare department or other social service agencies.

When establishing Home and School Associations, the UNA field-workers first had to secure the support of principals. When a field-worker approached the principal at the Nathaniel Hawthorne Elementary School, the principal told him that a parents' group at the school had failed in the past and the mothers would not be able to organize effectively. The worker wrote in his notes that the principal tried to discourage him by warning that "because these people can't read or write and they feel their clothing is inadequate, they will not attend meetings." When the worker spoke with local women, they blamed the principal's prejudices for their problems organizing a mothers' group. One mother told the staffer that the principal "thinks Negroes in this area . . . don't have any community interest, and cannot see any further than they are at the present." She believed the school needed a "strong Negro principal" who had faith in, and would work cooperatively with, local parents.[144]

When field-workers turned their attention to recruiting members for Home and School Associations, they learned about the major obstacles that working-class African American women had to overcome to join neighborhood associations. Organizers began by enlisting one or two women already recognized as community leaders and bringing these women with them to canvass the neighborhood, knocking on doors and asking others to join the group. More than half of the neighborhood women they spoke with expressed support for the idea of a Home and School Association, but stated that they could not attend meetings because of their jobs or their need to care for small children. Several women promised to attend the first meeting, but did not show up. When the UNA staffer met women who harbored great hostility toward the schools, he tried to convince them that joining a Home and School Association would enable them to improve the quality of their children's education.[145]

That each Home and School Association managed to recruit a core group of six to fourteen women who regularly attended meetings and twenty to forty others who helped with or attended events attests to some working-class African American women's strong commitment to working collectively to facilitate their children's education in spite of the severe problems that they faced. Over the course of the school year, members of Home and School Associations sometimes discussed being so poor that they found it difficult to get enough to eat. A few faced threats of eviction from their homes, and several had been deserted by their husbands or had suffered from domestic violence. Many women attended meetings after spending all day at their jobs, and some participated while coping with health problems or caring for family members with chronic illnesses. During Mary Shepard's tenure as president of the Hawthorne group, she cared for her nine children, sued her mentally ill husband for child support in the domestic relations court, and engaged in a struggle to obtain welfare benefits. That so many women like Mrs. Shepard took such an active role in organizing parents suggests that they experienced a rare sense of collective power in Home and School Associations that they treasured. Mothers believed that they could achieve goals as a group that they could not achieve as individuals and felt that the sacrifices they made to be part of their associations were worth the cost. Even the Hawthorne principal ultimately acknowledged their accomplishments, informing them at one end-of-year meeting that they had worked hard and had "good ideas."[146]

Because women who joined Home and School groups overcame significant obstacles to participate in their associations, they frequently became angry and frustrated when the other mothers in their neighborhoods did not make similar efforts to attend.[147] The cleavages and alliances within working-class African American communities were dynamic and complex, shifting according to the issue at hand. Distinctions between long-standing residents and new arrivals, the solidly working-class and the very poor, drug users and nonusers, drinkers and teetotalers, welfare recipients and the steadily employed, churchgoers and nonchurchgoers were frequently blurred. Employed residents gossiped about welfare recipients on the street, but formed bonds with them at church. Long-standing residents were sometimes suspicious of recent migrants, but cultivated relationships with them in community organizations such as block groups. In Home and School Associations, women mingled regardless of their employment histories, migration status, or recreational pursuits, aligning themselves in opposition to their neighbors who they believed did not exhibit a similar commitment to their children's education.[148]

Although Home and School members criticized mothers in their communities who did not participate in their educational organizing, they were far less contemptuous of men for not joining their organizations. When a field-worker asked one group whether they wished to include men in their meetings, the women stated emphatically that they did not. Following a long tradition of women's collective organizing, they believed that they had a special responsibility for promoting health, well-being, and education in their communities.[149] They told the staffer that their husbands and boyfriends would not attend meetings because they were "all tied up with working, and afterwards attending or watching on TV the baseball game." Women did not interpret men's lack of participation as a sign of their lack of commitment to their children. They emphasized that they would call on men to play auxiliary roles such as building tables for bake sales or lemonade stands.[150] In the same way that mothers took charge of their children's daily activities but valued and relied on fathers' contributions of child care, money, and discipline, they encouraged and expected men to support their collective educational organizing while keeping their associations under their control.

The Hawthorne and Meredith groups engaged in some of the same kinds of school-based activities pursued by white middle-class Home and School organizations, recruiting room mothers and holding hot-dog sales, bake sales, and chicken dinners to subsidize school trips and help purchase musical instruments.[151] However, in sharp contrast to white middle-class Home and School

Associations, they directed a great deal of their energy toward their neighborhoods. Regarding unsafe streets as a major impediment to their children's school attendance, they sought assistance directly from the city, hoping that Mayor Clark's liberal civil rights agenda would address their concerns. In 1953, the Hawthorne Home and School Association went to the mayor's office to request a traffic light for their neighborhood; several members arranged to leave their jobs early to attend the meeting. When the city denied this request, the group asked for a crossing guard.[152] The Meredith Home and School group also wanted a crossing guard, and when the city did not provide one, the mothers organized their own student safety patrol. Through biweekly cookie sales, they raised money to provide student volunteers with bright raincoats to wear while helping younger children cross busy streets.[153] The inability of the mothers at Meredith and Hawthorne to secure crossing guards and traffic lights for their neighborhoods served as a vivid example of city Democrats' resistance to the demands of working-class African American families. It is difficult to imagine that wealthy white mothers would have encountered such difficulties trying to protect their children.

Working-class African American mothers' Home and School organizations addressed the connections between health, housing, child care, and education. They strongly supported the government's provision of public housing; some mothers even joined committees attempting to influence its location.[154] One group sent a delegate to a Health and Welfare Council meeting to discuss the need for licensed day care facilities in their neighborhood. Some Home and School meetings addressed health issues. Mothers invited speakers to give presentations about such subjects as "Food and Finance," in which they discussed the struggle to prepare nutritious foods on low budgets and brought in medical professionals to show films about diseases such as cancer and tuberculosis, followed by question periods and discussions.[155] By inviting professionals to talk to their groups, they sought information that would enable them to create healthy and safe households that would improve their children's abilities to succeed in school.

Home and School Associations sought to forge more cooperative relationships with the police department. In private, many mothers were suspicious of police officers. At one meeting, they complained bitterly about the sergeant at 12th and Pine Streets who "yanks kids around" unnecessarily and engaged in conduct that was "rough and abusive to women." Yet by holding formal meetings with authorities who dealt with juvenile crime, mothers tried to ameliorate the adversarial relationship between law enforcement officials and their community. In the meetings, by sharing with authorities their concerns about gangs and discussing their own efforts to eradicate youth violence and vandalism,

mothers challenged the prevalent assumption that their neglect of their children encouraged criminal activities. Explaining how their families suffered
from the violence in their communities, they exposed the falsity of the premise
that white people were the primary victims of African American gangs and
youth crime.[156] Mothers refrained from discussing the police's notorious and
long-standing sexual abuse of African American women, but they underscored
the pervasive sexual violence in their neighborhoods by recounting incidents in
which their daughters had been raped or threatened by men.[157] Decades before feminist activists would draw public attention to rape and harassment,
working-class African American women informed law enforcement officials
that sexual violence should be taken seriously and constituted a serious and
punishable crime.[158]

Home and School group members sometimes came into conflict with field-
workers regarding the wide scope of their activities. When the Hawthorne
mothers wanted to write a letter supporting black city councilman Raymond
Pace Alexander's efforts to integrate Girard College, the UNA staffer agreed,
although he made them first check with the citywide Home and School Council
to make sure that the action was acceptable. The citywide body refused to take a
similar position, but allowed the group to write the letter.[159] The staffer proved
less flexible when the group sought to pursue activities that he believed lacked
an educational focus. Despite his stated commitment to letting mothers control
the organization, he found it difficult to cede authority completely, especially
when he did not agree with his group's choice of issues to address. The staffer
went so far as to convince the mothers not to organize a campaign to lobby the
state to close a local taproom because he did not believe that the issue was
appropriate for a Home and School Association. The mothers viewed ridding
the streets of the men and women who congregated outside taprooms, goading
and harassing passersby, as an integral part of their efforts to create safe streets
for their children's walk to school. Getting rid of the taproom would have also
helped prevent teenage children from frequenting it instead of going to school.
The worker told the group to form a separate organization to address the
problem. Three years later, in 1956, when he retired from his position, he
lamented the fact that the mothers still insisted on addressing community
issues that he believed did not belong in a Home and School Association. "The
group itself," he acknowledged, did "not see it this way." Mothers placed neighborhood issues at the center of their collective educational work because they
believed their children could not succeed in school if their neighborhoods were
unsafe and unhealthy.[160]

Working-class African American women's educational activism belied public
claims about their lack of interest in their children's schooling. Unable to sig-

nificantly alter school policies that discriminated against their children, mothers focused their attention on battles they believed they had some chance of winning. Although they agreed with scholars and public officials who charged that living in poverty hurt their children's chances of succeeding in school, they insisted that the problem stemmed not from their attitudes or family structures, but from government authorities' refusal to provide them with police protection, crossing guards, stop signs, streetlights, and well-located public housing.

Working-class African American women's deep and long-standing belief in the value of education inspired them to labor to facilitate their children's schooling in the face of massive resistance from education authorities. Although many teachers and principals strove to provide good instruction, a few schools stood out for encouraging African American students' achievement, and a significant contingent of black students overcame obstacles and secured college preparatory diplomas, in no other public institution did authorities engage in such explicit racial and class discrimination in their distribution of resources as they did in the public schools. Black children, and boys in particular, dropped out at extremely high rates after being confined mainly to nonacademic programs in the most underfunded and overcrowded schools in the city. With public schools failing to help most black students achieve academically, and school authorities blaming mothers for their children's problems, the education system played a major role in the gendered construction and maintenance of African American urban poverty.

In the face of pervasive institutional resistance, working-class African American women tried to take advantage of the opportunities in the education system and work around its edges to obtain decent schooling for their children. Belying white educators' harmful assertions that they were hostile or indifferent, many mothers met with teachers and principals and sometimes engaged in complicated negotiations to secure school transfers. Outside of school, mothers tried to obtain proper food, clothing, and child care so that their children could learn. Some resorted to welfare, viewing their reliance on public assistance as a way to help their children stay out of trouble and succeed in school. In Home and School Associations, women demanded that the city provide safe streets and decent housing to enable their children to get to school safely and pursue their studies until high school graduation. Without the political power and public resources required to fundamentally transform the schools or the labor market, working-class African American mothers tried to make the best of the educational opportunities that they had to secure brighter futures for their children.

CHAPTER FIVE

A Hospital of Their Own

In the early 1960s, Edwina Jordan lived in South Philadelphia with her young son and worked for the city water department. Mrs.
Jordan frequently worked "sixteen hours" a day while running her household
single-handedly. "You're trying to figure out, okay, if I pay the rent, how am I
paying the baby-sitter; if I'm paying the baby-sitter, how am I buying food. . . .
Then you've got all the other stress of raising, trying to educate . . . and on top of
it all, my son was hyperkinetic." Mrs. Jordan's efforts to care for her son were
complicated by her own health problems. Each month, she had a week of severe
menstrual cramps that forced her to spend "the first two to three days" of her
period in bed.

When Mrs. Jordan's son was toddler, she discovered that she was pregnant. "I
realized I could not handle two children. . . . One would have been two, two-
and-a-half, and the other would have been newborn. . . . I guess, maybe, if you
are home, and you don't have the stress or the worry or the frustration of being
their only support or the only one who's taking care of them, that may make a
difference." Lacking the institutional and social resources that she believed she
needed to raise a second child, Mrs. Jordan "ended up having an abortion."
Although abortion was illegal in Pennsylvania, she learned from a friend that a
woman in her neighborhood would perform one for a fee. The woman used a

"coat hanger" to induce a miscarriage. "I didn't really feel it," Mrs. Jordan recalled. "It was like a pinprick." Hours later, Mrs. Jordan began to suffer from complications. "I ended up in the hospital," she explained, "because all of the placenta didn't come down." The hospital admitted her and sent her to the surgical ward, where she underwent a dilation-and-curettage (D&C) procedure.[1]

Working-class African American women spent a great deal of time dealing with their own health problems as well as those confronted by their children, spouses, parents, and friends. Vulnerable to illness because of poverty and racism, and more likely than men to need medical attention at a young age, many women had very clear ideas about the kind of health care they required. While the National Association of Colored People (NAACP) sought to increase the numbers of black professionals hired in white hospitals and the Urban League tried to provide more women with prenatal care, working-class African American women focused their attention on the quality of the treatment they received from their local health care providers. They did not want to feel like "charity cases" when they sought medical care and resented receiving sub-standard treatment because of their race, marital status, or inability to pay. Many felt most comfortable at institutions that served and employed signifi-cant numbers of African Americans, particularly those that exhibited careful consideration for both their medical needs and their personal dignity.

Since most working-class African American women did not have health insurance and could not afford to visit private doctors, they invested their high expectations in Philadelphia's hospitals. Many became astute consumers of medical care and made carefully calculated decisions when choosing a hospital. Philadelphia's small African American hospital was rarely an option for them because it did not have the space or the resources to accommodate the large numbers of African Americans in the city who needed care.[2] White voluntary hospitals (private nonprofit institutions) gave free care to poor patients, but frequently provided them with second-rate treatment. At Philadelphia General Hospital (PGH), the city's public hospital, some doctors and nurses harbored racial prejudices and mistreated African American patients. However, the pub-lic hospital often responded positively to African American women's needs and adhered to policies that afforded them greater respect and privacy than they received in other institutions. Many working-class African American women chose PGH over all of the other hospitals in the city because they were attracted to its philosophy and its services.[3] They developed a deep trust of PGH and encouraged their friends and family to join them in seeking its care. In the process, they cultivated a strong sense of black ownership of the public hospital.

Of all the public institutions in postwar Philadelphia, PGH commanded the most widespread public respect and support for the services that it provided to the poor. The hospital had a prestigious professional staff and a philanthropic mission that Philadelphians from a range of backgrounds appreciated. Medical and nursing students competed fiercely to train at PGH, eager to gain exposure to the hospital's world-renowned staff and its patients' wide range of medical conditions. Civil rights activists faulted PGH for not hiring enough African American professionals, but they joined labor unions in recognizing the importance of the hospital's commitment to its service workers. Even when critics charged that PGH's policies encouraged African American women's immorality, no one suggested that the city should close or cease adequately funding the hospital. While few felt much affection for the meagerly funded welfare department or the city's increasingly decrepit and dangerous public housing, a public hospital with a national reputation that substantially helped low-income patients and workers commanded a broad range of public support.

Gender, Race, Poverty, and Health

Health problems were a major concern for working-class African American women. In the 1950s, the average life expectancy for African Americans was sixty-three compared to seventy for whites. Rates of premature birth and infant mortality were twice as high among African Americans as among whites, and African Americans were twice as likely as whites to die from tuberculosis, a contagious disease whose ravages were closely correlated with poverty, especially overcrowded housing and inadequate nutrition.[4] Within every class and racial group, health problems took a particular toll on women, who were especially susceptible to illness at a young age and usually took responsibility for caring for sick friends and family members.[5]

Working-class African American women identified direct connections between their poverty and poor health. Catherine Sanderson collapsed after years of overwork, low wages, and poor nutrition, and Bell Jackson's newborn baby contracted pneumonia because she could not afford to heat her apartment.[6] In turn, health problems frequently exacerbated women's poverty by preventing them from earning a living. Mrs. Sanderson had to quit her job after she got sick, and Corrine Elkins nearly lost hers because of heavy bleeding caused by her endometriosis, which returned after she stopped having children. "The blood flow was so heavy that . . . I was afraid things would just get out of hand," Mrs. Elkins recalled, explaining why she missed work when her condition flared up. When her supervisor told her that her "absenteeism had to stop," she resorted to drastic measures. The next time she began to bleed at her job, Mrs. Elkins "let it flow." She "sat on the toilet and the whole toilet turned red." Only by humiliating herself by showing her supervisor the bloody toilet bowl did Mrs. Elkins receive permission to take time off to seek medical treatment. Women who did not have Mrs. Elkins's confidence or an understanding boss frequently were fired when health problems interfered with their job performance.[7]

Health care providers could address the medical but not the social causes of women's illnesses. Doctors had a great deal to offer Mrs. Elkins: after a hysterectomy, she was able to resume full-time employment. Yet for many others, the results were more mixed because their health problems were inextricably linked to their poverty. Doctors could not provide much assistance to Mrs. Sanderson, whose sickness was caused by overwork and poor nutrition. Her doctor vouched for her need for welfare, but he could not provide her with the assistance she needed to address the causes of her illness. For women like Mrs. Sanderson, sustaining good health required not only medical care but also affordable housing, adequate nutrition, decent wages and working conditions, day care, and protection from domestic violence.

Creating a Black Hospital at PGH

Like other Philadelphians, most working-class African Americans viewed their choice of health care providers as an extremely important decision. The long history of racism in the medical profession made many African Americans wary of white health care professionals. From the nineteenth-century use of slaves and free blacks as subjects for dissection and medical experimentation to twentieth-century tragedies such as the Tuskegee Syphilis Study and the persistent sterilization abuse of poor black women, African Americans had good reason to look upon the medical profession with suspicion and mistrust.[8] Many working-class African Americans had received discriminatory treatment from white doctors and other medical professionals who had either refused to accept them as patients or had provided inadequate and demeaning care.[9]

In the postwar period, Philadelphia gained a national reputation for providing first-rate medical care; one historian has suggested that the city shed its long-standing reputation as a "city of homes" and became a "city of hospitals."[10] Working-class African Americans could seek care at one of the city's sixty-seven voluntary hospitals, which were supported by a combination of federal, state, local, and private funds, including payments from insurance companies. Voluntary hospitals had once mainly served poor people, but in the 1950s, as new technology attracted wealthier patients to hospitals, the growing number of insured patients became voluntary hospitals' primary clientele.[11] African Americans could also receive care at PGH, the public hospital, which was funded almost entirely by the city. Established in 1732 as the Philadelphia Almshouse,

Philadelphia General Hospital's administration building. Temple University Libraries, Urban Archives, Philadelphia, Pa.

PGH originally functioned as a hospital, insane asylum, and poorhouse. A century later, it moved from Center City to the Blockley township (which became West Philadelphia), where it earned the affectionate nickname, "Old Blockley." In 1920, the almshouse portion of the institution moved to a new location, and PGH began to focus exclusively on providing health care. In addition to city employees and other special cases, PGH only admitted medically indigent patients, treating one-third of all patients in the city who could not afford to pay for their care.[12]

African Americans who sought health care at PGH understood that it was one of the best public hospitals in the country. The hospital's twenty-seven buildings on twenty-six acres of land seemed outdated when compared to many voluntary hospitals' modern high-rise buildings, but PGH attracted a highly esteemed staff and had a reputation as a first-rate research and teaching institution.[13] The 1951 City Charter created a board of trustees, appointed by the mayor, who oversaw and managed the hospital. The trustees appointed an executive director who was responsible for the hospital's daily administration. Both the trustees and the executive director served under the city health commissioner, who oversaw PGH's expenditures and budget appropriations. Until the late 1950s, when the city adopted a controversial plan that contracted out care to local medical schools, patient care at PGH was run by "chiefs" of its medical services, prestigious specialists from around the country who donated their time to work at the hospital.[14] While few professionals felt attracted to stigmatized institutions such as the welfare department, medical and nursing students coveted positions at PGH because of its world-class doctors and opportunities to work with an enormous range of health conditions. In 1960, the hospital received over 450 applications for its 90 internship positions.[15] Nurses explained that "you had to be very scholastically skilled" to work at PGH and that the hospital provided such "good training" that students "could get a job anywhere" after they finished their education.[16] In the 1950s, PGH periodically received unflattering press coverage in sensationalist news articles about the overcrowding in its psychiatric and tuberculosis wards and the hospital's treatment of large numbers of unwed mothers. Yet the staff remained extremely loyal to PGH, and even Philadelphians who did not use or work at the hospital often expressed their appreciation for its services.[17] Stephanie Stachniewicz, who attended the PGH training school for nurses in the late 1940s, recalled, "When I was in the taxicab coming into training," the cabdriver said, " 'Oh, you're going to Philly General. That's a good place.' This was almost like second nature. Everyone was proud of this hospital."[18]

Philadelphia General Hospital maintained its high stature in the city because municipal authorities responded positively to its significant financial demands and provided it with adequate funding. The task was not easy because PGH was at a major financial disadvantage when compared to voluntary hospitals. While voluntary hospitals could count on payments from health insurers, most PGH patients lacked insurance and could not afford to pay for their medical care. Voluntary hospitals also benefited substantially from the 1946 federal Hill-Burton Act, which provided federal funds for the survey and construction of hospitals, and they received support for their care of the poor from the state government and the Philadelphia United Fund. Until 1959, when PGH finally received state funding for its treatment of low-income patients, the city had to fund the hospital almost single-handedly. The hospital was never entirely financially sound. Several departments periodically struggled when municipal budgets did not cover their patient loads, and the tuberculosis and psychiatric wards were overcrowded because the state shirked its responsibility for paying for treatment of these cases. Still, Mayor Clark made improvements at PGH a central campaign promise. Throughout the 1950s, the city allocated sufficient funds not only to meet the basic needs of most specialties but also to support modernization and expansion. Solid financial backing enabled PGH to retain its reputation as one of the best public hospitals in the nation.[19]

Very few African American doctors and graduate nurses worked at PGH, but their absence did not serve as a deterrent for African American patients because none of the city's major hospitals employed a significant number of black professionals. In the 1940s and 1950s, to protest the virtual ban on the employment of African American doctors and nurses in white hospitals, the Philadelphia NAACP joined in the national NAACP's vigorous hospital integration campaign.[20] In 1942, in response to pressure from the Philadelphia NAACP's Health Committee and African American churches, PGH's nurse-training school admitted its first black student. Four years later, PGH hired its first black intern. In 1953, city Democrats agreed to require medical schools that trained their students at PGH to build equal opportunity into their affiliation plans, a measure that produced small yet symbolically important results in diversifying the professional staff at the hospital. The greatest successes in staff integration came at the lowest ranks where the principle of equal opportunity in city jobs resulted in PGH's hiring a significant number of African American service workers.[21] Service positions at PGH were unionized city jobs with decent salaries, health insurance, vacations, and job security. With federal legislation preventing voluntary hospital workers from forming unions, comparable positions at voluntary hospitals paid very low wages and had few benefits.[22]

African Americans were much more likely than whites to choose PGH as their hospital. In the early 1950s, only four out of every one thousand whites in Philadelphia sought care at PGH, compared to thirty-five out of every one thousand African Americans.[23] Although whites occupied 61 percent of PGH's 1,970 beds on any given day, they were concentrated in the wards devoted to neurology, psychiatry, rehabilitation, and the treatment of alcoholism; specialties like these could not be found in voluntary hospitals, and such wards had very low turnover rates (see Table 5.1).[24] Working-class whites' minimal use of PGH reflected both their preference for their local hospitals and their desire to avoid seeking care at the public hospital. Many had a strong attachment to the local ethnic or religiously based voluntary hospitals that their families had frequented for many generations. German Americans frequently went to the Lankenau Hospital, Jews to Mount Sinai, and Italian Americans and Irish Americans to Catholic hospitals.[25] Some whites who qualified to receive free care at PGH avoided seeking treatment at the public hospital because they were embarrassed by their inability to pay. The shame they associated with visiting the public hospital was reinforced by publicity for hospital insurance that emphasized that responsible citizens—"real Americans"—were "too proud" to accept free care.[26]

Even though most white voluntary hospitals served poor black people, many African Americans still chose to receive care at the public hospital. In the late

Table 5.1. Percentage of Black Patients on Wards, Philadelphia General Hospital, March 28, 1949, and July 20, 1955

Ward	Percentage Black	
	1949	1955
Hospital average	42	53
Maternity	93	93
Children's medical	75	82
Gynecological	68	81
Children's surgical	36	80
Eye and laryngeal	50	78
Tuberculosis	57	64
Skin and venereal	42	60
Metabolic	38	58
Medical	48	53
Urological	47	52
Surgical	27	50
Orthopedic	22	50
Neurological	31	39
Psychopathic	24	36
Rehabilitation	25	35
Alcoholic	—	28

Source: Kling, Sander, and Sigmond, *Philadelphia General Hospital Survey*, table 40.

1950s, 72 percent of the patients admitted to PGH were African American, and the hospital treated nearly one-third of the city's African American patients.[27] Although it is possible that some African Americans sought care at PGH after voluntary hospitals turned them away, admissions records indicate that most African Americans chose the public hospital first. In 1955, African Americans comprised three-fourths of all walk-in cases at PGH. Only 3 percent of them had been referred by voluntary hospitals; most of the rest approached PGH on their own volition.[28]

African American women were largely responsible for the strong presence of black patients at PGH. Over twice as many black women as black men sought care at PGH: they were 71 percent of the hospital's African American admissions.[29] African American women's use of PGH revolved heavily around gender-specific health concerns such as childbirth, injuries from illegal abortions,

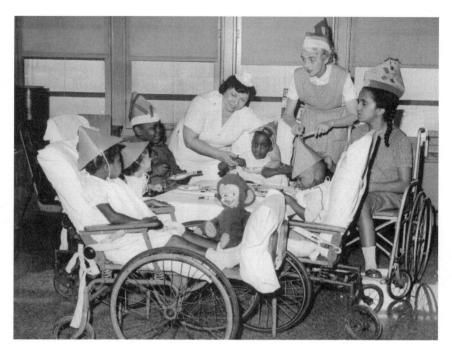

Children in the rehabilitation ward at Philadelphia General Hospital celebrate the Christmas holiday in 1964. Temple University Libraries, Urban Archives, Philadelphia, Pa.

gynecological problems, domestic abuse, and rape. They also tended to shoulder responsibility for securing health care for their children. By 1955, African Americans comprised 81 percent of the hospital's gynecology patients, 93 percent of its maternity patients, 82 percent of the patients in the children's medical department, and 80 percent of the patients in the children's surgical department (see Table 5.1).[30]

Childbirth brought extremely large numbers of African American women to PGH. Between 1931 and 1954, while the number of births in voluntary hospitals doubled, the number at PGH quadrupled, largely because of the increase in the number of African American women choosing to deliver their babies at the public hospital. Between 1946 and 1956, the number of births at PGH increased by 200 percent. By 1960, well over four thousand African American women annually delivered children at PGH, constituting 94 percent of the hospital's births.[31] Although the rising number of births partly reflected the increased birth rate, it also stemmed from African American women's assertive pursuit of PGH's care. Over 50 percent of PGH's obstetrics patients had been admitted to the hospital on at least one previous occasion, an extremely high readmission rate.[32] One 1962 study of pregnant African American women found a "strong attachment to the Philadelphia General . . . on the part of those who use it, because of the generally high regard in which the hospital is held and their own familiarity with it as well as that of friends and relatives."[33] African American women developed similar birthing communities at several voluntary hospitals. Sixty percent of women who gave birth at Temple University Hospital in North Philadelphia were black, and at Pennsylvania Hospital, located in Center City, which had a reputation as a "charity hospital" that welcomed poor patients, African Americans comprised 40 percent of the births. Still, the overwhelming predominance of African Americans among maternity patients at PGH made it seem uniquely their own.[34]

African American women's choice of PGH may have resulted from the hospital's location in West Philadelphia, an area of the city that housed 29 percent of the city's black population. As historian Vanessa Northington Gamble has explained, some hospitals in the United States that served large numbers of African Americans were "demographically determined," meaning that they had originally served whites but turned into black hospitals when African Americans moved into their surrounding areas.[35] In Philadelphia, this label suited Temple University Hospital, which served large numbers of African Americans from its surrounding North Philadelphia community. But PGH was not a demographically determined hospital. In 1957, only 36 percent of the African Americans admitted to PGH came from West Philadelphia. Fifty-two percent lived in North and South Philadelphia, areas of the city with more than adequate voluntary hospitals. Clearly, many African Americans traveled a great distance just to obtain care at PGH.[36]

African Americans' choice of PGH partly reflected the lack of adequately funded private institutions of their own that could accommodate them. Like European immigrants, African Americans established hospitals in the late-nineteenth and early-twentieth centuries to guard against discrimination.[37] Philadelphia's two historically black hospitals, Mercy and Douglass, which merged in 1948 to form Mercy-Douglass, provided important employment and training opportunities for African American doctors and nurses largely excluded from working in the city's white hospitals. Yet Mercy-Douglass could not serve large numbers of African American patients because it only had 104 beds. With Mercy-Douglass able to care for only 5 percent of the African Americans in Philadelphia who needed health care, most had to find other hospitals.[38]

Although Philadelphia's white voluntary hospitals did not exclude African Americans, they seldom made them feel welcome. Many had a long history of racial segregation and discrimination.[39] One 1946 Bureau of Municipal Research study concluded that, "no matter what the emergency," even "well-to-do" African Americans were frequently "unable to obtain adequate medical attention" from voluntary hospitals.[40] With the passage of the Hill-Burton Act, the federal government declined to prohibit racial discrimination in voluntary hospitals, allowing separate but equal hospital facilities.[41] A 1954 study conducted by the American Civil Liberties Union found de facto segregation still in effect in several of the forty-one Philadelphia hospitals that agreed to respond to the survey, and the organization received numerous complaints from African Americans about racial discrimination in hospitals. One such complaint came from Alphonso A. Woods, who charged that the Presbyterian Hospital discharged him against his will when he was vomiting and having bloody stools. He nearly passed out in the cab he took from Presbyterian to PGH.[42]

Philadelphia General Hospital maintained a formal commitment to racial equality that surpassed what most voluntary hospitals offered, but it did not ensure that African American patients would avoid being subjected to racism. The 1951 city charter required the public hospital to enforce a clear non-discrimination policy, and many white doctors and nurses at PGH publicly prided themselves on the "equitable" treatment they provided to all patients.[43] In 1954, one doctor proclaimed that when PGH "doctors or nurses approach the bedside of a patient, they . . . do not see color, race or creed, but only a creature of God in need of care." The hospital, he concluded, "makes all people equal."[44] A white nurse recalled the "marvelous feeling" of working at a public institution like PGH where "we didn't really pay any attention to color."[45]

Yet while white staff members described PGH as a nonracist institution, many black patients held a different view. Marcelle Blackwell almost died from a burst appendix when she was fifteen years old because a doctor at PGH refused to examine her and tried to force her to admit to the possibility of being pregnant. "I can't be pregnant, I'm not married," she protested, feeling insulted since she had been raised to believe that only "bad girls" had sex. When a second doctor came in to assess the situation, the first doctor told him that Miss Blackwell was pregnant even though he had still not examined her. The second doctor performed an exam, found the ruptured appendix, and rushed her to the operating room.[46] In the 1960s, when a mayor's committee interviewed patients at PGH (92 percent of whom were African American), it found that only 37 percent believed that "black people" received better treatment at PGH than at voluntary hospitals.[47] Many African American patients did not believe that the public hospital was free from racism.

What attracted most African American patients to PGH was the hospital's class and gender politics. Sixty-eight percent of the patients interviewed believed that PGH treated "poor people" better than the city's voluntary hospitals.[48] Whenever uninsured patients approached voluntary hospitals, they always faced the prospect of being interrogated about their financial circumstances and denied admission.[49] Ella Maxwell described being loudly quizzed about her welfare status by hospital clerks: "They got to embarrass you. You be sitting on one side of the room . . . a nurse she's way over here on the other side hollering . . . 'What name do the [welfare] check come under?' . . . All of the people sitting around, they hear it. It makes you feel bad."[50] The structure of voluntary hospitals institutionalized such embarrassing treatment. Uninsured patients frequently had to stay in separate charity wards, segregated from those able to pay. Mrs. Maxwell disparagingly remarked, "They treat you like you was on charity, like everybody's supposed to start giving you pieces of bread, bowls of soup."[51]

Philadelphia General Hospital provided all patients with medical care as a right. In addition to treating indigent patients and city employees, an essential component of the hospital's mission was to care for the patients suffering from conditions that other hospitals either refused or lacked the capacity to treat: tuberculosis, alcoholism, psychiatric problems, neurological diseases, and chronic illnesses.[52] While most other public institutions in the city strictly enforced residency requirements, PGH even treated recent arrivals.[53] City employees were treated in separate wards, but everyone else waited in the same lines, stayed in the same wards, and had equal access to the hospital's world-renowned doctors. The hospital's professional staff often boasted that they had no way of knowing the financial status of their patients.[54] Doctors and nurses wore formal attire and addressed every patient, no matter how downtrodden, as "Mr." or "Mrs."[55] Voluntary hospitals "do treat you different" if you are poor, observed Bell Jackson, but "Philadelphia General, they don't treat you too much different than they would a private patient."[56]

Philadelphia General Hospital cultivated a sense of entitlement to services among patients by trusting them and affording them a greater sphere of privacy than did other institutions. When patients first arrived at the hospital, clerks asked only for their age, name, and address before admitting them. Not until after they had been examined and diagnosed did patients have to furnish information about their financial circumstances. In 1960, when the welfare department tried to force PGH to release public assistance recipients' medical information without their consent, the hospital refused to comply, insisting that even the poorest patients deserved medical privacy.[57] Unlike welfare caseworkers, the PGH staff assessed patients' abilities to pay almost solely on the basis of their own descriptions of their financial situations. Admissions personnel routinely checked to make sure that patients did not own property, but they did not conduct extensive investigations into the wages earned by patients or their family members, or require patients to provide documentation of their financial resources, residency, or marital status. Until 1958, PGH charged all patients for care, but, aside from a few crackdowns on delinquent accounts, the hospital put forth little effort to collect the money owed on outstanding bills. In 1958, in recognition of most patients' inability to pay for their care, PGH began to charge fees on a sliding scale based on patients' financial circumstances. PGH charged less than voluntary hospitals did for comparable services and provided half of its care for free.[58]

African American single mothers found PGH a particularly attractive place to receive obstetrical care. Many voluntary hospitals subjected unmarried pregnant women to intrusive and judgmental questioning and reprimands. Mrs. Maxwell recalled nurses chastising her, "hollering . . . 'You pregnant? You pregnant *again?*'"[59] By contrast, PGH maintained a formal commitment to treating single mothers without questioning or punishing them for their sexual behavior. Clerks were instructed not to inquire about women's marital status until after their deliveries, and some of the hospital staff considered it a point of pride that they did not distinguish between single and married mothers in providing treatment.[60] Women responded positively to such policies: In 1957, more than one-third of the women who gave birth at PGH were unmarried mothers.[61]

As African Americans women repeatedly sought care at PGH and recommended the hospital to their family and friends, they created a strong sense of community at the hospital. Half of all patients discharged from PGH had at least one previous admission, and African Americans constituted 81 percent of the readmissions.[62] Many of these African Americans had first sought care at PGH after their mothers, grandmothers, aunts, cousins, and friends introduced them to its services. The women then carried on the tradition at PGH by bringing their friends and other family members to the hospital. With African Americans not only dominating many wards and waiting rooms, but also staffing secretarial, janitorial, and practical-nurse positions, they created a culture at the hospital that made it feel more like a vital part of the black community than like some of the alien or indifferent white-dominated institutions in the city.

In a self-perpetuating cycle, as increasing numbers of African American women and their families received care at PGH, white patients avoided the hospital. Between 1949 and 1955, the proportion of white patients in nearly every department diminished. The decrease was too large to reflect population changes in West Philadelphia. In several of the departments that offered services also found in voluntary hospitals, the decrease ranged from 20 to 40 percent (see Table 5.1).[63] Nathaniel C. Stewart, a PGH pharmacist, used the concept of the tipping point to explain the growing predominance of African

Americans at PGH: "As blacks reach a certain point in a group, whites leave the group."[64]

As African Americans returned to PGH over and over again to seek medical treatment, their confidence in the hospital increased. In the 1960s, three-quarters of the patients stated that even if they had enough money to obtain health care anywhere in the city, they would still choose PGH. Although they considered it "dirtier" than most hospitals, they believed that the care they received from PGH equaled, and sometimes even surpassed, the care they could have obtained at voluntary hospitals.[65] Many expressed a deep trust of the hospital based on their own and their families' past experiences using its facilities and their knowledge that PGH doctors were among the best in the world.[66] No one wanted to feel like a "charity case." Yet while whites associated "charity" and humiliation with the public hospital, many African Americans viewed PGH as one of the few institutions in the city that did not adhere to policies that demeaned them. They chose a familiar hospital that had a community of black patients and a mandate to assist them over more modern and unfamiliar voluntary hospitals that they expected to discriminate on the basis of class, gender, and race.

Selecting Health Care

One of the most striking aspects of working-class African American women's relationship with PGH was that they selectively and self-consciously used the hospital for prenatal care and childbirth in ways that medical personnel did not recommend. Doctors wanted patients to seek regular prenatal care during their pregnancies and arrive in plenty of time to give birth at the hospital when they went into labor. However, many pregnant black women visited prenatal clinics infrequently and chose to wait at home when they went into labor instead of immediately seeking medical treatment. At other public institutions, when women engaged in behaviors that contradicted government authorities' instructions, they faced reprimands or penalties. At PGH, doctors did not refuse to treat patients who disregarded their advice, a policy that solidified patients' sense of entitlement to the public hospital's care.

The most significant difference of opinion between doctors and African American women concerned prenatal care, which became an essential part of obstetrics practice over the course of the twentieth century. In 1919, 15 percent of all pregnant women in Philadelphia sought prenatal care, but in the postwar period, it became much more common, particularly among whites.[67] In 1960, only 4 percent of whites in Philadelphia, but 34 percent of African Americans, had received inadequate prenatal care, which doctors defined as a first prenatal visit in the third trimester or no prenatal care at all.[68] Since the lack of prenatal care was highly correlated with poverty, 67 percent of African American obstetrics patients at PGH had received inadequate prenatal care.[69]

Although medical professionals and health care advocates claimed that inadequate prenatal care caused high rates of infant mortality and prematurity, it is impossible to ascertain the degree to which prematurity was caused by women's lack of prenatal care and the degree to which it was caused by factors unrelated to health care such as dilapidated housing, poor nutrition, excess alcohol consumption, cigarette smoking, and drug use.[70] In 1956, more than half of the mothers who gave birth to premature infants had received no prenatal care, and three out of four had received inadequate care.[71] Yet because prenatal care could not address the adverse effects of racism and poverty, between 1959 and 1964, the proportion of African American women in Philadelphia who obtained inadequate prenatal care decreased from 34 to 30 percent while the black prematurity rate increased from 16 to 17 percent.[72] Still, doctors consistently encouraged women to receive prenatal care, and in 1958, the Philadelphia Urban League (PUL) joined them. Unique among civil rights organizations for its identification of health as a crucial part of the struggle for civil rights, the PUL opened a prenatal clinic in the basement of Ebenezer Baptist Church on Thursday afternoons. The clinic was staffed by volunteers from the Ebenezer Ladies' Auxiliary and physicians, nurses, and social workers from the Hahnemann and Kensington hospitals.[73]

African American women based their decision to avoid prenatal care on their own understanding of its costs and benefits, not on doctors' and activists' recommendations. Even women who had recently migrated from the South usually knew that doctors recommended prenatal care. Yet both new arrivals and long-standing residents often resisted seeking treatment. Their avoidance of prenatal care partly reflected their aversion to the options available to them. Some hospital clinics in the city had a history of racial discrimination. Most clinics were extremely overcrowded and did not have precise appointment schedules. Women showed up on an assigned day but then had to wait their turn to be seen by a doctor. For an average of three hours, they sat on hard wooden benches without reading materials or toys for children.[74] In the 1950s, the city constructed several new public health clinics that offered prenatal care, but many were underutilized because women did not know about their services or did not trust them. Hoping to attract low-income women to the freestanding clinics, the city did not invest in PGH's prenatal clinic, which had the worst conditions of any in the city. Doctors at PGH did not examine women or run tests at their first appointment, leading many patients to believe that their initial visit had provided no tangible benefit (other city clinics examined women on the initial visit, but did not perform tests until the second visit). The fact that PGH's clinic was always filled beyond its capacity, with its staff seeing an average of 125 to 150 patients each day, five days a week, demonstrates that many women were still motivated to obtain prenatal care. However, not surprisingly, over 20 percent of the clinic's patients did not return after their first visit, the highest attrition rate in the city.[75]

Other deterrents to obtaining prenatal care reflected the ordinary conditions of low-income women's lives: employment, poverty, poor health, and responsibility for children. Women with jobs could not afford to miss work, but none of Philadelphia's clinics provided evening or weekend appointments. Unable to afford taxis, many women with health problems could not walk to clinics, even in their own neighborhoods. Mothers found the three-hour waits extremely long because they had to amuse small children in the waiting rooms.[76] Women's attitudes toward their pregnancies also influenced their decisions regarding prenatal care. Those who did not welcome the prospect of having a child were disproportionately represented among those who did not obtain prenatal care because they often tried to ignore or hide their unwanted pregnancies for as long as possible. Many welfare recipients tried to conceal their pregnancies because they feared that their caseworkers would become angry. Teenagers sometimes tried to hide their pregnancies because they knew that they would be forced to quit school once their pregnancies were discovered.[77]

Of all the factors that influenced women's pursuit of prenatal care, the most crucial one was their evaluation of the benefits prenatal care would afford them. Those who sought prenatal care were not necessarily those who were the most excited about their pregnancies or the least bothered by the long waits and decrepit facilities. Rather, they usually believed that regular prenatal care would improve their health and help their babies. Some feared that they might have complications that only a doctor could detect, and others wanted advice, information, or dietary supplements. Women undergoing their first pregnancies often sought prenatal care because they wanted to become more familiar with what was happening to their bodies.[78] Those who avoided regular prenatal visits had often been pregnant before and doubted that regular prenatal care would benefit them markedly. They knew that doctors recommended prenatal care and even gave lip service to its importance. However, since they considered the purpose of prenatal care to be "checking that nothing is wrong," they did not see much use for it as long as they felt well.[79] Believing that the benefits of recommended appointments were minimal, and certainly not enough to justify the inconveniences and frustrations involved, they developed a common strategy, purposely visiting prenatal clinics only once or twice in the final months of their pregnancies. They sought prenatal care on their own terms, valuing their familiarity with the rituals of pregnancy over the formal medical practices of doctors.[80]

When the time came to give birth, many women continued to prioritize their own knowledge of their bodies over doctors' recommendations. Most women preferred a hospital birth to a home birth because they believed it would be safer if they had complications and wanted to be in the hospital for their recovery. Yet many women preferred to go through labor at home, to avoid what they described as "them doctors messing you around" during labor. Sounding much like women's health activists in the 1970s, working-class African American women often complained about their lack of autonomy and inability to move around during labor in the hospital. Gladys Robinson stayed at home because "if you can walk around the house, you can fight the pains better." Jacqueline Wallace hated the constraints of hospital beds, preferring to undergo labor at home, where "when you get tired of walking you just lie down and roll from side to side." Many women insisted that the baby knew when to come and should not be manipulated by doctors. Those who had previously delivered children at the hospital knew that doctors often subjected women to four or five vaginal examinations over the course of their labors and sometimes performed rectal examinations. Women could avoid these painful examinations by laboring at home.[81]

Birthing women frequently waited at home until they were in active labor. Most did not have friends who owned cars so they called taxis or the police to take them to the hospital. When their rides took a long time to come or labor progressed more quickly than women anticipated, they ended up arriving barely in time. Some women gave birth on the steps of PGH, in the emergency ward waiting room, in hospital elevators and hallways, or even inside their taxis outside the hospital. The PGH staff sent interns out with the police and kept a doctor's delivery bag in the emergency ward in preparation for the frequent last-minute deliveries. Women's refusal to go to the hospital when their contractions first started illustrates their confidence in their own abilities to handle their labors and their resistance to being confined to beds and placed under doctors' orders in the hospital.[82]

The Shaping of PGH's Services

As a public hospital that could not turn people away, PGH had to respond to patients' needs.[83] This imperative enabled working-class African American women to participate in shaping PGH's services. Patients' influence on the hospital began with the type of illnesses they presented. Those who approached PGH tended to be sicker than those at voluntary hospitals because of their more punishing lifestyles and their lack of health insurance and preventative care. In 1955, doctors classified almost half the PGH inpatient admissions as "emergency cases" with conditions so severe that they had to be hospitalized immediately. Voluntary hospitals, in contrast, admitted less than 10 percent of their patients on an emergency basis.[84] Philadelphia General Hospital also saw an unusually high number of patients who presented routine problems. In a pattern that still occurs with uninsured patients in the early twenty-first century, some patients went to the public hospital for the treatment of minor illnesses, care that most middle-class patients received from private doctors. Catherine Simon explained that she and her friends "used Philadelphia General as their doctor, more or less" and turned to the public hospital whenever they needed medical attention.[85] By seeking routine health care at PGH, women forced the hospital to become their pediatrician, gynecologist, and general provider of primary care.

In the postwar period, PGH expanded rapidly to accommodate patients' needs for its services and to secure new technology. The improvements began in the 1940s and continued when Mayor Clark and later Mayor Dilworth took office. Both Clark and Dilworth made PGH a priority. Under their administrations, the hospital hired more staff, provided day care for employees' children, and opened a new neurological building, tuberculosis ward, food service building, laboratory department, X-ray department, and operating suite. Outpatient visits soared after the construction of a new building with a much larger capacity and a range of new clinics. One 1962 hospital progress report summed up the extent of the transformation by noting, "There are virtually few departments and sections of the hospital which have not undergone general renovation and physical improvements in the past decade."[86] The improvements benefited medical professionals by providing them with more space and access to modern technology and helped patients by affording them an improved standard of care.

African American women's demands helped promote a significant proportion of the new construction and renovations at PGH. The most pressing situation was the extremely high number of women giving birth at the hospital. In 1949, PGH obstetricians were annually performing forty-seven deliveries per bed, more than double the rate of voluntary hospitals.[87] To compensate, the staff drastically reduced the length of patients' hospital stays. Prior to World War II, maternity patients typically stayed in hospitals from seven to ten days. After the war, hospitals throughout the nation discharged postpartum women and their infants more quickly, but PGH's practices shifted particularly dramatically. Most PGH patients stayed for less than four days after delivering, and in times of severe overcrowding, doctors sometimes had to send them home in an ambulance after only twenty-four hours.[88] Dissatisfied with their inability to provide proper care for birthing women, in 1953, hospital authorities spent over half-a-million dollars to renovate the Northern Division of PGH (previously the Philadelphia Hospital for Contagious Diseases) so that it could treat obstetrical patients.[89] When the Northern Division failed to attract large numbers of birthing women because it was inconveniently located and African American women did not feel the same attachment to it as they did to the main branch in West Philadelphia, health authorities devised a new plan to accommodate black women's preferences.[90] In 1958, PGH closed the Northern Division and constructed a modern new maternity ward at the main branch of the hospital to serve the thousands of African American women who insisted on delivering their children at "Old Blockley." One of the obstetrics nurses, describing her excitement about the new ward, explained, "It was such a big improvement" in patient care.[91]

The special needs presented by women's children prompted other investments by the hospital. Because so many women who gave birth at the hospital were impoverished, the most widespread problem was prematurity. In the late 1950s, with 23 percent of the hospital's babies born prematurely, PGH joined hospitals across the nation in adding a high-tech premature nursery that addressed the complex medical problems of premature infants.[92] Constructed in 1956, the nursery dramatically improved the outcomes for premature babies. Before the new nursery, nearly one out of every three premature infants born at PGH died within two days; with the new facility, only one in five died. After a few years, the hospital expanded the nursery from 32 to 62 bassinets.[93] In 1960, in response to the large numbers of African American mothers who returned to PGH during their children's lives to pursue various forms of pediatric care, the hospital established a new pediatrics clinic that was one of the finest in the country, offering specialties ranging from child psychiatry to orthopedics.[94]

PGH responded in a particularly striking and empathetic way to the huge numbers of women who sought treatment for complications from illegal abortions. In the 1960s, more than one in seven women admitted to the obstetrics department of PGH presented with complications from illegal abortions. The illegality of abortion in Pennsylvania dated back to 1860, and the fines for performing an abortion increased significantly in 1939. After World War II, legal and medical authorities intensified the surveillance and prosecution of underground abortion providers. Middle-class women frequently found private doctors or hospitals who would perform "therapeutic abortions," but working-class women like Edwina Jordan rarely had doctors who could help them. As a publicly funded institution, PGH had to adhere to some of the strictest abortion restrictions in the city, which severely limited the number of "therapeutic abortions" it could perform.[95]

A Hospital of Their Own **175**

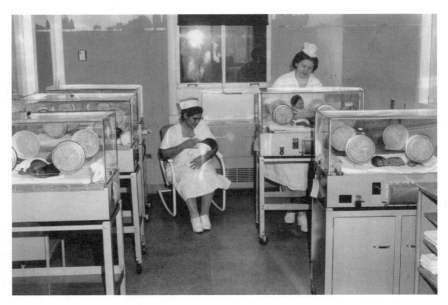

Philadelphia General Hospital's new high-tech nursery for premature babies opened in 1956. Temple University Libraries, Urban Archives, Philadelphia, Pa.

Thousands of women arriving at PGH presented with severe complications from illegal abortions. They ranged from young teenagers to women in their forties, and many had risked their lives when they or other women had tried to induce abortions by beating their bellies with boards or inserting sharp objects such as knitting needles, bicycle spokes, umbrella spokes, and coat hangers through their cervixes and into their uteruses. One of the local underground abortionists was known as the neighborhood "hackster," suggesting that her procedures often went awry.[96] Complications arose when the woman's uterus, bowel, or abdominal wall was punctured accidentally; in cases such as Mrs. Jordan's, when the placenta was not fully expelled during the induced miscarriage that followed the procedure; and especially when the lack of sterile instruments and conditions resulted in pelvic infections. In the late 1950s and 1960s, after word spread in working-class neighborhoods that potassium permanganate tablets could act as an abortifacient, PGH saw many cases in which this strategy caused major problems. Since potassium permanganate was an oxidizing agent, it could burn women's vaginas and sometimes burned their bladders.[97] Ira Gerstley, an obstetrician-gynecologist who joined PGH's staff in 1956, recalled numerous cases of "burned holes in the rectum" and "feces passing through the vagina" as a result of illegal abortions. He remained haunted by the suffering and death he witnessed, describing the patients who suffered from complications from illegal abortions as "the sickest women I ever saw."[98]

The policies at PGH mandated that women suffering from complications from illegal abortions receive medical and nursing treatment no different from the care they would receive for any other illness. Exhibiting a sensitivity rarely found in institutions during this period, the staff was instructed to avoid casting blame or moral judgment on patients suffering from abortion complications. One nurse explained that the women "were never categorized, they were never put to shame"; they were given the same standard of care afforded to other patients. She recalled nurses spending "many a twelve-hour shift with a girl" suffering from an illegal abortion, "sponging her down and trying to keep her alive."[99] Although some individual PGH doctors and nurses may not have upheld the policies mandating respectful treatment, PGH's institutional commitment provided women with a unique opportunity to receive humane care.

Victims of rape and domestic abuse who sought care from PGH met with more predictable responses from the hospital staff. Prior to the emergence of the women's movement in the late 1960s, the patterns and effects of violence against women were not widely known. Victims of domestic abuse who approached the hospital presented a wide range of injuries, including broken bones, bruises, black eyes, and severe wounds. One woman came to the hospital after her husband seriously injured her by stomping on her face with his cleated shoes. Since these incidents happened years before the establishment of women's shelters and domestic violence counseling services, after women received medical treatment for their injuries, the hospital staff sent them home where they frequently faced the husbands or boyfriends who had injured them.[100] Rape victims usually only approached the hospital if they had severe tears in their vaginas or had very heavy bleeding. Many were young and came to the hospital with their mothers. Most had been raped by someone they knew, but refused to identify their assailants to the hospital staff. They could receive extremely insensitive care if doctors suspected that they were frequently sexually active. Nurse Gloria Gay recalled that one doctor "joked" after performing a gynecological exam on a rape victim that "you could run a Mack truck up her." Such stereotypes about African American women's hypersexuality legitimized a common belief that they deserved to be raped or that rape was not a serious issue. Only in the 1970s did PGH, as an institution, acknowledge the severity of the problem of sexual violence. The hospital took responsibility for all of the rape victims in the city, treating almost one thousand rape cases each year. Three-quarters of the victims were African American women.[101]

"Illegitimate Illegitimacy" at PGH

In the postwar period, working-class African American women's assertive pursuit of health care at PGH became caught up in the battles over race and civil rights that raged throughout the city. Popular concern about patients taking advantage of public health care dated back at least to the early twentieth century; however, in the 1950s, it increasingly merged with the growing uproar over African American single mothers' "abuse" of the city's welfare system.[102] In 1958, City Revenue Commissioner Mortin E. Rotman launched a highly publicized investigation into what he called the "illegitimate claims of illegitimacy" made by maternity patients at PGH. Rotman began his probe after the release of a study concluding that nearly two-fifths of the hospital's maternity patients had provided false information about their financial circumstances to PGH admissions officers in order to obtain lower rates.[103] Most shocking to Rotman and others, 8 of the 238 women studied had told the hospital that they were single when there was "clear evidence" of "common-law marriage."[104] Reporters and municipal authorities did not seem to care that only 3 percent of all patients engaged in this alleged transgression. Nor did they discuss whether the women who were living with men and described themselves as "unmarried" were actually lying. The definition of common-law marriage used by white authorities to determine financial responsibility had little in common with the meaning of marriage to African Americans, who often referred to live-in mates as their "husbands" or "wives," but to whom the difference between living together and getting married in a church or at city hall remained significant.

Public officials and journalists echoed themes articulated in the discourse on welfare by portraying women's actions as both moral transgressions and a severe financial drain on taxpayers. Newspapers ran sensationalist stories about African American women's "immorality," with headlines such as "Phony Illegitimacy" and "Mothers Fake Illegitimacy to Evade Baby Bills at PGH."[105] According to Rotman, maternity patients who were living with men purposely set out to cheat the city and "escape responsibility" for their bills. "Not only is the city defrauded in these false claims of illegitimacy," he claimed, "but a child is branded for life."[106] The *Inquirer* described unmarried women who received health care at PGH as "deadbeats and moochers of free medical care," and the *Bulletin* condemned them for engaging in "about as low-class a human activity as could be imagined." Juxtaposing African American women's immorality with the general public's virtue, *Bulletin* editors pronounced it "shocking to those with any old-fashioned notions of morality that people can behave so shabbily" and found it "intolerable that the facilities of Philadelphia General and the tax money which supports it should be so abused."[107] Such statements reinforced the growing association of whiteness with moral superiority earned through the avoidance of public institutions and blackness with a deplorable reliance on the state. They bolstered the damaging stereotypes that proliferated throughout the city of African American women as immoral reproducers of "illegitimate" children.

Unlike the backlash against welfare, which commanded a steady stream of headlines, the public outcry about African American women's "abuse" of PGH did not last for long. To quell the controversy, the hospital announced plans to tighten its billing practices. It hired collection department investigators to screen patients' financial circumstances more closely while field-workers checked on patients' circumstances outside the hospital. Although the new practices diminished patients' sense of entitlement to services, health authorities did not introduce the same degree of scrutiny practised by the welfare department. Even under the new regime, hospital administrators did not require patients to provide documentation verifying their financial status before administering treatment and field-workers' investigations into patients' private lives were not routine; they only checked the "doubtful cases."[108] Patients continued to receive more privacy and respect at PGH than they did at other public institutions in the city.

The outcry about African American women's "immorality" at PGH focused on rare instances of alleged fraud and did not call into question the hospital's overarching mission or its programs. No one challenged the city's expenditure of millions of dollars on subsidized health care for the poor or suggested that it should restrict the services that it offered to unmarried mothers.[109] The lack of persistent and deeply rooted opposition may have partly reflected whites' recognition that if PGH did not serve poor black people, they would frequent white voluntary hospitals in higher numbers. It also reflected the greater public support for health care than for welfare, particularly health care provided by an institution such as PGH that was known to deliver it properly. While many Philadelphians viewed welfare grants as "handouts" that encouraged promiscuity and irresponsibility, high-quality publicly funded hospital care saved lives and could enable people to become "productive," employed citizens.

Of all the public institutions in postwar Philadelphia, PGH delivered services to working-class African American women most effectively and commanded the greatest public support. The hospital's expansive offerings and provision of health care as an entitlement fostered a deep sense of loyalty among professionals and patients alike. Health care professionals coveted positions at PGH because the hospital offered them an opportunity to become part of a community of first-rate doctors and nurses who treated a wide range of medical conditions. Many working-class African American women avoided voluntary hospitals because they preferred the public hospital's policies mandating equitable treatment of all patients regardless of their ability to pay.

The widespread public support for PGH demonstrates that public institutions serving large numbers of African American women and children were not inevitably stigmatized and denied financial resources. Public perceptions of the kind of assistance that state programs offered combined with popular beliefs about authorities' effectiveness in delivering services to shape public institutions' reputations. Even welfare programs commanded some public support when they were portrayed as providing vital assistance to "innocent" African American children. Before public housing became run-down and dangerous, it was welcomed by both liberal whites and African Americans who envisioned it helping solve the city's housing crisis and improving the conditions in low-income neighborhoods. And although many middle-class whites did not want to pay more taxes or send their children to public schools serving large numbers of African Americans, most agreed with the purpose of public education, hoping it would enable African Americans to become employable and upstanding citizens. The widespread respect for PGH reflected public support for the provision of health care to the poor and the hospital's reputation as a first-class medical institution.

Philadelphia General Hospital's most committed supporters remained the working-class African American women who turned and returned to the hospital for all their health care needs. The hospital's provision of health care as an entitlement enabled women who were degraded and stigmatized by most other public institutions in the city to feel like legitimate consumers of essential services. As an institution, PGH respected patients' privacy and attempted to respond positively to their needs. When working-class African American women made repeat visits to PGH and encouraged their family and friends to join them, they developed a deep trust of the hospital and formed a community of black patients in its wards and waiting rooms. Philadelphia General Hospital provided working-class African American women with a unique opportunity to create a niche for themselves in the city of hospitals. They seized the moment and turned PGH into their own hospital.

CONCLUSION

On foot and by bus, tens of thousands of African American women, with young children in tow and papers in hand, made their way from impoverished neighborhoods across Philadelphia to the doorsteps of public institutions to claim benefits and services for themselves and their families. They came despite the difficulty of gaining access to state programs and the inadequacy of the resources that fragmented, poorly funded agencies provided. After encountering rebuffs and routine denials, they came back, bringing more documents to prove their eligibility. They came despite the myriad restrictions surrounding public programs, the numerous burdens imposed, and the intrusive surveillance that accepting benefits frequently entailed. They knew that those who sought assistance were often publicly condemned as lazy, immoral, and dependent, and black mothers raising children alone were the most stigmatized of all. But still they came. City and state bureaucrats did not advertise the availability of most publicly funded benefits and services, especially in black neighborhoods, but women heard about government programs through word of mouth and community networks and learned how to navigate dauntingly complex bureaucracies. Between 1945 and the early 1960s, working-class African American women claimed public institutions for themselves.

African American women's movement without marches resembles other tidal changes in American social history, when masses of ordinary people—propelled by the common problems produced by poverty and prejudice and pulled by shared aspirations for dignity and opportunity—have turned toward the places and institutions that seemed to offer resources to improve their lives and their children's prospects. Difficult personal decisions made by myriads of individuals and families generated the Great Migration that carried generations of African Americans out of the impoverished, repressive Jim Crow South to Philadelphia and other northern and western cities where both political freedom and economic improvement seemed attainable. The persistence of racial and gender discrimination amid the new circumstances of urban life induced impoverished yet resilient and determined women to seek out and take hold of whatever public resources might be available to them. In ever-growing numbers, they proceeded to the doorsteps of public institutions—to "1801 Vine," the "DPA," and "PGH." Every woman whom officials turned away was replaced by another seeking similar services; every woman who succeeded in obtaining welfare benefits, court-ordered child support, an affordable apartment in public housing, health care, or education for her children was soon followed by many others. In linking their fate to public institutions, women turned state programs into battlegrounds over the distribution of power and resources in the postwar city.

Women's movement without marches reverberated through the halls and boardrooms of city and state institutions, made headlines in the press, and altered many vitally important aspects of daily life in African American neighborhoods. For women whose schooling had been truncated and whose job opportunities were limited, whose family budgets were ordinarily stretched so tightly that any unavoidable expense could precipitate a crisis, and whose relatives, friends, and neighbors were equally impoverished, the scanty resources provided by public institutions were crucial in enabling them to support themselves, maintain their bodily integrity, and fulfill their responsibilities to their children. Yet women's success in securing resources from public institutions rarely helped them escape from poverty. Taken together, the policies and programs that constituted the postwar welfare state sustained black women and children in a situation of chronic deprivation. Although Philadelphia General Hospital (PGH) sought to accommodate women's demands, several institutions responded to their assertive pursuit of resources by introducing restrictive new policies. A harsh public discourse condemning women's use of public institutions emerged as a powerful counterforce to their activism.

Women's movement into public institutions traversed a complicated terrain.

Public institutions were not integrated into a coherent social welfare system, but had grown up independently, forming a confusing patchwork of agencies and programs that remained full of gaping holes. Each program had its own eligibility requirements, rules and regulations, and institutional culture. Women made astute decisions when seeking public services, choosing programs that would help them cope more effectively with the most acute of the myriad problems that they faced: poor health, inadequate housing, limited education, discrimination in the labor market, and responsibility for the labor of social reproduction. Local institutions were not necessarily more responsive to their needs than federal ones, despite the fact that black Philadelphians had gained some political power in the city. Nor were federally funded programs necessarily more inclusive than local and state programs. Philadelphia General Hospital and the public schools were both controlled mainly by the city, but their approaches to serving African American women and children were diametrically opposed. The hospital provided high-quality services with few restrictions and was widely acknowledged to be the most effective and inclusive public institution in the city. By contrast, the underfunded public school system discriminated against African Americans and consistently failed to address working-class black mothers' concerns. Women developed strategies to maximize the benefits of public institutions while minimizing their drawbacks, traveling across the city to receive health care at PGH while attempting to transfer their children to better schools and avoid principals and teachers who blamed them for their children's problems.

In seeking resources for themselves and their families, many women chose to bypass private agencies because they preferred to receive assistance from the state. Their choice of public institutions partly reflected the sheer amount of aid provided by the government, which dwarfed what the private sector could or would provide. It also reflected the sense of entitlement that women felt to the assistance offered by publicly funded programs. No matter how many barriers government authorities tried to impose, women felt that they had a more legitimate claim on the services provided by the state than they did on those offered by private agencies. While Catholic schools dismissed "problem" students and voluntary hospitals could turn poor patients away, the public schools and the public hospital had to serve everyone who applied. Private charities could arbitrarily refuse to provide women with assistance, but if women brought all the required paperwork to a city welfare office and met objective standards for eligibility, caseworkers were obligated to serve them. If women met resistance or were unfairly denied benefits, they could advocate for themselves and their children and demand explanations. The fact that they were seeking services from a government agency made a real difference to poor women who lacked political clout and had little to fall back on aside from their status as citizens.

In asserting their entitlement to the benefits and services offered by public institutions, women refused to consider government assistance a form of undeserved charity. They did not yet speak of a "right" to welfare, education, or public housing; what political scientists and critical legal theorists call "rights talk" did not emerge among low-income women until the late 1960s. Still, they firmly believed that the government had an obligation to provide them with opportunities to secure basic necessities and a few of the conveniences and comforts promised by the expanding consumer economy. Many insisted that their reliance on the state was not shameful and that they did not deserve "to be treated . . . like dirt" because they received government assistance. Integral to their worldview was a belief that they and their children had a right to live with dignity and receive respectful treatment from other people.[1]

In the late 1960s and 1970s, the hopes, desires, and sense of entitlement that women expressed through their pursuit of assistance from public institutions became explicitly and publicly articulated by new groups of working-class, mostly nonwhite, women who organized collectively to demand social and political change. During these years, the Black Power movement gained increased visibility and influence in Philadelphia, and the black men who emerged as leaders emphasized black cultural pride and the need for African Americans to have control over the social, economic, and political institutions in their communities. With the exception of the public schools, Black Power activists did not focus on the state programs that were integral to working-class African American women's daily lives. But black women made social welfare programs and institutions a priority. In cities throughout the North and West, they publicized the struggles carried on in the trenches of public institutions and working-class homes, seeking to improve the government's delivery of services and fundamentally redefine the terms of public debate. Building on the language and tactics of the Black Freedom Movement, they sought to preserve, improve, and expand public institutions and dispel the demeaning stereotypes of African American women that circulated in the public press.

In 1967, low-income women in Philadelphia formed the Philadelphia Welfare Rights Organization (PWRO) to advocate for increased benefits and respect for public assistance recipients. The PWRO was a chapter of the National Welfare Rights Organization (NWRO), an activist group formed in 1967 that was led and established by welfare recipients, predominantly African Americans and Latinas, with support from civil rights activists and antipoverty advocates. Together with community-based and policy-oriented lawyers, the NWRO pursued an innovative litigation strategy that established a "right" to welfare for all mothers who qualified for assistance.[2] Between 1967 and 1971, hundreds of low-income women in Philadelphia joined the PWRO, which grew from 330 to 3,000 members. George Wiley, the executive director of the NWRO, called the PWRO "the most dynamic local group in the country." The PWRO lobbied for improvements in slum housing, demanded more respect from caseworkers, picketed landlords who would not rent to welfare recipients, staged sit-ins at the Philadelphia Department of Public Assistance, sought and won credit at local department stores, and orchestrated statewide demonstrations that resulted in increased welfare allowances. With the help of Community Legal Services (CLS), a legal aid program for low-income citizens founded in 1966 by Philadelphia lawyer William R. Klaus, the organization successfully pressured the state to remove the one-year residency requirement for welfare and helped reduce the rejection rate for new public assistance applicants from 50 to 31 percent.[3]

In the early 1970s, PWRO members created an Education Committee to address the problems their children faced in the public schools. The committee embarked on an investigation of the public school system's funding policies and determined that it had not complied with the federal law requiring it to concentrate the funds received under Title I of the 1965 Elementary and Secondary Education Act on economically disadvantaged students. Community Legal Services helped the Education Committee sue the Philadelphia school system and secure more funds for the instruction of low-income students.[4] Other groups of working-class women targeted specific schools for improvements. For example, in the 1970s, black, white, and Puerto Rican mothers who had children living near Edison High School in North Philadelphia's Kensington neighborhood joined forces to lobby the board of education to construct a new school. Edison was the oldest operating high school in the city, and it was dingy, ill-equipped, and unsafe. For years, mothers engaged in petition drives, letter-writing, rallies, and numerous meetings, trying to convince the board to build a new school. The board ultimately agreed to construct the school, but its plans were constantly delayed because of fierce resistance from local whites who did not want a school serving a diverse student population in or near their neighborhoods.[5]

Public housing tenants joined the growing numbers of women demanding more control over the institutions that materially shaped their lives. In 1968, CLS filed a suit on behalf of thirteen women who challenged the Philadelphia Housing Authority's (PHA) policy banning unmarried mothers with two or more children from public housing. In an out-of-court settlement, the PHA pledged to abolish its restrictions on unmarried mothers, process all applications expeditiously, give written notice of the reasons it rejected applicants, and provide a right of appeal.[6] The same year, residents of Richard Allen and Tasker Homes successfully campaigned for the right to form tenant councils. Through their councils, tenants won the right to pay their monthly rent in two installments instead of one and convinced authorities to accord them preferential treatment when awarding jobs within public housing. Managers pledged to limit home visits, give tenants notice before conducting inspections, and charge them only for damage to apartments that was intentional or malicious instead of imposing fines for problems that developed in the normal course of everyday life. In 1969, tenants used their newfound leverage with the PHA to convince the Authority to allow them to organize a citywide Resident Advisory Board.[7]

Philadelphia's racially biased system of law enforcement became another target for African American women seeking to reform public institutions in the city. In 1967, they founded the Council of Organizations on Philadelphia Police Accountability and Responsibility (COPPAR) to collect and investigate complaints of racial discrimination and rampant brutality in the police department. Led by Mary Rouse, a working-class mother whose son had suffered from a police beating, COPPAR pulled together a coalition of neighborhood groups, poverty organizations, and antiwar activists to support its efforts. To increase public awareness of the problems in the police department and exert pressure on legal authorities, COPPAR collected and disseminated information on incidents in which the police used excessive force. In 1971, thanks in part to COPPAR's activism, the U.S. Commission on Civil Rights began to conduct hearings on the Philadelphia Police Department. The committee concluded that the police had failed to respect the rights of minority citizens and used the arrest process as "a means of humiliation, harassment, or an instrument of indiscriminate community control." It recommended that the federal Department of Justice investigate the police department and called on the city to reestablish an external police-review board and employ citizens' groups to guide and monitor police policies and practices.[8]

Of all the public institutions from which working-class black women sought essential services, PGH proved the most vulnerable to budgetary pressures. In the late 1960s and 1970s, the hospital faced a serious financial crisis as an unintended result of major shifts in public policy. The establishment of Medicare and Medicaid changed the system of health care funding by subsidizing services for the elderly and medically indigent at private hospitals and clinics. With rising standards of care requiring substantial capital expenditures, the city fought with the medical schools in Philadelphia over rates of compensation for physicians and services. The hospital became increasingly expensive to operate and its facilities deteriorated. In 1976, the Democratic mayor, Frank Rizzo,

On February 25, 1976, protesters marched from Philadelphia General Hospital to City Hall to oppose the closing of the hospital. Temple University Libraries, Urban Archives, Philadelphia, Pa.

announced plans to close PGH, inspiring a groundswell of community opposition. Labor unions, doctors, nurses, welfare rights activists, health care advocates, black churches, and patients joined forces to keep PGH open, organizing marches, public demonstrations, and work stoppages. Yet PGH was closed in 1977, and Philadelphia lost an institution that had been a bedrock of the black community and a touchstone for the entire city.[9]

From the movement without marches to the numerous organized movements with marches, low-income women's insistence that they deserved the same rights and privileges as other U.S. citizens confronted a wall of resistance built on deeply rooted beliefs about gender, race, wage-earning, and citizenship held by conservatives and liberals alike. Embedded within this worldview was a belief in a social compact in which the benefits people received from the state were rewards for the contributions they made by paying taxes. Steady employment was the fulcrum of citizenship, enabling workers in stable jobs, who were predominantly white men, to qualify for first-class government benefits such as unemployment insurance and old-age pensions. Those who did not have a steady employment history or were not married to eligible wage earners had to engage in lengthy application processes to qualify for second-class benefits such as General Assistance that provided much less support than the first-class programs. Single mothers who did not hold jobs were in the worst position because their ability to access ADC was contingent on their adherence to specific rules of behavior. Undergirding this unequal distribution of resources was

Conclusion **187**

the belief that wage earners were merely taking out what they had paid into the system, while everyone else received assistance "given" to them as charity. In fact, government policy, more than past contributions, determined how much support people received. None of the programs created by the 1935 Social Security Act provided workers with the amount of money they had paid into the system, and old-age pensions and unemployment insurance replaced a higher percentage of income for low-wage workers than for better-off workers. Still, many public officials and ordinary people insisted that recipients of first-class benefits had paid their own way, while recipients of second-class benefits were "dependent" on the state.[10]

Over the course of the 1950s, as large numbers of African American women claimed ADC and more white middle-class mothers entered the labor force, public officials from all political persuasions increasingly portrayed single mothers who received government assistance not merely as second-class citizens but as the very antithesis of the upstanding "taxpayer." Democratic judges and Republican newspaper editors drew stark comparisons between low-income African American women and "taxpayers," describing the two groups as polar opposites whose values, behaviors, and interests were diametrically opposed. They described poor black women not only as "dependent" on the state, but also as taking money directly from "taxpayers," whose hard-earned dollars allegedly supported women's freewheeling lifestyles. The discourse portrayed African American women who relied on government programs as a threat to upstanding citizens, while casting white wage earners, the main beneficiaries of the postwar welfare state, as the aggrieved and exploited victims.

Although civil rights activists and white liberals who supported social welfare spending did not join in promoting demeaning images of mothers of "illegitimate" children wasting "taxpayers'" money, they rarely addressed the specific struggles of working-class African American women. The reform-oriented mayors Joseph Clark and Richardson Dilworth advocated the construction of public housing and improvements at PGH, but largely ignored the controversies brewing over welfare and the segregation and underfunding of the public schools in African American neighborhoods. Most civil rights activists focused on the elimination of racial discrimination, lobbying most assertively for public policies and programs that would benefit middle-class African American families and working-class African American men. With both white reformers and black activists rarely defending the rights of unmarried mothers publicly, the popular outcry about African American women's "illicit" uses of state resources remained largely unchallenged.

Civil rights activists and liberal reformers did not simply overlook African American women's struggles in public institutions. Rather, their political platforms often explicitly marginalized or stigmatized women who headed their own households and received government assistance. As Ruth Feldstein has argued, postwar racial liberalism depended upon gender conservatism—a commitment to normative gender roles and white middle-class ideals of motherhood.[11] Liberal social scientists and journalists subscribed to theories about "cultural deprivation" that placed the blame for African Americans' difficulties on black culture and single-parent households. Even when unmarried African American mothers confronted explicit sex discrimination in their efforts to secure admission to public housing, civil rights activists focused only on the barriers facing families headed by black men. Holding ambivalent attitudes about black mothers' paid and unpaid labors on behalf of their children, social workers and welfare advocates responded to their growing access to publicly funded social services by seeking to diminish the number of women who received government assistance.

By the early 1960s, the link between government social programs and immoral African Americans had become firmly established in the public mind, leading some whites in Philadelphia to question their support for the Democratic Party, which they identified with civil rights and public welfare services. Despite prominent Democrats' forceful condemnations of African American women's "abuse" of public programs, the legacy of the New Deal as a Democratic initiative, combined with the city government's civil rights agenda and African Americans' strong support for Democrats in electoral politics, left Democrats vulnerable to charges that they supported African Americans' exploitation of the social welfare system, the city coffers, and the state treasury. The linking of the Democratic Party with African Americans and public welfare helped alienate many working-class whites who had been part of the New Deal coalition, as they came to resent the special treatment they believed African Americans received from the government through civil rights initiatives and antipoverty programs. In 1959, political scientist James Reichley observed that in Philadelphia "smoldering hostility toward the Negroes is a sentiment present among all of the city's white groups," particularly those with low incomes who did not benefit from Democratic social welfare programs either because they were not poor enough to qualify or were too proud to apply for racially stigmatized government benefits.[12]

During the 1960s and 1970s, the racialized opposition to welfare programs and support for the interests of "taxpayers" that congealed in Philadelphia and other cities during the 1950s became a principal theme in the national political discourse. It emerged in full force in 1962, when a set of severe welfare cutbacks in Newburgh, New York, became front-page news across the country. Newburgh's flamboyant city manager, Joseph Mitchell, became an overnight sensation and catapulted Aid to Dependent Children (ADC) to the forefront of state and federal politics when he charged that his city had become a "welfare resort" for black newcomers who used ADC as a "reward for promiscuity." Mitchell described welfare as the "taxpayers' burden," and white newspapers depicted Newburgh's ADC recipients "mooching" money from hard-working men. In 1965, the national debate became even more heated with the release of the highly controversial, yet enduringly powerful, Moynihan Report, which blamed African Americans' poverty and reliance on welfare on "the Negro family structure" and the "tangle of pathology" that single mothers allegedly perpetuated.[13] Guy Drake's 1970 song featuring a welfare recipient making payments on a Cadillac became a major hit, and Ronald Reagan's infamous 1976 depiction of a "welfare queen" reinforced the idea that promiscuous welfare recipients lived in idle luxury by exploiting white taxpayers.[14] In the late 1970s, an organized movement for "taxpayers' rights" emerged in twenty states, invoking the term "taxpayer" as a racial and gender code word for white male citizens that sometimes included white women and occasionally was extended to encompass middle-class nonwhite women and men.[15] Calls for "taxpayers' rights" implicitly defined wage earners and their families in direct opposition to African American women who relied on government assistance. Supporters of "taxpayers' rights" cast themselves as victims, wronged by both an overly activist government and promiscuous and lazy black women.

As the national discussion of welfare and taxes became increasingly stacked against low-income women, so did public policy. In the late 1960s, the majority of federal social welfare dollars went to the nonpoor, but the much more limited assistance provided to low-income women and their families came under attack. Between 1967 and 1988, Democratic-controlled Congresses and Republican presidents hammered out a conservative consensus and amended welfare policies six times. Each reform moved policy in a more punitive and restrictive direction, prioritizing the gainful employment of women with children and attempting—but largely failing—to promote marriage and two-parent households among the poor. During the same period, Congress passed stringent legislation designed to force women to establish paternity and enforce men's payment of child support. These punitive measures tended to disrupt relationships between parents and to reduce women's ability to protect themselves from domestic abuse, even though their financial benefits were often minimal.[16] A rising unmet demand for services marked other arenas as well. Working-class women confronted pressing needs for health care and affordable high-quality day care that politicians largely ignored. Even as public housing became more unsafe and run-down, waiting lists consistently exceeded 10,000 families. The public school system continued to fail generations of poor black students, leading them to drop out or to graduate without the skills demanded by the changing labor market.[17]

At the end of the twentieth century, Democrats and Republicans joined forces to eliminate poor mothers' right to welfare. Seizing the politically valuable antiwelfare platform, Democratic presidential candidate Bill Clinton pledged to "end welfare as we know it." A Republican Congress fulfilled Clinton's promise, passing the Personal Responsibility and Work Opportunity Reconciliation Act (PRA) in 1996.[18] The PRA introduced strict time limits on the receipt of welfare, mandatory establishment of paternity, and stringent employment requirements while failing to provide adequate subsidies for child care, health insurance, and education. The end of welfare reflected the increased acceptance and financial necessity of middle-class mothers' employment, a situation that made the provision of public assistance for poor mothers of color politically untenable. It dealt a fundamental blow to women's equality, diminishing their reproductive rights, economic security, and marital freedom. The elimination of welfare was part of the far-reaching late twentieth-century assault on low-income urban communities that was also visible in the dearth of public investment in job creation, public housing, health care, and public education, and the phenomenal growth in the prison system, which incarcerated unprecedented numbers of low-income racial-ethnic minorities for nonviolent offenses. The disinvestment in public services to the inner cities went hand in hand with the rise in mass incarceration.

In face of these assaults on public institutions and the urban poor, it is hard to remember a time when things were different. A time when the social welfare state was expanding, not contracting, serving to empower masses of low-income women. A time when women such as Corrine Elkins and Catherine Sanderson could assert themselves on the public stage, seeking to achieve their expansive conception of citizenship. Working-class African American women turned and returned to postwar public institutions because they felt entitled to government assistance and believed they could legitimately and unapologetically lobby state authorities. If they were continually disappointed in the services they received, it was because they saw tremendous potential in public institutions and steadfastly believed the government could do better. When women chafed at meager benefits and humiliating restrictions, they expressed their strong belief that public institutions should help them live with dignity and enable them to improve their lives and the prospects of their children. In these women's broad conception of their entitlements and their deep faith in the constructive capacity of the democratic state lies a radical vision of human rights and economic citizenship.

Appendix: Note on First-Person Sources

This book draws on a wide array of traditional primary sources: newspapers, census records, government documents, annual reports of public institutions and private agencies, sociological studies, maps, interview transcripts, and manuscript collections from social service, housing, education, and civil rights organizations. Its inspiration comes from the sources that allow us to hear working-class African American women's voices and provide a window into their daily lives. What follows is a discussion of my work with the sources that provided the richest first-person accounts: municipal court transcripts, oral history interviews, and social work studies of welfare recipients.

In 1997, I took my first extended research trip to Philadelphia. My work began in the Philadelphia City Archives, which had preserved hundreds of boxes of transcripts and bills of indictment from the cases tried in the municipal court between 1838 and 1987. The collection took up nearly 20,000 cubic feet, and many of the twentieth-century cases had never been touched. The transcripts and bills of indictment were stored in chronological order, in boxes that held approximately fifty cases each. I cast a wide net and studied randomly selected boxes from every five years between 1917 and 1962. Nonsupport cases were not included in these records, but the boxes held many Fornication and Bastardy and Assault and Battery cases. I also read cases in which abused women were tried for spousal murder and cases in which neighborhood disputes led women to press assault charges against each other. I compiled a database in which I recorded and described nearly 300 cases involving women. Some cases did not have any reliable racial markers, making it difficult for me to ascertain with certainty whether the participants were African American or white. I read the transcripts mainly for evidence of how men and women presented themselves in court as they sought to convince judges to rule in their favor. I relied on the court's *Annual Reports* for all statistical evidence, and I used a combination of *Annual Reports*, other court publications, oral history interviews, and social work studies to document how women interacted with legal authorities and forced changes in court policies.

A few days after I started working with the legal sources, I learned that the Philadelphia City Archives had received a grant to conduct a sampling project for all its court records after 1940. The records took up a great deal of storage space and were so voluminous that it was difficult for researchers to use them effectively. By preserving a small sample of the records and creating a searchable database, the archivists hoped to reduce the bulk and make the records more accessible to the public. I urged the archivists to save all of the records, arguing that they were one of the few extant sources in which we could hear the voices of working-class men and women. However, the decision had already been made, and the plans for the sampling project were underway. The archivists agreed to save the transcripts that I used in my work, but all other transcripts and bills of indictment after 1940 have been preserved selectively. Information on the sampling project and its methods can be found at: http://www.phila.gov/phils/Docs/otherinfo/sampling/PhaseI.htm and http://www.phila.gov/phils/Docs/otherinfo/sampling/PhaseII.htm.

In 1998, after working intensively in the archives in the Philadelphia area, I began conducting tape-recorded oral history interviews. I found my interview subjects at senior citizen centers located throughout Philadelphia that other researchers had recommended to me. The staff of the centers introduced me to women who were participating in activities on the days of my visits. We asked the women if they wanted to take part in my project, and I scheduled interviews with those who agreed. I began each interview asking the women if they had always lived in Philadelphia and then tried to let each interview take its own shape. I had a list of topics that I tried to cover (i.e., childhood, family life, education, neighborhoods, employment), but I did not go through the list methodically, preferring to let the women dictate the direction of our conversations as much as possible. My interviews did not generate as much detailed information about public institutions as they might have if I had asked more targeted questions. But because I learned about women's entire life histories, not just their relationship with the state, the interviews provided great insight into poverty's multidimensional roots.

I interviewed both white and African American women, but my most fruitful encounters were with the African American women. I expected the African American women to view me—a young white Jewish woman—with suspicion. Indeed, some of them refused outright to participate in my study. However, those who agreed to talk to me were quite forthcoming about intimate aspects of their lives. In some cases, I felt myself gaining their trust over the course of the interview as I encouraged them to talk freely and was able to communicate my familiarity with their experiences through my knowledge of African American history. But above all, black women's forthrightness attested to their generosity and their belief that the telling of their history mattered to future generations. The women whom I expected to trust me most readily, the Jewish women, were the hardest to interview. They seemed to view poverty as shameful and did not want to talk about their experiences. During our interviews, some of the Jewish women showed me photos of their grandchildren and talked about their children's successes instead of sharing the struggles that they had faced in their youth.[1]

The oral interviews provided me with the detailed portraits of Corrine Elkins and Catherine Sanderson that I used in the introduction and some of the other quotations scattered throughout the book. However, I used the interviews as supplementary sources; they were not the backbone of my evidence. I am well aware that my interview subjects' memories and self-censorship shaped our conversations. I did not press women to discuss parts of their lives they did not feel comfortable sharing, and I did not focus the interviews around public institutions. Finally, the women I interviewed were a self-selected group who had achieved some financial security and were actively participating in community life at senior centers. Many of the women in the written records did not end up in such favorable situations.

A trip to Bryn Mawr College in the summer of 1999 made me realize how wonderfully fortuitous it was to have located my study in Philadelphia, for the college has a rich archive of material on poor women in the city. Nine miles west of Philadelphia, Bryn Mawr is a Quaker institution dedicated to women's achievement and social service. In the postwar period, faculty and graduate students from the Department of Social Work and Social Research produced a body of work on Philadelphia's Aid to Dependent Children (ADC) recipients that I used in this book. The project began in 1959, when Jane C. Kronick, an ambitious young scholar getting her Ph.D. at Yale University, joined Bryn Mawr's social work faculty. Kronick was recruited to Bryn Mawr by Dean Katherine Lower, who had worked for Franklin D. Roosevelt during the New Deal and World War II and was well-connected to people in the federal government. Shortly after Lower hired Kronick, the Social Security Administration announced a new program providing grants for studies of welfare mothers. Lower invited two of her friends in Washington to come to Bryn Mawr to talk about the program and asked Kronick to apply for a grant. Several months later, Kronick received the administration's first grant.[2]

Kronick's study began in 1959 as an investigation of the meaning of "illegitimacy" among ADC recipients in Philadelphia. Kronick wanted to know whether the presence of "illegitimate" children had a substantial effect on family life. She studied 237 ADC case files (2 percent of the city's caseload), which she chose using a systematic random sampling method. Three years later, Kronick studied 119 of the 237 families in more depth by conducting home interviews. Wanting the predominantly black mothers to feel as comfortable as possible during the interviews, Kronick, a white woman, hired two African American women interviewers. One was an unmarried graduate student finishing her Master of Social Service Degree at Bryn Mawr. She had worked for the Department of Public Assistance (DPA), so she was familiar with ADC recipients' struggles. The other interviewer was a psychiatric caseworker who was married and the mother of a small boy. She knew little about ADC policies and frequently asked the women detailed questions about how the system functioned so that she could better understand their experiences. Such questions helped establish for the women that the study was not connected to the DPA. The fact that the interviewers dressed differently from caseworkers and did not seem concerned about whether ADC recipients had men's clothing lying around their houses also signaled the study's independence from the welfare department. And when several ADC recipients asked their caseworkers about the study, the caseworkers had not heard of it, further establishing that the project had nothing to do with the welfare system.[3]

Each ADC recipient participated in two interviews—one with each interviewer—and each interview lasted approximately two hours. The interviews were voluntary, but the nearly universal participation rate made Kronick wonder in retrospect if the women realized that they could refuse to take part in the study. The first interviewer focused on women's living conditions, their childhoods, and the experiences their families had had with ADC. The second interviewer examined women's situations when they applied for welfare, how they came to receive ADC benefits, the effect of the program on their lives, their interactions with community institutions, and their relationships with their children and neighbors. The second interview was tape recorded, and Kronick coded and analyzed the information compiled from both interviews. Although Kronick had hoped to compare the experiences of white and African American ADC recipients, the number of white recipients (nine) was too small to allow her to conduct a statistically significant comparison.

When Kronick analyzed her findings, the questions she asked reflected her engagement with contemporary social scientific scholarship and public discourse. During the postwar period, many scholars identified a "subculture" in which poor people lived and outlined the pernicious effects of a "culture of poverty."[4] The emphasis on culture in studies of poor racial minorities was a progressive response to previous emphases on biological difference because it suggested that environment, not biology, produced racial inequalities. Yet the cultural turn downplayed the role of racism and political economy in shaping the contours of people's lives. Several studies held culture responsible for the high rates of out-of-wedlock births among African Americans, and a significant body of scholarship argued that "hardcore," "multiproblem" ADC recipients who received welfare for an extended period of time belonged to a subculture that differed significantly from mainstream America. Others emphasized the high degrees of hostility and distrust within poor communities. Almost everyone assumed that childbearing by unmarried women was a major component of the culture of poverty and a significant social problem.[5] White newspapers and public officials sensationalized these discussions by portraying ADC recipients as irresponsible migrants from the South who had countless "illegitimate" children as a "way of life."

In a coauthored article in the social work journal *Child Welfare*, two reports to the Social Security Administration, and an unpublished paper, Kronick investigated the claims about poor African Americans that circulated in both social-scientific scholarship and public discourse and found most of them significantly flawed.[6] Disagreeing with conventional wisdom, she argued that ADC recipients who had children out of wedlock did not hail disproportionately from the South. She maintained that most women hated being on welfare, documented the prevalence of ill health among recipients, and showed that almost all of them had histories of employment. Their backgrounds helped Kronick argue that ADC recipients did not live in a distinct "culture of poverty" or a deviant lower-class "subculture." She compared women who had children in and out of wedlock and found that the women who had children out of wedlock tended to be the ones who had developed the most careful and effective strategies for managing their lives. Kronick described out-of-wedlock childbearing as a "woman's choice" and argued that the formation of single-parent households was an adaptive strategy—a rational response to women's past experiences with men who frequently beat them and did not provide consistently for their children's basic needs. Only in her analysis of ADC recipients' interpersonal relationships did Kronick follow dominant scholarly models of the period. She consistently emphasized women's social isolation, a focus that was in line with her contemporaries who underscored the considerable hostility and distrust among members of low-income communities.[7]

Kronick's work on ADC recipients never became widely known. Aside from the article in *Child Welfare*, she did not publish her findings in any academic journals. Kronick tried on several occasions to publish articles. She told me that they were rejected on "peculiar" grounds; for example, editors told her that there was "no data" in articles that contained both a correlation matrix and a factor analysis. She suspects that the problem was the timing, not the quality of the scholarship. Kronick tried to publish her papers shortly after the release of Assistant Secretary of Labor Daniel Patrick Moynihan's 1965 report, "The Negro Family: A Case for National Action." Moynihan's controversial statements about poor African American families' "tangle of pathology," characterized by high rates of delinquency, crime, and out-of-wedlock childbearing, caused an outcry among liberals and civil rights activists, who criticized him for blaming African Americans' family structure for urban poverty. Kronick portrayed ADC recipients in a much more sympathetic light than did Moynihan or the majority of postwar political commentators; however, in the shadow of the debate over the Moynihan report, she believes that academic journals considered her work much too controversial to publish.[8] Kronick's work was particularly vulnerable to criticism because she explored the high rates of domestic violence and hostile gender relationships in low-income African American communities. Since Kronick only analyzed working-class African American women's perspectives and rarely mentioned the social conditions that helped produce men's violence and mistreatment, her work could certainly have been interpreted as furthering a "blame-the-victim" approach.

I relied on Kronick's studies mostly for their rich demographic data. They document ADC recipients' ages, family size, employment histories, health problems, access to child care, and past relationships with men. The studies also contain important information about women's daily lives, documenting small yet crucial details such as the proportion of families who had enough chairs, dishes, or beds for all members of their households. I treated Kronick's theoretical arguments much differently. Some of the issues that she addressed were simply not important to my study. For example, she spent a great deal of time comparing women who had children out of wedlock with those who did not, a question that had no direct bearing on my research. In other cases, I disagreed with Kronick's interpretation of her evidence. For instance, in emphasizing women's isolation, she minimized the importance of women's communication networks; she mentioned this phenomenon several times but did not incorporate it into her larger framework of analysis. My account recognizes that support networks could not provide the resources that women needed to avoid relying on ADC, but suggests they could provide more limited assistance and frequently helped women negotiate the welfare system.

The usefulness of Kronick's research extends beyond her writings because she allowed Bryn Mawr graduate students in social work to use the casework and interview data for their Master's theses. These theses, which are held in the Bryn Mawr College archives, explore aspects of ADC recipients' lives that Kronick did not analyze in great detail. As in Kronick's studies, the questions the students asked reflected their engagement with postwar debates in social work regarding "illegitimacy," deviant "subcultures," and "multiproblem" families. However, I found several of the theses useful in my work. One study calculated what women cited as their greatest need: food, clothing, money, furniture, or housing. Another documented women's attitudes toward employment. A few used direct quotations from the interviews with ADC recipients. One thesis that I frequently cite, "A Concept of Alienation," by Judith Levy and Gail Shouse, contains many pages filled with block quotations, in which Levy and Shouse transcribed ADC recipients' answers to the interviewers' questions. The inclusion of these long excerpts enabled me to explore questions that differed from the issues that Levy and Shouse examined in their work. Unfortunately, none of the theses identified the race of the specific women whom they were quoting. However, since they studied populations that were either 85, 93, or 100 percent African American, the vast majority of ADC recipients quoted were black women.

Another study of ADC recipients that I used was Renee Berg's 1962 University of Pennsylvania Ph.D. dissertation in social work, "A Study of a Group of Unwed Mothers Receiving Aid to Dependent Children." Berg also published an article in *Child Welfare*, which was based on the dissertation. Before embarking on her Ph.D., Berg worked for ten years in the Baltimore Department of Public Welfare, with prostitutes and other women described as having "abnormal" sexual behavior. She first became familiar with ADC recipients in 1958, when, as a doctoral student, she had a position with the Philadelphia DPA supervising work-study students from the University of Pennsylvania School of Social Work. Many of the students whom Berg supervised worked with ADC recipients. Struck by the way the stories the students told her about their clients differed from popular stereotypes, Berg decided to base her doctoral dissertation on ADC recipients.

Berg's study was based on a smaller population than Kronick's, and it was more narrowly targeted. In 1961, she interviewed thirty Philadelphia ADC recipients: twenty-eight African American women and two white women. Berg only spoke with women who had received ADC for more than two years and who had two or more children born out of wedlock. She assembled her sample with the help of the DPA, which had recently taken a 10 percent sample of ADC cases and counted the children born in and out of wedlock. The DPA gave Berg three hundred cases in which there were two or more children born out of wedlock. Berg took the first seventy-nine active cases and then chose thirty from that group that seemed particularly difficult, those whom critics would label "hardcore" recipients for whom welfare was a "way of life." Compared to the typical ADC recipient, the women in Berg's study had been receiving ADC for a longer continuous period of time, had larger families, and more different fathers of their children.

Berg's study focused primarily on ADC recipients' roles as mothers and argued that they defied the popular stereotypes about poor women's maternal inadequacies. She described ADC recipients as thoughtful, extremely polite, and welcoming. Emphasizing the seriousness with which these women regarded their maternal responsibilities and their efforts to care for their children properly, she documented their engagement with community institutions such as schools and churches. In contrast to most political commentators, who viewed single motherhood as a moral transgression and a sign of irresponsibility, Berg argued that ADC recipients viewed their decisions to raise children out of wedlock as a fulfillment of a moral obligation. Although they did not have a great deal of hope for their own futures, they hoped that their reliance on ADC would provide better opportunities for their children.

Berg's focus on long-term recipients was valuable because they were the women often accused of engaging in particularly "deviant" and "antisocial" behaviors. She included many quotations documenting women's belief that their mothering work was a moral responsibility. Some of the statistical information that she compiled helped me understand women's relationships with schools and their use of prenatal care. However, Berg did not explore why the women she studied needed welfare or probe the problems they faced. She described several women who did not seem to be doing well—who lacked hope for the future, seemed disorganized, and lived in very disheveled homes— but she did not analyze the causes of their problems. The usefulness of Berg's study was limited by her focus on disproving popular stereotypes and her lack of attention to the economic and social problems that many ADC recipients faced in their lives.

When I included women's voices in this book, I used pseudonyms for those who spoke with me about their struggles with poverty. I used the real names of women who appeared in newspaper articles, but when no name was given, I used a pseudonym and indicated this usage in the endnotes. Most of the women quoted in the social work studies were anonymous, so I used pseudonyms when quoting them. I did not change the names of most social workers, nurses, academics, social welfare advocates, judges, lawyers, politicians, and other public officials. On the few occasions when I used a pseudonym for these professionals, I indicated the usage in the endnotes.

Some of the social work studies relied on interview transcripts that tried to capture poor African American women's accents and used dialect instead of Standard English. Yet when quoting middle-class persons who had accents or used regionally distinctive language, none of the sources attempted to represent their manner of speaking. To retain consistency, when quoting poor black women, I retained slang and colloquial expressions but changed improper spelling and dialect. For example, I used the terms "ain't" and "y'all," but I changed "tired of bein' seconds" to "tired of being seconds"; and I changed "they think the average person that's on relief is sittin' down with nothin' to do" to "they think the average person that's on relief is sitting down with nothing to do." To do otherwise would have singled out poor minority women's speech patterns and run the risk of perpetuating ethnocentric stigmas associated with their manner of speaking.

Readers who wish to view the original quotations can refer to the sources cited in the endnotes.

Notes

Abbreviations

CSHN	Center for the Study of the History of Nursing, Philadelphia
DPWF	Department of Public Welfare, Administrative Files, 1955–58
EELR	Floyd L. Logan (Educational Equality League) Records, 1922–78
FCR	Fellowship Commission Records, 1941–94
FNGR	Friends Neighborhood Guild Records, 1922–80
FS	Family Service of Philadelphia
GSR	Germantown Settlement Records, 1908–10, 1928, 1947–91
HADVR1	Housing Association of the Delaware Valley Records, 1909–75
HADVR2	Housing Association of the Delaware Valley Records, 1909–72
HWCR1	Health and Welfare Council, Inc., Records, 1922–69
HWCR2	Health and Welfare Council, Inc., Records, 1926–55
HWCR3	Health and Welfare Council, Inc., Records, 1928–66
HWCR-648	Health and Welfare Council, Inc., Records, Accession no. 648
JA	Philadelphia Jewish Archives Center
JFSR	Jewish Family Service Records
LC	Manuscript Division, Library of Congress, Washington, D.C.
MCPA	Medical College of Pennsylvania Archives, Philadelphia
NAACPR	National Association for the Advancement of Colored People, Philadelphia Branch Records, 1943–63
NARA	National Archives and Records Administration, College Park, Maryland
PC	Urban Archives Pamphlet Collection
PCA	Philadelphia City Archives
PEB	*Philadelphia Evening Bulletin*
PEBNC	*PEB* Newsclipping Collection
PGH-OH	Philadelphia General Hospital Oral History Interview Project
PMC-AR	*Philadelphia Municipal Court Annual Report*
PSA	Pennsylvania State Archives, Harrisburg
RAATS	Records of the Alumni Association Training School of the Philadelphia General Hospital
RNUL	Records of the National Urban League, 1900–1986
RSSA	General Records of the Social Security Administration, 1935–86
SSER	Philadelphia-Camden Social Service Exchange Records, 1911–70
UATU	Urban Archives, Temple University, Philadelphia
UCR	United Communities of Southeast Philadelphia Records, 1847–1978

ULPR1   Urban League of Philadelphia Records, 1935–63
ULPR2   Urban League of Philadelphia Records, 1960–67, Addition 1
WCR   Wharton Centre Records, 1913–68
WHS   Wisconsin Historical Society, Madison
WMMCPR   Women in Medicine and the Medical College of Pennsylvania Records
WOARR   Women Organized against Rape Records, 1973–95
WPSCR   West Philadelphia Schools Committee Records, 1961–70
YMCAR-C   YMCA of Philadelphia—Christian Street Records, 1943–64
YWCAR-SW   YWCA of Philadelphia—Southwest Belmont Branch Records, 1920–77

Introduction

1. This is an example of what Jacquelyn Dowd Hall has called an "open secret"; see Hall, "Open Secrets."

2. The life histories of Catherine Sanderson and Corrine Elkins are based on C.S. interview and C.E. interview. On women and oral histories, see Gluck and Patai, *Women's Words*; Armitage, *Women's Oral History*.

3. This book focuses on the instances in which women proactively sought services from government agencies, not on the cases in which the state ensnared them against their will. Although women did not comprise the majority of clients of all kinds of cases in the municipal court, they predominated among those who pressed nonsupport, fornication and bastardy, and assault and battery charges, which were the most common cases brought by working-class people during this period.

4. Sugrue, *Origins of the Urban Crisis*; Hirsch, *Making the Second Ghetto*; Self, *American Babylon*; Bauman, *Public Housing*; McKee, "Philadelphia Liberals."

5. Wilson, *The Truly Disadvantaged*. See also Neckerman, Aponte, and Wilson, "Family Structure, Black Unemployment, and American Social Policy"; Testa and Krogh, "The Effect of Employment on Marriage among Black Males."

6. Although *The "Underclass" Debate*, an influential 1993 collection of historical essays on urban poverty edited by Michael B. Katz, includes articles on education and family relationships, it does not comprehensively examine the role of gender or include analyses of health care or the legal system. Conversely, the excellent historical studies of education, health care, welfare, and the municipal courts rarely link these arenas to scholarship on urban poverty. Important exceptions include Katz's *The Price of Citizenship* and *Improving Poor People*.

7. On the prewar roots of this shift to public institutions, see Kathryn M. Neckerman, "The Emergence of 'Underclass' Family Patterns, 1900–1940," in Katz, *The "Underclass" Debate*, 194–219; Wolcott, *Remaking Respectability*, 226–40.

8. Kelley, *Race Rebels*, 6–7. See also Hunter, *To 'Joy My Freedom*. On welfare rights and tenants' rights, see Williams, *The Politics of Public Housing*; Orleck, *Storming Caesars Palace*; Nadasen, *Welfare Warriors*; Kornbluh, *The Battle for Welfare Rights*.

9. Opposition to African Americans' reliance on the government dated back to Reconstruction; however, in the postwar period, whites had more forms of state assis-

tance that they could decry, and they focused to a much greater extent on the unique culpability of black women. See Richardson, *Death of Reconstruction*.

10. On the roots of Republican efforts to use racism to win white support, see Wolfinger, *Philadelphia Divided*.

11. For interpretations of the New Right that emphasize the defense of race and class privilege, see Kruse, *White Flight*; Sugrue, *Origins of the Urban Crisis*; Lassiter, *The Silent Majority*; Self, *American Babylon*; MacLean, *Freedom Is Not Enough*; Wolfinger, *Philadelphia Divided*. On the role of libertarianism, religion, and anticommunism, see McGirr, *Suburban Warriors*; Critchlow, *Phyllis Schlafly and the Rise of Grassroots Conservatism*. On the issue of welfare in New Right discourse and policy proposals, see Kornbluh, *The Battle for Welfare Rights*.

12. The point is not that women necessarily led harder lives than men but that since gender played an important role in constructing urban poverty, men and women frequently struggled with different problems.

13. Stein, *City of Sisterly and Brotherly Loves*, 3. When using U.S. Census statistics in this book, I equate "nonwhite" with African American because African Americans made up the vast majority of this category in the city's population. Philadelphia City Planning Commission, *Population of Metropolitan Area Counties*, 2-1, 2-2; U.S. Department of Commerce, *U.S. Censuses of Population and Housing, 1960*, 21. Compared to neighboring cities such as New York, Philadelphia had a relatively small immigrant population; see Golab, *Immigrant Destinations*.

14. Bureau of Municipal Research, *Special Assimilation Problems*; Blumberg, *Migration as a Problem Area for Urban Social Work*, table 8.

15. Blumberg, *Migration as a Program Area for Urban Social Work*, tables 3, 4, 5. Nearly one third of all migrants had previously lived in cities of over 50,000 people. Another third came from farms or areas with populations of less than 1,000 people. For an excellent discussion of the similarities between new migrants and longtime residents, see Gregory, *The Southern Diaspora*, 104–8.

16. "Area between Washington Ave. and Christian Street, and between Broad Street and 11th Street," Box 23, Folder Hawthorne Home and School Association, August 26, 1952–July 22, 1953, UCR, UATU; Fish and Welburn, "Study of the Characteristics of Neighborhood, Housing, and Mobility," 18–19; "Marshall-Pemberton-Kenilsworth," 1956, Box 21, Folder KMP Records, UCR, UATU.

17. Fish and Welburn, "Study of the Characteristics of Neighborhood, Housing, and Mobility," 17–18; "An Urban Renewal Policy for North Philadelphia," 1958, Box 40, Folder 73, WCR, UATU; Bauman, *Public Housing*, 87; Wolfinger, *Philadelphia Divided*, 208; C.E. interview.

18. "The Jungle," *PEB*, February 3, 1957, section 2, pp. 1, 2; "Neighbors Disown North Philadelphia 'Jungle,'" *PEB*, February 17, 1957, 1, 14. The term "jungle" was applied to African American neighborhoods in other cities during this period as well as to communities of white southern migrants; see Guy, "The Media, the Police, and Southern White Migrant Identity"; Durr, *Behind the Backlash*, 197.

19. Johnson, "Black Philadelphia in Transition," 62; Gregg, *Sparks from the Anvil of*

Oppression, 221; Fish and Welburn, "Study of the Characteristics of Neighborhood, Housing, and Mobility," 19.

20. Warner, *The Private City*, 173.

21. "Review of Public Housing Policies," June 25, 1956, Box 282, Folder 4921, HADVR1, UATU; Levy and Shouse, "Concept of Alienation," 36, 42, 87; Bauman, *Public Housing*, 149–51; Bauman, Hummon, and Muller, "Public Housing," 281.

22. Bauman, *Public Housing*, 146–50, 152–53; Lavell, *Philadelphia's Non-White Population*; Lewis J. Carter, "Urban Renewal and Non-White Families in Philadelphia," paper presented to the National Urban League's Urban Renewal Institute, Elizabeth, N.J., April 19–20, 1956, Box 13, Folder 227, ULPR1, UATU; Wolfinger, *Philadelphia Divided*, 188–90. On these trends nationally and in other major cities, see Self, *American Babylon*; Jackson, *Crabgrass Frontier*; Sugrue, *Origins of the Urban Crisis*; Hirsch, *Making the Second Ghetto*. On African American suburbanization, see Wiese, *Places of Their Own*.

23. Urban League of Philadelphia, *Selected Health and Welfare Characteristics of Negro Philadelphians: 1961* (Philadelphia, 1962). On the historical relationship between employment and motherhood among African American women, see Jones, *Labor of Love, Labor of Sorrow*; Lemke-Santangelo, *Abiding Courage*, 107–32.

24. Adams et al., *Philadelphia*, 30–32, 39; Bauman, *Public Housing*, 22; Goldstein, "The Wrong Side of the Tracts," 2.

25. Bauman, *Public Housing*, 57.

26. Countryman, *Up South*, 53; Bauman, *Public Housing*, 162.

27. Abrams, *Home Ownership for the Poor*, 18–19; Bauman, *Public Housing*, 83; Bauman, Hummon, and Muller, "Public Housing," 279. For an excellent discussion of Philadelphia's labor market in the postwar period, see Whalen, *From Puerto Rico to Philadelphia*, 138–44.

28. McKee, "Philadelphia Liberals," 283–84, 356; Sullivan, *Build Brother Build*, 67; Countryman, *Up South*, 62–68; Bauman, *Public Housing*, 84–87; Abrams, *Home Ownership for the Poor*, 18–19. African Americans also lacked the opportunities that immigrants could find in "ethnic niches"; see Waldinger, *Still the Promised City*; Suzanne Model, "The Ethnic Niche and the Structure of Opportunity: Immigrants and Minorities in New York City," in Katz, *The "Underclass" Debate*, 161–93. One of the best accounts of racial discrimination in employment is Sugrue, *The Origins of the Urban Crisis*, 91–123.

29. On domestic work, see Clark-Lewis, *Living In, Living Out*; Rollins, *Between Women*; Palmer, *Domesticity and Dirt*.

30. For a cogent and thorough analysis of the limitations of 1950s civil rights activism in addressing the problems of the working class that focuses on the NAACP, see Countryman, *Up South*, esp. 48–79. In a different account, Johnson focuses on the civil rights agitation in black churches, arguing that African Americans' fears of being identified as communists in the midst of the Cold War led them to focus on organizing internally instead of mounting large protests; see Johnson, "Black Philadelphia in Transition," 249–52, 262–65.

31. "Intergroup understanding," quoted in Countryman, *Up South*, 28–29.

32. On the struggle for jobs throughout the country, see MacLean, *Freedom Is Not Enough*.

33. For a more detailed account, see Countryman, *Up South*, 35–38.

34. Countryman, *Up South*, 59–63.

35. On selective patronage, see Countryman, *Up South*, 101–10, 118–19; McKee, "Philadelphia Liberals," 308–21; Sullivan, *Build Brother Build*, 70–84.

36. Countryman, *Up South*, 41, 44–46.

37. Rothman, Rosenthal, Bowman, and Hebb, *Philadelphia Government*, 26–27; McKee, "Philadelphia Liberals," 285–86.

38. Weigley, *Philadelphia*, 653–57; Pennsylvania Economy League, "History of Philadelphia's City Government," Report 365, February 1973, 11–15, Box A-1601, File PEL, "History of Philadelphia's City Government," Report #365, February 1973, PCA; City of Philadelphia, *Annual Report of the Personnel Department, 1953*, 3–5, 9.

39. Countryman, *Up South*, 50; Reichley, *Art of Government*, 70. African Americans were overrepresented in the municipal sector because many talented African Americans who were denied opportunities in the private sector sought jobs working for the city. Consequently, African Americans scored disproportionately high on civil service examinations.

40. Between 1940 and 1960, the white home ownership rate increased from 43 to 68 percent. Lavell, *Philadelphia's Non-White Population—1960: Report No. 2, Housing Data*; Elfriede F. Hoeber, "Facts on the Housing Situation of Negroes in the Philadelphia Metropolitan Area" (1958), Box 7, Folder 15, HADVR2, UATU. Philadelphia had an exceptionally high rate of home ownership among both races because of the profusion of low-cost housing in semidetached and attached row houses; see Courtney C. Smith Jr., "Philadelphia Housing," Box 8, Folder 22, HADVR2, UATU. On the upper echelons of those in city employment, see Ershkowitz and Zikmund, *Black Politics in Philadelphia*, 124.

41. On support networks, see Lemke-Santangelo, *Abiding Courage*, 49–68; Grossman, *Land of Hope*, 133–37; Phillips, *Alabama North*, 139–45. For a classic sociological study, see Stack, *All Our Kin*.

42. Johnson, "Black Philadelphia in Transition," 282, 283–87, 292–93.

43. Ibid., 273–74, 282, 289–90, 297–98, 330. For an important analysis of African Methodist Episcopal churches in the early twentieth century and their relationship to migration and community formation, see Gregg, *Sparks from the Anvil of Oppression*.

44. Mays and Nicholson, *The Negro's Church*, 219.

45. Johnson, "Black Philadelphia in Transition," 297–99; Minutes of the Meeting of the Poplar Area Community Council, January 17, 1955, Box 85, Folder 130, FNGR, UATU; J.P. interview.

46. Masur, "Reconstructing the Nation's Capital." On twentieth-century activists' "dual agenda" of civil rights and social welfare services, see Hamilton and Hamilton, *Dual Agenda*.

47. The term "under-class" was first used in 1963 by Swedish social scientist Gunnar Myrdal, who described chronic unemployment and underemployment as one of its

defining features. In the 1970s, the term "underclass" (without a hyphen) was used more widely by journalists, and in the 1980s, many scholars began to use the term; see Myrdal, *The Challenge to Affluence*, 34–49; George Russell, "The American Underclass," *Time*, August 19, 1977, 12–18; Auletta, *The Underclass*. For an important historical analysis of the term and its uses, see Michael B. Katz, "The Urban 'Underclass' as a Metaphor of Social Transformation," in Katz, *The "Underclass" Debate*, 3–23.

48. For a broad definition of the working class, see Kelley, *Race Rebels*, 12–13. Thanks to Joe Trotter for helping me formulate my views on women's labor. Feminist labor historians have shown that we need to expand our conception of "work" beyond formal employment in order to capture the myriad forms of unpaid labor that women perform on a daily basis in their homes and communities; see Boris and Kleinberg, "Mothers and Other Workers."

49. Important works on public housing include Hirsch, *Making the Second Ghetto*; Sugrue, *Origins of the Urban Crisis*; Bauman, *Public Housing*; Hunt, "What Went Wrong with Public Housing in Chicago?" Important works on the history of social welfare policy include Gordon, *Pitied but Not Entitled*; Brown, *Race, Money, and the American Welfare State*; Goodwin, *Gender and the Politics of Welfare Reform*; Mittelstadt, *From Welfare to Workfare*.

50. Mitchell, "Silences Broken, Silences Kept." I have also been influenced by Hine, "Black Migration to the Urban Midwest."

51. On the need for gendered studies of men, see Trotter, *Black Milwaukee*, 315.

52. On working-class white women in Philadelphia, see Levenstein, "The Gendered Roots of Modern Urban Poverty"; Levenstein, "Hard Choices at 1801 Vine"; Broder, *Tramps, Unfit Mothers, and Neglected Children*. Studies of working-class white women elsewhere include Igra, *Wives without Husbands*; Stadum, *Poor Women and Their Families*.

53. On the Puerto Rican experience in Philadelphia, see Whalen, *From Puerto Rico to Philadelphia*. In 1960, 14,424 Philadelphians were born in Puerto Rico or had Puerto Rican parents; see City of Philadelphia, *Philadelphia's Puerto Rican Population*, 6.

54. Low-income women in postwar Philadelphia occasionally engaged in militant collective protests, such as when the federal government tried to evict them from public housing after World War II. However, protests initiated by poor black women in Philadelphia were rare during this period. Studies of other cities have pointed to some collective protest among low-income black women in the immediate postwar period; see Shockley, "*We, Too, Are Americans*"; Williams, *The Politics of Public Housing*. There is also a burgeoning literature on women's activism in postwar labor unions, which includes Gabin, *Feminism and the Labor Movement*; Cobble, *The Other Women's Movement*; Deslippe, *Rights, Not Roses*.

Chapter One

1. Quoted in Levy and Shouse, "Concept of Alienation," 22–23. I use the term "marriage" to describe legal unions between men and women. I use the term "husband" more loosely, as the women themselves did, to refer to any long-term partner.

2. All figures are approximate and have been compiled from the following sources: Pennsylvania Department of Public Welfare, *Trends: Annual Report, 1960*, 16–17; Kronick, "Attitudes toward Dependency," 2; Philadelphia County Board of Assistance, "Study of Characteristics of Regular Segment of Aid to Dependent Children Families," Box 20, Folder 300, ULPR2, UATU; Philadelphia County Board of Assistance, "Summary Statistical Report," October 1963, Box 20, Folder 295, ULPR2, UATU. When using the summary statistical report, I only considered ADC cases, not the briefly adopted ADC-UP program. If I had incorporated ADC-UP, the figures would have been even higher.

3. Most historical accounts of welfare focus on either welfare policy or the 1960s welfare rights movement; the politics of the daily struggles of women seeking to survive on welfare have been overlooked. On welfare rights in Philadelphia, see Countryman, *Up South*, 271–82. More generally, see West, *The National Welfare Rights Movement*; Nadasen, *Welfare Warriors*; Kornbluh, *The Battle for Welfare Rights*; Orleck, *Storming Caesars Palace*. Studies of welfare policy include Gordon, *Pitied but Not Entitled*; Goodwin, *Gender and the Politics of Welfare Reform*; Brown, *Race, Money, and the American Welfare State*.

4. On Mothers' Assistance in Philadelphia, see Hall, *Mothers' Assistance in Philadelphia*. In Chicago, see Goodwin, *Gender and the Politics of Welfare Reform*. Nationally, see Gordon, *Pitied but Not Entitled*, 37–64.

5. Gordon, *Pitied but Not Entitled*, 12–13, 293–99.

6. The proportion of the federal contribution increased over the course of the postwar period; see Commonwealth of Philadelphia, *Origin and Development of Public Assistance* (1955), 39. No other state in the nation had a program controlled so tightly at the state level; see William B. Tollen, "A Point of View on Reorganization of Public Welfare Services in Pennsylvania" (July 10, 1962), Box 3, Folder 92, HWCR3, UATU; Health and Welfare Council, Public Assistance Committee, Minutes, April 18, 1961, Box 4, Folder 99, HWCR3, UATU; Braun, "The Development of Public Assistance," 39, 41, 44–45. Each Pennsylvania county had a local Board of Public Assistance, which consisted of a politically diverse group of local citizens (11 in Philadelphia) appointed by the governor to oversee the program. The board had a minimal role in administering the program. See Braun, 43–44. In 1958, the Pennsylvania Department of Welfare and the Pennsylvania Department of Public Assistance merged to form the Pennsylvania Department of Public Welfare.

7. Commonwealth of Pennsylvania, *Pennsylvania Public Assistance Statistics, May 1939*, 17–18; Commonwealth of Pennsylvania, *Pennsylvania Public Assistance Review: Third Quarter 1943*, 8, 10–11.

8. Charles S. Johnson and Associates, "The Negro Population in Philadelphia" (Council of Social Agencies, 1942), Box 2, Folder 9, HWCR2, UATU. Pennsylvania was one of only nine states in which a significant number of nonwhite children received grants between 1942 and 1948. The others were Florida, Illinois, Missouri, Nebraska, New York, North Dakota, Oklahoma, and Rhode Island. See Bell, *Aid to Dependent Children*, 55.

9. Philadelphia County Board of Assistance, "Study of Characteristics of Regular Segment of Aid to Dependent Children Families." Although a few men received ADC grants, women and their children were the vast majority of recipients. In 1956, on the national level, 60 percent of the ADC caseload was white and 40 percent was nonwhite, with African Americans comprising 94 percent of the nonwhite recipients; see Coll, *Safety Net*, 199.

10. On the myth that ADC attracted southern migrants, see Jacqueline Jones, "Southern Diaspora: Origins of the Northern 'Underclass,' " in Katz, *The "Underclass" Debate*, 44–45; Levenstein, "From Innocent Children to Unwanted Migrants and Unwed Moms," 18–19.

11. On the similarities in the experiences of migrants and long-standing residents, see Gregory, *The Southern Diaspora*, 104–6.

12. Kronick, "Attitudes toward Dependency," 19; Norton and Vernon, "A Study of a Random Sample of Mothers of Legitimate and Illegitimate Children," 137.

13. Health and Welfare Council, Inc., "Report of the Public Assistance Committee" (1962), Box 11, Folder 4, series 6, JFSR, JA; Ritti, *The "Welfare Explosion."*

14. Studies of race and the U.S. welfare state include Brown, *Race, Money, and the American Welfare State*; Lieberman, *Shifting the Color Line*. On suitable home laws and other restrictions, see Bell, *Aid to Dependent Children*; Reese, *Backlash against Welfare Mothers*.

15. U.S. Bureau of the Census, *U.S. Censuses of Population and Housing: 1960*, 21, 317. All U.S. Census statistics cited in this book equate "nonwhites" with African Americans. On income disparities by race, see also "Distribution of Income for White & Non-White Persons with Income—PSMA—1950 & 1960, in Constant 1960 Dollars (no. in 1000's)," Box 7, Folder 5, HADVR1, UATU.

16. Goldsmith, "Working the System," 77–87, 103, 179. Initially, an automobile was allowed only if a person was deemed to have a specific need for one and if the vehicle was not expensive. After a policy change in 1956, women did not have to demonstrate a specific need for a car, but their cars could not be less than 5 years old or worth more than $500. See Commonwealth of Pennsylvania, *Public Assistance Review* (1956), 6. If welfare recipients owned or were making mortgage payments on homes, liens were taken out against these properties for the dollar amount of the public assistance received. If recipients ever sold their homes, they had to reimburse the government for the money they had collected. This rule remained in place until 1995. For an important contemporary comparison of black and white poverty, see Oliver and Shapiro, *Black Wealth/White Wealth*.

17. On unemployment insurance, see Lieberman, *Shifting the Color Line*, 177–215; Abramovitz, *Regulating the Lives of Women*, 215–40, 273–305.

18. Between 1930 and 1960, as young white families moved to the suburbs and African Americans in their childbearing years migrated to Philadelphia, the number of white children aged seven to fifteen residing in the city decreased by 30 percent while the number of black children increased by 201 percent; see *PMC-AR, 1960*, 37–38; Nightingale, *On the Edge*, 197.

19. Statistic regarding household heads is from Adams et al., *Philadelphia*, 62. The available information makes more precise statistical comparison impossible. The data tend to understate the differences in the experiences of white and black women because more of the white female household heads were widows with older children. Statistic regarding children out of wedlock is from 1955; see Health and Welfare Council, Family Division, Advisory Committee Minutes, September 16, 1958, Box 12, Folder 85, HWCR1, UATU. On racial differences in out-of-wedlock childbearing, see Solinger, *Wake Up Little Susie*.

20. Levy and Shouse, "Concept of Alienation," 76; Ladner, *Tomorrow's Tomorrow*, 213–23. See also Hicks, "'In Danger of Becoming Morally Depraved.'" On the stigma faced by both white and African American women who sought assistance at a Philadelphia home for unwed mothers, see Barron, "Illegitimately Pregnant."

21. Westerfield, "Reasons for Discharge," 41, 43; Ladner, *Tomorrow's Tomorrow*, 213–23; Berg, "Study of a Group of Unwed Mothers," 108–9; Levy and Shouse, "Concept of Alienation," 76. For a contemporary study, see Kaplan, *Not Our Kind of Girl*.

22. Quoted in Levy and Shouse, "Concept of Alienation," 23.

23. McMurray, "Employment Experiences and Attitudes," 31; "Image of Recipients Wrong," *Philadelphia Inquirer*, September 14, 1961, 1, 52; Kronick interview. Studies of the historical relationship between black women's employment and motherhood include Jones, *Labor of Love, Labor of Sorrow*; Lemke-Santangelo, *Abiding Courage*, 107–32. For important conceptual frameworks, see Glenn, Chang, and Forcey, *Mothering*.

24. Kronick, "Attitudes toward Dependency," 43. All statistics from Kronick's study reflect the ADC population in the early 1960s; see Appendix. On unemployment, see Russell, "Study of White and Nonwhite Female Unemployment," 45, 47, 56. Russell found that in the lowest-income groups of African Americans, women were more likely than men to be unemployed. Statistics on women's job distribution, calculated from all employed women who reported their occupation to the U.S. Census, are in U.S. Department of Commerce, *U.S. Censuses of Population and Housing: 1960*, 243, 317.

25. One study based on Kronick's data found 32 percent of ADC recipients stating that they did not hold jobs because of health problems; see McMurray, "Employment Experiences and Attitudes," 39. A different study found 29 percent of ADC recipients citing illness or the disability of the wage earner as the precipitating event in their application for welfare; see Department of Public Assistance, Philadelphia County Board, *Annual Report, 1951*, 15. On health problems and ADC recipients more generally, see Kronick, "Attitudes toward Dependency," 68; Health and Welfare Council, Family Division, Advisory Committee Minutes, December 17, 1957, Box 12, Folder 84, HWCR1, UATU; Allis, Becker, Henderson, and Myers, "Wants of AFDC Mothers," 58, 69.

26. Quoted in Levy and Shouse, "Concept of Alienation," 82.

27. Most women said that lack of day care prevented them from leaving ADC, not that it impelled them to seek ADC in the first place; see McMurray, "Employment Experiences and Attitudes," 39.

28. One 1961 DPA study found that 60 percent of all ADC families had 3 children or less, 10 percent had 4 children, and 27 percent had 5 or more children. Kronick found

slightly higher numbers of children living in women's households: 50 percent of women in her study had 3 children or less in their homes, 18 percent had 4 children, and 32 percent had 5 or more children. See Philadelphia County Board of Assistance, "Study of Characteristics of Regular Segment of Aid to Dependent Children Families"; Kronick, "Family Life and Economic Dependency," 53; Department of Public Assistance, Philadelphia County Board, *Annual Report, 1951*, 13.

29. Kronick, "Attitudes toward Dependency," 70. See also Commonwealth of Pennsylvania, Philadelphia County Board of Assistance, *Toward Family Renewal: Annual Report, 1958*.

30. Josephine Milton, "Summary of Skits and Statistical Information," 1962, Box 40, Folder 83, WCR, UATU; "Finding Good Day Care Centers Is Working Mothers' Problem," *PEB*, September 3, 1957, 58; "We Need More Day Care Centers," *PEB*, September 4, 1957, 28. For a general history of day care in Philadelphia, see Rose, *A Mother's Job*.

31. Quoted in Levy and Shouse, "Concept of Alienation," 24.

32. Ibid., 31–32.

33. Levy and Shouse, "Concept of Alienation," 83–85, quotation on 83.

34. Kronick, "Family Life and Economic Dependency," 65–66; Kronick interview.

35. Quoted in Berg, "Study of a Group of Unwed Mothers," 95.

36. Ibid., 95.

37. Ibid., 95; see also 93–95, 109.

38. Quoted in Levy and Shouse, "Concept of Alienation," 92.

39. Solinger, *Wake Up Little Susie*, 148–86; M. Leo Bohanon, "The Urban League of Philadelphia," June 11, 1962, Box 7, Folder Philadelphia, HWCR-648, UATU; Barron, "Illegitimately Pregnant," 333–37.

40. Quoted in Berg, "Study of a Group of Unwed Mothers," 94.

41. Gay interview; Van Dyke interview; J.P. interview; J.E.J. interview; M.G. interview; V.F. interview; Lemke-Santangelo, *Abiding Courage*, 145.

42. Jane C. Kronick, "A Woman's Choice: A New Interpretation of Illegitimacy among the Poor," 9–10, quotation on 10, unpublished manuscript, n.d., in author's possession; Kronick, "Attitudes toward Dependency," 21, 37–38, 41–42. Eight percent of ADC recipients were under 25 years old, 38 percent were between 26 and 35, and 37 percent were between 36 and 46. Thirty-nine percent of ADC recipients reported at least one desertion, which they described as a breakup in which men had unilaterally decided to leave. Forty-four percent had experienced at least one separation in which they said they had participated in the decision to split up. In a significant shift from the Mothers' Assistance clientele, only 15 percent of ADC recipients in 1960 were widows.

43. Kronick, "Attitudes toward Dependency," 33. Berg estimated that the total proportion of children receiving ADC who were born out of wedlock was between 40 and 50 percent; see Berg, "Study of a Group of Unwed Mothers," 20.

44. Kronick, "Attitudes toward Dependency," 37.

45. See, for example, Wilson, *The Truly Disadvantaged*, 82–92, 95–106, 145–46; Neckerman, Aponte, and Wilson, "Family Structure, Black Unemployment, and American Social Policy"; Testa and Krogh, "The Effect of Employment on Marriage."

46. Quoted in M.B.M. interview; author's e-mail correspondence with Jane Kronick, March 29, 2000; Ladner, *Tomorrow's Tomorrow*, 36–37, 236. On similar attitudes held by working-class whites in the late-nineteenth and early-twentieth centuries, see Igra, *Wives without Husbands*, 64.

47. Kronick, "Family Life and Economic Dependency," 68, 71; Kronick, "A Woman's Choice," 9–10; Ladner, *Tomorrow's Tomorrow*, 37, 236; Kronick interview; author's e-mail correspondence with Jane Kronick, March 29, 2000. Studies of poor whites in the first half of the twentieth century have shown that it was not uncommon for employed men to withhold money from women and children; see Kathryn M. Neckerman, "The Emergence of 'Underclass' Family Patterns, 1900–1940," in Katz, *The "Underclass" Debate*, 211–13; Gordon, *Heroes of Their Own Lives*; Stadum, *Poor Women and Their Families*.

48. Quoted in L.W. interview.

49. Kronick, "A Woman's Choice," 10–11, quoted on 11; Kronick, "Attitudes toward Dependency," 39, 41–42. There were probably also women who chose not to share experiences of abuse with interviewers or who were abused by men other than the fathers of their children (the men they were questioned about).

50. For an important discussion of low-income abusive men's struggles in the late twentieth century, see Raphael, *Saving Bernice*, 140–50.

51. Quotation from Savitz, *Factors Influencing Crime Rates of Negroes*, 9; Johnson, "Black Philadelphia in Transition," 144.

52. Kronick, "Attitudes toward Dependency," 37.

53. Ibid., 41–42.

54. Quoted in C.S. interview. See also J.P. interview; A.B. interview; G.J. interview. Similarly, on poor whites in the early twentieth century, see Stadum, *Poor Women and Their Families*, 98.

55. Nightingale, *On the Edge*, 59; Abrahams, *Deep Down in the Jungle*, 28–29; author's e-mail correspondence with Jane Kronick, March 29, 2000; Ladner, *Tomorrow's Tomorrow*, 36–37, 236; L.L. interview; E.O.K. interview.

56. Fifteen percent of the women interviewed for Kronick's study stated that men's unemployment or insufficient earnings was the precipitating event in their application for welfare. However, we do not know how many of these women were living with men and separated in order to receive welfare. See Kronick, "Attitudes toward Dependency," 43.

57. Ladner, *Tomorrow's Tomorrow*, 47–48.

58. Bane, "Household Composition and Poverty." For an overview of the literature, see Zinn, "Family, Race, and Poverty in the Eighties."

59. Statistics are based on a statistical analysis of a random sample of women over age 18 in Philadelphia who appeared in households where the head was a sample line person in the United States Census. The sample was extracted through the Integrated Public Use Microdata Series (IPUMS). Poverty was calculated by using Mark J. Stern's poverty index, which is useful because it adjusts for changes in social expectations as well as inflation; see Stern, "Poverty and the Life Cycle."

60. For a similar argument regarding single motherhood and poverty in the lives of working-class Jewish women in early twentieth-century New York, see Igra, *Wives without Children*, 65.

61. Quoted in Levy and Shouse, "Concept of Alienation," 20.

62. Kronick, "Attitudes toward Dependency," 43–45; Levy and Shouse, "Concept of Alienation," 20; Department of Public Welfare, Minutes of State Hearing, #525 448-D, August 26, 1958, Box 12, DPWF, PSA.

63. Commonwealth of Pennsylvania, *Public Assistance Review: Annual Summary, December 1947*, 3–30; Levy and Shouse, "Concept of Alienation," 78–79; Philadelphia Welfare Rights Organization, "Get It Together: Philadelphia Welfare Rights Handbook," 2–3, Box 7, Folder Philadelphia Welfare Rights Organization, HWCR-648, UATU; Philadelphia Welfare Rights Organization, "PWRO Handbook," Box 326, Folder 6287, HADVR1, UATU.

64. Quoted in Levy and Shouse, "A Concept of Alienation," 78–79.

65. See, for example, ibid., 78–79.

66. Many of the women quoted in Levy and Shouse, "A Concept of Alienation," adopted this shorthand; Kronick interview; Kronick, "Attitudes toward Dependency," 44.

67. In 1951, the DPA accepted only 37 percent of all applicants; by the late 1950s, it accepted nearly half of the applicants; see Department of Public Assistance, Philadelphia County Board, *Annual Report, 1951*, 12; Philadelphia County Board of Assistance, "Summary Statistical Report," January 1961, Box 34, Folder 56, SSER, UATU; "Number on Dole near Postwar Peak," *Philadelphia Inquirer*, September 10, 1961, 1, 28. On the increased availability of federal monies for welfare in the 1950s, see Commonwealth of Pennsylvania, *Origin and Development of Public Assistance* (1958), 26, 39; Coll, *Safety Net*, 176–82.

68. Pennsylvania ranked twenty-second of all U.S. states in the monetary value of its ADC provisions; see Commonwealth of Pennsylvania, *Public Assistance Allowances*; Commonwealth of Pennsylvania, *Public Welfare Report*, 73, 74; Health and Welfare Council, Family Division, "Memorandum on Public Assistance," February 13, 1959, Box 12, Folder 85, HWCR1, UATU. Each fiscal year, state welfare authorities returned to the Pennsylvania legislature when their appropriation ran dry to seek more money. Although the legislature frequently granted additional funds over the course of the year, instead of using the funds to increase the monetary value of grants, welfare authorities usually put the money toward adding more needy people to the program. See Health and Welfare Council, Public Assistance Committee, Minutes, April 18, 1961, Box 4, Folder 99, HWCR3, UATU.

69. Kronick, "Attitudes toward Dependency," 47, 61; Levy and Shouse, "Concept of Alienation," 37; "Excerpts from: A Policy Statement on Standards of Public Assistance (The Woodbury Report)," February 19, 1957, Box 325, Folder 6276, HADVR1, UATU; "It's Possible to Live on Relief, But High Rents Make It Tough," *PEB*, June 7, 1959, 32.

70. Kronick, "Attitudes toward Dependency," 58.

71. Kornbluh, "To Fulfill Their Rightly Needs," 84.

72. Levy and Shouse, "Concept of Alienation," 44–46. On the surplus food program in Philadelphia, see Rothman, Jacob, and Deaton, *Philadelphia Government*, 142.

73. Levy and Shouse, "Concept of Alienation," 41, 47–49, 51, quotation on 48; Allis, Becker, Henderson, and Meyers, "Wants of AFDC Mothers," 53, 55, 68; "2d Hand Clothes for Reliefers Called a 'Badge of Shame,'" *PEB*, April 13, 1952, 10; Kronick, "Attitudes toward Dependency," 47, 61.

74. Levy and Shouse, "Concept of Alienation," 37; Kronick interview.

75. Levy and Shouse, "Concept of Alienation," 38, 50. More generally, see Caplovitz, *The Poor Pay More*.

76. In 1956, the DPA took a small step toward changing these policies by allowing recipients to own life insurance policies with net cash values of $500 or less. If recipients' policies exceeded this amount, they had a six-month grace period to give them up, enabling women to receive ADC for a short time without liquidating their insurance. See Commonwealth of Pennsylvania, *Public Assistance Review* (1956), 6.

77. Restrictions on additional income had not always been a part of welfare programs. Mothers' Assistance administrators had expected women and children to supplement their grants through employment. See Commonwealth of Pennsylvania, *Pennsylvania Public Assistance Review: Third Quarter 1943*, 4, 5; Hall, *Mothers' Assistance*, 32–34; Commonwealth of Pennsylvania, *Report of the Mothers' Assistance Fund*, 7, 57–58. On similar Mothers' Assistance policies in Chicago, see Goodwin, *Gender and the Politics of Welfare Reform*, 7, 169–72. It is difficult to discern exactly when restrictions on outside earnings were instituted. According to Blanch Coll's national study, in 1942, women could still keep extra income. See Coll, *Safety Net*, 119. One 1945 Pennsylvania report claimed that restrictions had been implemented; see Commonwealth of Pennsylvania, *Current Living Costs*. According to a 1947 report, prior to 1947, ADC covered only four out of fifteen "essential living requirements" (food, clothing, fuel, and shelter) and ADC recipients could use income that they earned in addition to their grants to cover the other nine requirements recognized by the DPA (laundry, garbage and refuse disposal, transportation to a source of essential medical care or employment training, housekeeping service, household furnishings, life insurance, school expenses, and a telephone). In 1947, when ADC grants increased in value (ostensibly to cover food, clothing, incidentals, rent, ice, electricity, heat and light, water, garbage, and refuse disposal), policies were rewritten to specify that additional income could only be used to cover expenses incidental to the holding of a job such as transportation, special work clothes, necessary tools, and a telephone. An additional $10.00 a month was also granted to cover employed women's "increased need for food, clothing, and incidentals" as well as care for children (only if there were no relatives who could perform this service for free). See Commonwealth of Pennsylvania, *Public Assistance Review: Annual Summary, December 1947*, 36–37. See also Arthur J. Brown to Margaret Nim, November 25, 1947, Box 12, Folder 89, HWCR1, UATU.

78. Philadelphia County Board of Assistance, *A Report on Dependent Children Families*; Commonwealth of Pennsylvania, *Pennsylvania Public Assistance Review: Second Quarter 1944*, 12. On employment requirements, see also Pennsylvania Citizens Association for

Health and Welfare, "What's Wrong with Pennsylvania's Public Assistance Program?" Box 11, DPWF, PSA. Welfare authorities left a major loophole in their employment policy by stipulating that women with children under thirteen years old could not hold jobs that required them to work outside of their households when their children were at home.

79. Levy and Shouse, "Concept of Alienation," 30; E.O.K. interview; Department of Public Assistance, Philadelphia County Board, *Annual Report, 1947*, 9; Family Division, Advisory Committee Minutes, October 21, 1952, Box 11, Folder 80, HWCR1, UATU. On the shift toward an emphasis on employment on the national level, see Mittelstadt, *From Welfare to Workfare*.

80. Quoted in Levy and Shouse, "Concept of Alienation," 72.

81. Quoted in ibid., 31.

82. Ibid., 103.

83. Philadelphia County Board of Assistance, *Toward Family Renewal*.

84. Commonwealth of Pennsylvania, *Pennsylvania Public Assistance Statistics Summary: 1932–1940*, 43–44.

85. Ibid.

86. On the development of medical care policies, see Commonwealth of Pennsylvania, *Origin and Development of Public Assistance* (1958), 15, 20, 23–24, 28–29.

87. Quoted in Levy and Shouse, "Concept of Alienation," 56. Although Levy and Shouse refer to this ADC recipient as a man, the recipient describes being pregnant, leading me to conclude that this is a typographical error.

88. Ibid., 60–61, 101–2.

89. Pennsylvania Department of Public Welfare, *Trends: Annual Report, 1960*, 17.

90. Levy and Shouse, "Concept of Alienation," 49.

91. Hunter, *To 'Joy My Freedom*, 15–17, 28, 58–59, 74, 76, 223, 224; Clark-Lewis, *Living in, Living Out*, 123–46; Phillips, *Alabama North*, 95–96.

92. Quoted in Levy and Shouse, "Concept of Alienation," 31.

93. Twenty states enacted employment requirements in the late 1940s and 1950s; see Reese, *Backlash against Welfare Mothers*, 209.

94. U.S. Department of Commerce, *Sixteenth Census of the United States: 1940*, 52; U.S. Department of Commerce, *U.S. Censuses of Population and Housing: 1960*, 317. Such figures do not take into account the women who performed domestic work "under the table" and did not report it to census takers.

95. Kronick interview. On similar practices in the 1990s, see Edin, *There's a Lot of Month Left at the End of the Money*.

96. Burt, "Centralization and Decentralization," 51; Urban League of Philadelphia, "Suggested Areas Needing Consideration and Action by the Urban League of Philadelphia, Its Member Organizations, and Other Community Groups . . . Public Assistance," April 3, 1959, Box 5, Folder 170, ULPR2, UATU. On the education of social workers throughout the country, see Bell, *Aid to Dependent Children*, 38.

97. "50% of Case Workers Resign in Frustration," *Philadelphia Inquirer*, September 15,

1961, 1, 14; Pennsylvania Economy League, *Improving the State Public Assistance Program*, 77, 85.

98. Although the welfare department required caseworkers to ferret out wrongdoing, it also exhibited compassion for low-income Philadelphians. At the main welfare office at Broad and Spring Garden streets, the staff spent so much of their own money helping walk-in clients buy food and take the bus to find jobs that they began to hold cake sales to raise money for a slush fund. See "Image of Recipients Wrong," *Philadelphia Inquirer*, September 14, 1961, 1, 52.

99. Braun, "The Development of Public Assistance in Philadelphia," 44–45, quotation on 45.

100. Levy and Shouse, "Concept of Alienation," 28, 34, quotation on 34; G.P. interview.

101. Quoted in Levy and Shouse, "Concept of Alienation," 24.

102. Quoted in ibid., 40.

103. Kronick, "A Woman's Choice," 10–11; Kronick, "Family Life and Economic Dependency," 86; Kronick, "Attitudes toward Dependency," 39; Van Dyke interview; G.J. interview; Ladner, *Tomorrow's Tomorrow*, 185–86. Contemporary studies suggesting a similar relationship between women's attitudes toward marriage and their experiences with men include Leadbeater, Ross, Way, and Arden, "Why Not Marry Your Baby's Father?"; Edin, "Why Poor Mothers Don't Marry."

104. Quoted in L.W. interview. Similarly, see G.J. interview; C.S. interview; J.E.J. interview; Levy and Shouse, "Concept of Alienation," 104.

105. Kronick, "A Woman's Choice," 11; Kronick interview. Contemporary studies suggest that we must not overestimate women's ability to use welfare to escape domestic violence since many women who rely on welfare continue to depend on men who abuse them; see Raphael, *Saving Bernice*, 23–24.

106. Kronick interview; Bellama et al., "Use of Resources by Recipients," 50; Levy and Shouse, "Concept of Alienation," 71, 103.

107. Quoted in Levy and Shouse, "Concept of Alienation," 103.

108. Quoted in ibid., 71. Similarly, see Allis, Becker, Henderson, and Meyers, "Wants of AFDC Mothers," 33.

109. Quoted in Levy and Shouse, "Concept of Alienation," 25.

110. See, for example, "State Arrests 357 Fathers in Drive on Welfare Frauds," *PEB*, March 10, 1959, 29. Midnight raids were outlawed by the Supreme Court in 1967; see Abramovitz, *Regulating the Lives of Women*, 335.

111. Quoted in "Relief Chiselers Face New Drive," *PEB*, February 12, 1952, 1, 44, quotation on 44. Similarly, see Kronick interview; C.E. interview; M.C. interview.

112. Levy and Shouse, "Concept of Alienation," 68.

113. Quoted in ibid., 25.

114. Ibid., 68, 86, quotation on 86.

115. Kronick, "Attitudes toward Dependency," 64.

116. Allis, Becker, Henderson, and Meyers, "Wants of AFDC Mothers," 31, 45–46,

52–54. It is difficult to determine how long women stayed on welfare. Kronick found that over half of the women had been on assistance for more than six years; see Kronick, "Attitudes toward Dependency," 48. According to one DPA study, only 25 percent of ADC recipients had been on assistance for seven years or more; see Philadelphia County Board of Assistance, "Study of Characteristics of Regular Segment of Aid to Dependent Children Families." A different study found that the average length of time on assistance was three years; see Health and Welfare Council, Inc., "Report of the Public Assistance Committee," November 1962, Box 11, Folder 4, series 6, JFSR, JA.

117. Quoted in Levy and Shouse, "Concept of Alienation," 43.

118. Berg, "Study of a Group of Unwed Mothers," 49–54, 103–5, quotation on 104; Levy and Shouse, "Concept of Alienation," 71.

119. Weigley, *Philadelphia*, 651–60; Countryman, *Up South*, 46.

120. Bauman, *Public Housing*, 161; Jimmy Brown, "Hoodlums Flaunt KKK Sign, Wreck South Phila. Home," October 15, 1960, newsclipping (publication not stated), in Clippings—Blacks: Housing, Prior to 1962, PEBNC, UATU. Many other examples of housing incidents include those in Box 22, Folders 1–6, FCR, UATU; Box 4, Folders 94–96, NAACPR, UATU. Resistance to integration had long-standing roots; see Wolfinger, *Philadelphia Divided*, 11–12, 85.

121. Johnson, "Police-Black Community Relations." On Buffalo, see Wolcott, "Recreation and Race."

122. Savitz, *Factors Influencing Crime Rates of Negroes*, 8; Johnson, "Police-Black Community Relations."

123. In the 1920s, northern whites had frequently expressed their discomfort with the migration of African Americans by criticizing their "deplorable" housing and health conditions and condemning domestic workers for contaminating their households with germs; see "Negro Congestion Menace to Health," *Philadelphia Public Ledger*, July 9, 1923, 2; "Four More Blocks under Quarantine in War on Smallpox," *North American*, May 22, 1923, 2; McBride, *Integrating the City of Medicine*, 57, 63. Similarly, in the post–Civil War South, see Hunter, *To 'Joy My Freedom*, 187–218. On the roots of public opposition to government provisions for African Americans, see Richardson, *The Death of Reconstruction*, 122–245.

124. Sub-Committee to the Philadelphia District Committee of the Health and Welfare Council on the Report of Robert Lowe Kunzig, Deputy Attorney General, "The 1952 Investigation of the Relief Program in Philadelphia" 1953, Box 12, Folder 81, HWCR1, UATU; "Special Court Set Up to Try Relief Chiselers," *PEB*, September 21, 1952, 3; "8% of Reliefers Here Ineligible, Prober Reports," *PEB*, April 13, 1952, 1, 10. On postwar crackdowns in other cities, see Bell, *Aid to Dependent Children*, 60–63, 68, 72; Nadasen, *Welfare Warriors*, 6. In 1947, Pennsylvania Republican Governor James H. Duff expressed concern about "chiseling," but the Philadelphia media coverage was not racialized; see "Duff Relief Probe Aided by Andrews," *PEB*, January 3, 1947, 7; "Relief and Decent Living," *PEB*, January 21, 1947, 12B. See also Philadelphia Health and Welfare Council, Family Division, Advisory Committee, Minutes, January 1947, Box 11, Folder 78, HWCR1, UATU.

125. On fraud, see "Analytic Comments: Pennsylvania AFDC Review," 1963, Box 14, Folder 620.63, RSSA, NARA. On media coverage throughout the country, see Bell, *Aid to Dependent Children*, 62.

126. Quoted in "Woman Soup Worker Jailed for $5,344 Relief Fraud," *PEB*, August 11, 1952, 3; "Working Woman Got $5,344 Relief: Given Six Months," *Philadelphia Tribune*, August 12, 1952, 3. In his astute study of the postwar migration of southern whites and African Americans, James Gregory overlooks the way that white resistance to black migration frequently centered on public institutions such as welfare and the schools; see Gregory, *The Southern Diaspora*, 66–79.

127. Quoted in "More Than $4 Million Is Recovered by State from Relief Chiselers," *Philadelphia Inquirer*, July 21, 1957, 1, 6, quotation on 1.

128. On postwar social scientific scholarship, see, for example, Orleck, *Storming Caesars Palace*, 84–86; Curran, "The Culture of Race, Class, and Poverty."

129. Kallick quoted in "Unwed Mothers on Relief Shocking to Judge Kallick," *PEB*, January 4, 1959, 7. See also "Let's Have It," *PEB*, August 12, 1958, 16; "Swollen Relief Costs," *PEB*, December 11, 1958, 24; "Hard-Core Families: A Festering Empire," *Greater Philadelphia Magazine* 51:5 (June 1960), 17–18, 50–55.

130. On the *Bulletin*, see Binzen, *Nearly Everybody Read It*, 2–11, 16–17. On the *Inquirer*, see Mainwright, *The History of the Philadelphia Inquirer*. On differences between the two, see Reichley, *The Art of Government*, 63–64; Weigley, *Philadelphia*, 690–91.

131. "Wanton Illegitimacy Compounds Problems of Child Assistance," *Philadelphia Inquirer*, September 11, 1961, 1, 28; "Unwed Mother of 3 Received $5,493 in State Aid: She Grew Up on Relief," *PEB*, March 16, 1961, 10.

132. "Blanc Wants State to Deny Public Aid to Unwed Mothers," *PEB*, July 9, 1958, 66; "Blanc Urges Restrictions on Aid to Unwed Mothers," *Philadelphia Inquirer*, December 11, 1958, 49; "DA's Man Tells How Unwed Mothers Spend Relief Money on Liquor and Friends," *PEB*, August 2, 1959, 15; "Blanc Calls on State to Stop Relief Funds to Unwed Mothers after Second Child," *PEB*, December 10, 1958, 1; "Number on Dole near Postwar Peak," *Philadelphia Inquirer*, September 10, 1961, 1, 28. Suitable home laws specifically targeted African Americans because they raised children out of wedlock more frequently than whites did. Public officials in several southern states instituted suitable home laws as retribution for black civil rights organizing. See Bell, *Aid to Dependent Children*; Solinger, *Wake Up Little Susie*, 58, 192–94; Levenstein, "From Innocent Children," 12, 15.

133. Quoted in "Magistrate Blasts Relief for Unwed Mothers," *PEB*, December 14, 1958, 30. Similarly, see "Subsidized Slatterns," *PEB*, March 21, 1961, 44; "Judge Would Ban Relief for Parents Having 3 Illegitimate Children," *PEB*, March 17, 1961, 6.

134. Quoted in "Blanc Calls on State to Stop Relief Funds." Similarly, see "Wanton Illegitimacy"; "Judge Shocked at Payoffs," *Philadelphia Inquirer*, September 13, 1961, 1.

135. "Subsidized Slatterns."

136. "Disturbing Relief Roll Rise," *PEB*, December 4, 1960, section 2, p. 6.

137. "Patience Abused," *PEB*, December 12, 1958, 20.

138. Historical analyses of the two-tiered structure of government social welfare and

housing provisions include Radford, *Modern Housing*, Jackson, *Crabgrass Frontier*; Gordon, *Pitied but Not Entitled*.

139. Goldsmith, "Working the System," 171–201.

140. All quotations from Binzen, *Whitetown U.S.A.*; "might be to admit," on 103, "too lazy," on 111, "we had to do without," on 229.

141. "58 Million Taxes Paid by Negro," *Philadelphia Tribune*, October 31, 1959, 1, 5.

142. Quoted in "Should Unwed Mothers Get Welfare Aid?" *Philadelphia Afro-American*, January 10, 1959, 20.

143. Quoted in Levy and Shouse, "Concept of Alienation," 69.

144. "North Philadelphia Needs Training, Not Study," *Philadelphia Independent*, February 23, 1963, newsclipping, Box 50, EELR, UATU.

145. Ashton quoted in "Should Unwed Mothers Get Welfare Aid?" *Philadelphia Afro-American*, January 10, 1959, 20. On Stout, see "Judge Would Ban Relief for Parents Having 3 Illegitimate Children," *PEB*, March 17, 1961, 6; "J. K. Stout, Pioneering Judge in Pennsylvania, Is Dead at 79," *New York Times*, August 24, 1998, <http://www.law.stanford.edu/library/wlhbp/articles/stoutobit.pdf> (May 23, 2006).

146. Mittelstadt, *From Welfare to Workfare*, 83–84, 88–91; Levenstein, "From Innocent Children," 12, 15.

147. Mittelstadt, *From Welfare to Workfare*, 84, 98–99. On the national level, this shift was particularly discernible after the 1961 controversy over welfare in Newburgh, New York; see Mittelstadt, 91–104; Levenstein, "From Innocent Children."

148. Feldstein, *Motherhood in Black and White*, 142–51; Mittelstadt, *From Welfare to Workfare*, 144; Orleck, *Storming Caesars Palace*, 86.

149. Quoted in Brown, *Race, Money, and the American Welfare State*, 200. Similarly, see Mittelstadt, *From Welfare to Workfare*, 99.

150. National Urban League, "Urban League Chief Cites 'Built-In' Welfare Problems at Moreland Commission Hearing on Public Aid," n.d., circa 1962–1963, Box 5, Folder 171, ULPR2, UATU. On the Urban League, see also Mittelstadt, *From Welfare to Workfare*, 8, 83–85, 98–99. For sympathetic black press coverage, see "No Profit in Babies at $30 Per Month," *Philadelphia Tribune*, October 24, 1959, 1, 11.

151. Solomon P. Gethers to Charles C. Beckett, memorandum, November 13, 1963, Box 5, Folder 172, ULPR2, UATU; Urban League of Philadelphia, "A Statement on Public Assistance in Pennsylvania and Philadelphia," n.d., circa 1962–1963, Box 5, Folder 171, ULPR2, UATU.

152. Solomon P. Gethers to Charles C. Beckett, memorandum, November 13, 1963, Box 5, Folder 172, ULPR2, UATU.

153. Sailer quoted in "Image of Recipients Wrong," *Philadelphia Inquirer*, September 14, 1961, 1, 52, quotation on 1. Lourie quoted in "Judge Shocked at Payoffs," *Philadelphia Inquirer*, September 13, 1961, 1, 10.

154. "Report Disputes Theory of Relief Families Here," *PEB*, January 12, 1960, 9; "Few on Relief Rolls Cheat, Studies Show," *Philadelphia Daily News*, December 10, 1962, 24; "Beliefs on Child Aid Refuted by Survey; Philadelphia Cost 19 Million," *Philadelphia*

Sunday Inquirer, July 9, 1961, 1, 23; "Judge Shocked at Payoffs," *Philadelphia Inquirer*, September 13, 1961, 1, 10; Commonwealth of Pennsylvania, Department of Public Welfare, "Children of Illegitimate Birth Receiving Assistance under the Pennsylvania Aid to Dependent Children Program, and Birthrate on the Rolls," April 24, 1959, Box 34, Folder 59, SSER, UATU.

155. On the discourse on government assistance for single mothers prior to World War II, see Gordon, "Putting Children First."

156. "It's Possible to Live on Relief, but High Rents Make It Tough," *PEB*, June 7, 1959, 32. Similarly, see "Judge Shocked at Payoffs," *Philadelphia Inquirer*, September 13, 1961, 1, 10; "Welfare Chief Raps 'Punishment' Demands by Police," *Philadelphia Inquirer*, December 10, 1958, 51. On rehabilitation nationally, see Mittelstadt, *From Welfare to Workfare*. In Philadelphia, see "50% of Case Workers Resign in Frustration"; "Aid Overhaul Needed to End Shortcomings," *Philadelphia Inquirer*, September 16, 1961, 5.

157. "Two Relief Proposals," *PEB*, August 22, 1958, 10.

158. "Visitors Defend Relief System," *PEB*, April 25, 1952, 1, 30; "Aid Overhaul Needed to End Shortcomings," *Philadelphia Inquirer*, September 16, 1961, 1, 5; "Statement by Leon S. Rosenthal," December 9, 1958, Box 12, Folder 85, HWCR1, UATU.

159. "50% of Case Workers Resign in Frustration."

160. "Aid Overhaul Needed to End Shortcomings," *Philadelphia Inquirer*, September 16, 1961, 1, 5.

161. On the increased emphasis on employment for ADC recipients, see Mittelstadt, *From Welfare to Workfare*.

162. Quoted in Levy and Shouse, "Concept of Alienation," 40.

163. Ibid., 49, 68; Kronick interview; Berg, "Study of a Group of Unwed Mothers," 71–73; "Beliefs on Child Aid Refuted by Survey."

164. Kronick interview; Levy and Shouse, "Concept of Alienation," 62, 69.

165. Quoted in Levy and Shouse, "Concept of Alienation," 49.

166. Quoted in ibid., 49.

167. Ibid., 41, 47–49, 51, quotation on 47; Allis, Becker, Henderson, and Myers, "Wants of AFDC Mothers," 53, 55, 68; "2d hand Clothes for Reliefers Called a 'Badge of Shame,' " *PEB*, April 13, 1952, 10; Kronick, "Attitudes toward Dependency," 47, 61.

168. Quoted in Levy and Shouse, "Concept of Alienation," 51. On the effects of consumerism on poor African American children, see Nightingale, *On the Edge*, 135–65.

169. Levy and Shouse, "Concept of Alienation," 48, 99, quoted on 48. On working-class African American women's pursuit of respectability, see Wolcott, *Remaking Respectability*; Harley, "When Your Work Is Not Who You Are," 46. In Philadelphia specifically, see Allis, Becker, Henderson, and Myers, "Wants of AFDC Mothers," 68; Berg, "Study of a Group of Unwed Mothers," 56.

170. Quoted in Levy and Shouse, "Concept of Alienation," 45, 46.

171. Quoted in ibid., 48.

172. Kornbluh, "To Fulfill Their 'Rightly Needs' "; on postwar consumption more generally, see Cohen, *Consumer's Republic*.

Chapter Two

1. Case 447, November 18, 1947, PCA.

2. In his analysis of African American women's suits against men in the post–Civil War era, Dylan C. Penningroth observed: "Black women's lawsuits represented a startling, brilliant use of the legal system and its attitudes about gender"; see Penningroth, *The Claims of Kinfolk*, 181. Some of the best legal accounts of race and sex discrimination in the legal system include Crenshaw, "Mapping the Margins"; Crenshaw, "Demarginalizing the Intersection of Race and Sex"; Roberts, "Rape, Violence, and Women's Autonomy." For historical accounts of sexism in the courts, see Pleck, *Domestic Tyranny*; Igra, "Likely to Become a Public Charge." On the legal system as both a resource and a constraint for the working-class, see Odem, *Delinquent Daughters*; Hicks, " 'In Danger of Becoming Morally Depraved.' "

3. On the tradition of working-class women's activism surrounding domestic violence, see Penningroth, *Claims of Kinfolk*, 180–81; Edwards, *Gendered Strife and Confusion*, 180–83; Gordon, *Heroes of Their Own Lives*, 250–88, Pleck, *Domestic Tyranny*, 137–41.

4. Similarly, on men's experiences with the court, see Willrich, "Home Slackers"; Igra, *Wives without Husbands*, 47–54.

5. Steinberg, *Transformation of Criminal Justice*.

6. The best historical treatment of the municipal courts is Willrich, *City of Courts*.

7. Shenton, *History and Functions of the Philadelphia Municipal Court*, 66, 80–81; PMC-AR, *1949*, A19.

8. M.B.M. interview.

9. Keast, *Juvenile and Domestic Relations Branches of the Municipal Court*, 6–24.

10. The court documented the racial breakdown of new clients in 1954 in *PMC-AR, 1957*, 242. On similarities between white and black women's experiences in court, see Levenstein, "Hard Choices at 1801 Vine."

11. The juvenile division had the court's only black judge, Juanita Kidd Stout, the first African American woman appointed to a court of record in the nation.

12. Since this book focuses on women's proactive use of public institutions, this chapter explores the most common instances in which they approached the court seeking assistance. The instances in which the legal system ensnared women against their will influenced their use of the court but are not the main subject of this chapter.

13. In the 1940s, Pennsylvania, Maryland, and Massachusetts courts considered fornication and bastardy a criminal action. In eight states, the courts did not allow unmarried women to prosecute the fathers of their children for support at all. Other states heard these cases but dealt with them in civil court; see Selma Holz, "Legal Aspect of Illegitimacy," Senior Research Project, 1940, 53–54, Box 35, Folders 81–85, SSER, UATU. Not until 1963 did the Philadelphia courts begin to hear the cases as civil rather than criminal proceedings; see *PMC-AR, 1963*, 19.

14. *PMC-AR, 1959*, 318.

15. *PMC-AR, 1964*, 221. Although a few cases of nonsupport each year were brought by husbands against wives, their numbers were very small.

16. Because some women went to the magistrates courts instead of the municipal court when seeking protection from violence, the statistics cited in the text do not capture the full extent of women's pursuit of legal assistance. Records documenting women's cases in the magistrates' courts are not available. The statistics on women's assault and battery cases from the municipal court were very inconsistent, but the best available data shows an average of 627 cases each year between 1953 and 1958; see *PMC-AR, 1959*, 203. For an example of the difficulties in reading the data, see *PMC-AR, 1953*, A16, 156. In the late 1950s and early 1960s, the number of assault and battery cases dropped sharply, without any explanation from the court. Given the tremendous variance in previous statistics, it is likely that the drop at least partially reflected changes in the court's recording of the cases.

17. Rosen, *The World Split Open*, 186. Linda Gordon found that poor women's complaints about domestic abuse in social service agencies increased in the 1930s and 1940s, but her account suggests that they rarely approached the legal system; see Gordon, *Heroes of Their Own Lives*, 250–60, 280–81. On women who brought domestic violence cases to court in the 1920s, see Pleck, *Domestic Tyranny*, 137–44. On the significant number of women who brought suits against abusive men in mid-nineteenth-century Philadelphia, see Steinberg, *Transformation of Criminal Justice*, 46–47, 69.

18. Contemporary discussions of the relationship between domestic violence and poverty include Raphael, *Saving Bernice*; Brandwein, *Battered Women, Children, and Welfare Reform*.

19. *PMC-AR, 1952*, 155–56. Similarly, in the nineteenth century, see Steinberg, *Transformation of Criminal Justice*, 69.

20. "Municipal Court Judges Decries 'Assembly-Line Justice,'" *PEB*, February 17, 1957, 1, 6; *PMC-AR, 1950*, 132, 135; "Court Backlog Boosts Aid to Unwed Mothers Here," *PEB*, May 15, 1959, 34. Similarly, see Pleck, *Domestic Tyranny*, 136–38.

21. *PMC-AR, 1959*, 318–19.

22. Discussions of the family wage include Gordon, *Pitied but Not Entitled*, 53.

23. First quotation in *PMC-AR, 1954*, 153; second quotation in *PMC-AR, 1957*, 197. Similarly, see *PMC-AR, 1954*, 152; *PMC-AR, 1950*, 134; Pleck, *Domestic Tyranny*, 8–9, 128–29.

24. *PMC-AR, 1957*, 207. On the close historical relationship between the court's insistence on support orders and the government's provision of financial assistance, see Willrich, *City of Courts*, 152–55, 171.

25. Quoted in "Unwed Mothers Speak Their Piece," *Philadelphia Afro-American*, January 31, 1959, 3.

26. "Court Slashes Backlog in Distributing Support Checks," *Philadelphia Inquirer*, January 4, 1959, 14.

27. In 1959, the court tried to improve the process by sending out checks more quickly when men paid in cash at 1801 Vine; see "In Municipal Court Holidays Bring Added Work . . . Held-up Checks," *Philadelphia Independent*, December 28, 1958, 3.

28. *PMC-AR, 1960*, 210–11.

29. Ibid., quotation on 211.

30. *PMC-AR, 1957,* 237. Similarly, in early twentieth-century New York, see Igra, *Wives without Husbands,* 47–54.

31. "Wanted: Solomon with an Adding Machine as HCL Plagues Estranged Couples," *PEB,* August 28, 1946, 14.

32. On the relationship between men and the court, see Willrich, "Home Slackers."

33. Holz, "Legal Aspects of Illegitimacy," 159.

34. *PMC-AR, 1959,* 196; "Bonnelly Acts to Clear Up Support Cases," *PEB,* March 8, 1959, 3.

35. "Bonnelly Acts to Clear Up Support Cases." On the early twentieth-century roots of such rhetoric, see Willrich, *City of Courts,* 150.

36. Quoted in Levy and Shouse, "Concept of Alienation," 54.

37. On women's responsibility for tracking down men, see Levy and Shouse, "Concept of Alienation," 23, 53. Similarly, in early twentieth-century New York, see Igra, "Likely to Become a Public Charge."

38. Quoted in Levy and Shouse, "Concept of Alienation," 53.

39. *PMC-AR, 1960,* 210–11; *PMC-AR, 1961,* 215.

40. Similarly, see Igra, "Likely to Become a Public Charge," 59–81.

41. C.E. interview. Similarly, see G.J. interview; Holz, "Legal Aspect of Illegitimacy," 130–31.

42. *PMC-AR, 1959,* 389.

43. On postwar public assistance policy, see *PMC-AR, 1953,* A23; *PMC-AR, 1957,* 201.

44. Igra, *Wives without Husbands,* 44, 97, 122, quotation on 44; Igra, "Likely to Become a Public Charge," 73.

45. Quoted in Levy and Shouse, "Concept of Alienation," 81.

46. C.E. interview.

47. J.E.J. interview; "Runaway Husbands," *PEB,* October 7, 1956, section 2, pp. 1, 2. In 1950, only 14 percent of wives who pressed charges in the domestic relations court had jobs; see *PMC-AR, 1950,* 173.

48. J.E.J. interview.

49. Quoted in Levy and Shouse, "Concept of Alienation," 81; *PMC-AR, 1957,* 205–6.

50. H.C. interview.

51. J.P. interview.

52. *PMC-AR, 1959,* 219.

53. Quoted in Levy and Shouse, "Concept of Alienation," 23; C.E. interview; Barron, "Illegitimately Pregnant," 259–61; *PMC-AR, 1950,* 173; *PMC-AR, 1957,* 208, 228–29.

54. *PMC-AR, 1952,* 158.

55. Case 2, November 6, 1946, PCA. See also Case 1177, June 5, 1947, PCA; Case 121, February 19, 1948, PCA.

56. Sanderson quoted in C.S. interview, Elkins quoted in C.E. interview. See also Gordon, *Heroes of Their Own Lives,* 257–64, 271–85. For a contemporary study of women prisoners in New York City that argues that African American women who placed a high value on being married and having a conventional family life often found it particularly difficult to leave violent relationships, see Richie, *Compelled to Crime.*

57. *PMC-AR, 1950,* 173. See also Pleck, *Domestic Tyranny,* 137.

58. *PMC-AR, 1957,* 237.

59. *PMC-AR, 1944,* A62–A63; *PMC-AR, 1949,* 261; *PMC-AR, 1934,* 276–77; *PMC-AR, 1939,* l, 310–12; Health and Welfare Council, Children's Division, "Committee on Illegitimacy, 1946–1947," May 29, 1947, Box 34, Folder 75, SSER, UATU.

60. *PMC-AR, 1957,* 236–37, quotations on 237.

61. *PMC-AR, 1947,* 166–67, 178–79. On drunkenness also being a factor in these cases, see *PMC-AR, 1954,* 172; *PMC-AR, 1957,* 236–37.

62. *PMC-AR, 1952,* 153–56.

63. M.B.M. interview.

64. J.E.J. interview; Van Dyke interview.

65. *PMC-AR, 1953,* 166.

66. "Police Brutality Sweeps Philly Area," *Philadelphia Tribune,* April 20, 1946, 1; "Police Directive Barring Brutality Overdue—NAACP," *Philadelphia Tribune,* September 30, 1950, 2; "150 New Police, 1 Negro," *Philadelphia Tribune,* November 1, 1950, 4; "Police Brutality," *Philadelphia Tribune,* September 9, 1952, 4; "Dilworth Edict on Illegal Evidence Stirs Criticism," *Philadelphia Tribune,* March 22, 1952, 1; "Protest of Police Brutality Draws Crowd to Meeting," *Philadelphia Tribune,* August 15, 1959, 1; Johnson, "Black Philadelphia in Transition," 127–74. Accounts of raids include "Door in Court," *Philadelphia Afro-American,* November 12, 1955, 1; "Feds Seize 16 in Philly's Biggest Dope Suspect Net," *Philadelphia Afro-American,* April 22, 1950, 1; "Special Squad Snares 10 Dope Suspects in Week's Roundup," *Philadelphia Afro-American,* February 15, 1958, 3; "Woman, 77, Freed: Beer Man Held in Digits Raid," *Philadelphia Afro-American,* June 14, 1958, 3; "50 Suspects Nabbed in Raids throughout City," *Philadelphia Tribune,* August 1, 1959, 1; "21 Nabbed As Cops Turn Out Germantown Party," *Philadelphia Afro-American,* June 14, 1958, 3.

67. Johnson, "Police-Black Community Relations."

68. Quotations from "400 Riot at 20th and Norris, Manhandle Dozen Policemen," *PEB,* July 26, 1951, 16. Similarly, see "Arrest of Women Starts a Row," *PEB,* August 4, 1952, 3; "13 Police Beaten When 1000 Riot to Stop an Arrest," *PEB,* June 24, 1951, 1, 16; "8 Trying to Free Woman Seized at Police Station," *Philadelphia Inquirer,* October 21, 1951, 8. For a similar prewar case, see "Mob Fights Cops, 70 Fined $10 Each," *PEB,* August 2, 1934, 1, 2. On grassroots resistance elsewhere prior to World War II, see Rabinowitz, "The Conflict between Blacks and the Police."

69. "Rookie Cops Held for Court on Charges on Mother of 7," *Philadelphia Tribune,* April 18, 1959, 1. Similarly, see "Plaintiff Called 'Liar,'" *Philadelphia Tribune,* December 20, 1947, 1, 2; "Matron Threatens Suit against Police," *Philadelphia Tribune,* October 11, 1952, 1; "Woman Claims Policemen Beat Her into 'Unconsciousness,'" *Philadelphia Tribune,* December 12, 1959, 1; "Suspended Policeman Held on Criminal Attack Charge," *Philadelphia Tribune,* September 22, 1959, 1; "Beautician Says Digits Planted on Her by Cops," *Philadelphia Tribune,* April 7, 1959, 1; "Cops Slapped, Bruised Her, Woman Cries," *Philadelphia Tribune,* August 6, 1955, 1, 3; "Attny Blasts Woman in Police Rape Case," *Philadelphia Tribune,* September 15, 1959, 1. For similar occurrences elsewhere,

see Shockley, *"We, Too, Are Americans,"* 203; Green, *Battling the Plantation Mentality*, 81–83, 86–88.

70. Gay interview; *PMC-AR, 1952,* 155; M.B.M. interview. On similar occurrences in Boston, see Gordon, *Heroes of Their Own Lives*, 280–81.

71. Brown, *Law Administration*, esp., 141–42, 148–49, quotation on 142. For the term "white man's law" and a discussion of racial discrimination in the legal system, see Savitz, *Factors Influencing Crime Rates of Negroes*, 8.

72. "Judge Bonnelly Clarifies Statement about Migrants," *Philadelphia Afro-American*, August 1, 1959, 1; "Blanc Wants State to Deny Public Aid to Unwed Mothers," *PEB*, July 9, 1958, 66; "Seed-Bed of Delinquency," *PEB*, October 18, 1958, 6; "Blanc Calls on State to Stop Relief Funds to Unwed Mothers after Second Child," *PEB*, December 10, 1958, 1; "Foundling Assistance," *PEB*, July 11, 1958, 10. Other articles, often not as explicitly racialized, blamed both parents. On the national juvenile delinquency scare, see Gilbert, *Cycle of Outrage*. On the blaming of mothers' employment, see Phillips, *Alabama North*, 153.

73. Quoted in "Blanc Asks Cut in State Aid to Unwed Mothers," *Philadelphia Inquirer*, July 9, 1958, 61. See also "Blanc Asks for Law to Equalize Funds in Murder Trial Defense," *Philadelphia Inquirer*, July 10, 1958, 29; "Blanc Urges Restrictions on Aid to Unwed Mothers," *Philadelphia Inquirer*, December 11, 1958, 49.

74. Quoted in "Myers Defends His Curfew Court and Tells Why He Blows His Stack," *PEB*, October 23, 1960, 18. For curfew trials, see also "Mothers Face Curfew Action," *PEB*, December 28, 1955, 4; "23 Mothers Face Curfew Crackdown," *Philadelphia Inquirer*, December 28, 1955, 1, 4; "D-Day for Parents," *PEB*, December 29, 1955, 10; "Court Imposes Curfew Fines on 18 Mothers," *PEB*, December 30, 1955, 1.

75. Quoted in "Violators' Parents Flayed by Myers at Curfew Court," *PEB*, June 20, 1958, 9. Similarly, see "Unwed Mother of 7 Arouses Ire of Municipal Court," *Philadelphia Inquirer*, October 18, 1958, 13.

76. C.E. interview.

77. *PMC-AR, 1950,* 134.

78. Ibid., 135. Court officials also sometimes required men and women to undergo medical and psychiatric evaluations.

79. Holt, "Legal Aspects of Illegitimacy," 116–17.

80. *PMC-AR, 1952,* 153–56.

81. Quoted in "Unwed Mother of 7." This was a delinquency hearing, and "Mary Sapp" is a pseudonym.

82. *PMC-AR, 1953,* 166.

83. For "busted my head open," see Case 127, February 18, 1948, PCA. For knife wounds, see Case 631 and Case 632, May 22, 1957, PCA. See also Case 653 and Case 654, February 7, 1938, PCA; Case 648, May 22, 1957, PCA; Case 952, May 26, 1958, PCA; Case 691, June 3, 1947, PCA; Case 1177, June 5, 1947, PCA; Case 69, February 16, 1948, PCA. It is not clear from the records which of these cases involved African Americans and which involved whites.

84. Testimony of prosecutrix's mother in Cases 146, 147, 148, February 6, 1948, PCA.

85. *PMC-AR, 1929*, 52–53; Committee on the Philadelphia Relief Study, *Philadelphia Relief Study*, 17.

86. The law initially made welfare recipients' wives, husbands, children, fathers, mothers, grandparents, and grandchildren liable for support. In 1945, grandparents and grandchildren were removed from liability; see *PMC-AR, 1939*, xxxiii; Commonwealth of Pennsylvania, *Origin and Development of Public Assistance* (1955), 16, 21.

87. Prior to World War II, several private social welfare agencies in Philadelphia joined the welfare department in pressuring women to press nonsupport charges so that these organizations could avoid providing them with financial assistance. On the different approaches to court action taken by Philadelphia social service agencies, see Committee on Illegitimacy, Minutes, June 4, 1934, Box 2, Folder 47, HWCR3, UATU; Hunter, *Juvenile Division of the Municipal Court*, 43, 100–102; Johnson, *Domestic Relations Division of the Municipal Court*, 10. The Philadelphia Family Society usually referred women to seek Mothers' Pensions or ADC instead of referring them to court; see Ralph Ormsby, "A Brief History of Family Service of Philadelphia, 1879–1959," FS; Society for Organizing Charity, *Out of a Crisis: Annual Report* (Philadelphia: 1920), 11–12. The Jewish Welfare Society seems to have advocated court action in the 1920s and welfare in the 1930s; see "Report of Executive Director, Jewish Welfare Society," February 15, 1932, Box 2, Folder 1, series 4, JFSR, JA; "Report of Executive Director to Board Meeting," November 12, 1923, Box 1, Folder 1, series 1, JFSR, JA. On agencies that discouraged women's pursuit of court action, see Holz, "Legal Aspects of Illegitimacy," 16; Lundberg, *Unmarried Mothers in the Municipal Court*, 14–15. On the significant pressure for women to seek legal action in early twentieth-century New York, see Igra, "Likely to Become a Public Charge," 61–64, 66–68.

88. *PMC-AR, 1949*, A44.

89. Pennsylvania also followed the Uniform Reciprocal Support Act, which made it possible for authorities to seek support from fathers who lived in states that had reciprocal legislation; see Commonwealth of Pennsylvania, *Origin and Development of Public Assistance* (1955), 28; Reese, *Backlash against Welfare Mothers*, 41–42; Brown, *Race, Money, and the American Welfare State*, 175. Federal legislation encouraged ADC recipients to press charges, but it did not make legal action a condition of eligibility. Only with the 1974 Child Support Act did federal law mandate that mothers cooperate in establishing paternity in order to receive welfare. On the development of national policies, see Coll, *Safety Net*, 182–86; Mink, *Welfare's End*, 71–101.

90. Philadelphia County Board of Assistance, *Report on Dependent Children Families*; *PMC-AR, 1957*, 199–201; *PMC-AR, 1949*, 148–49, 155; *PMC-AR, 1954*, A23; *PMC-AR, 1957*, 235; "Bonnelly Acts to Clear Up Support Cases"; "Smith Demands State Probe of Relief to Unwed Mothers," *PEB*, August 6, 1958, 40; Health and Welfare Council, Family Division, Advisory Committee Minutes, September 16, 1958, Box 12, Folder 85, HWCR1, UATU.

91. "Lawyers Urge Family Court," *PEB*, June 13, 1950, 68.

92. *PMC-AR, 1954*, 157–59. The municipal court had concurrent jurisdiction with the magistrates' court over cases of assault and battery, and from its inception, it took over

the adjudication of many types of cases previously handled by the magistrates' court; see Ervin, *Magistrates' Courts of Philadelphia*, 155. In 1968, Philadelphia reorganized its entire court system and established a Family Court, which opened in 1969; see *Court of Common Pleas of Philadelphia, Family Court Division, Report 1968 to 1970*, 1–2.

93. *PMC-AR*, 1953, A16.

94. *PMC-AR*, 1954, 158.

95. *PMC-AR*, 1959, 188–90, 203, quotation on 203; *PMC-AR*, 1954, 158; *PMC-AR*, 1952, 153–58.

Chapter Three

1. M.B.M. interview.

2. On "way stations," see Bauman, *Public Housing*, 52.

3. Bauman, *Public Housing*, xiii, 135; Wallace, *Housing and Social Structure*, 4, 9–10.

4. Many historians have tried to account for the problems that developed in postwar public housing. For the most multifaceted examination, see Hunt, "What Went Wrong," (2000). Accounts that emphasize the problems associated with income limits include Radford, *Modern Housing for America*; Wood, *The Beautiful Beginnings*; Bauman, *Public Housing*. On the importance of site selection, see Hirsch, *Making the Second Ghetto*; Sugrue, *Origins of the Urban Crisis*, 57–88; Bauman, *Public Housing*. On architecture, see Yancey, "Architecture, Interaction, and Social Control"; Newman, *Defensible Space*. My analysis is one of the few to foreground tenants' daily experiences; it also emphasizes the deleterious effects of the top-down, punitive management style, the program's inadequate funding, and the poor locations. For an account of tenants' collective activism, see Williams, *The Politics of Public Housing*.

5. On public housing prior to 1937, see Bauman, *Public Housing*, 22–39; Radford, *Modern Housing for America*, 111–44. On the two-tiered system, see Radford, *Modern Housing*, 2–3, 177, 189–94, 197–98.

6. Wright, *Building the Dream*, 227; Bauman, *Public Housing*, 44; Philadelphia Housing Authority, *To Better Living: Report of the Philadelphia Housing Authority (July 1, 1950–June 30, 1952)*, 19.

7. Bauman, *Public Housing*, 90, 94–95, 101–3, 136, 140, 172. In 1951, the 1949 Housing Act was restricted to 50,000 annual units. The 1954 Act capped construction at 35,000 units targeted primarily at people displaced by slum clearance programs, at a time when housing advocates were arguing that the country annually needed 400,000 units of public housing. For an excellent discussion of the origins and importance of the 1949 Housing Act, see von Hoffman, "A Study in Contradictions."

8. Bauman, *Public Housing*, 49–50.

9. Ibid., 50–51.

10. "The Philadelphia Housing Authority Presents Richard Allen Homes," pamphlet, Folder Richard Allen Homes, 1945–1967, PEBNC, UATU.

11. "Laborer with Six Children First Allen Homes Lessee," *Philadelphia Tribune*, February 24, 1942, 1, 2; "New Life Opens for Widow's Child As First Allen Homes Lease Is

Signed," *Philadelphia Record*, February 25, 1942, 3; "New Homes, New Health, New Fun, New Happiness," *PEB*, August 1, 1942, 8. Similarly, in the 1950s, see "Everything Very Wonderful for Rosen Homes Residents," *Philadelphia Tribune*, August 2, 1955, 1, 2; "Rosen Homes Families Finding Happiness in New Apartments," *Philadelphia Tribune*, August 6, 1955, 1, 2.

12. "Glenwood's 1st Tenants Due Tuesday," *Philadelphia Record*, September 29, 1940, 1. See also "A Preview of Low-Rent Housing," *Philadelphia Record*, August 21, 1940, 2; "New Homes, New Health."

13. On Lamberton, see Wolfinger, *Philadelphia Divided*, 63–70. Examples of positive media coverage include "New Homes, New Health" and "First Housing Projects Here Pay Dividends in Happiness," *PEB*, June 11, 1949, 6. Although newspapers often praised public housing, by emphasizing how it disproved its opponents' dire predictions, they reminded readers about conservative misgivings even as they sought to paint public housing in a positive light; see "Homes Evade Doom," *PEB*, July 6, 1949, 13; "Richard Allen Homes," *PEB*, July 27, 1949, 13.

14. "First Housing Projects Here Pay Dividends"; "Bright Spot in Public Housing," *PEB*, June 24, 1948, 20F. On links made between public housing and communism, see Radford, *Modern Housing for America*, 200; Bauman, *Public Housing*, 137; Parson, *Making a Better World*. Parson demonstrates the crippling effects of the association between public housing and communism in Los Angeles and illustrates how the Cold War decline in organizing on the Left resulted in public housing losing its most significant advocates.

15. Bauman, *Public Housing*, 113, 131, 175–76.

16. Ibid., 111–14.

17. Hunt, "What Went Wrong," 421–22; D. Bradford Hunt, "Warren J. Vinton's Public Housing Career," paper delivered at the Urban History Association's Second Biennial Urban History Conference, Milwaukee, Wis., October 8, 2004.

18. The mayor appointed two members of the board, the city controller appointed another two, and these four members appointed the fifth.

19. Philadelphia Housing Authority, *Biennial Report: 1960–1961*, 1–23; "Energy Makes the Man," *Philadelphia Inquirer*, October 19, 1959, 29.

20. Philadelphia Housing Authority, *20 Years of Service*, 19.

21. Williams, *The Politics of Public Housing*, 30.

22. Quoted in "What Happens at a Project in a Blighted Area," *PEB*, April 29, 1956, section 2, p. 5; South Philadelphia Coordinating Council, Petition to the Honorable James H. Duff, Box 21, Folder Neighborhood Betterment Club, 1951–1955, UCR, UATU; Wharton Neighborhood Block Council, *Newsletter* 24 (February 1959), Box 44, Folder 132, WCR, UATU; Wharton Neighborhood Block Council, *Newsletter* 25 (March 1959), Box 44, Folder 132, WCR, UATU; Wharton Centre, "Housing Neighborhood," n.d., Box 6, Folder 93, WCR, UATU; South Philadelphia Coordinating Council, Petition to the Honorable James H. Duff, Box 21, Folder Neighborhood Betterment Club, 1951–1955, UCR, UATU; Wharton Neighborhood Block Council, *Newsletter* 24 (February 1959), Box 44, Folder 132, WCR, UATU; Wharton Neighborhood Block Council, *News-*

letter 28 (June 1959), Box 44, Folder 132, WCR, UATU. On the NAACP and Urban League, see Countryman, *Up South*, 76–78; Bauman, *Public Housing*, 68–69, 75.

23. On these trends in postwar social-scientific scholarship, see Curran, "The Culture of Race, Class, and Poverty"; O'Connor, *Poverty Knowledge*, 99–112.

24. Philadelphia Housing Authority, *To Better Living*, 14–15, quotation on 15. On these expectations for public housing, see Bauman, *Public Housing*, 115–17.

25. Philadelphia Housing Authority, *Public Housing: Report to the Community* 3:5 (1953), 3. The PHA emphasized that public housing reduced rates of juvenile delinquency, even though its own studies illustrated that in many areas more children were arrested within public housing than from the surrounding neighborhood. For public statements, see Philadelphia Housing Authority, *Public Housing: Report to the Community* 2:7 (August 1952), 3; Philadelphia Housing Authority, *To Better Living*, 15; "Bright Spot in Public Housing." For indicators that juvenile delinquency rates were higher in public housing than in its surrounding neighborhoods, see Philadelphia Housing Authority, "Arrest Cases of Boys 7–17 Years Inclusive by Project Residence" and "Arrest Cases of Girls 7–17 Years Inclusive by Project Residence," circa 1955, Box 281, Folder 4887, HADVR1, UATU.

26. "First Housing Projects Here Pay Dividends in Happiness."

27. Bauman, *Public Housing*, 151. To get apartments, some single mothers employed male friends or brothers to pose as their husbands. See Levy and Shouse, "Concept of Alienation," 36, 42.

28. Committee on Public Housing Policy, "Basic Policies for Public Housing," 27a. African Americans were overrepresented among applicants prior to the 1950s; see Wolfinger, *Philadelphia Divided*, 66. On Chicago, see Hirsch, *Making the Second Ghetto*, 231.

29. Bauman, *Public Housing*, 52.

30. Quoted in Bauman, *Public Housing*, 47.

31. On integration attempts in Chicago, see Hunt, "What Went Wrong," 101–52.

32. Questionnaires on Public Housing: A collection of completed questionnaires sent out to social workers by the Committee on Public Housing in 1956 to get feedback on public housing in Philadelphia, Box 282, Folders 4924–4933, HADVR1, UATU (hereafter cited as Questionnaires); "Memo to the Files of Committee on Public Housing Policy from Howard W. Hallman," Box 282, Folder 4933, HADVR1, UATU; Committee on Housing Policy, "Basic Policies for Public Housing," 25–26.

33. George J. Dunn to Joseph L. Devine, "Problem Families," May 29, 1957, Box 283, Folder 4937, HADVR1, UATU; "Per George J. Dunn's Memorandum of May 20, 1957," 1957, Box 285, Folder 5006, HADVR1, UATU. Authorities also enforced a furniture requirement to prevent very poor families with no visible or easily identifiable social "problems" from getting in; see Committee on Social Service in Public Housing, Minutes, April 21, 1960, Box 285, Folder 5007, HADVR1, UATU.

34. Countryman, *Up South*, 76.

35. Ibid., 14–17.

36. Philadelphia Housing Authority, "Comments on Survey—Basic Policies for Public

Housing for Low-Income Families in Philadelphia," 1957, 7–8, Box 283, Folder 4956, HADVR1, UATU; Robert Johnson, "Review of the Integration Program for the Philadelphia Housing Authority," 1957, 51–52, 73–74, Box 236, Folders 3542–3548, HADVR1, UATU. On white tenants' protests against racial integration in Chicago, see Hirsch, "Massive Resistance in the Urban North."

37. Johnson, "Review of the Integration," 84–85. The first African American director was Osborne McLain, who headed the Social Service Division.

38. Countryman, *Up South*, 76–77; Bauman, *Public Housing*, 121–23; "Summary Report on 1954 Occupancy Trends in Developments of the Philadelphia Housing Authority," January 11, 1955, Box 45, Folder 148, WCR, UATU; Committee on Public Housing Policy, "Basic Policies for Public Housing," 27a; Johnson, "Review of the Integration," table 2. On similar policies in Chicago, see Hirsch, *Making the Second Ghetto*, 230–36. In Philadelphia, one exception was Arch Homes, opened in 1952, which was the first truly integrated public housing in the city.

39. Countryman, *Up South*, 77. The most complete account of the controversy is Bauman, *Public Housing*, 160–69.

40. "Georgia" quoted in "Public Housing Dilemma: What Next for the City?" *PEB*, April 29, 1956, section 2, pp. 1, 4; "These Arguments Heard Most Often at Site Hearings," *PEB*, April 29, 1956, section 2, p. 5; Wolfinger, *Philadelphia Divided*, 199–200; Bauman, *Public Housing*, 163.

41. On the limits of the liberal civil-rights agenda in addressing the needs of working-class African Americans, see Countryman, *Up South*.

42. Armstrong Association, Catholic Housing Council, Committee on Democracy in Housing, Friends Race Relations Committee, National Association for the Advancement of Colored People, Philadelphia District Health and Welfare Council, Philadelphia Federation of Settlements, and Philadelphia Housing Association, press release, May 3, 1956, Box 281, Folder 4900, HADVR1, UATU.

43. Harry J. Greene to Walter E. Alessandroni, April 24, 1956, Box 9, Folder 196, NAACPR, UATU.

44. Bauman, *Public Housing*, 169; Countryman, *Up South*, 77–78.

45. Philadelphia Housing Authority, Citizens' Council, and Philadelphia Housing Association, Minutes, September 25, 1957, Box 282, Folder 4905, HADVR1, UATU; Committee on Public Housing Policy, Minutes, July 9, 1957, Box 283, Folder 4940, HADVR1, UATU.

46. See "Marchers Fight Tasker Rent Raise," *PEB*, May 21, 1949, 20.

47. Quoted in "Hill Creek No Slum," *PEB*, June 2, 1956, 6.

48. Quoted in "Hill Creek Is the Prettiest Project but Many Are Moving from It," *PEB*, April 29, 1956, section 2, p. 5. The surname "Park" is a pseudonym; the article identified the man only as "Jim." On whites' fearing that they would experience a "loss of social status" if they moved into public housing, see Advisory Committee on Community Relations to the Philadelphia Housing Authority, Minutes, February 8, 1954, Box 82, Folder 106, FNGR, UATU. See also Wallace, *Housing and Social Structure*, 78.

49. Bauman, *Public Housing*, 171. Abbottsford, Passyunk, Bartram Village, Wilson

Park and Schuylkill Falls became nearly half African American by 1968. Liddonfield and Hill Creek remained predominantly white.

50. Philadelphia District Health and Welfare Council, Inc., Committee on Social Service in Public Housing, Minutes, February 16, 1961, Box 4, Folder 113, HWCR3, UATU; Emily J. Achtenberg, Housing Association of Delaware Valley, "Public Housing Handbook" (1968), Box 286, Folder 5044, HADVR1, UATU; Bauman, *Public Housing*, 204; Mark K. Joseph to CAC Chairmen and Housing Aides, DPA Housing Liaison Agents, Field Workers for Area-Wide Council, Governor's Branch Officers, Welfare Rights Organization Members, Other Persons Interested in Public Housing, May 22, 1968, Box 285, Folder 5005, HADVR1, UATU. On single mothers' collective efforts to gain admittance to public housing in Durham, N.C., see Greene, *Our Separate Ways*, 135.

51. Large families of all kinds found it particularly difficult to gain access to public housing because less than 1 percent of all apartments in Philadelphia had five bedrooms and only 6 percent had four bedrooms, leaving twenty times as many families on waiting lists for four- and five-bedroom apartments as there were available apartments. Large families on the waiting list complained that vacancies in large apartments were usually filled with current residents who had more children. Health and Welfare Council, Inc., Family Division, Committee on Social Service in Public Housing, Minutes, September 176, 1959, Box 4, Folder 110, HWCR3, UATU; "Review of Public Housing Policies," June 25, 1956, Box 282, Folder 4921, HADVR1, UATU.

52. Married couples occupied 49 percent of the units in Philadelphia's public housing, separated and divorced tenants occupied 26 percent, widows 15 percent, and unmarried persons 4 percent. A few of these widows, divorcees, and separate household heads may have been men. See untitled, circa 1962, Box 281, Folder 4890, HADVR1, UATU.

53. "Characteristics of Low-Income Households in the Philadelphia Region, 1960: Rent-to-Income Ratios," Box 7, Folder 9, HADVR1, UATU.

54. During World War II, the government ordered a temporary hold on evictions but resumed the practice after the war, inciting organized protests among tenants who wanted to retain their subsidized apartments; see "613 Tenants Face Eviction Because of High Income," *PEB*, January 30, 1949, 1, 2; "Allen Homes Evictions Held to Be Mandatory," *Philadelphia Inquirer*, January 28, 1949, 3; "Allen Folk to Combat Evictions," *Philadelphia Tribune*, July 5, 1949, 1; "Pickets March," *Philadelphia Tribune*, October 10, 1942, 3. On similar protests in New York and Baltimore, see Schwartz, "Tenant Unions," 430–34; Williams, *Politics of Public Housing*, 74–75.

55. Quoted in Kronick, "Attitudes toward Dependency," 56; M.B.M. interview.

56. On restrictions on the admission of welfare recipients, see Hazel M. Leslie to Joseph W. Brown, October 19, 1967, and Hazel M. Leslie to Thomas J. McCoy, November 27, 1967, Box 326, Folder 6286, HADVR1, UATU.

57. The Department of Public Assistance even charged that the PHA discouraged welfare recipients from getting jobs by refusing to lower their rents immediately when they found employment. Philadelphia Housing Authority, Management Division, untitled, 1962, Box 282, Folder 4919, HADVR1, UATU; Committee on Housing Policy, "Basic Polices for Public Housing," 23; Health and Welfare Council, Inc., Family Divi-

sion, Committee on Social Services in Public Housing, Minutes, April 21, 1960, Box 4, Folder 111, HWCR3, UATU; Health and Welfare Council, Inc., Family Division, Committee on Social Service in Public Housing, Minutes, December 17, 1959, Box 4, Folder 11, HWCR3, UATU; Commonwealth of Pennsylvania, *Public Assistance Review* (1953), 4–5; Committee on Social Service in Public Housing, Minutes, April 21, 1960, Box 285, Folder 5007, HADVR1, UATU.

58. Quoted in Bauman, *Public Housing*, 135.

59. Ibid.

60. On racial similarities, see Levenstein, "The Gendered Roots of Modern Urban Poverty," 134–92. The main racial difference was that white public housing was usually constructed in more economically stable neighborhoods than African American public housing.

61. Philadelphia Housing Authority, Family Discussion Group, March 20, 1961, Box 82, Folder 109, FNGR, UATU; Lewis and Guinessy, *Helping the Poor Housekeeping Family*, 156.

62. "Richard Allen Homes."

63. Quoted in "New Homes, New Health."

64. Quoted in ibid.

65. "Everything Very Wonderful for Rosen Homes Residents," quotation on 2.

66. Philadelphia Housing Authority, "Report of Activities Conducted in Community Buildings," October 1955, Box 10, Folder 177, ULPR1, UATU; Philadelphia Housing Association, "1955 Report of Community Activities," Box 282, Folder 4920, HADVR1, UATU; Philadelphia Housing Authority, *Report for 1955*, 8.

67. Williams, *Politics of Public Housing*, 51–53.

68. "Concert Today at Allen Homes," *PEB*, April 13, 1958, section 3, p. 7

69. Philadelphia Housing Authority, *20 Years of Service*, 23.

70. In Baltimore, tenant organizations began in the 1940s; see Williams, *Politics of Public Housing*, 63–86. On tensions between black women tenants and a black manager, see Williams, *Politics of Public Housing*, 67–70.

71. Quotation is from a social worker paraphrasing Mrs. Davenport, Philadelphia Housing Authority, Housekeeping Discussion Group, April 17, 1961, Box 82, Folder 109, FNGR, UATU.

72. Quoted in Levy and Shouse, "Concept of Alienation," 39; Wallace, *Housing and Social Structure*, 64, 79.

73. M.B.M. interview.

74. Social worker quoting tenants, Philadelphia Housing Authority, Family Discussion Group, February 6, 1961, Box 82, Folder 109, FNGR, UATU, "Alice Moore" is a pseudonym; "What Happens at a Project in a Blighted Area." See also "What Happens When Public Housing Is Erected in a Neighborhood of Privately-Owned Homes," *PEB*, April 29, 1956, 1, 4. Although the article focused on Wilson Park, which mainly housed whites, it discussed policies governing daily life in public housing that were adopted by managers throughout the city.

75. Lewis and Guinessy, *Helping the Poor Housekeeping Family*, 40, 76–77, 80, 84.

76. Philadelphia District Health and Welfare Council, Inc., Committee on Social Service in Public Housing, Minutes, November 17, 1960, Box 285, Folder 5008, HADVR1, UATU.

77. Public Housing Authority, Family Discussion Group, February 19, 1961, Box 82, Folder 109, FNGR, UATU; "What Happens When Public Housing Is Erected."

78. Wallace, *Housing and Social Structure*, 76; "What Happens When Public Housing Is Erected." Similarly, on spying in St. Louis in the 1960s, see Rainwater, *Behind Ghetto Walls*, 113–14.

79. Wallace, *Housing and Social Structure*, 55.

80. M.B.M. interview; Health and Welfare Council, Inc., Family Division, Committee on Social Service in Public Housing, Minutes, April 21, 1960, Box 4, Folder 111, HWCR3, UATU; Health and Welfare Council, Inc., Family Division, Committee on Social Service in Public Housing, Minutes, January 21, 1960, Box 4, Folder 111, HWCR3, UATU; Committee on Social Service in Public Housing, Minutes, April 21, 1960, Box 285, Folder 5007, HADVR1, UATU.

81. Philadelphia Housing Authority, Family Discussion Group, May 25, 1961, Box 82, Folder 109, FNGR, UATU.

82. Quoted in Levy and Shouse, "Concept of Alienation," 93. See also M.B.M. interview; Health and Welfare Council, Inc., Family Division, Committee on Social Service in Public Housing, Minutes, January 21, 1960, Box 4, Folder 111, HWCR3, UATU.

83. Quoted in Levy and Shouse, "Concept of Alienation," 89, 78–79.

84. Bauman, Hummon, and Muller, "Public Housing," 282–83; Questionnaires.

85. Bauman, Hummon, and Muller, "Public Housing," 284; "What Happens When Public Housing Is Erected"; M.B.M. interview. On such policies, nationally, see Wood, *Beautiful Beginnings*, 21–22.

86. M.B.M. interview.

87. M.B.M. interview. Similarly, see "Tasker Homes Up in the Air over Curb on TV Antennas," *PEB*, July 21, 1958, 33.

88. This was one of the central messages of a 1956 report commissioned by the PHA; see Wallace, *Housing and Social Structure*.

89. Bauer, "The Dreary Deadlock of Public Housing."

90. On the politics of the 1950s, see Hunt, "How Did Public Housing Survive the 1950s?"; von Hoffman, "A Study in Contradictions."

91. Radford, *Modern Housing for America*, 200; Committee on Public Housing Policy, "Basic Policies for Public Housing," 5, 14. They anticipated having the funds for approximately 13,000 units and estimated that they needed 70,000.

92. Radford, *Modern Housing for America*, 190–92, 200.

93. For an interesting account, see Hunt, "Was the 1937 U.S. Housing Act a Pyrrhic Victory?" 208–9, 213–14.

94. Questionnaires; Philadelphia Housing Authority, Family Discussion Group, April 3, 1961, Box 82, Folder 109, FNGR, UATU; Federal Public Housing Authority, *The Livability Problems of 1,000 Families*, 31.

95. Questionnaires; Philadelphia Housing Authority, Family Discussion Group, May 1,

1961, Box 82, Folder 109, FNGR, UATU; Philadelphia Housing Authority, *Public Housing: Report to the Community* 4:2 (May 1954), 9.

96. For an excellent account of this process in Chicago, see Hunt, "What Went Wrong," 420–58.

97. In 1955, the PHA made plans to replace the fifteen-year-old ranges and fridges at Richard Allen, Johnson, and Tasker, assuring the public that it would be cheaper to install new ones than to continue to make repairs on the old ones; see Philadelphia Housing Authority, *Report for 1955.*

98. Committee on Public Housing Policy, "Basic Policies for Public Housing," 32; "Maintenance Subcommittee Report," Box 286, Folder 5053, HADVR1, UATU.

99. Health and Welfare Council, Inc., Family Division, Committee on Social Service in Public Housing, Minutes, April 21, 1960, Box 4, Folder 111, HWCR3, UATU; Levy and Shouse, "Concept of Alienation," 39. On working-class African American women's protests against utility bills in the 1960s in Durham, N.C., see Greene, *Our Separate Ways*, 183.

100. "What Happens When Public Housing Is Erected."

101. "A Spick-and-Span Spot," *PEB*, June 5, 1947, 14.

102. "Richard Allen Homes"; "Bright Spot in Public Housing."

103. "A Spick-and-Span Spot"; "Everything Very Wonderful for Rosen Homes Residents."

104. "Maintenance Committee Report," January 29, 1957, Box 281, Folder 4886, HADVR1, UATU.

105. Philadelphia Housing Authority, "Comments on Survey"; "Special Meeting to Discuss Conference with Charles Slusser, PHA Administrator," Minutes, January 7, 1958, Box 218, Folder 4877, HADVR1, UATU.

106. Quoted in Levy and Shouse, "Concept of Alienation," 40.

107. Social worker paraphrasing Mrs. Davenport, Philadelphia Housing Authority, Housekeeping Discussion Group, April 17, 1961, Box 82, Folder 109, FNGR, UATU. On gossip, see Levy and Shouse, "A Concept of Alienation," 90; Johnson, "Review of the Integration," 88; Questionnaires; Rainwater, *Behind Ghetto Walls*, 114.

108. Quoted in Levy and Shouse, "Concept of Alienation," 39. On noise, see also Federal Public Housing Authority, *The Livability Problems of 1,000 Families*, 62–63.

109. Levy and Shouse, "Concept of Alienation," 39; Dorothy S. Montgomery, Philadelphia Housing Association, "High-rise or Low-rise in Public Housing?," speech, NAHO Regional Conference, Pittsburgh, Pa., May 23, 1952, Box 283, Folder 4964, HADVR1, UATU; Johnson, "Review of the Integration," 87–88; Philadelphia Housing Authority, Housekeeping Discussion Group, April 17, 1961, Box 82, Folder 109, FNGR, UATU.

110. Philadelphia Housing Authority, *Biennial Report: 1960–1961*, 14; Philadelphia Housing Authority, "1955 Report of Community Activities," Box 282, Folder 4920, HADVR1, UATU.

111. Philadelphia Housing Authority, "Report of Activities Conducted in Community Buildings," October 1955, Box 10, Folder 177, ULPR1, UATU.

112. "Low Rent: Richard Allen Homes," 1945, Box 24, Folder Philadelphia Housing Association, YMCAR-C, UATU; Philadelphia District Health and Welfare Council, *Use of Community Facilities*. In 1952, Richard Allen tenants became so frustrated by their lack of resources that they raised funds to install a recreation center and gymnasium in the basement of a nearby church; see Philadelphia Housing Authority, *Public Housing: Report to the Community* 11:4 (April 1952), 6.

113. Wharton Centre, "Rosen-Johnson Housing Neighborhood," draft, n.d., Box 6, Folder 93, WCR, UATU. The problem had a different configuration in more economically stable neighborhoods with better and less crowded recreation facilities. In those cases, tenants frequently were not welcome at nearby recreation centers. See Health and Welfare Council, *Use of Community Facilities*. On similar shortages of recreation space in public housing in Chicago, see Hunt, "What Went Wrong," 353.

114. Philadelphia Housing Authority, Family Discussion Group, May 1, 1961, Box 82, Folder 109, FNGR, UATU. Similarly in Chicago, see Venkatesh, *American Project*, 24.

115. Social worker paraphrasing Mrs. Murphy, Philadelphia Housing Authority, Family Discussion Group, Richard Allen Homes, February 6, 1961, Box 82, Folder 109, FNGR, UATU.

116. "First Housing Projects Pay Dividends in Happiness"; Wallace, *Housing and Social Structure*, 74; Philadelphia Housing Authority, Family Discussion Group, May 1, 1961, Box 82, Folder 109, FNGR, UATU; Levy and Shouse, "Concept of Alienation," 40; Questionnaires.

117. On high-rises, see Bristol, "The Myth of Pruitt Igoe"; Bauman, Hummon, and Muller, "Public Housing," 285.

118. Wallace, *Housing and Social Structure*, 91; Montgomery, "High-rise or Low-rise."

119. Quoted in Levy and Shouse, "Concept of Alienation," 40.

120. By the 1970s, after constant breakdowns and several serious injuries and deaths of young boys on elevators (after they jumped into the shaft and plunged to the bottom), the PHA shut down some elevators in public housing completely, declaring them unsafe for personal use. See "S. Phila. Boy, 8, Hurt by Fall in Elevator Shaft," *PEB*, January 6, 1969, 15; "Project Loses Elevator Use," *Philadelphia Daily News*, April 9, 1976, 19; "Boy, 3, Killed In Elevator Shaft," *PEB*, September 2, 1975, 3; "Perils Haunt Housing Projects Where Boy Died in Fall," *PEB*, September 3, 1975, 51; "Boy, 2, Falls to His Death in Elevator," *PEB*, October 4, 1978, 12. Similarly, in Chicago, see Hunt, "What Went Wrong," 358–60.

121. "Residents of 1,500 Blocks Get Out Brooms for Cleanups," *PEB*, April 16, 1961, 14; Wharton Centre, *A Directory of Resources* (1956); "Beechwood-Norwood," 1954–1955, Box 45, Folder 139, WCR, UATU. Men headed anywhere from 16 to 30 percent of block groups. Less than half of the groups also had a significant male presence in their membership. See Clean Block Campaign, Captains List, 1954, Box 24, Folder Clean Block Campaign Citizens' Committee, YMCAR-C, UATU; "Block Captains for Cleanup Campaign," n.d., Box 10, Folder 59, GSR, UATU; "1958 Roster, South Philadelphia Clean Block Committee," Box 24, Folder Clean Block Committee—South Phila.,

YMCAR-C, UATU. For earlier examples of women's neighborhood organizing, see Hunter, *To 'Joy My Freedom*, 137–42; Wolcott, *Remaking Respectability*, 134–55; Gordon, *Pitied but Not Entitled*, 67–143.

122. Alphonso Johnson, Eugene Boyer, Luther Cherry, "A Report on the 211 Block of Stewart Street," 1957, Box 45, Folder 140, WCR, UATU; *Wharton Neighborhood Block Council Newsletter* 11 (1957), Box 44, Folder 131, WCR, UATU; 2100 Block Sharswood Street Improvement Club to Department of Licenses and Inspections, July 29, 1957, Box 44, Folder 125, WCR, UATU; "Fixing Up and Beautifying Our Homes," n.d., Box 40, Folder 77, WCR, UATU; Alphonso Johnson, Eugene Boyer, and Luther Cherry to Commissioner Samuel Baxter, May 9, 1957, Box 44, Folder 125, WCR, UATU; Minutes of the South Philadelphia Clean Block Association, September 28, 1959, Box 56, Folder 212, YWCAR-SW, UATU; Eugene Boyer to Department of Traffic, August 23, 1957, Box 44, Folder 125, WCR, UATU; "Beechwood-Norwood," 1954–1955, Box 45, Folder 139, WCR, UATU; "Residents of 1,500 Blocks Get Out Brooms"; Alphonso Johnson and Eugene Boyer to Hall W. Crooks, April 7, 1958, Box 44, Folder 126, WCR, UATU. The Neighborhood Garden Association of Philadelphia sponsored the flower-box campaigns; see Neighborhood Garden Association of Philadelphia, *Report of Activities for the Year 1955*, Box 45, Folder 139, WCR, UATU.

123. "Area Fights Liquor Permit," *Philadelphia Inquirer*, August 13, 1959, 4. For similar protests, see "In Protest of Tavern," *Philadelphia Afro-American*, April 19, 1958, 1, 2; "Taproom Fight Won," *Philadelphia Afro-American*, August 16, 1958, 1, 2; "North Philly Citizens Fight Move to Open Another Bar," *Philadelphia Tribune*, November 21, 1942, 1; "Liquor Bd. Nixes Shift of Taproom," *Philadelphia Tribune*, December 20, 1947, 1, 5; "Citizens Protest Official Indifference to Lawlessness," *Philadelphia Tribune*, August 13, 1955, 5.

124. "A Report to the Residents of the East Poplar Area Who Attended the November 23rd Meeting on Crime and Delinquency," 1953, Box 85, Folder 128, FNGR, UATU. Similarly, see Rosetta Payton and Wilson Long to Inspector Allen Ballard, May 17, 1957, Box 44, Folder 125, WCR, UATU; Poplar Area Community Council, Minutes of Meeting, December 19, 1955, Box 85, Folder 130, FNGR, UATU; "North Newkirk St. Residents Demand Better Area Policing," *Philadelphia Tribune*, August 15, 1959, 11; "Neighbors Protesting Burglaries," *Philadelphia Tribune*, July 7, 1959, 2. On women's fears, see also Levy and Shouse, "Concept of Alienation," 86–87, 94.

125. Field notes, January 12, 1953, Box 21, Folder NBC, December 20, 1952–November 9, 1953, UCR, UATU.

126. Nightingale, *On the Edge*, 15.

127. Allesandroni quoted in Bauman, *Public Housing*, 176; "Girls, 9 Molested in Project, At Home; Two Suspects Sought," *Philadelphia Tribune*, July 28, 1959, 13; "600 Quizzed about Murder," *PEB*, August 17, 1958, 3; "Man Admits Killing Guard at Project," *PEB*, August 19, 1958, 1; M.B.M. interview.

128. "Johnson Homes: Bouquets," *Philadelphia Inquirer*, April 16, 1978, 1-L, 8-L, quotation on 8-L; "First Housing Projects Here Pay Dividends in Happiness."

Chapter Four

1. Social worker paraphrasing Hattie Parker in "Hawthorne Project," Box 23, Folder Hawthorne Home and School Association, September 29, 1952–July 7, 1953, UCR, UATU. "Hattie Parker" is a pseudonym.

2. Odell, *Educational Survey Report*, 74, 343–44; Sanzare, *History of the Philadelphia Federation of Teachers*, 44, 48; Thompson, "The Socio-Political Context of the Philadelphia Public Schools," 160.

3. Important historical studies exploring African Americans' commitment to education include Anderson, *The Education of Blacks in the South*; Franklin, *The Education of Black Philadelphia*; Homel, *Down from Equality*; Shaw, *What a Woman Ought to Be and to Do*; Cecelski, *Along Freedom Road*; Douglas, *Jim Crow Moves North*; Dougherty, *More Than One Struggle*.

4. Quoted in Berg, "Study of a Group of Unwed Mothers," 91.

5. Quoted in ibid., 90.

6. Quoted in ibid., 89.

7. For a good summary of the debates regarding the effects of formal schooling on economic achievement, see Mirel, *The Rise and Fall of an Urban School System*, ix–x. Important works include Katz, *The Irony of Early School Reform*; Ravitch, *The Revisionists Revised*; Katz, *Reconstructing American Education*, 136–59. Studies of the effects of schooling on African Americans' future prospects include Margo, *Race and Schooling in the South*; Harrison, *Education, Training, and the Urban Ghetto*. Recent work on the construction of racialized poverty includes Sugrue, *The Origins of the Urban Crisis*; Hirsch, *Making the Second Ghetto*; Bauman, *Public Housing*; Self, *American Babylon*. Some of the few works that explore the historical relationship between education and urban poverty include Licht, *Getting Work*; Harvey Kantor and Barbara Brenzel, "Urban Education and the 'Truly Disadvantaged': The Historical Roots of the Contemporary Crisis, 1945–1990," in Katz, *The "Underclass Debate*," 366–402; Katz, *Improving Poor People*. For a study that emphasizes the need for both jobs and training, see McKee, "Philadelphia Liberals."

8. Odell, *Educational Survey Report*, 167.

9. Figures are based on African American males and females ages fourteen to seventeen in the labor force in Philadelphia's standard metropolitan statistical area; see U.S. Department of Commerce, *Census of Population*, part 40, pp. 651, 652. Only 33 percent of seventeen-year-old African American men were in the labor force at all. Since 42 percent had dropped out of school, that left at least 9 percent unaccounted for, many of whom were also likely unemployed. This data set had a preponderance of whites, reflecting both the difficulties of locating poor African Americans and the fact that the figures cover the entire Philadelphia standard metropolitan area, which included many white neighborhoods on the outskirts of the city. A few of the many public discussions of the increasing need for youth to secure high school diplomas to qualify for employment include Tony Bok, "Jobs for School Youth," 1963, Box 53, Folder 10, WCR, UATU;

"Those Who Quit School Are Witnesses to Toll of Frustration and Boredom," *PEB*, January 8, 1964, 1, 32.

10. Odell, *Educational Survey Report*, 167, 171. I did not include students classified as "other" or "unknown" when calculating the unemployment rate cited in the text. See Tables 4.1 and 4.2 for more information and comprehensive statistics.

11. My findings contradict James Gregory's argument that a high school diploma did not significantly improve African Americans' employment prospects; see Gregory, *The Southern Diaspora*, 106–7. On the value of education for African Americans in Chicago, see Neckerman, *Schools Betrayed*, 59.

12. See, for example, Binzen, *Whitetown U.S.A.*, 149; "Add Anderson: A Man of Economy but Critics Say He Slights Teachers," *PEB*, June 25, 1962, 1, 12.

13. Binzen, *Whitetown U.S.A.*, 273–75, quotation on 275.

14. The state's responsibility increased over the course of the postwar period. In 1949, 73 percent of the funding came from real-estate taxes, 14 percent from the state, 5 percent from personal-property taxes, and 6 percent from mercantile taxes. In 1959, 55 percent came from the city's real-estate tax, 32 percent from the state, 3 percent from property taxes, 7 percent from general business taxes, and 2 percent from federal subsidy. See School District of Philadelphia, *One Hundred Forty-First Annual Report of the Board of Public Education*, 10. Federal government contributions for foreign language and science programs increased with the passage of the National Defense Education Act in 1958.

15. William H. Wilcox, "Who Should Set Tax Rates for Philadelphia's Schools?," 1963, Box 24, Folder 95, ULPR2, UATU; Binzen, *Whitetown U.S.A.*, 274–75.

16. Weigley, *Philadelphia*, 680. The board members were officially appointed by judges from the Court of Common Pleas, but the judges followed Anderson's recommendations. On the board, see Binzen, *Whitetown U.S.A.*, 274; United States Commission on Civil Rights, *Civil Rights U.S.A.*, 122–23; Greater Philadelphia Movement, *A Citizens Study of Public Education*, 24; "School Survey Cites Need for $38 Million in Budget Boost in '60," *PEB*, March 9, 1965, 1, 54; "Taking the Easy Way Doesn't Work," *Philadelphia Daily News*, February 11, 1957, 5. This method of school board selection was unique. In New York City, Chicago, Baltimore, and San Francisco, the mayor appointed the board. In Los Angeles, Detroit, Cleveland, St. Louis, and Boston, the board was chosen in nonpartisan elections. Only Washington, D.C., and Pittsburgh had boards appointed by judges. See U.S. Commission on Civil Rights, *Civil Rights U.S.A.*, 121–22. Only in 1965 did Philadelphia voters approve a referendum that replaced the fifteen-member board with a nine-member board appointed by and accountable to the mayor. The referendum also gave the new school board greater fiscal control by transferring authority to levy school taxes from the state legislature to the city. See Birger, "Race, Reaction, and Reform," 32.

17. Quoted in Birger, "Race, Reaction, and Reform," 27. Similarly, see Petshek, *Challenge of Urban Reform*, 40.

18. Franklin, *The Education of Black Philadelphia*, 29–86.

19. "Negro Pupils Top 50% Mark in City Schools," *PEB*, August 30, 1962, 1, 16.

20. Urban League of Philadelphia, "Statement Presented to the Special Committee on Non-Discrimination of the Board of Public Education," April 24, 1963, Box 20, Folder 1, EELR, UATU; "Summary of Testimony Given at Public Hearings before the Special Committee on Non-Discrimination of the Philadelphia Board of Public Education," 1963, Box 20, Folder 1, EELR, UATU.

21. For an important analysis of segregation in twentieth-century northern schools, see Douglas, *Jim Crow Moves North*. On Chicago, see Neckerman, *Schools Betrayed*. In Philadelphia, public discussions frequently employed the term "de facto" to describe the segregation in the schools, thereby distinguishing conditions in Philadelphia from those in the South prior to *Brown v. Board of Education*. Yet in many cases, the segregation in the North was intentional. The West Philadelphia Schools Committee called it "de facto discrimination." See "Statement of the West Philadelphia Schools Committee, to the District One Subcommittee Appointed to Review the Non-Discrimination Policy of the School District of Philadelphia," 1963, Box 1, Folder 1963 Statements of the WPSC, WPSCR, UATU. See also "Summary of Testimony Given at Public Hearings before the Special Committee on Non-Discrimination of the Philadelphia Board of Public Education" 1963, Box 20, Folder 1, EELR, UATU; Educational Equality League, "Report," 1953, Box 1, Folder 4, EELR, UATU; U.S. Commission on Civil Rights, *Civil Rights U.S.A.*, 129–37; "Benjamin Franklin High Called Jim Crow School," *Philadelphia Inquirer*, October 7, 1951, 15; "Germantown Parents Alarmed about Segregation in Schools," *Philadelphia Tribune*, February 4, 1958, 1, 2.

22. U.S. Commission on Civil Rights, *Civil Rights U.S.A.*, 133–35.

23. U.S. Commission on Civil Rights, *Civil Rights U.S.A.* On educational discrimination in the North more generally, see Douglas, *Jim Crow Moves North*.

24. On the limitations of the settlement, see Franklin, *Education of Black Philadelphia*, 200–201.

25. Special Committee on Nondiscrimination, *Report of the Special Committee on Nondiscrimination*, 20; "City's Teacher Recruiter Sells 'Challenge' in Filling Vacancies at 'Difficult Schools,'" *PEB*, December 1, 1961, 1.

26. When calculating overcrowding, a "black" or a "white" school was defined as one whose student body was at least 70 percent black or at least 70 percent white; see *Report of the Special Committee on Nondiscrimination*, 12. On teacher vacancies, see Odell, *Educational Survey Report*, 115. On crowding, see "Population Shifts Overcrowd 10 of City's 18 High Schools," *PEB*, January 24, 1960, 3; "4,407 Pupils on Part-Time in City's Public Schools," *PEB*, March 15, 1956, 20; "Schools to Put 4,465 Pupils on Part-Time," *PEB*, August 23, 1961, 29.

27. School District of Philadelphia, *One Hundred Forty-First Annual Report of the Board of Public Education*, 22–41. When calculating per-pupil expenditures, I subtracted substantial funding for construction and new equipment provided by the board since such funds were often one-time grants. On unequal funding, see also "Tioga Group Blasts Education Board's New School Plan," *Philadelphia Tribune*, April 30, 1960, 1, 9. In 1959,

African Americans comprised 30 percent of the city's high school students and 50 percent of its elementary students.

28. "$80 Million Spent in Phila. for Schools," *PEB*, May 17, 1959, special section "Schools—Class of '59," p. 18.

29. Saunders, *School Facilities Survey*; Odell, *Educational Survey Report*, 76; Urban League of Philadelphia, "Statement Presented to the Special Committee on Non-Discrimination of the Board of Public Education," 1963, Box 20, Folder 1, EELR, UATU.

30. Binzen, *Whitetown U.S.A.*, 168; "Boards Pinch Pennies on Libraries yet Find the Dollars for Sports," *PEB*, March 24, 1961, 1, 20, 22.

31. "Public Hearings Called on School Expansion," *PEB*, September 25, 1962, 3; U.S. Commission on Civil Rights, *Civil Rights U.S.A.*, 134; Clapper, "School Design"; "Pre-fabricated Classrooms Expand Schools at Low Cost to City," *PEB*, December 15, 1957, section 2, p. 1.

32. On educators' long-standing views of schools as agents of socialization serving societal goals, see Katz, *The Irony of Early School Reform*; Katz, *Reconstructing American Education*, esp. 154; Spring, *The Sorting Machine Revisited*, 11, 57–58.

33. On the process through which schools increasingly sought to serve not only academic and vocational functions but also "custodial ones," see Angus and Mirel, *The Failed Promise of the American High School*. On tracking, see also Ravitch, *The Troubled Crusade*, 43–45. For an excellent contemporary analysis of tracking, see Oakes, *Keeping Track*.

34. Philadelphia school authorities did not call it "tracking," nor did they acknowledge its extent; see U.S. Commission on Civil Rights, *Civil Rights U.S.A.*, 113–14.

35. For critiques of intelligence tests, see Franklin, *Education of Black Philadelphia*, 47–48, 130–33.

36. "Some Poor Students Hide Brains to Gain Prestige among Their Pals," *PEB*, April 7, 1960, 1, 8; "Tioga Group Blasts Education Board's New School Plan," *Philadelphia Tribune*, April 30, 1960, 1, 9. Similarly, see "Children Hungry for Learning Often Mislabeled 'Sick, Disturbed,'" *PEB*, February 3, 1966, 1, 12. For IQ scores broken down by race, see Odell, *Educational Survey Report*, 35.

37. "Job Training Gives Dropouts a Second Chance," *PEB*, July 7, 1963, 13. The *Bulletin* did not give Lucille's last name so I used a pseudonym.

38. Special Committee on Nondiscrimination, *Report of the Special Committee on Nondiscrimination*, 16.

39. "Many IQs Dip after 4 Years of Schooling, Report Says," *PEB*, January 22, 1965, 4; Binzen, *Whitetown U.S.A.*, 166–67; "No Student Is Just 'Average,'" *Philadelphia Daily News*, January 31, 1957, 5; Sanzare, *History of the Philadelphia Federation of Teachers*, 47; Binzen, *Whitetown U.S.A.*, 167–68. Binzen states that teachers in schools that served working-class whites lowered standards because they did not believe the students would succeed if they pursued challenging academic work; see *Whitetown U.S.A.*, 171. Yet looking at the system as a whole, racial discrepancies in achievement were significant. In 1963, just over one-third of the schools with 70 percent or more black students

reached the city's median sixth-grade level of achievement in reading and arithmetic compared to over 90 percent of the schools with 30 percent or fewer African American students. See Odell, *Educational Survey Report*, 58–59.

40. Countryman, *Up South*, 64.

41. "Are the Schools Really Better past City Line?" *PEB*, September 25, 1959, 1, 3.

42. Special Committee on Nondiscrimination, *Report of the Special Committee on Nondiscrimination*, 7.

43. Odell, *Educational Survey Report*, 134.

44. Special Committee on Nondiscrimination, *Report of the Special Committee on Nondiscrimination*, 15; Odell, *Educational Survey Report*, 108.

45. Odell, *Educational Survey Report*, 140–41.

46. "No Student Is Just 'Average,'" *Philadelphia Daily News*, January 31, 1957, 5. See also "Those Who Quit School Are Witnesses to Toll of Frustration and Boredom," *PEB*, January 8, 1964, 1, 32.

47. "More Negroes Than Ever Teach Here, Board Says," *PEB*, December 16, 1962, 3. On black and white teachers' differential treatment of black students, see Franklin, *Education of Black Philadelphia*, 192.

48. "Where Children Learn Confidence," *PEB*, February 4, 1962, section 2, pp. 1, 2. Similarly, see "Children Hungry for Learning."

49. Hayre was appointed acting principal in 1955 and was fully appointed as principal in 1956. Thompson, "The Socio-Political Context of the Philadelphia Public Schools," 192–93; Hayre and Moore, *Tell Them We Are Rising*, 62; Franklin, *Education of Black Philadelphia*, 207.

50. J.E.J. interview; Franklin, *Education of Black Philadelphia*, 207. In 1973, Marcus Foster was tragically murdered by the Symbionese Liberation Army.

51. School District of Philadelphia, *Great Cities School Improvement Program*, 9, 10, 11–60; "How Good?," *Sunday Bulletin Magazine*, April 21, 1963, 5; Binzen, *Whitetown U.S.A.*, 57–58, 79–80, 82, 190.

52. Greater Philadelphia Movement, *A Citizens Study of Public Education*, 46–47; Odell, *Educational Survey Report*, 190–91; Marechal-Neil E. Young to the Editor, *Evening and Sunday Bulletin*, November 16, 1962, Box 1, Folder 1962 correspondence, WPSCR, UATU.

53. "The City's No. 1 School Problem," *PEB*, June 7, 1959, section 2, p. 7; "7,000 Pupils Drop Out of Public Schools Each Year, Survey by Board Shows," *PEB*, September 26, 1962, 10; "Urgent Needs of Youth Place Heavy Load on Schools," *Philadelphia Inquirer*, November 21, 1963, 41.

54. "2 Grade Schools Here Plan to Use Readers That Break the Color Line," *PEB*, October 24, 1963, 1, 43; "Negro Culture Given Short Shrift in Many Histories in Schools Today," *PEB*, October 22, 1963, 1, 37; "Phila. Schools to Add Course about Bigotry," *PEB*, July 6, 1960, 3.

55. Sanzare, *History of the Philadelphia Federation of Teachers*, 48–53, Liveright quoted on 50. On behavior problems in schools, see also "Schools Adopt Tough Policy with Rowdies," *PEB*, February 14, 1957, 1, 10.

56. Sanzare, *History of the Philadelphia Federation of Teachers*, 43.

57. For examples of the extensive press coverage of youth gangs, see "Four in Teenage Gang Held in Burglaries Totaling $1,000," *PEB*, May 6, 1958, 81; "46 Youths Held as 500 Terrorize Area in Fight," *Philadelphia Inquirer*, November 11, 1954, 1, 9; "15 in Gang Fight Held for Rioting," *PEB*, November 11, 1954, 1, 3; "Police Keep Tense Guard in N. Phila. against Gang Warfare, Junior Grade," *PEB*, April 4, 1954, 19, 29. On youth gangs in New York City, see Schneider, *Vampires, Dragons, and Egyptian Kings*.

58. "Roving Gangs Invade City High Schools," *PEB*, March 4, 1954, 1; "Cops in the Schools," *PEB*, March 5, 1954, 16; "City Teachers Fear Reprisal by Principals, Ryan Says," *PEB*, May 9, 1964, 8; "200 Pupils Riot, Damage Autos," *PEB*, September 23, 1955, 1, 2; "Police Break Up Teen Mob, Clamp Curfew across City to Curb Rising Gang Feuds," *Philadelphia Inquirer*, November 13, 1954, 1, 13; "The Schools Face Facts," *PEB*, May 10, 1956, 26; "Attacks on Teachers Rare, Police and Schools Insist," *PEB*, February 25, 1958, 1.

59. "Pupils Behave When Police Watch School," *PEB*, April 2, 1959, 3; "The Big Story in the Big Cities," *U.S. News and World Report*, December 19, 1958, 46–54. Three of the schools with police presence served a predominantly black student body, two served both whites and African Americans, and the remaining five served mostly whites.

60. Odell, *Educational Survey Report*, 41, 45, 51. Dropout statistic for African American girls was calculated by including most girls classified as leaving school because they were "incapacitated or dead" as dropouts because most of them were "incapacitated" because of pregnancy. See Table 4.6.

61. Schneider, *Vampires, Dragons, and Egyptian Kings*, 107–13. Sociologists suggest that low-income boys today continue to face unique problems in the classroom because teachers often treat them in strict and uncompromising ways; see Lopez, *Hopeful Girls, Troubled Boys*; Ferguson, *Bad Boys*.

62. "Education Comes Hard for 33% of City Pupils," *PEB*, April 4, 1960, 1, 9.

63. "Migration from South Is a Cause of School Problem, Educator Says," *PEB*, April 6, 1960, 1, 19; "The Slow Learners," *PEB*, April 5, 1960, 34

64. "Education Comes Hard," quotation on 9.

65. On twentieth-century liberal scholarship on African American family life, see Feldstein, *Motherhood in Black and White*. Specifically on cultural deprivation, see Ravitch, *The Troubled Crusade*, 150. On the cultural-deprivation discourse used by school authorities in Boston and Milwaukee, see Theoharis, "They Told Us Our Kids Were Stupid," 19, 25; Dougherty, *More Than One Struggle*, 64–70.

66. "Migration from South Is a Cause of School Problem."

67. First part of the quotation is the *Bulletin* explaining the findings disclosed by Wetter. See "Education Comes Hard." Second part of the quotation (beginning with "These children . . . live in Negro ghettoes") is from "Migration from South Is a Cause of School Problem."

68. "Education Comes Hard." The publicity surrounding "slow learners" justified an experimental approach to poor black children, adopted in several schools, that focused on improving their self-esteem; see "Teachers of Low IQ Pupils Steer a Middle Course in Rating Abilities," *PEB*, April 5, 1960, 1, 52.

69. "Schools Fight Parents Who Retard Pupils," *PEB*, September 29, 1963, 28.

70. In 1961, Conant's *Slums and Suburbs* called for increased school funding, curriculum development, higher salaries for teachers, and jobs for youth. In 1966, Coleman's *Equality of Educational Opportunity* identified a complex interaction between the social composition of schools, the skills of the teachers, and students' family backgrounds and suggested that racial integration would increase African American achievement. Still, as education scholar Diane Ravitch has observed: "The most important point to filter through the public prints was that 'schools don't make a difference.' . . . Student achievement is determined largely by family background and scarcely at all by teachers, books, and facilities." See Ravitch, *The Troubled Crusade*, 169; Conant, *Slums and Suburbs*; Coleman, *Equality of Educational Opportunity*. For analysis of liberal and conservative responses to Coleman, see Mirel, *The Rise and Fall of an Urban School System*, vii.

71. For a contemporary perspective, see Patricia Hill Collins, "Shifting the Center: Race, Class, and Feminist Theory," in Glenn, Chang, and Forcey, *Mothering*, 54–55.

72. Educational Equality League, "Many Giant Steps Have Been Taken in 41 Years Because Public Education Must Survive," n.d., Box 1, Folder 1, EELR, UATU. See also Franklin, *Education of Black Philadelphia*, 137–48, 188–89, 200.

73. On textbooks, see "Urges Integrated Group Help Board of Education Pick Proper Textbooks," *Philadelphia Independent*, July 16, 1960, 5. On tracking, see "Children in Happy Homes Learn Faster, Wetter Says," *PEB*, September 8, 1963, 11. The 400 ministers also lobbied for equitable conditions in white and African American schools; see "The Ministers' School Plan," *PEB*, August 23, 1963.

74. WPSC records are held at the Urban Archives, Temple University, Philadelphia. Another group, the Citizens Committee on Public Education, brought together representatives from political groups, churches, unions, the chamber of commerce, and universities to attend lectures on topics such as school finances and teacher shortages and to campaign for a new school survey to be conducted in the early 1960s. See Resnik, *Turning on the System*, 35–41.

75. "Tioga Group Blasts Education Board's New School Plan," *Philadelphia Tribune*, April 30, 1960, Box 48, EELR, UATU; Florence Cohen to Friend, January 2, 1964. Box 41, Folder 86-A, WCR, UATU; "School to Shift 100 Pupils in Integration Move Here," *PEB*, May 3, 1961, 24.

76. Teachers Union of Philadelphia, *Teachers Union NEWS* 6:1 (September 1951), 2.

77. Urban League of Philadelphia, "A Statement on the Proposed Building Plan of the Board of Public Education," 1962, Box 61, Folder Annual Report Source Materials, Urban League of Philadelphia, 1962–1964, RNUL, part 2, series 5, LC; Franklin, *Education of Black Philadelphia*, 171; "Philadelphia Urban League," December 8, 1960, and "Urban League Sponsors Career Conference at Benjamin Franklin High School," n.d., both in Box 8, Folder 134, ULPR1, UATU. In the late 1960s, community control of the schools became a major goal and source of activism of Philadelphia's Black Power movement; see Countryman, *Up South*, 223–57.

78. On EEL victories, see Educational Equality League, "Many Giant Steps Have Been

Taken in 41 Years Because Public Education Must Survive," n.d., Box 1, Folder 1, EELR, UATU. See also Franklin, *Education of Black Philadelphia*, 137–48, 188–89, 200.

79. Board of Public Education, *For Every Child*, 16.

80. On the maintenance of segregated housing, see Hirsch, "Massive Resistance in the Urban North."

81. In 1958, a group of black mothers in New York City staged a school boycott to protest the racially inferior education that their children received, but most low-income women in Philadelphia did not directly challenge the school board's policies. See Adina Back, "Exposing the 'Whole Segregation Myth': The Harlem Nine and New York City's School Desegregation Battles," in Theoharis and Woodard, *Freedom North*, 65–91. On women's educational activism in the East Bay Area of northern California in the postwar period, see Lemke-Santangelo, *Abiding Courage*, 170–74. For an excellent account of educational organizing in Boston in the 1960s, see Theoharis, "They Told Us Our Kids Were Stupid." For a single example of mothers in Philadelphia lobbying the board for a new school in the postwar period, see Resnik, *Turning on the System*, 125.

82. "The Big Story in the Big Cities," *U.S. News and World Report*, December 19, 1958, 46–54; "Report of the Action Research Project: West Philadelphia High School, 1961," Box 1, Folder 1961 Publications, Action Research Project, WPSCR, UATU; *Civil Rights U.S.A.*, 146–47; "Transfers Help Integrate City Schools, Study Shows," *PEB*, December 18, 1962, 9; "City Schools Accused of Segregation Laxity," *PEB*, January 16, 1961, 16.

83. " 'Open Schools' Policy Permits Pupil Shifts," *PEB*, June 4, 1959, 3; School District of Philadelphia, Board of Public Education, *Procedures for Admission and Transfer of Pupils*, Administrative Bulletin no. 24, 1956, Box 20, Folder 18, EELR, UATU.

84. School District of Philadelphia, *Procedures for Admission and Transfer of Pupils*.

85. Quoted in U.S. Commission on Civil Rights, *Civil Rights U.S.A.*, 143.

86. To prevent parents from securing such illegal transfers, the board instructed principals to "scrutinize with great care any change of address reported by pupils or parents" by requiring them to present bills of sales or long-term rental agreements to verify their moves; see School District of Philadelphia, *Procedures for Admission and Transfer of Pupils*. See also U.S. Commission on Civil Rights, *Civil Rights U.S.A.*, 142–43; Poplar Area Community Council, "Draft of Resolution to Be Sent to the Board of Education," January 16, 1956, Box 85, Folder 130, FNGR, UATU; "Taking the Easy Way Doesn't Work," *Philadelphia Daily News*, February 11, 1957, 5.

87. For a thorough discussion of these debates, see Douglas, *Jim Crow Moves North*.

88. "The Many Faces of Integration," *Philadelphia Daily News*, February 5, 1957, 5; U.S. Commission on Civil Rights, *Civil Rights U.S.A.*, 152.

89. "The Big Story in the Big Cities," *U.S. News and World Report*, December 19, 1958, 46–54; U.S. Commission on Civil Rights, *Civil Rights U.S.A.*, 145–53.

90. "Summary of Testimony Given at Public Hearings before the Special Committee on Non-Discrimination of the Philadelphia Board of Public Education," 1963, Box 20, Folder 1, EELR, UATU.

91. In 1961, the archdiocese reported that of the 149,061 students in the Catholic

schools, only 1,000 were not Catholic; see U.S. Commission on Civil Rights, *Civil Rights U.S.A.*, 117. See also Odell, *Educational Survey Report*, 6–7; "Parochial Pupils Outnumber Public Rolls in One City Area," *PEB*, May 13, 1960, 9; National Council of the Churches of Christ in the U.S.A., *Churches and Church Membership in the United States*, table 34, part 2. On enrollment in Philadelphia's Catholic school system during the twentieth century, see Donaghy, *Philadelphia's Finest*, 233; "Catholics Add 15,000 Pupils," *PEB*, August 25, 1956, 5.

92. Binzen, *Whitetown U.S.A.*, 241, 245, 248; Weigley, *Philadelphia*, 682–83.

93. Binzen, *Whitetown U.S.A.*, 241, 248, 251–55.

94. The statistic covered all parochial schools, which included a few Quaker institutions. The number of African Americans enrolled rose from 4,000 in 1953 to 15,000 in 1962. See "15,000 Negroes Enrolled in Parochial Schools Here," *PEB*, October 3, 1963, 31. On white parents sending children to Catholic schools to avoid African Americans, see Luconi, *From Paesani to White Ethnic*, 131. Paula S. Fass has argued that Catholic schools had a history of racial discrimination, particularly prior to the 1960s; see *Outside In*, 217–26.

95. "Negro Pupils Deepen Deficits of Parish Schools," *PEB*, March 2, 1969, 4.

96. In 1953, 6,400 students in Philadelphia attended school only for half the day, mostly in elementary schools in poor African American neighborhoods. In 1956, 4,407 students attended part-time. See "4,407 Pupils on Part-Time in City's Public Schools"; Special Committee on Nondiscrimination, *Report of the Special Committee on Nondiscrimination*, 11.

97. C.E. interview. Similarly, see G.J. interview; J.E.J. interview; A.P. interview; E.O.K. interview.

98. Commission on Secondary Schools of the Middle States Association of Schools and Colleges, "Report of the Visiting Committee on the Evaluation of the Benjamin Franklin High School," April 1951, Box 20, Folder 26, EELR, UATU. In 1960, 50 percent of Philadelphia's nonwhites and 44 percent of whites aged twenty-five and older had no schooling beyond the eighth grade. U.S. Census statistic cited in Odell, *Educational Survey Report*, 26.

99. Berg, "Study of a Group of Unwed Mothers," 57. See also "Hawthorne Project," Box 23, Folder Hawthorne Home and School Association, July 28, 1953–August 2, 1954, UCR, UATU.

100. Quoted in Levy and Shouse, "Concept of Alienation," 100.

101. Ibid., 62.

102. U.N.A. Student Field Work Report, Process Record, "Meredith Home and School Association Project," October 20, 1953–November 11, 1953, Box 23, Folder Meredith Home and School Association, UCR, UATU.

103. Berg, "Study of a Group of Unwed Mothers," 57. See also "Hawthorne Project," Box 23, Folder Hawthorne Home and School Association, July 28, 1953–August 2, 1954, UCR, UATU.

104. "Hawthorne Association," Box 23, Folder Hawthorne Home and School Associa-

tion, September 26, 1952–July 22, 1953, UCR, UATU. In 1955, the school district began to advise that only principals administer corporal punishment.

105. "Pupil's Mother Accused of Striking Teacher," *PEB*, November 27, 1963, 23; G.J. interview.

106. Quoted in Levy and Shouse, "Concept of Alienation," 99.

107. C.S. interview.

108. Quoted in Levy and Shouse, "A Concept of Alienation," 99; J.P. interview.

109. Quoted in Levy and Shouse, "A Concept of Alienation," 48.

110. Kronick interview.

111. On women's efforts to counter negative stereotypes of their mothering in Boston, see Theoharis, "They Told Us Our Children Were Stupid."

112. Both Bonds and Harris quoted in "Urgent Needs of Youth Place Heavy Load on Schools," *PEB*, November 21, 1963, 41.

113. Quoted in Allis, Becker, Henderson, and Myers, "Wants of AFDC Mothers," 33.

114. Levy and Shouse, "Concept of Alienation," 48–49, quotation on 49. See also Allis, Becker, Henderson, and Myers, "Wants of AFDC Mothers," 53, 55, 68; "2nd Hand Clothes for Reliefers Called a 'Badge of Shame,'" *PEB*, April 13, 1952, 10; Kronick, "Attitudes toward Dependency," 47, 61.

115. Odell, *Educational Survey Report*, 95.

116. "Residents' Pleas Spur Police Action on Icebox 'Tomb,'" *Philadelphia Inquirer*, August 9, 1958, 9.

117. Neighborhood Council Meeting Minutes, October 15, 1952, Box 9, Folder 21, GSR, UATU; C.E. interview.

118. J.P. interview; J.E.J. interview.

119. C.E. interview.

120. L.L. interview.

121. C.S. interview. Similarly, see J.E.J. interview.

122. Quoted in "Report of the Action Research Project: West Philadelphia High School, 1961," Box 1, Folder 1961 Publications, Action Research Project, WPSCR, UATU. See also C.E. interview. Similarly, in New York, see Conant, *Slums & Suburbs*, 19; Marya Mannes, "School Trouble in Harlem," *The Reporter*, February 5, 1959, 16.

123. Odell, *Educational Survey Report*, 41; "In Our Town," *PEB*, April 17, 1950, 4; "Philadelphia's Teen Mothers: How Can We Keep Them in School?" *PEB*, April 24, 1967, 18. For a comparison of pregnancy policies at schools throughout the nation, see Glenn C. Atkyns, "Trends in the Retention of Married and Pregnant Students in American Public Schools," *Sociology of Education* 41:1 (1968): 57–65. The Berean Institute offered education programs for single mothers, but it only reached a small number of young women; see Health and Welfare Council, *Resources, Programs and Projects*, 7; "We Can Keep Them Studying—but It's Expensive," *PEB*, April 25, 1967, 46.

124. Odell, *Educational Survey Report*, 41, 45.

125. This statement reflects my reading of the rich sociological literature on teenage pregnancy. Studies have demonstrated that most teenage mothers have mainstream

goals, but many feel incapable of fulfilling them. A good job and a stable marriage to an upstanding employed man often seem out of reach to girls growing up in impoverished inner-city neighborhoods. One of the best sociological studies of teenage motherhood is Kaplan, *Not Our Kind of Girl*.

126. Solinger, *Wake Up Little Susie*, 54, 207–11. In Philadelphia, it remained difficult for welfare recipients (particularly unmarried ones) to get contraception throughout the 1960s because of the intense opposition from Catholic officials; see American Friends Service Committee, *Family Planning Services*.

127. J.E.J. interview.

128. J.P. interview; C.E. interview. See also Ladner, *Tomorrow's Tomorrow*, 178–204; Gloria L. Joseph, "Black Mothers and Daughters: Traditional and New Perspectives," in Bell-Scott et al., *Double Stitch*, 96–99.

129. "Those Summer Jobs Are Hard to Find," *PEB*, May 15, 1959, 22.

130. See, for example, Gay interview; J.E.J. interview; J.P. interview. Similarly, in the East Bay area, see Lemke-Santangelo, *Abiding Courage*, 146.

131. J.E.J. interview.

132. C.E. interview.

133. Ibid.

134. Quoted in Berg, "Study of a Group of Unwed Mothers," 91. Similarly, see Levy and Shouse, "Concept of Alienation," 24.

135. E.O.K. interview. Similarly, see L.L. interview. On mothers' attempts to pursue jobs that enabled them to care for their children at the same time, see Hunter, *To 'Joy My Freedom*, 56–57; Clark-Lewis, *Living In, Living Out*, 168.

136. Quoted in Berg, "Study of a Group of Unwed Mothers," 90.

137. Quoted in ibid., 90.

138. Johnson, "Black Philadelphia in Transition," 285–86, 288, 290, 295, 297–98.

139. Wharton Centre, *A Directory of Resources (Wards 28, 29, 32, 47)* (Philadelphia, 1956), Box 41, no folder, WCR, UATU. In 1949, four additional African American elementary and junior high schools had Home and School Associations and two were in the process of organizing them. It is not clear whether, or how long, these groups continued into the 1950s. See Henrietta Collins to Charles E. Perry, May 26, 1949, Box 2, Folder 24, FNGR, UATU. A Home and School Association operated in the 1950s at the racially mixed McCall school.

140. It is not clear how many other working-class black Home and School groups had contact with social welfare organizations. A Wharton Centre social worker tried to get involved with the Douglass group after it had already been formed, and the Reynolds group seems to have had at least some contact with the Wharton Centre. However, I have not found records from any other groups. See Singerly-Douglass P.T.A., October 25, 1951, Box 30, Folder 83, WCR, UATU; Reynolds Home and School Association Mother's Club, flyer, 1961, Box 39, Folder 70-B, WCR, UATU.

141. "Hawthorne Project," Box 23, Folder Hawthorne Home and School Association, September 26, 1952–July 22, 1953, UCR, UATU. "Junior Gets a Break As Home and School Team Up for His Good," *PEB*, December 25, 1949, section MI, p. 6; "Pupils Tell of

Personal Problems," *PEB*, February 4, 1962, section 2, p. 2; Molly Ladd-Taylor traces the origins of middle-class Parent Teacher Associations (PTAs) and their shift from focusing on a broad range of issues in the early twentieth century to a narrow focus on parental education and the schools in the 1920s. She found incidents of racial discrimination within the PTA in the early twentieth century; see Ladd-Taylor, *Mother-Work*, 43–73.

142. On Philadelphia, see Binzen, *Whitetown U.S.A.*, 275–76; Resnik, *Turning on the System*, 122–23. Nationally, see Cutler, *Parents and Schools*, 167, 175.

143. Quoted in United Neighborhood Association, "Evaluation Institution," 1951, Box 20, Folder UNA Staff Evaluation Initiatives, UCR, UATU. For roots of this middle-class approach to neighborhood organizing, see Schlossman and Sedlak, "The Chicago Area Project Revisited." The Hawthorne group was started by a student intern and then passed to a full-time field-worker.

144. "Hawthorne Project," Box 23, Folder Hawthorne Home and School Association, September 26, 1952–July 22, 1953, UCR, UATU.

145. U.N.A. Student Field Work Report, Process Record, "Meredith Home and School Association Project," October 20, 1953–November 11, 1953, Box 23, Folder Meredith Home and School Association, UCR, UATU; "Hawthorne Project," Box 23, Folder Hawthorne Home and School Association, July 28, 1953–August 2, 1954, UCR, UATU; "Hawthorne Project," Box 23, Folder Hawthorne Home and School Association, September 26, 1952–July 22, 1953, UCR, UATU; Singerly-Douglass P.T.A., October 25, 1951, Box 30, Folder 83, WCR, UATU.

146. U.N.A. Student Field Work Report, Process Record, "Meredith Home and School Association Project," October 20, 1953–November 11, 1953, Box 23, Folder Meredith Home and School Association, UCR, UATU; "Hawthorne Project," Box 23, Folder Hawthorne Home and School Association, July 28,1953–August 2, 1954, UCR, UATU; "Hawthorne Project," Box 23, Folder Hawthorne Home and School Association, September 26, 1952–July 22, 1953, UCR, UATU; Singerly-Douglass P.T.A., October 25, 1951, Box 30, Folder 83, WCR, UATU.

147. "Hawthorne Project," Box 23, Folder Hawthorne Home and School Association, September 26, 1952–July 22, 1953, UCR, UATU.

148. Conclusions based on my examination of the records of low-income African Americans' block groups and Home and School Associations. For an interesting contemporary analysis of divisions within low-income African American communities, see Anderson, *Code of the Street*.

149. For earlier examples, see Hunter, *To 'Joy My Freedom*, 137–42; Wolcott, *Remaking Respectability*, 134–55; Gordon, *Pitied but Not Entitled*, 67–143; Ladd-Taylor, *Mother-Work*, 62–63.

150. For the field-worker's words, see "Mothers' Summer Club," Box 23, Folder Mothers' Summer Club, July 1954–September 1954, UCR, UATU. The Mothers' Club was made up of Home and School Association members who wished to continue their organizing during the summer months.

151. On fundraising, see Singerly-Douglass P.T.A., October 25, 1951, Box 30, Folder 83, WCR, UATU; "Thousands of Dollars Given by Hopkins Association to Aid School

Children," July 28, 1949, newsclipping, no publication given, Box 5, Folder 85, WCR, UATU; "Hawthorne Project," Box 23, Folder Hawthorne Home and School Association, July 28,1953–August 2, 1954, UCR, UATU; "Summary of the Activity of the Hawthorne Home and School Association, September 27, 1955–June 19, 1956," Box 23, Folder Hawthorne Home and School Association, September 26, 1952–July 22, 1953, UCR, UATU. On room mothers, see Hawthorne Project, Minutes of the Meeting of Room Mothers, March 10, 1953, and "Room Mothers," both in Box 23, Folder Hawthorne Home and School Association, September 26, 1952–July 22, 1953, UCR, UATU; Reynolds Home and School Association Mother's Club, flyer, 1961, Box 39, Folder 70-B, WCR, UATU.

152. "Hawthorne Project," Box 23, Folder Hawthorne Home and School Association, September 26, 1952–July 22, 1953, UCR, UATU.

153. "Safety Patrol Gets Raincoats," Box 23, Folder Meredith Home and School Association, UCR, UATU; U.N.A. Student Field Work Report, Process Record, "Meredith Home and School Association Project," October 20, 1953–November 11, 1953, Box 23, Folder Meredith Home and School Association, UCR, UATU.

154. "December Meeting, Hawthorne Home and School Association," Box 22, Folder Hawthorne Home and School Association, September 7, 1954–June 5, 5 (folder error), UCR, UATU; Kathryn Young to President of Douglass School Parent-Teachers Association (name unclear on copy), June 30, 1950, Box 47, Folder 166, WCR, UATU.

155. "Hawthorne Project," Box 23, Folder Hawthorne Home and School Association, July 28, 1953–August 2, 1954, UCR, UATU; "March Meeting, Hawthorne Home and School Association," March 23, 1955, flyer, Box 22, Folder Hawthorne Home and School Association, September 7, 1954–June 5, 5 (folder error), UCR, UATU.

156. "Hawthorne Project," Box 23, Folder Hawthorne Home and School Association, September 26, 1952–July 22, 1953, UCR, UATU.

157. "Hawthorne Project," Box 23, Folder Hawthorne Home and School Association, July 28, 1953–August 2, 1954, UCR, UATU.

158. For historical roots of African American women's efforts to protect themselves from sexual violence, see Edwards, *Gendered Strife and Confusion*, 199–200, 204–6, 210–13.

159. On the campaign to integrate Girard College, see Franklin, *Education of Black Philadelphia*, 203; Countryman, *Up South*, 168–74.

160. "Hawthorne Project," Box 23, Folder Hawthorne Home and School Association, September 26, 1952–July 22, 1953, UCR, UATU; "Summary of the Activity of the Hawthorne Home and School Association, September 27, 1955–June 19, 1956, Box 23, Folder Hawthorne Home and School Association, September 26, 1952–July 22, 1953, UCR, UATU.

Chapter Five

1. J.E.J. interview.
2. On African American hospitals, see Gamble, *Making a Place for Ourselves*.
3. This contradicts several accounts of public hospitals in other cities that portray

them as institutions that patients turned to only as a last resort; see Dowling, *City Hospitals*; Morton, *And Sin No More*, 106–21. The best examination of the role of public hospitals in the twentieth-century city is Opdycke, *No One Was Turned Away*.

4. City of Philadelphia, Department of Public Health, *Annual Report, 1954*; Philadelphia Department of Public Health, Community Health Services, *Philadelphia Annual Statistical Report 1960*; "TB Perils 100,000 in No. Philly," *Philadelphia Tribune*, April 4, 1959, 11; M. Leo Bohanon, "The Urban League of Philadelphia," 1962, Box 7, Folder Philadelphia, HWCR-648, UATU; "Selected Social and Economic Facts on the Non-White Population of Philadelphia" 1961, Box 18, Folder Philadelphia 1961, RNUL, part 2, series 2, LC. In the first third of the twentieth century, U.S. health researchers studied the relationship between social class and health. However, the onset of World War II and the Cold War curtailed their efforts to produce national or local health statistics tabulated according to social class, occupation, and neighborhood. See Kreiger and Foe, "Measuring Social Inequalities."

5. Today, although women have a longer life expectancy than men from their social group, they still report more ill health than men, use primary care and hospital services more often than men, and suffer more long-term disability; see Doyal, "Hazards of Hearth and Home," 143; "More Women Are Losing Insurance Than Men," *New York Times*, August 31, 2001, A13.

6. Levy and Shouse, "Concept of Alienation," 79; C.S. interview.

7. C.E. interview.

8. Gamble, "Under the Shadow of Tuskegee"; Roberts, *Killing the Black Body*, 90–91; Reagan, *When Abortion Was a Crime*, 207.

9. McBride, *Integrating the City of Medicine*, 169; Levy and Shouse, "Concept of Alienation," 56, 101–2; Gay phone interview; Mrs. H. J. Mills, Committee on Illegitimacy, "Report of Hospitals Dealing with Unmarried Mothers," April 12, 1943, Box 3, Folder 61 (Child Placing Division), HWCR3, UATU.

10. The term "hospital city" was coined by Philadelphia historian Guain McKee.

11. Opdycke, *No One Was Turned Away*, 97; Rosenberg, *The Care of Strangers*; Stevens, *In Sickness and in Wealth*, 105. Between 1931 and 1954, inpatient admissions to Philadelphia's hospitals increased over 50 percent. One out of every thirteen Philadelphians was hospitalized in 1931; by 1954, the ratio was one in eight. See Kling, Sander, and Sigmond, *Philadelphia General Hospital Survey*, 60–61.

12. Kling, Sander, and Sigmond, *Philadelphia General Hospital Survey*, 107.

13. Health and Welfare Council, "To Close or Rejuvenate?—The Dilemma of Public Hospitals Today," n.d., Box 4, Folder PGH Situation, HWCR-648, UATU; Stachniewicz and Axelrod, *Double Frill*, 12–13; Rosenberg, "From Almshouse to Hospital," 179; Stachniewicz interview; Philadelphia General Hospital, *Report of Activities 1941–1946*, ii.

14. Robinson and Silverman, *The Reorganization of Philadelphia General Hospital*.

15. "Ten-Year Report—PGH, 1952–1962," 4, Box A-5431, Folder 80.17y, PCA.

16. "Scholastically skilled" in R.M. phone interview, August 21, 2007; "good training" in Givens interview.

17. Testament to the loyalty and deep sense of community that the hospital engen-

dered, annual PGH staff reunions were still occurring in 2005, nearly 30 years after the hospital closed. The reunions attracted former executives, nurses, doctors, staff, and patients. See O'Donnell, *Provider of Last Resort*, 107. Negative press coverage includes "No Bed Available for TB Victim," *PEB*, January 15, 1952, 26; "Jurors Condemn PGH Crowding," *Philadelphia Inquirer*, December 31, 1953, 30; "Another Jury Finds Fault with PGH," *PEB*, September 4, 1953, 3. Discussions of "illegitimacy" include "False Claims of Illegitimacy Probed at PGH," *Philadelphia Inquirer*, August 8, 1958, 5; "Phony Illegitimacy," *PEB*, August 8, 1958, 8; "Mothers Fake Illegitimacy to Evade Baby Bills at PGH," *PEB*, October 14, 1958, 11; "Rotman Says PGH Is Cheated by Fake Unwed Mothers," *PEB*, August 7, 1958, 4; "Maternity Patients at PGH Accused of Fraud When Listing Marital Status," *Philadelphia Inquirer*, October 15, 1958, 26.

18. "Oral History Interview with Stephanie Stachniewicz," May 23, 1994, 15, PGH-OH, UATU.

19. On Hill-Burton, see Stevens, *In Sickness and in Wealth*, 216–19. On the funding of Philadelphia hospitals, see "Summary of Report of the Policy Committee on Medical Care for the Needy," 1957, Box 17, Folder 136, HWCR1, UATU. On changes to the state allocations in the late 1950s that enabled PGH to secure more funds, see "$3 Million Health Grant Okd for City," *PEB*, November 10, 1959, 1, 2; "PGH Will Get $7.8 Million in State Budget," *PEB*, March 1, 1959, 1, 9. On PGH's reputation, see Peter (no surname provided) to George R. Clark, letter, March 11, 1955, Box A-477, File Philadelphia General Hospital, PCA.

20. McBride, *Integrating the City of Medicine*, 150. PGH hired its first African American doctor in 1936.

21. Ibid., 149–51, 170–74; "Medic Lowers Bar Here Traditional in Operating Room Ban on Negroes," *Philadelphia Tribune*, August 20, 1936, 1; "Dr. F. D. Stubbs Is Given Post at Phila. General," *Philadelphia Tribune*, May 29, 1936, 1; "New York Opens All Its Hospitals to Race Nurses: Phila. Gen. Balks," *Philadelphia Tribune*, December 12, 1942, 2; "Speakers in 31 Churches Push Drive for Entrance to Phila. General School," *Philadelphia Tribune*, June 20, 1942, 3; "Philadelphia General Superintendent Explains Nursing Restrictions," *Philadelphia Tribune*, April 14, 1938, 1; "First Intern Is Assigned to Phila. General," *Philadelphia Tribune*, July 16, 1946, 1; Philadelphia Fellowship Commission, "Five Year Study of the Selection of Medical Students," 1957, Box 9, Folder 188, NAACPR, UATU. In the 1960s and 1970s, black congressman Robert N. C. Nix Sr. and black lawyer Sadie T. Mossell-Alexander, the chairperson of the city's Human Relations Commission, led an aggressive effort in conjunction with the Equal Employment Opportunity Commission to integrate the staff of Philadelphia hospitals; see McBride, *Integrating the City of Medicine*, 196–98. On racial integration in the nursing profession during and after World War II, see Hine, *Black Women in White*, 162–93.

22. On unionization in city jobs, see City of Philadelphia, *Annual Report of the Civil Service Commission and Personnel Department*, 1955. On contract negotiations, see City of Philadelphia, "On the Job: The Story of Philadelphia's Personnel Department," 1959, Box A-604, Folder 147.6, PCA; "Agreement between the City of Philadelphia and Phila-

delphia District Council No. 33," 1952, Box A-604, Folder 147.9, PCA; City of Phila-delphia, *Annual Report of the Personnel Department, 1953*; City of Philadelphia, *Annual Report of the Civil Service Commission and Personnel Department, 1956*. On voluntary hospitals, see Opdycke, *No One Was Turned Away*, 86; Stevens, *In Sickness and in Wealth*, 164–66; "Low Wages, Few Benefits Are Lot of Non-Professional Hospital Workers," *Philadelphia Tribune*, August 1, 1959, 1, 2.

23. Kling, Sander, and Sigmond, *Philadelphia General Hospital Survey*, vii, 90, table 40.

24. Ibid., 90, table 40.

25. McBride, *Integrating the City of Medicine*, 6–7; Stevens, *In Sickness and in Wealth*, 8; Rosenberg, *Care of Strangers*, 111–13; C.P. interview.

26. Opdycke, *No One Was Turned Away*, 91.

27. Kling, Sander, and Sigmond, *Philadelphia General Hospital Survey*, 111. The 72 percent statistic is based on calculations that did not include "special patients" such as city employees and inmates of municipal institutions; see Bureau of Municipal Research and Pennsylvania Economy League, *Philadelphia General Hospital Admission Policies and Procedures, Part I*, 1a.

28. Those who had been referred by voluntary hospitals were mainly whites; see Kling, Sander, and Sigmond, *Philadelphia General Hospital Survey*, 97, table 66. Although PGH's admissions procedure required patients to demonstrate an "inability to obtain health care elsewhere," this proviso referred to their financial circumstances (i.e., that they did not have the money to pay for health care elsewhere). PGH did not require patients to seek health care at another hospital and be denied care before receiving treatment. See Bureau of Municipal Research and Pennsylvania Economy League, *Philadelphia General Hospital Admissions Policies and Procedures, Part I*, 5.

29. Bureau of Municipal Research and Pennsylvania Economy League, *Philadelphia General Hospital Admissions Policies and Procedures: Part II*, 3a.

30. Gay interview; Kling, Sander, and Sigmond, *Philadelphia General Hospital Survey*, 90, table 40.

31. Kling, Sander, and Sigmond, *Philadelphia General Hospital Survey*, 64–65; Norman R. Ingraham, F. Lloyd Mussells, and Leonard J. Zimet, "Public Responsibility for Maternity Care in Philadelphia: Report of Study of Application of Recommendations of the Duane Report to the Publicly Financed Maternity Care Program, with Special Reference to the Maternity Service of the Northern Division of the Philadelphia General Hospital," n.d., circa 1957, Box A-5430, Folder 80.54a, PCA; Division of Statistics and Research, "Philadelphia Live Birth Report 1960, Individual Hospital Statistics," Box A-5429, Folder 80.3a, PCA. The rate of increase in births in the voluntary hospital sector did not keep pace with the public hospital.

32. Bureau of Municipal Research and Pennsylvania Economy League, *Philadelphia General Hospital Admissions Policies and Procedures: Part II*, 12a.

33. Herman, *Prenatal Care Attitudes and Practices*, 36.

34. Division of Statistics and Research, "Philadelphia Live Birth Report 1960"; Gay interview.

35. Gamble, *Making a Place for Ourselves*, xv.

36. Bureau of Municipal Research and Pennsylvania Economy League, *Philadelphia General Hospital Admissions Policies and Procedures: Part II*, 18a.

37. Gamble, *Making a Place for Ourselves*, 12–14.

38. Rudwick, "A Brief History of Mercy-Douglass Hospital," 61–63; McBride, *Integrating the City of Medicine*, 142–43, 190–91; "The City's Health Problems," *Philadelphia Tribune*, May 15, 1948, 4; "Oral History Interview with Octavia Dickens, M.D.," March 20 and 30, 1988, Black Women's Physicians Project, WMMCPR, MCPA; Rice and Jones, *Public Policy and the Black Hospital*, 63. The success of civil rights activists' efforts to integrate African American medical professionals into white hospitals contributed to the demise of many African American hospitals; see Gamble, *Making a Place for Ourselves*; McBride, *Integrating the City of Medicine*; Rice and Jones, *Public Policy and the Black Hospital*.

39. On discrimination prior to World War II, see Alexander and Simpson, "Negro Hospitalization"; McBride, *Integrating the City of Medicine*, 125–46; Brown, *Law Administration*; "Segregation at U of P Hospital Now Practiced," *Philadelphia Tribune*, December 8, 1932, 1; "Council Moves to Curb Hospital Jim-Crowism," *Philadelphia Tribune*, December 3, 1936, 3.

40. Brown, *Law Administration and Negro-White Relations*, 53; McBride, *Integrating the City of Medicine*, 148–49; Levy and Shouse, "Concept of Alienation," 56, 103.

41. Stevens, *In Sickness and in Wealth*, 217–19, 254. Civil rights activists challenged the way that Hill-Burton licenced discrimination. In 1964, the Supreme Court forced the Department of Health, Education, and Welfare to require that discrimination could not be practiced in any part of an institution receiving Hill-Burton funds. See Rice and Jones, *Public Policy and the Black Hospital*, 94; Gamble, *Making a Place for Ourselves*, 81, 90–96; Dowling, *City Hospitals*, 160.

42. McBride, *Integrating the City of Medicine*, 169.

43. "Oral History Interview with Stephanie Stachniewicz," 98–99.

44. Pascal F. Lucchesi, "Tribute to Blockley," *Philadelphia Medicine* (July 10, 1954), series 3, Box 5, Folder 1, RAATS, CSHN. See also R.M. phone interview, August 21, 2007.

45. Stephanie Stachniewicz quoted in "Oral History Interview with Nathaniel Stewart," December 14, 1993, 39, PGH-OH, UATU.

46. M.B.M. interview.

47. Committee on Municipal Hospital Services, *Report of the Mayor's Committee*, 103. Patients were interviewed in the following clinics: medicine, pediatrics, physical medicine and rehabilitation, surgery, gynecology, dental, eye, prenatal, and dermatology.

48. Committee on Municipal Hospital Services, *Report of the Mayor's Committee*, 103.

49. Opdycke, *No One Was Turned Away*, 108–9. In Philadelphia, see, for example, Levy and Shouse, "Concept of Alienation," 102.

50. Quoted in Levy and Shouse, "Concept of Alienation," 56.

51. Ibid.; Stevens, *In Sickness and in Wealth*, 112, 253–54; Opdycke, *No One Was Turned Away*, 108–9.

52. Kling, Sander, and Sigmond, *Philadelphia General Hospital Survey*, iv; Zimet, *The Role of the Philadelphia General Hospital*; "200 Live at PGH: No Other Place to Go," *PEB*, June 27, 1954, 17.

53. City of Philadelphia, Department of Public Health, *Philadelphia Health Bulletin* (June 1949); Bureau of Municipal Research and Pennsylvania Economy League, *Philadelphia General Hospital Admissions Policies and Procedures, Part I*, 4–5; Bureau of Municipal Research and Pennsylvania Economy League, *Philadelphia General Hospital Admissions Policies and Procedures, Part III*, 6–7.

54. Gay interview; Stachniewicz interview. On similar practices in New York City, see Opdycke, *No One Was Turned Away*, 64.

55. R.M. phone interview, August 21, 2007.

56. Quoted in Levy and Shouse, "Concept of Alienation," 101.

57. Isador Kranzel to A. C. LaBoccetta, May 26, 1960, memorandum, Box A-224, Folder ADM-Depts-Public Health-Philadelphia General Hospital, PCA.

58. Bureau of Municipal Research and Pennsylvania Economy League, *Philadelphia General Hospital Admissions: Part I*, 4–5; Bureau of Municipal Research and Pennsylvania Economy League, *Philadelphia General Hospital Admissions: Part III*, 1–7, 10–11. PGH calculated poverty on a slightly more generous scale than the Department of Public Assistance: PGH's "subsistence budgets" were 10 percent higher than those calculated by the welfare department. For the few crackdowns on delinquent accounts, see *Annual Report Philadelphia General Hospital, 1950*; "Phila. General Starts Suits to Collect 6,000 Unpaid Bills," *PEB*, August 1, 1950, 10; "City Brings 235 Suits to Collect Hospital Bills," *PEB*, November 27, 1951, 3; "City Moves to Collect $10,000 in Hospital Bills," *PEB*, June 1, 1951, 52. For public discussions of delinquent accounts, see "Only 2% Paid in Full at PGH," *PEB*, November 13, 1953, 52; "Hemphill Says PGH Patients Owe $17 Million," *Philadelphia Inquirer*, December 18, 1963, 17; "City May Drop Old PGH Bills," *PEB*, December 4, 1962, 30.

59. Quoted in Levy and Shouse, "Concept of Alienation," 56. See also Levy and Shouse, "Concept of Alienation," 101–2; Gay phone interview; Mrs. H. J. Mills, Committee on Illegitimacy, "Report of Hospitals Dealing with Unmarried Mothers," April 12, 1943, Box 3, Folder 61 (Child Placing Division), HWCR3, UATU. See also Health and Welfare Council, Committee on Illegitimacy, Minutes, January 6, 1943, Box 2, Folder 55, HWCR3, UATU; Health and Welfare Council, Committee on Unmarried Parents, "Service of Maternity Care Agencies," January 15, 1953, Box 14, Folder 116, HWCR1, UATU; Lear phone interview.

60. Gay interview; Stachniewicz interview; "The Unwed Mother," *PEB*, August 18, 1957, section 2, pp. 1, 2.

61. "Only 6 Per Cent at PGH Pay Own Money," *PEB*, December 18, 1958, 2.

62. Kling, Sander, and Sigmond, *Philadelphia General Hospital Survey*, 94; Bureau of Municipal Research and Pennsylvania Economy League, *Philadelphia General Hospital Admissions: Part II*, 12a.

63. Kling, Sander, and Sigmond, *Philadelphia General Hospital Survey*, 90, table 40.

64. "Oral History Interview with Nathaniel C. Stewart," 39; "Oral History Interview

with Walter J. Lear," 22, December 22, 1993, PGH-OH, UATU. Between 1940 and 1960, the white population of West Philadelphia decreased by one-third, a loss of 106,400 persons; see Schein et al., *Demographic and Health Resources*, 10.

65. Committee on Municipal Hospital Services, *Report of the Mayor's Committee*, 104. See also Givens interview; Gay interview; Stachniewicz interview.

66. "Poor Like PGH Service Despite Dingy Facilities," *Philadelphia Inquirer*, April 26, 1970, 26.

67. Whittier Center, "Study of Health of Negro Babies Born in 1922 in Wards 24, 30, 36, and 47 of Philadelphia, Pa.," 25, Pamphlet 360–11, PC, UATU; Division of Statistics and Research, "Philadelphia Live Birth Report 1960"; Lawrence D. Longo and Christina M. Thomsen, "Prenatal Care and Its Evolution in America," in Sophie Colleau, compiler and editor, "Childbirth: The Beginning of Motherhood," 1982, Proceedings of the Second Motherhood Symposium, Women's Studies Research Center, University of Wisconsin-Madison.

68. City of Philadelphia, Department of Public Health, Community Health Services, "Live Births: Philadelphia and Selected Hospitals, 1964," 1965, Box A-5429, Folder 80.3a, PCA.

69. Perhaps reflecting PGH's tendency to serve extremely impoverished white patients, the few white women who delivered children at PGH had the lowest rates of prenatal care: 82 percent had not received adequate prenatal care.

70. On the limitations of prenatal care, see Strong, *Expecting Trouble*; Tew, *Safer Childbirth?*, 86–141.

71. On prematurity, see Community Health Services, "Live Births: Philadelphia and Selected Hospitals, 1964." Prematurity was usually defined as a condition in which a baby either had a birth weight of under 5 pounds 8 ounces or was born prior to thirty-seven weeks of gestation. Some definitions of prematurity did not take the gestational age of the infant into account and only judged according to weight. See Division of Statistics and Research, "Philadelphia Live Birth Report, 1960." In 1961 and 1962, infant mortality rates were 23 per 1,000 for whites and 40 per 1,000 for African Americans; see Urban League of Philadelphia, "Prenatal Care for Low-Income Women in the City of Philadelphia: Report on a Citizen's Survey of Six Prenatal Care Clinics," 1954, 1–2, Box 1, Folder 34, ULPR2, UATU.

72. Community Health Services, "Live Births: Philadelphia and Selected Hospitals, 1964."

73. Urban League of Philadelphia, "Prenatal Care for Low-Income Women"; "Community Group Opens New 'Expectant Mothers' Clinic," *North Philadelphia Neighborhood Newspaper*, n.d., newsclipping, Box 1, Folder 14, ULPR1, UATU; Urban League of Philadelphia Press Release, "A Community Helps Itself," n.d., Box 4, Folder 74, ULPR1, UATU; "North Phila. Area Clinic Set Up to Combat Infant Deaths," *PEB*, March 11, 1958, 30.

74. "Public Health Clinics Turn Away Mothers," *Philadelphia Tribune*, November 8, 1952, 9, 14; Urban League of Philadelphia, "Prenatal Care for Low-Income Women"; Herman, *Prenatal Care Attitudes and Practices*, 33–36.

75. Urban League of Philadelphia, "Prenatal Care for Low-Income Women," 3–4.

76. Ibid., 4; Herman, *Prenatal Care Attitudes and Practices*, 31–35; Berg, "Study of a Group of Unwed Mothers," 67.

77. Herman, *Prenatal Care Attitudes and Practices*, 27, 33–35; Berg, "Study of a Group of Unwed Mothers," 67, 77–78.

78. Herman, *Prenatal Care Attitudes and Practices*, 35.

79. Ibid., 10–11; Berg, "Study of a Group of Unwed Mothers," 67. Similarly, see Bernstein and Sauber, *Deterrents to Early Prenatal Care*, 95, 108.

80. Herman, *Prenatal Care Attitudes and Practices*, 10; Berg, "Study of a Group of Unwed Mothers," 68.

81. Quoted in Frankel, *Childbirth in the Ghetto*, 66, 67, 97; R.M. phone interview, August 21, 2007.

82. Frankel, *Childbirth in the Ghetto*, 67, 95; Stachniewicz interview; Gay interview; R.M. phone interview, August 21, 2007. In 1960, PGH stopped sending interns with the police because it took too long for the police to pick up the interns on the way to women's houses; see Board of Trustees, Philadelphia General Hospital, Minutes, January 27, 1960, Box A-224, File ADM-Depts-Public Health-Philadelphia General Hospital, PCA.

83. On the responsiveness of public hospitals, see Opdycke, *No One Was Turned Away*.

84. Kling, Sander, and Sigmond, *Philadelphia General Hospital Survey*, 95–96.

85. "Oral History Interview with Catherine Simon," June 1, 1994, 1, PGH-OH, UATU. On public health clinics, see City of Philadelphia, Mayors Committee on Medical Care for the Needy, "Program, Part VI: Immediate Program for Health Centers," 1956, Box A-501, File Administration—Committees—Policy Committee on Medical Care for the Needy, PCA.

86. "Ten Year Report—PGH, 1952–1962," quotation on 3, Box A-5431, Folder 80.17y, PCA; Philadelphia General Hospital, "Annual Report," 1954, typescript, Box A-477, File Philadelphia General Hospital, PCA; City of Philadelphia, Department of Public Health, Office of Health Education, *Public Health Views* 4:1 (1956), 13–16.

87. Kling, Sander, and Sigmond, *Philadelphia General Hospital Survey*, 65.

88. City of Philadelphia, Department of Public Health, Division of Health Protection, Maternal and Child Health Services, *Annual Report, 1960*.

89. Ingraham, "Public Responsibility for Maternity Care," 4–7.

90. On the problems with the Northern Division, see Philadelphia Department of Public Health, Division of Health Protection, Maternal and Child Health Section, *Annual Report, 1960*; "Philadelphia General Hospital, Northern Division, Staff Evaluation of Duane Report," 1957, Box 4, Folder Department of Public Health PGH, HWCR-648, UATU.

91. R.M. phone interview, August 21, 2007; "Ten Year Report—PGH, 1952–1962," Box A-5431, Folder 80.17y, PCA.

92. City of Philadelphia, Department of Public Health, *Annual Report, 1959*, 49; Philadelphia General Hospital, *Annual Report, Board of Trustees, 1960*. On the treatment of prematurity nationally, see Silverman, *Retrolental Fibroplasia*, 71–72; Silverman, *Dunham's Premature Infants*, 443–48.

93. "City Battles to Save the Lives of Premature Babies," *PEB*, December 9, 1956, section 2, pp. 1, 2; City of Philadelphia, Department of Public Health, *Public Health Views* 4:4 (1956); "Ten Year Report—PGH, 1952–1962," Box A-5431, Folder 80.17y, PCA.

94. Philadelphia General Hospital, "Annual Report," 1954, typescript, Box A-477, File Philadelphia General Hospital, PCA; City of Philadelphia, Department of Public Health, Office of Health Education, *Public Health Views* 4:1 (1956); "Ten Year Report—PGH, 1952–1962"; Board of Trustees, Philadelphia General Hospital, Minutes, May 25, 1960, Box A-2221, Folder Administration—Boards—Philadelphia General Hospital, PCA.

95. "Hospitals Are Relaxing Criteria for Abortions," *PEB*, December 15, 1969, 1, 25. On illegal abortions treated at Cook County Hospital in Chicago, see Reagan, *When Abortion Was a Crime*, 138, 209–11. On abortion, see also Ross, "African American Women and Abortion," 268; Davis, *Women, Race, and Class*, 204; Stachniewicz interview.

96. J.P. interview.

97. Attie and Goldwater, "Motherless"; Frankel, *Childbirth in the Ghetto*, 64. See also Reagan, *When Abortion Was a Crime*, 209; Ross, "African American Women and Abortion," 273.

98. Gorney, *Articles of Faith*, 25–26, quotation on 26.

99. R.M. phone interview, August 21, 2007.

100. Gay interview; Stachniewicz interview.

101. Gay interview; Stachniewicz interview; M.M. interview; "Oral History with Catherine Simon," 51–53; Linda Meyer and Nan Carroll, "PGH and the Rape Victim," 1976, and Kathleen M. Flanagan, "Testimony before City Council," 1976, both in Box 5, Folder PGH: ER Procedures, 1973–1974, WOARR, UATU. The large numbers of rape cases and need for sensitive and comprehensive treatment motivated grassroots activists to locate Philadelphia's first rape-crisis center at PGH.

102. "No Check on City Hospital Patients," *PEB*, April 22, 1932, 3; "Hospital Non-Resident Patients Declared Few," *PEB*, December 7, 1932, 3; Brosco, "Sin or Folly," 88–89.

103. The study that made the news found that 72 percent of obstetrics patients had received free care. Yet a more comprehensive study of 1,000 PGH admissions found that the percentage of cases receiving free care in the obstetrics ward (50 percent) was similar to that in all other wards (49 percent). See Bureau of Municipal Research and Pennsylvania Economy League, *Philadelphia General Hospital Admission Policies and Procedures: Part II*, vi.

104. "Mothers Fake Illegitimacy." See also "Maternity Patients at PGH Accused of Fraud."

105. "Mothers Fake Illegitimacy"; "False Claims of Illegitimacy Probed"; "Phony Illegitimacy"; "Rotman Says PGH is Cheated."

106. Quoted in "False Claims of Illegitimacy."

107. "PGH to Tighten Billing Practice at Start of Year," *Philadelphia Inquirer*, December 23, 1958, 21; "Phony Illegitimacy."

108. "PGH to Tighten Billing Practice at Start of Year."

109. In 1976, the *Bulletin* conducted a poll that found that the majority of residents in both the suburbs and the city opposed the plan to close PGH. Fifty-seven percent stated that they were opposed to the closing, 19 percent said they were indifferent, 16 percent supported it, and 8 percent had no opinion. In the city proper, even higher numbers supported the hospital, with 62 percent opposing the closing. The city closed the hospital in 1977. See "Closing PGH Opposed by Majority in Poll," *PEB*, April 22, 1976, 23.

Conclusion

1. Quoted in Levy and Shouse, "Concept of Alienation," 56.

2. Kornbluh, *The Battle for Welfare Rights*; Nadasen, *Welfare Warriors*.

3. Countryman, *Up South*, 276–81, Wiley quoted on 281; Kornbluh, *The Battle for Welfare Rights*, 122; Philadelphia Welfare Rights Organization, *Straight Talk* 1:13 (December 1967), 1; Kornbluh, "Black Buying Power," 205–6; Goldberg, "Class Action," 229.

4. Goldberg, "Class Action," Sanders quotation on 226. On women's educational organizing in other cities, see Theoharis, "They Told Us Our Kids Were Stupid"; Adina Back, "Exposing the 'Whole Segregation Myth': The Harlem Nine and New York City's School Desegregation Battles," in Theoharis and Woodard, *Freedom North*, 65–91; Jeanne Theoharis, "'I'd Rather Go to School in the South': How Boston's School Desegregation Complicates the Civil Rights Paradigm," in Theoharis and Woodard, *Freedom North*, 125–51.

5. Luttrell, *Women in the Community*, 90–99. The racially charged battles over the school location received a great deal of coverage in the Philadelphia press. See, for example, "Edison Biracial Protest Set to Disprove Rizzo," *PEB*, March 21, 1974, 13; "Edison High 'Alternative' Draws Flak from Parents," *PEB*, May 15, 1979, 1, 10. The new Edison was not constructed until 1988. For a discussion of a different 1970s parent-advocacy group run by a multiracial group of parents from a variety of class backgrounds, see Fernandez, "Parents' Influence on School Policy and Practice."

6. Housing Association of Delaware Valley, "Revision of Housing Authority's Admission Policies and Procedures," 1968, memorandum, Box 277, Folder 4793, HADVR1, UATU; Mark K. Joseph to CAC Chairmen and Housing Aids, DPA Housing Liaison Agents, Field-workers for Area-Wide Council, Governor's Branch Officers, Welfare Rights Organization Members, Other Persons Interested in Public Housing, May 22, 1968, Box 285, Folder 5005, HADVR1, UATU; Bauman, *Public Housing*, 204. On single mothers' collective efforts to gain admittance to public housing in Durham, N.C., see Greene, *Our Separate Ways*, 135.

7. Bryan, "Public Housing Modernization," 172, 178; "Biography: Rose Wylie," Box 30, Folder 6 National Tenants Organization, 1972, George Wiley Papers, WHS; Countryman, *Up South*, 279–80.

8. Countryman, *Up South*, 290–93, quotation on 293.

9. O'Donnell, *Provider of Last Resort*, 70, 77–78, 95; "Protest: Crowd Chants 'Recall,'" *PEB*, February 25, 1976, 1, 3. On working-class women's health care activism elsewhere, see Morgen, "It's the Whole Power of the City."

10. For outstanding analyses of the role of employment in the distribution of benefits, see Katz, *Price of Citizenship*; Kessler-Harris, *In Pursuit of Equity*. One of the best treatments of single mothers is Gordon, *Pitied but Not Entitled*. For an important account of unemployment insurance, see Abramovitz, *Regulating the Lives of Women*, 273–311.

11. Feldstein, *Motherhood in Black and White*.

12. Reichley, *Art of Government*, 78–80, quotation on 79. For an account of the role of racism in fostering Philadelphia whites' disaffection with the Democratic Party that does not explore gender and social welfare programs, see Wolfinger, *Philadelphia Divided*.

13. Levenstein, "From 'Innocent Children' to Unwanted Migrants and Unwed Moms"; Rainwater and Yancey, *The Moynihan Report and the Politics of Controversy*; Feldstein, *Motherhood in Black and White*, 142–52.

14. Nadasen, *Welfare Warriors*, 196.

15. For a useful account of tax revolts, see Self, *American Babylon*, 281–89, 317–26.

16. Mink, *Welfare's End*, 34–36, 74, 85.

17. Adams et al., *Philadelphia*, 17–18, 59, 109–10.

18. Mink, *Welfare's End*, 1–5.

Appendix

1. For a discussion of the challenges researching Jewish poverty in postwar Philadelphia, see Lisa Levenstein, "The Problem of Jewish Poverty," paper presented at the Feinstein Center for American Jewish History, 2000, in author's possession.

2. Author's e-mail correspondence with Jane Kronick, June 16, 2006.

3. Kronick, "Attitudes toward Dependency," 9–18.

4. The classic account of the culture of poverty is in Lewis, *The Children of Sanchez*.

5. On postwar social work debates, see Curran, "The Culture of Race, Class, and Poverty." On postwar social scientific scholarship on poverty more generally, see O'Connor, *Poverty Knowledge*, 99–123.

6. Kronick's second report to the Social Security Administration, "Family Life and Economic Dependency," was largely a theoretical piece deeply engaged with social scientific debates about nuclear families and interpersonal relationships. The most useful parts for my purposes were the case studies in the appendix, which focused on women's relationships with other people.

7. Kronick, Norton, and Sabesta, "The Legitimacy Status of Children"; Kronick, "Attitudes toward Dependency"; Kronick interview; Kronick, "A Woman's Choice."

8. Author's e-mail correspondence with Jane Kronick, May 25, 2000; On the Moynihan report, see Lee and Yancey, *The Moynihan Report and the Politics of Controversy*.

Bibliography

Primary Sources

Manuscript and Archival Collections

Center for African American History and Culture, Temple University, Philadelphia,
    Pennsylvania
    Philadelphia Tribune Newsclipping File
Center for the Study of the History of Nursing, Philadelphia
    Records of the Alumni Association Training School of the Philadelphia General
      Hospital
Family Service of Philadelphia
Manuscript Division, Library of Congress, Washington, D.C.
    Records of the National Urban League, 1900–1986
Medical College of Pennsylvania Hahnemann University Archives, Philadelphia
    Women in Medicine and the Medical College of Pennsylvania Records
National Archives and Records Administration, College Park, Maryland
    General Records of the Social Security Administration, 1935–86
    Records of the Public Housing Administration, 1933–76
Pedagogical Library, Philadelphia Board of Education
    School District of Philadelphia, Board of Public Education Annual Reports
Pennsylvania State Archives, Harrisburg
    Department of Public Welfare, Administrative Files, 1955–58
Philadelphia City Archives
    Clerk of Quarter Sessions
    Department of Personnel
    Department of Public Health
    Department of Public Welfare
    Housing Authority
    Municipal Court
    Office of the Mayor
    Police Department
Philadelphia Jewish Archives Center
    Jewish Family Service Records
Urban Archives, Temple University, Philadelphia
    Crime Commission of Philadelphia Records, 1951–74
    Fellowship Commission Records, 1941–94

Free Library Pamphlet Collection

Friends Neighborhood Guild Records, 1922–80

Germantown Settlement Records, 1908–10, 1928, 1947–91

Health and Welfare Council, Inc., Records, 1922–69

Health and Welfare Council, Inc., Records, 1926–55

Health and Welfare Council, Inc., Records, 1928–66

Health and Welfare Council, Inc., Records, Accession no. 648

Housing Association of the Delaware Valley Records, 1909–72

Housing Association of the Delaware Valley Records, 1909–75

Floyd L. Logan (Educational Equality League) Records, 1922–78

National Association for the Advancement of Colored People, Philadelphia Branch
Records, 1943–63

Negro Migrant Study Records, 1923–24

Philadelphia-Camden Social Service Exchange Records, 1911–70

Philadelphia Evening Bulletin Newsclipping Collection

Philadelphia General Hospital Oral History Interview Project

United Communities of Southeast Philadelphia Records, 1847–1978

Urban Archives Pamphlet Collection

Urban League of Philadelphia Records, 1935–63

Urban League of Philadelphia Records, 1960–67, Addition 1

West Philadelphia Schools Committee Records, 1961–70

Wharton Centre Records, 1913–68

Women Organized against Rape Records, 1973–95

YMCA of Philadelphia-Christian Street Records, 1943–64

YWCA of Germantown Records, 1785, 1869–1983

YWCA of Philadelphia—Kensington Branch Records, 1891–1981

YWCA of Philadelphia—Southwest Belmont Branch Records, 1920–77

Wisconsin Historical Society, Madison

George Wiley Papers

Government Publications

City of Philadelphia, Board of Public Education, Special Committee on Nondiscrimination.
*Report of the Special Committee on Nondiscrimination of the Philadelphia Board of Public
Education, Submitted to the Board of Public Education, July 23, 1964*. Philadelphia, 1964.

City of Philadelphia, Commission on Human Relations. *Philadelphia's Puerto Rican Population: A Descriptive Summary Including 1960 Census Data*. Philadelphia, 1964.

Commonwealth of Pennsylvania, Department of Labor and Industry. *Employment Trends
in Philadelphia*. Harrisburg, 1933.

Commonwealth of Pennsylvania, Department of Public Assistance. *Current Living Costs
as Related to Standards of Public Assistance in Pennsylvania*. Harrisburg, 1945.

———. *Origin and Development of Public Assistance in Pennsylvania*. Harrisburg, 1955.

———. *Origin and Development of Public Assistance in Pennsylvania*. Harrisburg, 1958.

———. *Pennsylvania Public Assistance Review: Third Quarter, 1943*. Harrisburg, 1943.

———. *Pennsylvania Public Assistance Review: Second Quarter, 1944*. Harrisburg, 1944.

———. *Pennsylvania Public Assistance Statistics, December—1939*. Harrisburg, 1939.

———. *Pennsylvania Public Assistance Statistics Summary: 1932–1940*. Harrisburg, 1940.

———. *Public Assistance Review: Annual Summary, December 1947*. Harrisburg, 1948.

———. *Public Assistance Review*. Harrisburg, 1953.

———. *Public Assistance Review*. Harrisburg, 1956.

———. *Statistical Report on the Medical Program of the Department of Public Assistance*. Harrisburg, 1941.

Commonwealth of Pennsylvania, Department of Public Welfare. *Public Assistance Allowances Compared With the Cost of Living at a Minimum Standard of Health and Decency*. Harrisburg, 1960.

———. *Public Assistance Review: Annual Summary, December 1958*. Harrisburg, 1959.

———. *Public Welfare Report: June 1, 1958–May 31, 1960*. Harrisburg, 1960.

———. *Report to the General Assembly of Pennsylvania of the Mothers' Assistance Fund, 1922*. Harrisburg, 1923.

Commonwealth of Pennsylvania, Department of Welfare. *Fifth Biennial Report of the Secretary of Welfare, 1929–1930*. Harrisburg, 1930.

———. *Report of the Mothers' Assistance Fund to the General Assembly of Pennsylvania*. Harrisburg, 1926.

———. *Report of the Mothers' Assistance Fund to the General Assembly of Pennsylvania 1928*. Harrisburg, 1928.

———. *Sixth Biennial Report of the Secretary of Welfare: June 1, 1930 to May 31, 1932*. Harrisburg, 1932.

Commonwealth of Pennsylvania, State and Local Welfare Commission. *A Brief History and Description of Public Welfare in Pennsylvania*. Harrisburg, 1961.

Federal Public Housing Authority, National Housing Agency. *The Livability Problems of 1,000 Families*. Washington, D.C., 1945.

Joint State Government Commission to the General Assembly of the Commonwealth of Pennsylvania. *Public Assistance in Pennsylvania: Organization, Administration and Policy Problems*. Harrisburg, 1951.

National Center for Education Statistics. *120 Years of American Education: A Statistical Portrait*. Thomas D. Snyder, ed. Washington, D.C.: National Center for Education Statistics, 1993.

Odell, William R. *Educational Survey Report for the Philadelphia Board of Public Education*. Philadelphia: Board of Public Education, 1965.

Philadelphia City Planning Commission. *Population of Metropolitan Area Counties: 1790–1960; Population of Philadelphia Sections and Wards, 1860–1960*. Philadelphia, 1963.

———. *Recent Historical Trends in Population, Housing, and Socio-Economic Characteristics of Philadelphia Planning Analysis: Sections and Subsections, 1930–1940–1950–1960*. Philadelphia, 1966.

Philadelphia County Board of Assistance. *A Report on Dependent Children Families Receiving Aid from the Department of Public Assistance, Philadelphia County Board, 1953*. Philadelphia, 1953.

Philadelphia Housing Authority. *20 Years of Service: The Story of Public Housing in Philadelphia, 1937–1957.* Philadelphia: Gelmans, 1957.

Philadelphia School District, Board of Public Education. *For Every Child: The Story of Integration in the Philadelphia Public Schools.* Philadelphia, 1960.

——. *Great Cities School Improvement Program: Progress Report, September 1960–June 1962.* Philadelphia, 1963.

U.S. Commission on Civil Rights. *Civil Rights, U.S.A.: Public Schools, Cities in the North and West, 1962.* New York: Greenwood Press, 1968.

U.S. Department of Commerce, Bureau of the Census. *Census of Population, 1960.* Vol. 1, *Characteristics of the Population*, pt. 40, *Pennsylvania.* Washington, D.C.: U.S. Government Printing Office, 1961.

——. *Fourteenth Census of the United States, Taken in the Year 1920.* Vol. 4, *Population, 1920: Occupations.* Washington, D.C.: U.S. Government Printing Office, 1923.

——. *Sixteenth Census of the United States, 1940. Population.* Vol. 3, *The Labor Force.* Washington, D.C.: U.S. Government Printing Office, 1943.

——. *U.S. Censuses of Population and Housing: 1960. Final Report PHC (1)-116. Census Tracts. Philadelphia, Pa.–N.J. Standard Metropolitan Statistical Area.* Washington, D.C.: U.S. Government Printing Office, 1961–62.

Zimet, Leonard J. *The Role of the Philadelphia General Hospital within the Pattern of Providing Services to the Medically Needy.* Philadelphia: Department of Public Health, 1955.

Annual Reports

City of Philadelphia
    Bureau of the Police
    Civil Service Commission and Personnel Department
    Department of Public Health
    Department of Public Health, Division of Health Protection, Maternal and Child
        Health Services
    Office of the Mayor
Family Society of Philadelphia
Pennsylvania Department of Public Welfare, Philadelphia County Board of Assistance,
    Office of Public Assistance
Philadelphia General Hospital
Philadelphia Housing Authority
Philadelphia Municipal Court
School District of Philadelphia, Board of Public Education

Newspapers

Philadelphia Afro-American
Philadelphia Evening Bulletin
Philadelphia Inquirer
Philadelphia Tribune

Author's Interviews

Audiotapes in author's possession.

INTERVIEWS WITH NURSES, SOCIAL WORKERS, AND ACADEMICS

Gay, Gloria. Philadelphia, August 6, 1999.
Givens, Verdie. Philadelphia, June 22, 2000.
Kronick, Jane C. Haverford, Pennsylvania, December 27, 1999.
Stachniewicz, Stephanie. Philadelphia, June 20, 2000.
Van Dyke, Norma. Philadelphia, June 25, 1999.

PSEUDONYMOUS INTERVIEWS

A.B. Philadelphia, June 22, 2000.
A.B.B. Philadelphia, July 8, 1999.
A.P. Philadelphia, June 19, 2000.
B.M. Philadelphia, July 9, 1999.
B.N. Philadelphia, July 9, 1999.
C.B. Philadelphia, July 21, 1999.
C.D. Philadelphia, August 11, 1999.
C.E. Philadelphia, July 6, 1999; July 7, 1999.
C.F. Philadelphia, July 15, 1999.
C.P. Philadelphia, June 14, 2000.
C.S. Philadelphia, August 24, 1999.
E.B. Philadelphia, August 22, 1999.
E.C. Philadelphia, August 22, 1999.
E.H. Philadelphia, August 9, 1999.
E.K. Philadelphia, July 13, 1999.
E.O.K. Philadelphia, June 14, 2000.
E.R.W. Philadelphia, August 20, 1999.
E.S. Philadelphia, June 19, 2000.
F.R. Philadelphia, August 11, 1999.
F.S. Philadelphia, August 13, 1999.
G.J. Philadelphia, July 9, 1999.
G.P. Philadelphia, June 19, 2000.
H.C. Philadelphia, July 22, 1999.
H.M. Philadelphia, August 11, 1999.
I.G. Philadelphia, August 20, 1999.
J.E.J. Philadelphia, July 6, 1999.
J.P. Philadelphia, July 13, 1999.
L.L. Philadelphia, August 10, 1999.
L.M. Philadelphia, August 13, 1999.
L.W. Philadelphia, June 22, 2000.
M.A.G. Philadelphia, July 14, 1999.

M.A.M. Philadelphia, August 12, 1999.
M.B.M. Philadelphia, June 27, 2000.
M.C. Philadelphia, July 15, 1999.
M.F. Philadelphia, June 19, 2000.
M.G. Philadelphia, July 1, 1999.
M.J. Philadelphia, August 17, 1999.
M.M. Philadelphia, August 10, 1999.
S.M. Philadelphia, July 14, 1999.
V.B. Philadelphia, June 19, 2000.
V.F. Philadelphia, August 9, 1999.
W.J.P. Philadelphia, July 20, 1999.

PHONE INTERVIEWS

Dees, Gerald. January 22, 2001.
Gay, Gloria. November 21, 2000.
Lear, Walter J. November 8, 2000.
R.M. August 21, 2007.
R.M. August 28, 2007.

Oral History Interview Collections

PHILADELPHIA GENERAL HOSPITAL ORAL HISTORY INTERVIEW PROJECT
Transcripts in Urban Archives, Temple University, Philadelphia, Pennsylvania

Lear, Walter J. Philadelphia, December 22, 1993.
Simon, Catherine. Philadelphia, June 1, 1994.
Stachniewicz, Stephanie. Philadelphia, May 23, 1994.
Stewart, Nathaniel. Philadelphia, December 14, 1993.
Troncelliti, Manrico. Philadelphia, February 7, 1994.
Weintraub, Tina. Philadelphia, June 4, 1994.

BLACK WOMEN'S PHYSICIANS PROJECT
Transcript in Women in Medicine and the Medical College of Pennsylvania Records,
  Medical College of Pennsylvania Hahnemann University Archives, Philadelphia,
  Pennsylvania

Dickens, Octavia, M.D. Philadelphia, March 20 and 30, 1988.

Books, Articles, Manuals, Reports, and Theses

Alexander, Virginia, and George E. Simpson. "Negro Hospitalization." *Opportunity* 15:8
  (1937): 231–32.
Allis, Octavia, Paul Becker, William Henderson, and Ruth Meyers. "Wants of AFDC
  Mothers." Master of Social Service thesis, Bryn Mawr College, 1968.

American Friends Service Committee. *Family Planning Services for Medically Indigent Families in Philadelphia*. Philadelphia, 1970.

Auletta, Ken. *The Underclass*. New York: Vintage, 1982.

Ballama, Mariam H., Stefania Chmielewski, Marjorie T. McGrane, Frances R. Rogg, and Paula Sklarz. "Use of Resources by Recipients of Aid to Families with Dependent Children in Meeting Family Needs." Master of Social Service thesis, Bryn Mawr College, 1964.

Bauer, Catherine. "The Dreary Deadlock of Public Housing." *Architectural Forum* 106:5 (1957): 140–42; 219, 221.

Berg, Renee M. "A Study of a Group of Unwed Mothers Receiving Aid to Dependent Children." Ph.D. diss., University of Pennsylvania, 1962.

———. "Utilizing the Strengths of Unwed Mothers in the AFDC Program." *Child Welfare* 43 (1964): 333–39.

Berman, Lynne M., and Diana C. Carson. "A Study of Religion in the Lives of AFDC Recipients." Master of Social Service thesis, Bryn Mawr College, 1965.

Bernstein, Blanche, and Mignon Sauber. *Deterrents to Early Prenatal Care and Social Services among Women Pregnant Out-of-Wedlock*. Albany: New York State Department of Social Welfare, 1960.

Blumberg, Leonard. *Migration As a Program Area for Urban Social Work: A Pilot Study of Recent Negro Migrants into Philadelphia*. Philadelphia: Urban League of Philadelphia, 1958.

Braun, Peter J. "The Development of Public Assistance in Pennsylvania." Master of Governmental Administration thesis, University of Pennsylvania, 1963.

Brown, G. Gordon. *Law Administration and Negro-White Relations in Philadelphia*. Philadelphia: Bureau of Municipal Research of Philadelphia, 1947.

Bureau of Municipal Research and Pennsylvania Economy League. *The Magistrates' Courts of Philadelphia*. Rev. ed. Philadelphia, 1958.

———. *Philadelphia General Hospital Admissions Policies and Procedures: Part I*. Philadelphia, 1958.

———. *Philadelphia General Hospital Admissions Policies and Procedures: Part II, Social and Economic Data Relating to Sample of Inpatient Groups*. Philadelphia, 1958.

———. *Philadelphia General Hospital Admissions Policies: Part III, Rating and Collection Process*. Philadelphia, 1958.

———. *Special Assimilation Problems of Underprivileged In-migrants to Philadelphia*. Philadelphia, 1962.

Burt, Samuel. "Centralization and Decentralization of Function and Staff in Twelve Local Public Assistance Organizations." Master of Government Administration thesis, University of Pennsylvania, 1943.

Coleman, James S. *Equality of Educational Opportunity*. Washington, D.C.: U.S. Department of Health, Education, and Welfare, Office of Education, 1966.

Committee on Municipal Hospital Services. *Report of the Mayor's Committee*. Philadelphia, 1970.

Committee on the Philadelphia Relief Study. *The Philadelphia Relief Study: A Study of the Family Relief Needs and Resources of Philadelphia*. Philadelphia, 1926.

Committee on Public Housing Policy. "Basic Policies for Public Housing for Low Income Families in Philadelphia." Philadelphia: Philadelphia Housing Association, 1957.

Conant, James B. *Slums and Suburbs: A Commentary on Schools in Metropolitan Areas*. New York: McGraw-Hill, 1961.

Emerson, Haven. *Philadelphia Hospital and Health Survey, 1929*. Philadelphia: Philadelphia Hospital and Health Survey, 1930.

Ervin, Spencer. *The Magistrates' Courts of Philadelphia*. Philadelphia: Thomas Skelton Harrison Foundation, 1931.

Fish, Rose, and Evelyn Welburn. "A Study of the Characteristics of Neighborhood, Housing, and Mobility of Families Receiving Aid to Dependent Children in Philadelphia and Their Relationship to Illegitimacy." Master of Social Service thesis, Bryn Mawr College, 1961.

Ford, Bacon, and Davis. *Survey of Hospitals in Metropolitan Philadelphia*. New York: Ford, Bacon and Davis, 1946.

Frankel, Barbara. *Childbirth in the Ghetto: Folk Beliefs of Negro Women in a North Philadelphia Hospital Ward*. San Francisco: R&E Research Associates, 1977.

Gilkyson, Claude. "Life Insurance Regulations Relating to Public Assistance Recipients with Special Reference to the Commonwealth of Pennsylvania." Master of Governmental Administration thesis, Wharton School of Finance and Commerce, University of Pennsylvania, 1949.

Greater Philadelphia Movement. *A Citizens Study of Public Education in Philadelphia: Part A, 1962*. Philadelphia: Greater Philadelphia Movement, 1962.

———. *A Citizens Study of Public Education in Philadelphia: Part B, 1962*. Philadelphia: Greater Philadelphia Movement, 1962.

Hall, Elizabeth Louise. *Mothers' Assistance in Philadelphia, Actual and Potential Costs: A Study of 1010 Families*. Hanover, N.H.: Sociological Press, 1933.

Hallman, Howard W. *Relocation in Philadelphia*. Philadelphia: Philadelphia Housing Association, 1958.

Health and Welfare Council, Inc., Philadelphia District. *Use of Community Facilities in Developments of the Philadelphia Housing Authority*. Philadelphia, 1955.

Health and Welfare Council, Inc., Research Department. *Resources, Programs and Projects for Training and Employment of Youth in Philadelphia*. Philadelphia, 1962.

Herman, Mary. *Prenatal Care Attitudes and Practices: A Study of Women Living in West Philadelphia*. Philadelphia: Health and Welfare Council, 1962.

Horne, S. Hamill. "A Study of the Differences among Persons Seeking Economic Aid at a Family Service Agency." Master of Social Services thesis, Bryn Mawr College, 1959.

Hunter, Joel. *Juvenile Division of the Municipal Court of Philadelphia*. Philadelphia: Thomas Skelton Harrison Foundation, 1931.

Hussey, Miriam. *Personnel Policies during a Period of Shortage of Young Women Workers in*

Philadelphia. Philadelphia: Industrial Relations Unit, Wharton School of Finance and Commerce, University of Pennsylvania, 1958.

Johnson, Fred R. *Domestic Relations Division of the Municipal Court of Philadelphia*. Philadelphia: Thomas Skelton Harrison Foundation, 1931.

Keast, W. R. Morton. *The Juvenile and Domestic Relations Branches of the Municipal Court*. Philadelphia, 1941.

Kling, Vincent C., Hans K. Sander, and Robert M. Sigmond. *Philadelphia General Hospital Survey*. Philadelphia: Vincent G. Kling, Architect, AIA: 1956.

Kronick, Jane C. "Attitudes toward Dependency: A Study of 119 ADC Mothers." Graduate Department of Social Work and Social Research, Bryn Mawr College, 1962.

———. "Family Life and Economic Dependency: A Report to the Welfare Administration." Graduate Department of Social Work and Social Research, Bryn Mawr College, 1965.

———. "A Woman's Choice: A New Interpretation of Illegitimacy among the Poor." Unpublished manuscript in author's possession, n.d.

Kronick, Jane C., Dolores G. Norton, and Elizabeth V. Sabesta. "The Legitimacy Status of Children Receiving AFDC." *Child Welfare* 42 (1963): 339–44.

Lavell, Martha. *Philadelphia's Non-White Population—1960: Report No. 2, Housing Data*. Philadelphia: Commission on Human Relations, 1962.

Levy, Gail, and Judith Shouse. "A Concept of Alienation: A New Approach to Understanding the AFDC Recipient." Master of Social Service thesis, Bryn Mawr College, 1965.

Lewis, Harold, and Mildred Guinessy. *Helping the Poor Housekeeping Family in Public Housing*. Philadelphia: Friends Neighborhod Guild, 1963.

Lewis, Oscar. *The Children of Sanchez: The Autobiography of a Mexican Family*. New York: Random House, 1961.

Lundberg, Emma O. *Unmarried Mothers in the Municipal Court of Philadelphia*. Philadelphia: Thomas Skelton Harrison Foundation, 1931.

Luttrell, Wendy. *Women in the Community: A Curriculum Manual for Students and Teachers*. Philadelphia: Lutheran Settlement House Women's Program, 1983.

Mays, Benjamin Elijah, and Joseph William Nicholson. *The Negro's Church*. New York: Institute of Social and Religious Research, 1969.

McMurray, Georgia Louisa. "Employment Experiences and Attitudes toward Work among Fifty Negro Mothers Receiving Aid to Dependent Children." Master of Social Service thesis, Bryn Mawr College, 1962.

Montgomery, Dorothy S. *Relocation and Its Impact on Families*. Philadelphia: Philadelphia Housing Association, 1960.

Mossell, Sadie T. "The Standard of Living among One Hundred Negro Migrant Families in Philadelphia." Ph.D. diss., University of Pennsylvania, 1921.

Myrdal, Gunnar. *The Challenge to Affluence*. New York: Pantheon, 1963.

National Council of the Churches of Christ in the U.S.A., Bureau of Research and Survey. *Churches and Church Membership in the United States: An Enumeration and*

Analysis by Counties, States, and Regions. Series C, no. 8. New York: National Council of Churches, 1957.

Norton, Dolores Griffin, and Elizabeth Ann Vernon. "A Study of a Random Sample of Mothers of Legitimate and Illegitimate Children Receiving Aid to Dependent Children from the Philadelphia County Board of Assistance." Master of Social Service thesis, Bryn Mawr College, 1960.

O'Reilly, Charles T., and Margaret Pembroke. *Chicago's ADC Families*. Chicago: Loyola University School of Social Work, 1960.

Palmer, Gladys L. *Philadelphia Workers in a Changing Economy*. Philadelphia: University of Pennsylvania Press, 1956.

Paschkis, Margaret Melanie. "Parent Education in Philadelphia." Master's of Arts thesis, Bryn Mawr College, 1940.

Paul, Ruth Francis. "Negro Women in Industry: A Study of the Negro Industrial Woman in the Clothing, Cigar and Laundry Industries of Philadelphia." Master's thesis, Temple University Teachers College, 1940.

Pennsylvania Economy League, State Division. *Improving the State Public Assistance Program*. Harrisburg, 1952.

Ritti, Richard. *The "Welfare Explosion": Management Practice or Management Policy?* University Park: Pennsylvania State University, 1973.

Rothman, Edwin, Edgar Rosenthal, Emma L. Bowman, and Leigh B. Hebb. *Philadelphia Government: 1956*. Philadelphia: Bureau of Municipal Research and Pennsylvania Economy League, Eastern Division, 1956.

Rothman, Edwin, Marjorie L. Jacob, and Phillip L. Deaton. *Philadelphia Government*. 6th ed. Philadelphia: Pennsylvania Economy League, Eastern Division, and Bureau of Municipal Research, 1963.

Rudwick, Elliot M. "A Brief History of Mercy-Douglass Hospital in Philadelphia." *Journal of Negro Education* 20:1 (1951): 50–66.

Saunders, Harry B. *School Facilities Survey*. Philadelphia, 1965.

Savitz, Leonard D. *Factors Influencing Crime Rates of Negroes*. Philadelphia: Commission on Human Relations, 1962.

Shenton, Clarence B. *History and Functions of the Municipal Court of Philadelphia*. Philadelphia: Thomas Skelton Harrison Foundation, 1930.

Vice Commission of Philadelphia. *A Report on Existing Conditions with Recommendations to the Honorable Rudolph Bankenburg, Mayor of Philadelphia*. Philadelphia, 1913.

Wallace, Anthony F. C. *Housing and Social Structure: A Preliminary Survey, with Particular Reference to Multi-Story, Low-Rent Public Housing Projects*. Philadelphia: Philadelphia Housing Authority, 1956.

Westerfield, Anne R. "Reasons for Discharge of Illegitimate Children to Their Own Mothers from a Children's Agency." Master of Social Service thesis, Bryn Mawr College, 1955.

Wolfgang, Marvin E. "Criminal Homicide with Special Reference to Philadelphia, 1948–1952." Ph.D. diss., University of Pennsylvania, 1955.

Worthington, George J., and Ruth Topping. *Specialized Courts Dealing with Sex Delinquency: A Study of Procedure in Chicago, Boston, Philadelphia, and New York*. New York: Bureau of Social Hygiene, 1925.

Secondary Sources

Abrahams, Roger D. *Deep Down in the Jungle . . . : Negro Narrative Folklore from the Streets of Philadelphia*. Hatbom, Penn.: Folklore Associates, 1964. Rev. ed. Chicago: Aldine Publishing Company, 1970.

Abramovitz, Mimi. *Regulating the Lives of Women: Social Welfare Policy from Colonial Times to the Present*. Boston: South End Press, 1988.

Abrams, Charles. *Home Ownership for the Poor: A Program for Philadelphia*. New York: Praeger, 1970.

Adams, Carolyn, David Bartelt, David Elesh, Ira Goldstein, Nancy Kleniewski, and William Yancey. *Philadelphia: Neighborhoods, Division, and Conflict in a Postindustrial City*. Philadelphia: Temple University Press, 1991.

Anderson, Elijah. *Code of the Street: Decency, Violence, and the Moral Life of the Inner City*. New York: W. W. Norton, 1999.

——. *Streetwise: Race, Class, and Change in an Urban Community*. Chicago: University of Chicago Press, 1990.

Anderson, James D. *The Education of Blacks in the South, 1860–1935*. Chapel Hill: University of North Carolina Press, 1988.

Angus, David L., and Jeffrey E. Mirel. *The Failed Promise of the American High School: 1890–1995*. New York: Teachers College Press, 1999.

Armitage, Susan H., ed. *Women's Oral History: The Frontiers Reader*. Lincoln: University of Nebraska Press, 2002.

Attie, Barbara, and Janet Goldwater. "Motherless: A Legacy of Loss from Illegal Abortions." New York: Filmakers Library, 1993. Videocassette.

Bane, Mary Jo. "Household Composition and Poverty." In *Fighting Poverty: What Works and What Doesn't*, edited by Sheldon H. Danziger and Daniel H. Weinberg, 209–301. Cambridge: Harvard University Press, 1986.

Barron, Dana. " 'Illegitimately Pregnant': Unmarried Mothers and Poverty in Philadelphia, 1920–1960." Ph.D. diss., University of Pennsylvania, 1995.

Bauman, John F. *Public Housing, Race, and Renewal: Urban Planning in Philadelphia, 1920–1974*. Philadelphia: Temple University Press, 1987.

Bauman, John F., Norman P. Hummon, and Edward K. Muller. "Public Housing, Isolation, and the Urban Underclass: Philadelphia's Richard Allen Homes, 1941–1965." *Journal of Urban History* 17:3 (1991): 264–92.

Beito, David T. *From Mutual Aid to the Welfare State: Fraternal Societies and Social Services, 1890–1967*. Chapel Hill: University of North Carolina Press, 2000.

Bell, Winifred. *Aid to Dependent Children*. New York: Columbia University Press, 1965.

Bell-Scott, Patricia, Beverly Guy-Sheftall, Jacqueline Jones Royster, Janet Sims-Wood,

Miriam DeCosta-Willis, and Lucille P. Fultz. *Double Stitch: Black Women Write about Mothers and Daughters*. Boston: Beacon Press, 1991. Reprint, New York: Harper Collins, 1993.

Binzen, Peter. *Whitetown, U.S.A.* New York: Random House, 1970.

Binzen, Peter, ed. *Nearly Everybody Read It: Snapshots of the Philadelphia Bulletin*. Philadelphia: Camino Books, 1998.

Biondi, Martha. *To Stand and Fight: The Struggle for Civil Rights in Postwar New York City*. Cambridge: Harvard University Press, 2003.

Birger, Jon S. "Race, Reaction, and Reform: The Three R's of Philadelphia School Politics, 1965–1971." Master's thesis, Temple University, 1994.

Boris, Eileen, and S. J. Kleinberg. "Mothers and Other Workers: (Re)Conceiving Labor, Maternalism, and the State." *Journal of Women's History* 15:3 (2003): 90–117.

Brandwein, Ruth A., ed. *Battered Women, Welfare and Poverty*. Boston: Northeastern Press, 2000.

Bristol, Katherine. "The Myth of Pruitt Igoe." *Journal of Architectural Education* 44:3 (1991): 163–71.

Broder, Sherri. *Tramps, Unfit Mothers, and Neglected Children: Negotiating Family Life in Late Nineteenth-Century Philadelphia*. Philadelphia: University of Pennsylvania Press, 2002.

Brosco, Jeffrey. "Sin or Folly: Child and Community Health in Philadelphia, 1900–1930." Ph.D. diss., University of Pennsylvania, 1994.

Brown, Michael K. *Race, Money, and the American Welfare State*. Ithaca: Cornell University Press, 1999.

Bryan, Jack. "Public Housing Modernization." *Journal of Housing* 28:4 (1971): 167–78.

Caplowitz, David. *The Poor Pay More: Consumer Practices of Low-Income Families*. New York: Free Press, 1967.

Carson, Carolyn Leonard. "And the Results Showed Promise . . . Physicians, Childbirth, and Southern Black Migrant Women, 1916–1930: Pittsburgh as a Case Study." In *Women and Health in America: Historical Readings*, edited by Judith Walzer Leavitt, 347–70. 2d ed. Madison: University of Wisconsin Press, 1999.

Cecelski, David S. *Along Freedom Road: Hyde County, North Carolina, and the Fate of Black Schools in the South*. Chapel Hill: University of North Carolina Press, 1994.

Clapper, Michael. "School Design, Site Selection, and the Political Geography of Race in Postwar Philadelphia." *Journal of Planning History* 5:3 (2006): 241–63.

Clark-Lewis, Elizabeth. *Living in, Living Out: African American Domestics and the Great Migration*. New York: Kodansha, 1994.

Cobble, Dorothy Sue. *The Other Women's Movement: Workplace Justice and Social Rights in Modern America*. Princeton: Princeton University Press, 2003.

Cohen, Lizabeth. *A Consumer's Republic: The Politics of Mass Consumption in Postwar America*. New York: Knopf, 2003.

Coll, Blanche D. *Safety Net: Welfare and Social Security, 1929–1979*. New Brunswick, N.J.: Rutgers University Press, 1995.

Collins, Patricia Hill. *Black Feminist Thought: Knowledge, Consciousness, and the Politics of Empowerment*. New York: Routledge, 1991.

Coontz, Stephanie. *The Way We Never Were: American Families and the Nostalgia Trap*. New York: Basic Books, 1992. Reprint, 2000.

Countryman, Matthew J. "Civil Rights and Black Power in Philadelphia, 1940–1971." Ph.D. diss., Duke University, 1998.

———. *Up South: Civil Rights and Black Power in Philadelphia*. Philadelphia: University of Pennsylvania Press, 2005.

Crenshaw, Kimberle. "Demarginalizing the Intersection of Race and Sex: A Black Feminist Critique of Antidiscrimination Doctrine, Feminist Theory and Antiracist Politics." *University of Chicago Legal Forum* 139 (1989): 147–67.

———. "Mapping the Margins: Intersectionality, Identity Politics, and Violence Against Women of Color." *Stanford Law Review* 43 (1991): 1243–99.

Critchlow, Donald T. *Phyllis Schlafly and Grassroots Conservatism: A Woman's Crusade*. Princeton: Princeton University Press, 2005.

Curran, Laura. "The Culture of Race, Class, and Poverty: The Emergence of a Cultural Discourse in Early Cold War Social Work (1946–1963)." *Journal of Sociology and Social Welfare* 30:3 (2003): 15–38.

Cutler, William W., III. *Parents and Schools: The 150-Year Struggle for Control in American Education*. Chicago: University of Chicago Press, 2000.

Davis, Angela. *Women, Race, and Class*. New York: Vintage Books, 1983.

Deslippe, Dennis A. *Rights, Not Roses: Unions and the Rise of Working-Class Feminism, 1945–1980*. Urbana and Chicago: University of Illinois Press, 2000.

Diamond, Andrew. "Rethinking Culture on the Streets: Agency, Masculinity, and Style in the American City." *Journal of Urban History* 27:5 (2001): 669–85.

Dill, Bonnie Thorton. *Across the Boundaries of Race and Class: An Exploration of Work and Family among Black Female Domestic Servants*. New York: Garland, 1994.

Donaghy, Thomas J. *Philadelphia's Finest: A History of Education in the Catholic Archdiocese, 1692–1970*. Philadelphia: American Catholic Historical Society, 1972.

Dorn, Sherman. *Creating the Dropout: An Institutional and Social History of School Failure*. Westport, Conn.: Praeger, 1996.

Dougherty, Jack. *More Than One Struggle: The Evolution of Black School Reform in Milwaukee*. Chapel Hill: University of North Carolina Press, 2004.

Douglas, Davison M. *Jim Crow Moves North: The Battle over Northern School Segregation, 1865–1954*. New York: Cambridge University Press, 2005.

Dowling, Harry F. *City Hospitals: The Undercare of the Underprivileged*. Cambridge: Harvard University Press, 1982.

Doyal, Leslie. "Hazards of Hearth and Home." In *Women's Health: Readings on Social, Economic, and Political Issues*, edited by Nancy Worcester and Mariamne Whatley, 143–56. 3d ed. Dubuque, Iowa: Kendall/Hunt Publishing, 2000.

Drake, St. Clair, and Horace R. Cayton. *Black Metropolis: A Study of Negro Life in a Northern City*. New York: Harcourt, Brace, 1945.

Du Bois, W. E. B. *The Philadelphia Negro: A Social Study*. Philadelphia: University of Pennsylvania Press, 1899. Reprint, Philadelphia: Temple University Press, 1996.

Durr, Kenneth D. *Behind the Backlash: White Working-Class Politics in Baltimore, 1940–1980*. Chapel Hill: University of North Carolina Press, 2003.

Edin, Kathryn. *There's a Lot of Month Left at the End of the Money: How Welfare Recipients Make Ends Meet in Chicago*. New York: Garland, 1993.

———. "Why Poor Women Don't Marry or Remarry." *American Prospect* 11:4 (2000): 26–31.

Edwards, Laura. *Gendered Strife and Confusion: The Political Culture of Reconstruction*. Urbana and Chicago: University of Illinois Press, 1997.

Egemonye, Uche. "Treat Her Like a Lady: Judicial Paternalism and the Justification for Assaults against Black Women, 1865–1910." In *Lethal Imagination: Violence and Brutality in American History*, edited by Michael A. Bellesiles, 283–94. New York: New York University Press, 1999.

Ershkowitz, Miriam, and Joseph Zikmund II, eds. *Black Politics in Philadelphia*. New York: Basic Books, 1973.

Fass, Paula S. *Outside In: Minorities and the Transformation of American Education*. New York: Oxford University Press, 1989.

Feldstein, Ruth. *Motherhood in Black and White: Race and Sex in American Liberalism, 1930–1965*. Ithaca, N.Y.: Cornell University Press, 2000.

Ferguson, Ann Arnett. *Bad Boys: Public Schools and the Making of Black Masculinity*. Ann Arbor: University of Michigan Press, 2000.

Fernandez, Happy (Gladys) Craven. "Parents' Influence on School Policy and Practice: A Narrative of the Philadelphia Parents Union for Public Schools, 1980–1982." Ph.D. diss., Temple University, 1984.

Fine, Michelle. *Framing Dropouts: Notes on the Politics of an Urban Public High School*. Albany: State University of New York Press, 1991.

Franklin, Vincent P. *The Education of Black Philadelphia: The Social and Educational History of a Minority Community, 1900–1950*. Philadelphia: University of Pennsylvania Press, 1979.

———. "Operation Street Corner: The Wharton Centre and the Juvenile Gang Problem in Philadelphia, 1945–1958." In *W. E. B. DuBois, Race, and the City: "The Philadelphia Negro" and Its Legacy*, edited by Michael B. Katz and Thomas J. Sugrue, 195–216. Philadelphia: University of Pennsylvania Press, 1998.

———. "'Voice of the Black Community': The *Philadelphia Tribune*, 1912–1941." *Pennsylvania History* 4:51 (1984): 261–84.

Gabin, Nancy F. *Feminism in the Labor Movement: Women and the United Auto Workers, 1935–1975*. Ithaca, N.Y.: Cornell University Press, 1990.

Gamble, Vanessa Northington. *Making a Place for Ourselves: The Black Hospital Movement, 1920–1945*. New York: Oxford University Press, 1995.

———. "Under the Shadow of Tuskegee: African Americans and Health Care." In *Tuskegee's Truths: Rethinking the Tuskegee Syphilis Study*, edited by Susan M. Reverby, 431–42. Chapel Hill: University of North Carolina Press, 2000.

Gibson, Karen Joyce. "Income, Race, and Space: A Comparative Analysis of the Effects of Poverty Concentration on White and Black Neighborhoods in the Detroit and Pittsburgh Metropolitan Areas." Ph.D. diss., University of California-Berkeley, 1996.

Gilbert, James. *Cycle of Outrage: America's Reaction to the Juvenile Delinquent in the 1950s.* New York: Oxford University Press, 1986.

Gilens, Martin. *Why Americans Hate Welfare: Race, Media, and the Politics of Antipoverty Policy.* Chicago: University of Chicago Press, 1999.

Glenn, Evelyn Nakano, Grace Chang, and Linda Rennie Forcey, eds. *Mothering: Ideology, Experience, and Agency.* New York: Routledge, 1994.

Gluck, Sherna Berger, and Daphne Patai, eds. *Women's Words: The Feminist Practice of Oral History.* New York: Routledge, 1991.

Golab, Caroline. *Immigrant Destinations.* Philadelphia: Temple University Press, 1997.

Goldberg, Gertrude S. "Class Action, Community Organization, and School Reform: Part I." *Freedomways* 17:4 (1977): 224–38.

Golden, Janet, and Charles E. Rosenberg. *Pictures of Health: A Photographic History of Health Care in Philadelphia, 1860–1945.* Philadelphia: University of Pennsylvania Press, 1991.

Goldsmith, Julie D. "Working the System: Clients' Use and Experience of Social Welfare Institutions in Philadelphia, 1940 to the Present." Ph.D. diss., University of Pennsylvania, 1998.

Goldstein, Ira. "The Wrong Side of the Tracts: A Study of Residential Segregation in Philadelphia, 1930–1980." Ph.D. diss., Temple University, 1985.

Goldstein, Ira, and William L. Yancey. "Public Housing Projects, Blacks, and Public Policy: The Historical Ecology of Public Housing in Philadelphia." In *Housing Desegregation and Federal Policy*, edited by John Goering, 262–89. Chapel Hill: University of North Carolina Press, 1986.

Goodwin, Joanne L. *Gender and the Politics of Welfare Reform: Mothers' Pensions in Chicago, 1911–1929.* Chicago: University of Chicago Press, 1997.

Gordon, Linda. *Heroes of Their Own Lives: The Politics and History of Family Violence.* New York: Penguin, 1988.

——. *Pitied but Not Entitled: Single Mothers and the History of Welfare, 1890–1935.* New York: Free Press, 1994.

——. "Putting Children First: Women, Maternalism, and Welfare in the Early Twentieth Century." In *U.S. History as Women's History: New Feminist Essays*, edited by Linda Kerber, Alice Kessler-Harris, and Kathryn Sklar, 63–86. Chapel Hill: University of North Carolina Press, 1995.

——. "The 'Underclass' and the U.S. Welfare State." *Socialist Register* (1995): 163–87.

Gordon, Linda, ed. *Women, the State, and Welfare.* Madison: University of Wisconsin Press, 1990.

Gordon, Linda, and Nancy Fraser. "A Genealogy of *Dependency*: Tracing a Keyword of the U.S. Welfare State." *Signs: Journal of Women in Culture and Society* 19 (1994): 308–36.

Gorney, Cynthia. *Articles of Faith: A Frontline History of the Abortion Wars.* New York: Simon and Schuster, 1998.

Green, Laurie B. *Battling the Plantation Mentality: Memphis and the Black Freedom Struggle*. Chapel Hill: University of North Carolina Press, 2007.

Greene, Christina. *Our Separate Ways: Women and the Black Freedom Movement in Durham, North Carolina*. Chapel Hill: University of North Carolina Press, 2005.

Gregg, Robert. *Sparks from the Anvil of Oppression: Philadelphia's African Methodists and Southern Migrants, 1890–1940*. Philadelphia: Temple University Press, 1993.

Gregory, James N. *The Southern Disapora: How the Great Migrations of Black and White Southerners Transformed America*. Chapel Hill: University of North Carolina Press, 2005.

Grossman, James R. *Land of Hope: Chicago, Black Southerners and the Great Migration*. Chicago: University of Chicago Press, 1989.

Guy, Robert. "The Media, the Police, and Southern White Migrant Identity in Chicago, 1955–1970." *Journal of Urban History* 26:3 (2000): 329–49.

Hall, Jacquelyn Dowd. "Open Secrets: Memory, Imagination, and the Refashioning of Southern Identity." *America Quarterly* 50:1 (1998): 109–24.

Hamilton, Dona Cooper, and Charles V. Hamilton. *The Dual Agenda: Race and Social Welfare Policies of Civil Rights Organizations*. New York: Columbia University Press, 1997.

Hardin, Clara A. "The Negroes of Philadelphia: The Cultural Adjustment of a Minority Group." Ph.D. diss., Bryn Mawr College, 1945.

Hardy, Charles Ashley, III. "Race and Opportunity: Black Philadelphia during the Era of the Great Migration, 1916–1930." Ph.D. diss., Temple University, 1989.

Harley, Sharon. "For the Good of Family and Race: Gender, Work, and Domestic Roles in the Black Community." *Signs: Journal of Women in Culture and Society* 15:2 (1990): 336–49.

———. "When Your Work Is Not Who You Are: The Development of a Working-Class Consciousness among Afro-American Women." In *Gender, Class, Race, and Reform in the Progressive Era*, edited by Noralee Frankel and Nancy S. Dye, 42–55. Lexington: University Press of Kentucky, 1991.

Harris, Kathleen Mullan. *Teen Mothers and the Revolving Welfare Door*. Philadelphia: Temple University Press, 1997.

Harrison, Bennett. *Education, Training, and the Urban Ghetto*. Baltimore: Johns Hopkins University Press, 1972.

Hayre, Ruth Wright, and Alex Moore. *Tell Them We Are Rising: A Memoir of Faith in Education*. New York: John Wiley and Sons, 1997.

Hershberg, Theodore, ed. *Philadelphia: Work, Space, Family and Group Experience in the Nineteenth Century*. New York: Oxford University Press, 1981.

Hicks, Chery D. "'In Danger of Becoming Morally Depraved': Single Black Women, Working-Class Black Families, and New York Wayward Minor Laws, 1917–1928." *University of Pennsylvania Law Review* 151:6 (2003): 2077–121.

Hine, Darlene Clark. "Black Migration to the Urban Midwest: The Gender Dimension, 1915–1945." In *The Great Migration in Historical Perspective: New Dimensions of Race,*

Class, and Gender, edited by Joe William Trotter Jr, 127–46. Bloomington: University of Indiana Press, 1991.

———. *Black Women in White: Racial Conflict and Cooperation in the Nursing Profession, 1890–1950*. Bloomington and Indianapolis: Indiana University Press, 1989.

Hirsch, Arnold R. *Making the Second Ghetto: Race and Housing in Chicago, 1940–1960*. 2d ed. Chicago: Chicago University Press, 1998.

———. "Massive Resistance in the Urban North: Trumbull Park, Chicago, 1953–1966." *Journal of American History* 82:2 (1995): 522–50.

Hirsch, Arnold R., and Raymond A. Mohl, eds. *Urban Policy in 20th Century America*. New Brunswick: Rutgers University Press, 1993.

Homel, Michael W. *Down from Equality: Black Chicagoans and the Public Schools, 1920–41*. Urbana and Chicago: University of Illinois Press, 1984.

Hunt, D. Bradford. "How Did Public Housing Survive the 1950s?" *Journal of Policy History* 17:2 (2005): 193–216.

———. "Was the 1937 Housing Act a Pyrrhic Victory?" *Journal of Planning History* 4:3 (2005): 195–221.

———. "What Went Wrong with Public Housing in Chicago? A History of the Chicago Housing Authority, 1933–1982." Ph.D. diss., University of California-Berkeley, 2000.

———. "What Went Wrong with Public Housing in Chicago? A History of the Robert Taylor Homes." *Journal of the Illinois State Historical Society* 94:1 (2001): 96–123.

Hunter, Tera W. *To 'Joy My Freedom: Southern Black Women's Lives and Labors after the Civil War*. Cambridge: Harvard University Press, 1997.

Igra, Anna R. "Likely to Become a Public Charge: Deserted Women and the Family Law of the Poor in New York City." *Journal of Women's History* 11:4 (2000): 59–81.

———. *Wives without Husbands: Marriage, Desertion, and Welfare in New York, 1900–1935*. Chapel Hill: University of North Carolina Press, 2007.

Jackson, Kenneth T. *Crabgrass Frontier: The Suburbanization of the United States*. New York: Oxford University Press, 1985.

Johnson, Karl Ellis. "Black Philadelphia in Transition: The African-American Struggle on the Homefront during World War II and the Cold War Period, 1941–1963." Ph.D. diss., Temple University, 2001.

———. "Police-Black Community Relations in Postwar Philadelphia: Race and Criminalization in Urban Social Spaces, 1945–1960." *Journal of African American History* 89:2 (Spring 2004): 118–35.

Jones, Jacqueline. *Labor of Love, Labor of Sorrow: Black Women, Work and the Family from Slavery to the Present*. New York: Vintage Books, 1995.

Kaplan, Elaine Bell. *Not Our Kind of Girl: Unravelling the Myths of Black Teenage Motherhood*. Berkeley: University of California Press, 1997.

Katz, Michael B. *Improving Poor People: The Welfare State, the "Underclass," and Urban Schools as History*. Princeton: Princeton University Press, 1995.

———. *In the Shadow of the Poorhouse: A Social History of Welfare in America*. New York: Basic Books, 1986.

———. *The Irony of Early School Reform: Educational Innovation in Mid-Nineteenth Century Massachusetts*. Cambridge: Harvard University Press, 1968.

———. *The Price of Citizenship: Redefining the American Welfare State*. New York: Metropolitan Books, 2001.

———. *Reconstructing American Education*. Cambridge: Harvard University Press, 1987.

Katz, Michael B., ed. *"The Underclass" Debate: Views From History*. Princeton: Princeton University Press, 1993.

Katz, Michael B., and Lorrin R. Thomas. "The Invention of 'Welfare' in America." *Journal of Policy History* 10:4 (1998): 399–418.

Katznelson, Ira, and Margaret Weir. *Schooling for All: Class, Race, and the Decline of the Democratic Ideal*. New York: Basic Books, 1985.

Kelley, Robin D. G. *Race Rebels: Culture, Politics, and the Black Working Class*. New York: Free Press, 1994.

Kessler-Harris, Alice. *In Pursuit of Equity: Women, Men, and the Quest for Economic Citizenship in 20th-Century America*. New York: Oxford University Press, 2001.

———. *Out to Work: A History of Wage-Earning Women in the United States*. New York: Oxford University Press, 1982.

Kornbluh, Felicia. *The Battle for Welfare Rights: Politics and Poverty in Modern America*. Philadelphia: University of Pennsylvania Press, 2007.

———. "To Fulfill Their 'Rightly Needs': Consumerism and the National Welfare Rights Movement." *Radical History Review* 69 (1997): 76–113.

Krieger, Nancy, and Elizabeth Fee. "Measuring Social Inequalities in Health in the United States: A Historical Review, 1900–1950." *International Journal of Health Services* 26:3 (1996): 391–418.

Kruse, Kevin. *White Flight: Atlanta and the Making of Modern Conservatism*. Princeton: Princeton University Press, 2005.

Kunzel, Regina. *Fallen Women, Problem Girls: Unmarried Mothers and the Professionalization of Social Work, 1890–1945*. New Haven: Yale University Press, 1993.

Kusmer, Kenneth L. "African Americans in the City Since World War II." *Journal of Urban History* 21:4 (May 1995): 458–504.

———. *A Ghetto Takes Shape: Black Cleveland, 1870–1930*. Chicago: University of Illinois Press, 1976. Reprint, Chicago: Illini Books, 1978.

Ladd-Taylor, Molly. *Mother-Work: Women, Child Welfare, and the State, 1890–1930*. Urbana and Chicago: University of Illinois Press, 1994.

Ladner, Joyce A. *Tomorrow's Tomorrow: The Black Woman*. New York: Anchor Books, 1971.

Lassiter, Matthew D. *The Silent Majority: Suburban Politics in the Sunbelt South*. Princeton: Princeton University Press, 2006.

Leadbeater, Bonnie J. Ross, Niobe Way, and Anthony Arden. "Why Not Marry Your Baby's Father? Answers from African American and Hispanic Adolescent Mothers." In *Urban Girls: Resisting Stereotypes, Creating Identities*, edited by Bonnie J. Ross Leadbeater and Niobe Way, 193–209. New York: New York University Press, 1996.

Leavitt, Judith Walzer. *Brought to Bed: Childbearing in America, 1750–1950*. New York: Oxford University Press, 1986.

Lemann, Nicholas. *The Promised Land: The Great Black Migration and How It Changed America*. New York: Random House, 1991.

Lemke-Santangelo, Gretchen. *Abiding Courage: African American Migrant Women in the East Bay Community*. Chapel Hill: University of North Carolina Press, 1996.

Levenstein, Lisa. "From Innocent Children to Unwanted Migrants and Unwed Moms: Two Chapters in the Public Discourse on Welfare in the United States, 1960–1961." *Journal of Women's History* 11:4 (2000): 10–33.

———. "Hard Choices at 1801 Vine: Poor Women's Legal Actions against Men in Post–World War II Philadelphia." *Feminist Studies* 28:3 (Spring 2003): 141–63.

Lewis, Earl. *In Their Own Interests: Race, Class, and Power in Twentieth-Century Norfolk*. Berkeley: University of California Press, 1991.

Licht, Walter. *Getting Work: Philadelphia, 1840–1950*. Cambridge: Harvard University Press, 1992.

Lieberman, Robert C. *Shifting the Color Line: Race and the American Welfare State*. Cambridge: Harvard University Press, 1998.

Lightfoot, Sara Lawrence. *Worlds Apart: Relationships between Families and School*. New York: Basic Books, 1978.

Lopez, Nancy. *Hopeful Girls, Troubled Boys: Race and Gender Disparity in Urban Education*. New York: Routledge, 2003.

Luconi, Stefano. *From Paesani to White Ethnics: The Italian Experience in Philadelphia*. Albany: State University of New York Press, 2001.

Luttrell, Wendy. "The Edison School Struggle: The Reshaping of Working-Class Education and Women's Consciousness." In *Women and the Politics of Empowerment*, edited by Ann Bookman and Sandra Morgen, 136–56. Philadelphia: Temple University Press, 1988.

MacLean, Nancy. *Freedom Is Not Enough: The Opening of the American Workplace*. New York: Russell Sage Foundation; Cambridge: Harvard University Press, 2006.

Mainwright, Nicholas B. *The History of "The Philadelphia Inquirer."* Philadelphia: Philadelphia Inquirer, 1962.

Margo, Robert A. *Race and Schooling in the South, 1880–1950: An Economic History*. Chicago: University of Chicago Press, 1990.

Masur, Kate. "Reconstructing the Nation's Capital: The Politics of Race and Citizenship in the District of Columbia, 1862–1878." Ph.D. diss., University of Michigan, 2001.

May, Elaine Tyler. *Homeward Bound: American Families in the Cold War Era*. New York: Basic Books, 1993.

McBride, David. *Integrating the City of Medicine: Blacks in Philadelphia Health Care, 1910–1965*. Philadelphia: Temple University Press, 1989.

McGirr, Lisa. *Suburban Warriors: The Origins of the New American Right*. Princeton: Princeton University Press, 2001.

McKee, Guian Alexander. "Philadelphia Liberals and the Problem of Jobs, 1951–1980." Ph.D. diss., University of California-Berkeley, 2002.

Meyerowitz, Joanne J. *Women Adrift: Independent Wage Earners in Chicago, 1880–1930.* Chicago: University of Chicago Press, 1988.

Mink, Gwendolyn. *The Wages of Motherhood: Inequality in the Welfare State, 1917–1942.* Ithaca, N.Y.: Cornell University Press, 1995.

——. *Welfare's End.* Ithaca, N.Y.: Cornell University Press, 1998.

Mink, Gwendolyn, ed. *Whose Welfare?* Ithaca, N.Y.: Cornell University Press, 1999.

Mirel, Jeffrey. *The Rise and Fall of an Urban School System: Detroit, 1907–81.* Ann Arbor: University of Michigan Press, 1993.

Mitchell, Michele. "Silences Broken, Silences Kept: Gender and Sexuality in African-American History." *Gender & History* 11:3 (1999): 433–44.

Mittelstadt, Jennifer. *From Welfare to Workfare: The Unintended Consequences of Liberal Reform, 1945–1965.* Chapel Hill: University of North Carolina Press, 2005.

Morgen, Sandra. " 'It's the Whole Power of the City against Us!': The Development of a Political Consciousness in a Women's Health Care Coalition." In *Women and the Politics of Empowerment*, edited by Ann Bookman and Sandra Morgen, 97–115. Philadelphia: Temple University Press, 1988.

Morton, Marian J. *And Sin No More: Social Policy and Unwed Mothers in Cleveland, 1855–1990.* Columbus: Ohio State University Press, 1993.

Murray, Charles. *Losing Ground: American Social Policy, 1950–1980.* New York: Basic Books, 1984.

Nadasen, Premilla. "Expanding the Boundaries of the Women's Movement: Black Feminism and the Struggle for Welfare Rights." *Feminist Studies* 28:2 (2002): 271–301.

——. *Welfare Warriors: The Welfare Rights Movement in the United States.* New York: Routledge, 2005.

Neckerman, Kathryn M. *Schools Betrayed: Roots of Failure in Inner-City Education.* Chicago: University of Chicago Press, 1997.

Neckerman, Kathryn, Robert Aponte, and William Julius Wilson. "Family Structure, Black Unemployment, and American Social Policy." In *The Politics of Social Policy in the United States*, edited by Margaret Weir, Ann Schola Orloff, and Theda Skocpol, 397–420. Princeton: Princeton University Press, 1988.

Neighbors, Harold W. "Husbands, Wives, Family, and Friends: Sources of Stress, Sources of Support." In *Family Life in Black America*, edited by Robert Joseph Taylor, James S. Jackson, and Linda M. Chatters, 277–92. Thousand Oaks, Cal.: Sage Publications, 1997.

Nightingale, Carl Husemoller. *On the Edge: A History of Poor Black Children and Their American Dreams.* New York: Basic Books, 1993.

Oakes, Jeannie. *Keeping Track: How Schools Structure Inequality.* New Haven: Yale University Press, 1985.

O'Connor, Alice. *Poverty Knowledge: Social Science, Social Policy, and the Poor in Twentieth-Century U.S. History.* Princeton: Princeton University Press, 2001.

Odem, Mary E. *Delinquent Daughters: Protecting and Policing Adolescent Female Sexuality in the United States, 1885–1920.* Chapel Hill: University of North Carolina Press, 1995.

O'Donnell, Donna Gentile. *Provider of Last Resort: The Story of the Closure of the Philadelphia General Hospital*. Philadelphia: Camino Books, 2005.

Oliver, Melvin L., and Thomas M. Shapiro. *Black Wealth/White Wealth: A New Perspective on Racial Inequality*. New York: Routledge, 1995.

Opdycke, Sandra. *No One Was Turned Away: The Role of Public Hospitals in New York City Since 1900*. New York: Oxford University Press, 1999.

Orleck, Annelise. *Storming Caesars Palace: How Black Mothers Fought Their Own War on Poverty*. Boston: Beacon Press, 2005.

Osofsky, Gilbert. *Harlem: The Making of a Ghetto: Negro New York, 1890–1930*. New York: Harper and Row, 1966.

Palmer, Phyllis. *Domesticity and Dirt: Housewives and Domestic Servants in the United States, 1920–1945*. Philadelphia: Temple University Press, 1989.

Parson, Don. *Making a Better World: Public Housing, the Red Scare, and the Direction of Modern Los Angeles*. Minneapolis: University of Minnesota Press, 2005.

Pascoe, Peggy. *Relations of Rescue: The Search for Female Moral Authority in the American West, 1874–1939*. New York: Oxford University Press, 1990.

Patterson, James T. *America's Struggle against Poverty, 1900–1980*. Cambridge: Harvard University Press, 1981.

Pearson, Jessica, Nancy Thoennes, and Esther Ann Griswold. "Child Support and Domestic Violence: The Victims Speak Out." *Violence Against Women* 5:4 (1999): 427–48.

Penningroth, Dylan C. *The Claims of Kinfolk: African American Property and Community in the Nineteenth-Century South*. Chapel Hill: University of North Carolina Press, 2003.

Petshek, Kirk R. *The Challenge of Urban Reform: Policies and Programs in Philadelphia*. Philadelphia: Temple University Press, 1973.

Phillips, Kimberley L. *Alabama North: African-American Migrants, Community, and Working-Class Activism in Cleveland*. Urbana and Chicago: University of Illinois Press, 1999.

Piven, Frances Fox, and Richard A. Cloward. *Regulating the Poor: The Functions of Public Welfare*. New York: Pantheon Books, 1971. Rev. ed. New York: Vintage Books, 1993.

Pleck, Elizabeth. *Domestic Tyranny: The Making of American Social Policy against Family Violence from Colonial Times to the Present*. New York: Oxford University Press, 1987.

Pritchett, Wendell. *Brownsville, Brooklyn: Blacks, Jews, and the Changing Face of the Ghetto*. Chicago: University of Chicago Press, 2002.

Quadagno, Jill. *The Color of Welfare: How Racism Undermined the War on Poverty*. New York: Oxford University Press, 1994.

Rabinowitz, Howard R. "The Conflict between Blacks and the Police in the Urban South, 1865–1900." *Historian* 39:1 (1976): 62–76.

Radford, Gail. *Modern Housing for America: Policy Struggles in the New Deal Era*. Chicago: University of Chicago Press, 1996.

Rainwater, Lee. *Behind Ghetto Walls: Black Family Life in a Federal Slum*. Chicago: Aldine Publishing Company, 1970.

Rainwater, Lee, and William L. Yancey. *The Moynihan Report and the Politics of Controversy*. Cambridge: M.I.T. Press, 1967.

Raphael, Jody. *Saving Bernice: Battered Women, Welfare and Poverty*. Boston: Northeastern Press, 2000.

Ravitch, Diane. *The Revisionists Revised: A Critique of the Radical Attack on the Schools*. New York: Basic Books, 1977.

———. *The Troubled Crusade: American Education, 1945–1980*. New York: Basic Books, 1983.

Reagan, Leslie J. *When Abortion Was a Crime: Women, Medicine, and the Law in the United States, 1867–1973*. Berkeley: University of California Press, 1997.

Reed, Adolph, Jr. "The Liberal Technocrat." *Nation* 246:5 (1988): 167–70.

Reese, Ellen. *Backlash against Welfare Mothers: Past and Present*. Berkeley: University of California Press, 2005.

Reese, William J. *The Origins of the American High School*. New Haven: Yale University Press, 1995.

Reichley, James. *The Art of Government: Reform and Organization Politics in Philadelphia*. New York: Fund for the Republic, 1959. Reprint, Dubuque, Iowa: Brown Reprints, 1972.

Resnik, Henry S. *Turning on the System: War in the Philadelphia Public Schools*. New York: Pantheon Books, 1970.

Rice, Mitchell F., and Woodrow Jones Jr. *Public Policy and the Black Hospital: From Slavery to Segregation to Integration*. Westport, Conn.: Greenwood Press, 1994.

Richardson, Heather Cox. *The Death of Reconstruction: Race, Labor, and Politics in the Post–Civil War North, 1865–1901*. Cambridge: Harvard University Press, 2001.

Richie, Beth E. *Compelled to Crime: The Gendered Entrapment of Battered Black Women*. New York: Routledge, 1996.

Roberts, Dorothy E. *Killing the Black Body: Race, Reproduction and the Meaning of Liberty*. New York: Pantheon, 1997.

———. "Racism and Patriarchy in the Meaning of Motherhood." *Journal of Gender and the Law* 1 (1993): 1–38.

Robinson, Marianna, and Corinne Silverman. *The Reorganization of Philadelphia General Hospital*. Tuscaloosa: University of Alabama Press, 1959.

Rodrique, Jessie M. "The Black Community and the Birth Control Movement." In *Gendered Domains: Rethinking Public and Private in Women's History*, edited by Dorothy O. Helly and Susan M. Reverby, 244–60. Ithaca, N.Y.: Cornell University Press, 1992.

Rollins, Judith. *Between Women: Domestics and Their Employers*. Philadelphia: Temple University Press, 1985.

Rose, Dan. *Black American Street Life: South Philadelphia, 1968–1971*. Philadelphia: University of Pennsylvania Press, 1987.

Rose, Elizabeth. *A Mother's Job: The History of Day Care, 1890–1940*. New York: Oxford University Press, 1999.

Rosen, Ruth. *The World Split Open: How the Modern Women's Movement Changed America*. New York: Viking, 2000.

Rosenberg, Charles. "From Almshouse to Hospital: The Shaping of Philadelphia General Hospital." Chap. 1 in Rosenberg, *Explaining Epidemics and Other Studies in the History of Medicine*, 178–214. New York: Cambridge University Press, 1992.

———. *The Care of Strangers: The Rise of America's Hospital System.* New York: Basic Books, 1987.

Ross, Loretta J. "African American Women and Abortion, 1880–1970." In *Mothers and Motherhood: Readings in American History*, edited by Rima D. Apple and Janet Golden, 259–77. Columbus: Ohio State University Press, 1997.

Russell, John Forbes. "A Study of White and Nonwhite Female Unemployment Rates in Philadelphia." Master's thesis, Department of Social Work and Social Research, Bryn Mawr College, 1974.

Salvaggio, John. *New Orleans' Charity Hospital: A Story of Physicians, Politics, and Poverty.* Baton Rouge: Louisiana State University Press, 1992.

Sanzare, James. *A History of the Philadelphia Federation of Teachers, 1941–1973.* Philadelphia: Health and Welfare Fund, 1977.

Schein, Lawrence, Mary M. Bruce, Philip S. Murray, and Linda O. Sims. *Demographic and Health Resources Profile of West Philadelphia.* Philadelphia: West Philadelphia Community Mental Health Consortium, 1970.

Schlossman, Steven, and Michael Sedlak. "The Chicago Area Project Revisited." *Crime and Delinquency* 29:3 (1983): 398–462.

Schneider, Eric C. *Vampires, Dragons, and Egyptian Kings: Youth Gangs in Postwar New York.* Princeton: Princeton University Press, 1999.

Schwartz, Joel. "Tenant Unions in New York City's Low-Rent Housing, 1933–1949." *Journal of Urban History* 12:4 (1986): 414–44.

Seder, Jean. *Voices of Kensington: Vanishing Mills, Vanishing Neighborhoods.* McLean, Va.: EPM Publications, 1990.

Segal, Geraldine. *Blacks in the Law: Philadelphia and the Nation.* Philadelphia: University of Pennsylvania Press, 1983.

Self, Robert O. *American Babylon: Race and the Struggle for Postwar Oakland.* Princeton: Princeton University Press, 2003.

Shockley, Megan Taylor. *"We, Too, Are Americans": African American Women in Detroit and Richmond, 1940–1954.* Urbana and Chicago: University of Illinois Press, 2004.

Silverman, William A. *Dunham's Premature Infants.* 3d ed. New York: Paul B. Hoeber, 1961.

———. *Retrolental Fibroplasia: A Modern Parable.* New York: Grone and Stratton, 1980.

Solinger, Rickie. *Wake Up Little Susie: Single Pregnancy and Race before Roe v. Wade.* New York: Routledge, 1992.

Spear, Allan H. *Black Chicago: The Making of a Negro Ghetto, 1890–1920.* Chicago: University of Chicago Press, 1967.

Spring, Joel. *The Sorting Machine Revisited: National Education Policy Since 1945.* New York: Longman, 1989.

Stachniewicz, Stephanie, and Jean K. Axelrod. *The Double Frill: The History of the Philadelphia General School of Nursing.* Philadelphia: George F. Stickley, 1978.

Stack, Carol. *All Our Kin: Strategies for Survival in a Black Community*. New York: Harper & Row, 1974.

Stadum, Beverly. *Poor Women and Their Families: Hard Working Charity Cases, 1900–1930*. Albany: State University of New York, 1992.

Starr, Paul. *The Social Transformation of American Medicine*. New York: Basic Books, 1982.

Stein, Marc. *City of Sisterly and Brotherly Loves: Lesbian and Gay Philadelphia, 1945–1972*. Chicago: University of Chicago Press, 2000.

Steinberg, Allen. *The Transformation of Criminal Justice: Philadelphia, 1800–1880*. Chapel Hill: University of North Carolina Press, 1989.

Steinberg, Stephen. *Turning Back: The Retreat from Racial Justice in American Thought and Policy*. Boston: Beacon Press, 1995.

Stern, Mark J. "Poverty and the Life Cycle, 1940–1960." *Journal of Social History* 24:3 (1991): 521–39.

Stevens, Rosemary. *In Sickness and in Health: American Hospitals in the Twentieth Century*. New York: Basic Books, 1989.

Strong, Thomas H. *Expecting Trouble: The Myth of Prenatal Care in America*. New York: New York University Press, 2000.

Sugrue, Thomas J. "Affirmative Action from Below: Civil Rights, the Building Trades, and the Politics of Racial Equality in the United States, 1945–1969." *Journal of American History* 91:1 (June 2004): 145–73.

———. *The Origins of the Urban Crisis: Race and Inequality in Postwar Detroit*. Princeton: Princeton University Press, 1996.

Sullivan, Leon H. *Build Brother Build*. Philadelphia: Macrae Smith, 1969.

Testa, Mark, and Marilyn Krogh. "The Effect of Employment on Marriage among Black Males in Inner-City Chicago." In *The Decline in Marriage among African Americans*, edited by M. Belinda Tucker and Claudia Mitchell-Kernan, 59–95. New York: Russell Sage Foundation, 1995.

Tew, Marjorie. *Safer Childbirth?: A Critical History of Maternity Care*. 2d. ed. London: Chapman and Hall, 1995.

Theoharis, Jeanne. "They Told Us Our Kids Were Stupid: Ruth Batson and the Educational Movement in Boston." In *Groundwork: Local Black Freedom Movements in America*, edited by Jeanne Theoharis and Komozi Woodard, 17–44. New York: New York University Press, 2005.

Theoharis, Jeanne F., and Komozi Woodard, eds. *Freedom North: Black Freedom Struggles outside the South, 1940–1980*. New York: Palgrave Macmillan, 2003.

Thompson, Darlene A. "The Socio-Political Context of the Philadelphia Public Schools, 1912 to 1972: Viewed in Retrospect by Ruth Wright Hayre." Doctor of Education diss., Temple University, 1990.

Thompson, Heather Ann. *Whose Detroit? Politics, Labor, and Race in a Modern American City*. Ithaca, N.Y.: Cornell University Press, 2001.

Toll, Jean Barth, and Mildred S. Gillam, eds. *Invisible Philadelphia: Community through Voluntary Organizations*. Philadelphia: Atwater Kant Museum, 1995.

Trotter, Joe William, Jr. "African Americans in the City: The Industrial Era, 1900–1950." *Journal of Urban History* 21:4 (1995): 438–57.

———. *Black Milwaukee: The Making of an Industrial Proletariat: 1915–1945*. 2d ed. Urbana and Chicago: University of Illinois Press, 2007.

Trotter, Joe William, Jr., ed. *The Great Migration in Historical Perspective: New Dimensions of Race, Class, and Gender*. Bloomington: Indiana University Press, 1991.

Trotter, Joe William, Jr., and Eric Ledell Smith, eds. *African Americans in Pennsylvania: Shifting Historical Perspectives*. Harrisburg: Pennsylvania State University Press, 1997.

Tyson, Timothy B. *Radio Free Dixie: Robert F. Williams and the Roots of Black Power*. Chapel Hill: University of North Carolina Press, 1999.

Ventakesh, Sudhir Alladi. *American Project: The Rise and Fall of a Modern Ghetto*. Cambridge: Harvard University Press, 2000.

von Hoffman, Alexander. "A Study in Contradictions: The Origins and Legacy of the 1949 Housing Act." *Housing Policy Debate* 11:2 (2000): 299–326.

Waldinger, Roger. *Still the Promised City: African-Americans and New Immigrants in Post-Industrial New York*. Cambridge: Harvard University Press, 1996.

Walsh, Linda Vanderwerff. " 'A Special Vocation'—Philadelphia Midwives, 1910–1940." Ph.D. diss., University of Pennsylvania, 1992.

Weigley, Russel F., ed. *Philadelphia: A 300-Year History*. New York: W. W. Norton, 1982.

West, Guida. *The National Welfare Rights Movement: The Social Protest of Poor Women*. New York: Praeger, 1981.

Whalen, Carmen Teresa. *From Puerto Rico to Philadelphia: Puerto Rican Workers and Postwar Economies*. Philadelphia: Temple University Press, 2001.

Wiese, Andrew. *Places of Their Own: African American Suburbanization in the Twentieth Century*. Chicago: University of Chicago Press, 2004.

Williams, Rhonda Y. *The Politics of Public Housing: Black Women's Struggles against Urban Inequality*. New York: Oxford University Press, 2004.

———. " 'We're tired of being treated like dogs': Poor Women and Power Politics in Black Baltimore." *The Black Scholar* 31:3–4 (2001): 31–41.

Willrich, Michael. *City of Courts: Socializing Justice in Progressive Era Chicago*. New York: Cambridge University Press, 2003.

———. "Home Slackers: Men, the State, and Welfare in Modern America." *Journal of American History* 87:2 (2000): 460–89.

Wilson, William Julius. *The Truly Disadvantaged: The Inner City, the Underclass, and Public Policy*. Chicago: University of Chicago Press, 1987.

Wilson, William Julius, and Kathryn M. Neckerman. "Poverty and Family Structure: The Widening Gap between Evidence and Public Policy Issues." In *Fighting Poverty: What Works and What Doesn't*, edited by Sheldon H. Danziger and Daniel H. Weinberg, 232–59. Cambridge: Harvard University Press, 1986.

Wolcott, Victoria W. "Recreation and Race in the Postwar City: Buffalo's 1956 Crystal Beach Riot." *Journal of American History* 93:1 (2006): 63–90.

———. *Remaking Respectability: African American Women in Interwar Detroit*. Chapel Hill: University of North Carolina Press, 2001.

Wolfinger, James. *Philadelphia Divided: Race and Politics in the City of Brotherly Love.* Chapel Hill: University of North Carolina Press, 2007.

Wood, Elizabeth. *Beautiful Beginnings: The Failure to Learn; Fifty Years of Public Housing in America.* Washington, D.C.: National Center for Housing Management, 1982.

Wright, Gwendolyn. *Building the Dream: A Social History of Housing in America.* New York: Pantheon Books, 1981.

Yancey, William L. "Architecture, Interaction, and Social Control: The Case of a Large-Scale Public Housing Project." *Environment and Behavior* 3:1 (1971): 3–21.

Zinn, Maxine Baca. "Family, Race, and Poverty in the Eighties." *Signs: Journal of Women in Culture and Society* 14:4 (1989): 856–74.

Index

58–59, 212 (n. 68); and neighbors' informing against recipients of, 51; Newburgh, N.Y., cutbacks in, 189–90; newspapers on, 53–56, 58, 190; and nonsupport of families by men, 39–40, 43, 57, 74, 75–76, 77–78; and postwar racial politics, 52–59; pregnancy and recipients of, 38, 39, 172; and privacy issues, 49, 50, 51; and public housing, 103, 230 (n. 57); public opposition to, 6, 28, 33, 53–56, 58–62, 178, 189–90; public schools and recipients of, 143–44; racial discrimination in, 35; racialization of, 34–36; and recipients pushing boundaries of system, 46–52; research on, 33–34, 194–99; residency requirement for, 35, 43, 185; and restrictions on outside earnings, 45, 47, 48, 213 (n. 77); size of families on, 37, 209–10 (n. 28); statistics on, 4, 32, 35, 44, 208 (n. 9), 212 (n. 67); strain of generally, 31–32; and sustaining women in poverty, 44–46, 51–52, 61; and welfare rights movement, 185; and whites, 27, 36, 55, 208 (n. 9); women's need for, 36–42; and women's relationships with men, 32–33, 39–42, 47, 49–51, 61, 210 (n. 42). *See also* Philadelphia Department of Public Assistance; Welfare rights

Alcohol and drugs, 41, 78, 116, 118, 149, 155

Alessandroni, Walter E., 96, 100, 110, 113

Alexander, Raymond Pace, 52, 155

Alexander, Sadie Tanner Mossell, 52, 250 (n. 21)

Allen, Eleanor, 149–50

American Civil Liberties Union, 167

Anderson, Add, 125–26, 128, 151

Applegate, Henrietta, 101

Arch Homes, 93, 229 (n. 38)

Armstrong Association, 17, 134. *See also* Urban League

Ashton, Mamie, 56

Assault and battery cases, 28, 63–65, 68–70, 76–79, 83, 84, 85–87, 221 (n. 16), 225 (n. 92). *See also* Domestic violence

Automobile ownership, 43, 208 (n. 16)

Barnett, Pauline, 77

Barry, Irene, 38

Bartram Village, 92

Baylor, Anna, 38

Beauford, Janet, 146

Bell, Elsa, 60

Bell, Patricia, 38

Bell Telephone, 3, 17

Benjamin Franklin High School, 131, 136, 143

Berean Institute, 245 (n. 123)

Berg, Renee M., 198–99, 210 (n. 43)

Binzen, Peter, 125, 239 (n. 39)

Birth control. *See* Contraception

Black Power Movement, 184, 242 (n. 77)

Blacks. *See* African Americans; Working-class African American women

Blackwell, Marcelle, 39–40, 66, 107, 110, 167

Blackwell, Molly, 56

Blanc, Victor, 54, 81

Block groups, 116, 150, 234 (n. 121)

Board of Education, 125–26, 128, 132, 139, 140, 237 (n. 16)

Bok Technical School, 132

Bonds, Joe, 146

Bonnelly, Adrian, 53

Bridges, Lulu, 56

Brown, G. Gordon, 80–81

Brown v. Board of Education, 122, 238 (n. 21)

Bryant, Drayton, 103

Bryn Mawr College, 33–34, 195–98

Byrd, Harry, 111

Carson, Janice, 63–64, 70, 76

Carson, Vince, 63–64, 70

Carter, Jocelyn, 60
Caseworkers. *See* Aid to Dependent
    Children/welfare
Catholic schools, 122, 142, 183, 243–44
    (n. 91), 244 (n. 94). *See also* Private
    schools
Central High School for Boys, 132, 133
Chester A. Arthur Elementary School,
    135
Childbirth, 165–66, 169, 173, 174–75,
    256 (n. 103). *See also* Pregnancy
Child care: and community networks, 38,
    146–47, 149; difficulties in providing,
    5, 38, 46, 147, 149; and employment,
    37–38, 47; by grandmothers, 147, 149;
    parents' responsibilities for, 104; and
    welfare/ADC recipients, 38, 47, 59,
    191, 209 (n. 27). *See also* Day care
Children: adoption or foster care for, 38–
    39; aspirations of mothers for their
    children's education, 123, 144, 156;
    educational dimension of child rear-
    ing, 144–50; hospital care for, 164, 165,
    175; infant mortality, 171, 254 (n. 71);
    and informal adoptions, 39; and juve-
    nile delinquency, 52, 81, 82–83, 97,
    154–55, 228 (n. 25); out-of-wedlock
    children, 7, 29, 33, 36, 39, 53–54, 56,
    58, 81, 98–99, 178–79, 195–98, 210
    (n. 43), 217 (n. 132); physical punish-
    ment of, 144, 145, 147; premature
    infants, 171, 175, 176, 254 (n. 71); in
    public housing, 93, 105, 113–16; and
    risk of dropping out, 122, 136–37, 147–
    48, 156, 236 (n. 9), 241 (n. 60); size of
    ADC families, 37, 209–10 (n. 28); sta-
    tistics on white and black children in
    Philadelphia, 208 (n. 18); and tot lots,
    116, 150. *See also* Aid to Dependent
    Children/welfare; Childbirth; Child
    care; Public schools
Child support. *See* Financial support
    cases

Child Support Act (1974), 225 (n. 89)
CHR. *See* Commission on Human
    Relations
Churches: and civil rights movement, 18;
    community services provided by, 20,
    150; and efforts to integrate Phila-
    delphia General Hospital's nurse-
    training school, 163; and opposition to
    closing of Philadelphia General Hospi-
    tal, 187; and public schools, 139, 242
    (nn. 73–74); role of African American
    women in, 21; statistics on, 21
Citizens Committee on Public Education,
    242 (n. 74)
Civil rights movement: and Black Power
    Movement, 184, 242 (n. 77); and
    churches, 18, 204 (n. 30); and employ-
    ment discrimination, 17–18; and
    health care, 159, 252 (n. 41); illegiti-
    macy as issue avoided by, 7; and lack of
    attention to working-class African
    American women's needs, 7, 56–57,
    90, 100, 102, 122–23, 188–89; and
    public housing, 99–101; and public
    schools, 128, 139; and Truman, 52; and
    welfare/ADC, 56–57
Clark, Joseph S., 18, 52, 97, 99–100, 162,
    174, 188
Clark, Marcella, 146
Clinton, Bill, 191
Clothing, 44, 45, 51, 58, 60, 146
CLS. *See* Community Legal Services
Cohen, Wilbur, 59
Cole, Barbara, 83
Coleman, James, 138, 242 (n. 70)
Combs, Althea, 149
Commission on Civil Rights, U.S., 186
Commission on Human Relations
    (CHR), 17, 18, 102, 141
Community Legal Services (CLS), 102,
    185–86
Community networks: as alternative to
    welfare/ADC, 42; and child care, 38,

146–47, 149; and churches, 21; as dynamic and complex, 183; and information on financial support cases, 78; and information on Philadelphia General Hospital, 169; and information on school transfers, 140; and information on welfare/ADC, 43–44; limitations of, 8, 20, 38, 42, 51, 103, 108–110, 113; and public housing, 104–6, 108–110, 113; and welfare/ADC recipients, 38, 43, 50–51; for working-class families generally, 20

Conant, James B., 138, 242 (n. 70)

Consumer culture, 59–61

Contraception, 148

Cook, Barbara, 50

Cooper, Edna, 104

COPPAR. *See* Council of Organizations on Philadelphia Police Accountability and Responsibility

Coulter, Myrna, 107, 113, 114

Council of Organizations on Philadelphia Police Accountability and Responsibility (COPPAR), 186

Counts, Emma, 42

Court orders. *See* Support orders

Courts in Philadelphia, 65–66, 221 (n. 16), 225–26 (n. 92). *See also* Philadelphia Municipal Court

Crime: and gangs, 118, 122, 136, 146, 147, 150, 154–55; homicide, 116; municipal court approach to, 66; in North Philadelphia, 10, 116; and prisoners, 40–41, 191; in public housing, 114, 116, 118, 228 (n. 24); by public housing applicants, 99; whites' fears of black crime, 7. *See also* Domestic violence; Juvenile delinquency; Rape

Culture of poverty, 33, 196

C. W. Henry Elementary School, 127, 129

Darlington, S.C., 1–2

Davenport, Theresa, 107, 113

Day care, 37–38, 96, 154, 174, 190, 209 (n. 27). *See also* Child care

Deindustrialization, 4–5, 15

Democrats: and closing of Philadelphia General Hospital, 186–87; and judges, 68; and lack of attention to working-class African American women's needs, 7, 52, 100, 126, 188–91; and Philadelphia city government, 7, 18, 52, 54, 186–87; and public housing, 100; and public schools, 126; and welfare/ADC, 53, 81, 188–91

Desegregation. *See* Integration

Detroit, 27

Dialect, 199

Dickenson, Rossalyn, 60, 61, 146

Dilworth, Richardson, 52, 100, 126, 174, 188

Discrimination. *See* Racial discrimination; Sex discrimination

Dobbins Technical School, 132

Doctors. *See* Health care; Philadelphia General Hospital

Domestic violence: and alcohol abuse, 78; court cases on, 28, 63–65, 68–70, 76–79, 83, 84, 85–87, 221 (n. 16), 225 (n. 92); hospital treatment for victims of, 177; impact of, on African American women and children, 2, 4, 5, 8, 19, 20, 26, 37, 40, 77, 149; and jail sentences for violent men, 69, 70; and nonsupport cases, 70, 78, 82, 86; and peace bonds, 64, 69, 70; police response to victims of, 80; during pregnancy, 63; reconciliation favored by judges in cases of, 65, 69–71, 82, 85–86; statistics on, 221 (n. 16); and welfare/ADC recipients, 40, 215 (n. 105); women's avoidance of legal action for, 77; women's withdrawal of charges of, 78–79, 83

Domestic work, 1–3, 16, 32, 36, 37, 47, 48, 216 (n. 123)

Donnor, Josie, 150

DPA. *See* Philadelphia Department of Public Assistance

Drake, Guy, 190

Draper, Lucille, 132

Dropouts, 122, 136–37, 147–48, 156, 236 (n. 9), 241 (n. 60). *See also* Education; Public schools

Drug addiction. *See* Alcohol and drugs

Du Bois, W. E. B., 9

Dunn, George J., 98–99

Durham Elementary School, 132

Education: and black single mothers blamed for children's shortcomings, 138; child rearing's educational dimension, 144–50; mothers' aspirations for their children's education, 121, 122, 123, 144, 156; neighborhood activism as educational activism, 121–23, 150–56; statistics on educational attainment, 244 (n. 98); and upward mobility, 29, 123–26, 144, 156, 180, 237 (n. 11); of welfare/ADC recipients, 45–46; of working-class African American women, 22, 123, 142–43. *See also* Catholic schools; Private schools; Public schools

Educational Equality League (EEL), 139

EEL. *See* Educational Equality League

Elementary and Secondary Education Act (1965), 185

Elkins, Corrine, 2–3, 8, 10–11, 14–22, 73, 75, 77, 81, 135, 142, 147, 149, 159–60, 191, 194

Emlen Elementary School, 128, 129

Employment: of African American men, 71, 124, 236 (n. 9); of African Americans compared with whites, 124–26; of African American women, 14–20, 37–38, 47–48, 59, 71, 124, 147–49; at Bell Telephone, 3, 17; and child care, 37–38, 47; desegregation in, 17–18;

domestic work, 2–3, 16, 32, 36, 37, 47–48, 216 (n. 123); and educational attainment, 123–26, 134, 237 (n. 11); fair employment practices law, 18; and informal economy, 20, 32, 40, 45, 47, 48; manufacturing jobs, 15, 37; municipal jobs, 18–19, 205 (n. 39); occupational distribution for African Americans, 15–16; racial discrimination in, 17–18, 77, 124, 148; and selective patronage campaign against businesses, 18; summer jobs for adolescents, 148–49; unemployment of African American men, 4–5, 15, 39–40, 57, 124–26, 211 (n. 56); unemployment of African American women, 37, 124, 209 (n. 24); unemployment statistics, 15, 27, 124–26; welfare/ADC as alternative to low-paying jobs, 47–48, 61; welfare/ADC requirements on, 45–46, 191, 213 (n. 77), 214 (n. 78); welfare/ADC versus, 32, 37, 47–48, 59, 61, 149–50; of white women, 37, 59, 188. *See also* Unemployment insurance

European immigrants, 8, 11, 34, 53, 163, 166

Family wage ideology, 71

Fass, Paula S., 244 (n. 94)

Feldstein, Ruth, 189

Feminization of poverty, 42

Financial support cases: and domestic violence, 70, 78, 82, 86; fornication and bastardy cases, 68–71, 76, 83, 220 (n. 13); and noncompliance, 72–74; nonsupport cases, 22, 43, 46, 66, 68–78, 86, 87, 220 (n. 15); and support payments, 71–72, 221 (n. 27); women's decision on legal action for, 23, 75–78. *See also* Support orders

Food, 44–45, 50, 51, 58, 60–61, 78, 85, 144, 154

Ford Foundation, 135

Ickes, Harold, 98

Igra, Anna R., 74

Illegitimacy: African American community attitudes toward, 26; civil rights activists' avoidance of issue of, 7, 57; false claims of, 178–79; and juvenile delinquency, 81; newspapers on, 178–79; and Philadelphia General Hospital's care of African Americans, 29, 178–79; and public housing restrictions against unmarried mothers, 98–99; public opposition to, 53–54, 57, 178–79; research on, 195–98; statistics on, among whites and African Americans, 36; and welfare/ADC recipients, 33, 39, 53–54, 56, 57, 58, 210 (n. 43), 217 (n. 132)

Immigrants. See European immigrants

Infant mortality, 159, 171, 254 (n. 71)

Infants. See Children

Informal economy, 20, 32, 40, 45, 47, 48

Integration: in employment, 17–18; of Girard College, 155; of hospitals and hospital staffs, 18, 163, 250 (n. 21), 252 (n. 38); of Philadelphia Housing Authority staff, 100; of public housing, 98, 99–102; public opposition to integration of neighborhoods, 7, 52; of public schools, 126–28, 139, 141; and selective patronage campaign against businesses, 18

Intimate relationships. See Relationships between men and women

Jackson, Bell, 37–39, 43, 50, 51, 75, 109, 144, 159, 168

James Weldon Johnson Homes, 92, 93, 105, 118

Jews, 54, 76, 81, 163, 194, 212 (n. 60)

Jones, Alice, 47–48

Jordan, Beverly, 78, 146–47

Jordan, Edwina, 75, 148, 157, 175, 176

Judges. See Courts in Philadelphia; Philadelphia Municipal Court

Juvenile delinquency, 52, 81–83, 97, 154–55, 228 (n. 25). See also Crime

Kallick, Edward A., 53–54

Katz, Michael B., 202 (n. 6)

Kelley, Robin D. G., 6

Kidd, Lenora, 79–80

Kircher, Charles H., 96

Klaus, William R., 185

Kronick, Jane C., 33, 195–97, 209–10 (n. 28), 211 (n. 56), 216 (n. 116), 258 (n. 6)

Kunzig, Robert Lowe, 53

Labor force. See Employment

Ladd-Taylor, Molly, 247 (n. 141)

Lakenau Hospital, 163

Lamberton, Robert, 94

Larson, Loretta, 147

Law enforcement. See Police

Lawson, Helen, 38

Legal aid, 102, 185

Legal system. See Courts in Philadelphia; Philadelphia Municipal Court

Levy, Judith, 198

Liddonfield Homes, 93

Life expectancy, 159, 249 (n. 5)

Life insurance, 45, 213 (n. 76)

Liveright, Alice K., 136

Logan, Floyd L., 139

Louisiana, 56

Lourie, Norman V., 57–58

Lower, Katherine, 195

Low-income African American women. See Working-class African American women

Maryland, 220 (n. 13)

Massachusetts, 220 (n. 13)

Maxwell, Ella, 46, 168, 169

McKee, Guain, 249 (n. 10)

Medical care. See Health care; Philadelphia General Hospital

174, 179–80, 249–50 (n. 17); staff racism at, 167; therapeutic abortions at, 175; trustees and executive director of, 161; white patients at, 163, 164, 169–70, 254 (n. 69); women's and children's health services at, 164–66, 169, 170–77

Philadelphia Health and Welfare Council, 58, 100, 108, 154

Philadelphia High School for Girls, 132, 133

Philadelphia Housing Association, 96, 102, 113

Philadelphia Housing Authority (PHA): application process of, 98; on benefits of public housing, 97; citizen board of directors of, 96; and crime in public housing, 118; and design of public housing, 93–96; housekeeping policies of, 107–9; and integration of public housing, 100–102; integration of staff of, 100; and list of public housing units, 92–93; and maintenance of public housing, 111–13, 118, 233 (n. 97); and racial discrimination, 90, 98, 100, 102; and restrictions on overnight guests, 109–10; and restrictions on unmarried mothers, 90, 102, 185; and site-selection controversy, 100–101, 119; staff of, 96, 100; on substandard housing, 44; suit against, 102, 185–86; and tenants' economic circumstances, 110; and welfare recipients, 103. *See also* Public housing

Philadelphia Independent, 56

Philadelphia Inquirer, 7, 54, 178, 188

Philadelphia Municipal Court: approach of, to crime, 66; black women as plaintiffs in generally, 67–68, 86–87; and court interviewers, 82–83; divisions of, 66; and domestic violence cases, 28, 63–65, 68–70, 76–79, 84, 85–87, 221 (n. 16), 225 (n. 92); enforcement

of support orders of, 73–74; and family-wage system, 71; and fornication and bastardy cases, 68–71, 76, 83; judges' and working-class women's different perspectives on policies of, 65–74; judges' attitudes toward black women, 53–54, 68, 76, 81–83; location of, 66–67; men's responses to financial support policies of, 72–73; and noncompliance in support cases, 72–74; and nonsupport cases, 22, 43, 64, 66, 68–78, 86, 87, 220 (n. 15); photograph of, 67; and racism of legal system, 79–81; and reconciliation pressures in domestic violence cases, 65, 69–71, 82, 85–86; records of, 193–94; restrictive policy changes of, 83–87; and support orders, 22, 65, 70–74, 83, 84–85, 86; and support payments, 71–72, 221 (n. 27); testimony by women in, 83; and welfare/ADC, 64; and women's decision to pursue or avoid legal action, 22, 23, 75–79; women's seeking autonomy and privacy in dealings with, 82–83; women's use of, and changes in gender relationships, 64–65; and women's withdrawal of charges of domestic violence, 78–79, 83

Philadelphia Tribune, 55–56, 79

Philadelphia Urban League (PUL). *See* Urban League

Philadelphia Welfare Rights Organization (PWRO), 184–85. *See also* Welfare rights

Physical abuse. *See* Domestic violence

Physicians. *See* Health care; Philadelphia General Hospital

Police, 79–80, 136, 154–55, 186, 241 (n. 59), 255 (n. 82)

Poor African American women. *See* Poverty; Working-class African American women

newspapers on, 90, 94–95, 112, 227
(n. 13); in North Philadelphia, 89, 96;
photographs of, 93, 97, 106, 115, 117;
privacy issues in, 107, 109–10, 113;
protest by low-income women against
eviction from, 206 (n. 54), 230 (n. 54);
racial discrimination in, 90, 98, 100,
102; racial stigma of, 99–102; and
rape, 114, 116; and recreational
activities, 93, 105–6, 113–16, 118, 150,
234 (n. 113); rents for, 94, 96, 102–3,
106, 111, 112, 186; and Resident
Advisory Board, 186; and restrictions
on unmarried mothers, 90, 98–99,
102, 185; row housing, 89; safety in,
116–19, 234 (n. 120); segregation of,
89, 98, 99–101, 119, 238 (n. 21); sexual
harassment by staff of, 109; single
mothers as tenants of, 102, 230 (n. 52);
site-selection controversy in, 100–101,
119; statistics on, 92, 230 (n. 52); success of, as dependent on women's support, 90–91, 110; and tenant councils,
186; tensions among tenants in, 91,
113; turnover rates in, 118; unmarried
women's suit against Philadelphia
Housing Authority, 102, 185–86; and
upward mobility, 90; utilities for, 112;
waiting lists for, 98, 190; welfare recipients as tenants of, 103, 118, 230
(n. 57); white tenants of, 101–2, 231
(n. 60); women's care and ownership
of, 89, 91, 104–6, 110, 112; and
women's relationships with men, 109–
10. See also Philadelphia Housing
Authority

Public opposition: antiwelfare discourse
of African Americans, 55–56, 62; to
black migration, 137, 216 (n. 123), 217
(n. 126); to closing of Philadelphia
General Hospital, 187, 257 (n. 109); to
illegitimacy, 53–54, 57, 178–79, 217
(n. 132); to neighborhood integration,

7, 52; to rights of working-class African
American women, 7, 182, 187–91,
202–3 (n. 9); to school construction,
185; to welfare/ADC, 6, 28, 33, 53–56,
58–62, 178, 189–90. See also Whites

Public schools: African American students labeled as "culturally handicapped slow learners," 137–38, 241
(n. 68); African American teachers and
counselors in, 134, 139; and blame for
student problems placed on single
mothers, 138; and Board of Education,
125–26, 128, 130, 132, 139, 140, 237
(n. 16); boycott of, in New York City,
243 (n. 81); and clothing for students,
145–46; and collective organizing of
African American women, 185, 243
(n. 81); construction of new schools,
130–31, 185, 257 (n. 5); and corporal
punishment, 144, 245 (n. 104); curricula of, 124–26, 132–35; dropouts from,
122, 124, 136–37, 147–48, 156, 236
(n. 9), 241 (n. 60); funding for, 125–
26, 128, 130, 135, 185, 237 (n. 14); high
school curricula in, 133–35; inadequacies of generally, 121–22, 130, 135–
36, 183, 190–91; inexperienced
teachers and substitute teachers in,
122, 136; integration of, 126–28, 139,
141; map of elementary school zones,
129; mothers' interactions with educators, 122, 139–44, 156; and NAACP, 17,
128; and neighborhood activism, 121–
23, 150–56; newspapers on, 137–38;
open schools policy of, 140–43; overcrowding in, 128, 244 (n. 96); per-
pupil expenditures for, 128, 130; photographs of, 131, 133, 148; and pregnancy, 147; public opposition to construction of, 185; racial discrepancies
in achievement in, 239–40 (n. 39);
racial discrimination in, 29, 122–23,
126–34, 136, 139, 156, 183; and safety

USHA. *See* U.S. Housing Authority

U.S. Housing Authority (USHA), 92, 111

Violence. *See* Crime; Domestic violence;
Rape

Wagner-Steagall Act (1937), 91–92, 111

Wallace, Jacqueline, 173

Watson, Dolores, 144

Weinberg, Hazel, 76

Welfare. *See* Aid to Dependent Children/
welfare

Welfare rights, 6, 29, 43, 61, 184–85

West Philadelphia: black population of,
166; housing in, 11, 19; Philadelphia
General Hospital in, 161, 166; public
schools in, 130; white population of,
254 (n. 64)

West Philadelphia High School, 147,
148

West Philadelphia Schools Committee,
139

Wetter, Allen H., 137–38

Wharton Centre, 20, 150, 246 (n. 140)

Whites: and children born out of
wedlock, 36; collective educational
activism of, 185; dropout rates of, 136–
37; educational attainment of, 125,
126, 244 (n. 98); employed white
women, 37, 59, 188; and Home and
School Associations, 153–54; and
Home and School Council, 151; home
ownership by, 11, 205 (n. 40); life
expectancy of, 159; as Philadelphia
General Hospital patients, 163, 164,
169–70, 254 (n. 69); poverty of, 27,
42; and prenatal care, 170–71; public
housing avoided by working-class
whites, 99–102; public school construction opposed by, 185; relationships between poor white men and
women, 211 (n. 47); as single mothers,
36; unemployment of, compared with

African Americans, 124–26; and wel-
fare/ADC, 27, 36, 55, 208 (n. 9); in
West Philadelphia, 254 (n. 64);
working-class whites, 26–27, 55, 135,
189. *See also* Public opposition;
Taxpayers

Wickenden, Elizabeth, 59

Wiley, George, 185

Wilkins, Roy, 57

William M. Meredith Elementary School,
150–51, 153–54

William Penn High School, 3, 16–17,
135

Williams, Lucille, 40, 49

Williams, Rhonda Y., 105

Wilson, Cassandra, 45

Wilson, William Julius, 5

Wilson Park, 93, 94

Winters, Joyce, 40

Woods, Alphonso A., 167

Work. *See* Employment

Working-class African American women:
and confronting poverty in postwar
Philadelphia, 8–23; education of, 22,
123, 142–43; goals of, 24; health problems of, 23, 37, 46, 47, 59, 61, 157–60,
190, 209 (n. 25); interviews with, 194–
95; judges' attitudes toward, 53–54,
68, 76, 81–83; negative stereotypes of,
8, 26, 33–34, 54–56, 58–60, 177, 178–
79; research on, 193–99; and respectability, 4, 6, 24, 46, 60–66, 76, 83, 104,
105, 108, 112, 146, 154–55, 158, 168–
70, 184, 185, 191; and rights talk, 184;
and services of public institutions generally, 3–4, 6–7, 21–24, 26–29, 181–
84; as single mothers, 36, 39–42, 57,
190; struggles of generally, 5, 8, 24. *See
also* African Americans; Aid to Dependent Children/welfare; Council of
Organizations on Philadelphia Police
Accountability and Responsibility;
Education; Employment; Philadelphia

General Hospital; Philadelphia Municipal Court; Poverty; Public housing; Public schools; Relationships between men and women; Tenants' rights; Welfare rights

Working-class whites. *See* Whites